KU-176-179

TOM BURGIS is an investigations correspondent at the *Financial Times*, based in London. Previously, he was the paper's correspondent in Lagos and Johannesburg. He has filed stories from five continents and his work has appeared in the *Daily Telegraph*, *Independent*, *Guardian*, *Observer*, *New Statesman* and elsewhere. Awards for his journalism include an Award for Excellence for investigative reporting at the 2015 Society of Publishers in Asia Awards, the *FT*'s Jones-Mauthner Memorial Prize in 2013 and a place on the shortlist for the 2015 European Press Prize and the 2010 British Press Awards as Young Journalist of the Year. Before joining the *FT*, he did a stint in Chile and travelled the world covering globalisation and its discontents. He lives in London with his wife and daughter.

From the reviews of *The Looting Machine*:

'Explains lucidly how the oil and mineral bonanza subverts societies . . . particularly acute in analysing how multinationals connive in this institutionalised theft'
Sunday Times

'[Burgis] presents a lively portrait of the rapacious "looting machine" . . . Reads partly like a mystery thriller and partly like a court submission, with its detailed descriptions of corporate connections . . . a rich collage of examples showing the links between corrupt companies and African elites'
Economist

'A great scrapbook of exploitation. Burgis has the good sense not to present it in an alarmist way, but with an understatement that is far more powerful . . . [it] is in part a means of self-exoneration, a way of making amends to those he ultimately could not help'
Financial Times

'A powerful new book'
Nicholas Kristof, *New York Times*

'Transcends the tired binary debate about the root causes of the continent's misery'
Howard French, *Foreign Affairs*

'Burgis has managed to uncover a system responsible for the wholesale looting of Africa's mineral resources for the benefit of oligarchic and state interests around the world. Burgis, a gifted young journalist, has tracked down all these characters across some of Africa's most dangerous hotspots and beyond'   Misha Glenny, author of *McMafia*

'The great value lies in its fresh detail, storytelling and the characters'
Literary Review

'A chilling insight'   *Tablet*

'Africa is the site and victim of a colossal looting machine which Tom Burgis has analysed and described in this lucid impassioned analysis'
Chartist

THE
LOOTING
MACHINE

Warlords, Tycoons, Smugglers,
and the Systematic Theft
of Africa's Wealth

TOM BURGIS

WILLIAM
COLLINS

William Collins
An imprint of HarperCollins*Publishers*
1 London Bridge Street
London SE1 9GF
WilliamCollinsBooks.com

This William Collins paperback edition published in 2016

3

First published in Great Britain in 2015 by William Collins
Simultaneously published in the United States in 2015 by PublicAffairs™,
a Member of the Perseus Books Group

Copyright © Tom Burgis 2015

Tom Burgis asserts the moral right to
be identified as the author of this work

A catalogue record for this book
is available from the British Library

ISBN 978-0-00-752310-8

Editorial production by *Marra*thon Production Services www.marathon.net

Map © John Gilkes

Book design by Jane Raese
Set in 12-point Bulmer

Printed and bound in Great Britain by
Clays Ltd, St Ives plc

All rights reserved. No part of this publication may be reproduced,
stored in a retrieval system, or transmitted, in any form or by any
means, electronic, mechanical, photocopying, recording or
otherwise, without the prior permission of the publishers.

This book is sold subject to the condition that it shall not, by way of trade
or otherwise, be lent, re-sold, hired out or otherwise circulated without the
publisher's prior consent in any form of binding or cover other than
that in which it is published and without a similar condition including
this condition being imposed on the subsequent purchaser.

MIX
Paper from
responsible sources
FSC
www.fsc.org
FSC™ C007454

FSC™ is a non-profit international organisation established to promote
the responsible management of the world's forests. Products carrying the
FSC label are independently certified to assure consumers that they come
from forests that are managed to meet the social, economic and
ecological needs of present and future generations,
and other controlled sources.

Find out more about HarperCollins and the environment at
www.harpercollins.co.uk/green

FOR MY MOTHER AND FATHER,
AND THEIR KITCHEN TABLE

Contents

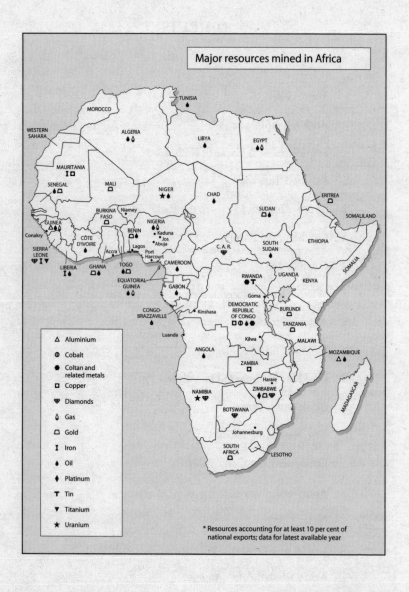

Major resources mined in Africa

Legend:
- △ Aluminium
- ☉ Cobalt
- ⬤ Coltan and related metals
- ▢ Copper
- ♦ Diamonds
- ◊ Gas
- ▢ Gold
- Ɪ Iron
- ♦ Oil
- ♦ Platinum
- T Tin
- ▼ Titanium
- ★ Uranium

* Resources accounting for at least 10 per cent of national exports; data for latest available year

Author's Note

IN LATE 2010 I started to feel sick. At first I put the constant nausea down to a bout of malaria and a stomach bug I'd picked up during a trip a few months earlier to cover an election in Guinea, but the sickness persisted. I went back to the UK for what was meant to be a week's break before wrapping up in Lagos, the Nigerian megacity where I was based as the *Financial Times*'s west Africa correspondent. A doctor put a camera down my throat and found nothing. I stopped sleeping. I jumped at noises and found myself bursting into tears. At the end of the week I was walking to a shop to buy a newspaper for the train ride to the airport when my legs gave way. I postponed my flight and went to another doctor, who sent me to a psychiatrist. In the psychiatrist's office I started to explain that I was exhausted and bewildered, and I was soon sobbing uncontrollably. The psychiatrist told me I had severe depression and that I should be admitted to a psychiatric ward immediately. There I was put on diazepam, a drug for anxiety, and antidepressants. After a few days in the hospital it became apparent that there was something else tormenting me in tandem with depression.

Eighteen months earlier I had travelled from Lagos to Jos, a city on the fault line between Nigeria's predominantly Muslim north and largely Christian south, to cover an outbreak of communal violence. I arrived in a village on the outskirts not long after a mob had set fire to houses and their occupants, among them children and a baby. I took photographs, counted bodies, and filed my story. After a few days trying to understand the causes of the slaughter, I set off for the next assignment. Over the months that followed, when images of the corpses flashed before my mind's eye, I would instinctively force them out, unable to look at them.

The ghosts of Jos appeared at the end of my hospital bed. The women who had been stuffed down a well. The old man with the broken neck.

The baby – always the baby. Once the ghosts had arrived, they stayed. The psychiatrist and a therapist who had worked with the army – both of them wise and kind – set about treating what was diagnosed as post-traumatic stress disorder (PTSD). A friend of mine, who has seen his share of horrors, devised a metaphor through which to better understand PTSD. He compares the brain to one of those portable golf holes with which golfers practise their putting. Normally the balls drop smoothly into the hole, one experience after another processed and consigned to memory. But then something traumatic happens – a car crash, an assault, an atrocity – and that ball does not drop into the hole. It rattles around the brain, causing damage. Anxiety builds until it is all-consuming. Vivid and visceral, the memory blazes into view, sometimes unbidden, sometimes triggered by an association – in my case, a violent film or anything that had been burned.

Steadfast family and friends kept me afloat. Mercifully, there were moments of bleak humour during my six weeks on the ward. When the BBC presenter welcoming viewers to coverage of the wedding of Prince William and Kate Middleton declared, 'You will remember where you were on this day for the rest of your life,' the audience of addicts and depressives in the patients' lounge broke into a chorus of sardonic laughter and colourful insults aimed at the screen.

The treatment for PTSD is as simple as it is brutal. Like an arachnophobe who is shown a drawing of a spider, then a video of one, then gradually exposed to the real thing until he is capable of fondling a tarantula, I tried to face the memories from Jos. Armed only with some comforting aromas – chamomile and an old, sand-spattered tube of sunscreen, both evocative of happy childhood days – I wrote down my recollections of what I had seen, weeping onto the paper as my therapist gently urged me on. Then, day after day, I read what I had written aloud, again and again and again and again.

Slowly my terror eased. What it left behind was guilt. I felt I ought to suffer as those who died had – if not in the same way, then somehow to the same degree. The fact that I was alive became an unpayable debt to the dead. Only after months had passed came a day when I realized that I had to choose: if I were on trial for the slaughter at Jos, would a jury of my peers – rather than the stern judge of my imaginings – find me guilty? I chose peace, to let the ghosts rest.

It was not, however, a complete exoneration. I had reported that 'ethnic rivalries' had triggered the massacres in Jos, as indeed they had. But rivalries over what? Nigeria's 170 million people are mostly extremely poor, but their nation is, in one respect at least, fabulously wealthy: exports of Nigerian crude oil generate revenues of tens of billions of dollars each year.

I started to see the thread that connects a massacre in a remote African village with the pleasures and comforts that we in the richer parts of the world enjoy. It weaves through the globalized economy, from war zones to the pinnacles of power and wealth in New York, Hong Kong and London. This book is my attempt to follow that thread.

A frozen moment when everyone sees
what is on the end of every fork.

—WILLIAM BURROUGHS, *Naked Lunch*

INTRODUCTION

A Curse of Riches

Opposite the New York Stock Exchange, at what the tourist information sign calls the 'financial crossroads of the world', the stately stone façade of 23 Wall Street evokes the might of the man whose bank it was built to house in 1913: J. P. Morgan, America's capitalist titan. The exterior is popular with Hollywood – it doubled as the Gotham City stock exchange in the 2012 film *The Dark Knight Rises* – but when I visited in late 2013 the red carpet lay grubby and sodden in the drizzle blowing in off the Atlantic. Through the smeared glass in the shuttered metal gates, all that was visible in the gutted interior where once a vast chandelier glittered were a few strip lights, stairways covered in plywood, and a glowing red 'EXIT' sign.

Despite its disrepair, 23 Wall Street remains an emblem of the elite, a trophy in the changing game of global commerce. The address of its current owners is an office on the tenth floor of a Hong Kong skyscraper. Formerly the site of a British army barracks, 88 Queensway has been transformed into the mirrored towers of Pacific Place, blazing reflected sunlight onto the financial district. The sumptuous mall at street level, air-conditioned against the dripping humidity outside, is lined with designer boutiques: Armani, Prada, Chanel, Dior. The Shangri La hotel, which occupies the top floors of the second of Pacific Place's seven towers, offers suites at $10,000 a night.

The office on the tenth floor is much more discreet. So is the small band of men and women who use it as the registered address for themselves and their network of companies. To those who have sought to track their evolution, they are known, unofficially, as 'the Queensway Group'.[1] Their interests, held through a web of complex corporate structure and secretive offshore vehicles, lie in Moscow and Manhattan, North Korea and Indonesia. Their business partners include Chinese state-owned corporations; BP, Total, and other Western oil companies; and Glencore, the giant commodity trading house based in a Swiss town. Chiefly, though, the Queensway Group's fortune and influence flow from the natural resources that lie beneath the soils of Africa.

Roughly equidistant – about seven thousand miles from each – between 23 Wall Street in New York and 88 Queensway in Hong Kong another skyscraper rises. The golden edifice in the centre of Angola's capital, Luanda, climbs to twenty-five storeys, looking out over the bay where the Atlantic laps at southern Africa's shores. It is called CIF Luanda One, but it is known to the locals as the Tom and Jerry Building because of the cartoons that were beamed onto its outer walls as it took shape in 2008. Inside there is a ballroom, a cigar bar, and the offices of foreign oil companies that tap the prodigious reservoirs of crude oil under the seabed.

A solid-looking guard keeps watch at the entrance, above which flutter three flags. One is Angola's. The second is that of China, the rising power that has lavished roads, bridges and railways on Angola, which has in turn come to supply one in every seven barrels of the oil China imports to fire its breakneck economic growth. The yellow star of Communism adorns both flags, but these days the socialist credentials of each nation's rulers sit uneasily with their fabulous wealth.

The third flag does not belong to a nation but instead to the company that built the tower. On a white background, it carries three grey letters: CIF, which stands for China International Fund, one of the more visible arms of the Queensway Group's mysterious multinational network. Combined, the three flags are ensigns of a new kind of empire.

In 2008 I took a job as a correspondent for the *Financial Times* in Johannesburg. These were boom times – or, at least, they had been. Prices for the commodities that South Africa and its neighbours possess in abundance had risen inexorably since the turn of the millennium as China, India and other fast-growing economies developed a voracious hunger for resources.

Through the 1990s the average price for an ounce of platinum had been $470.[2] A tonne of copper went for $2,600, a barrel of crude oil for $22. By 2008 the platinum price had tripled to $1,500, and copper was two and a half times more expensive, at $6,800. Oil had more than quadrupled to $95, and on one day in July 2008 hit $147 a barrel. Then the American banking system blew itself up. The shockwaves rippled through the global economy, and prices for raw commodities plunged. Executives, ministers and laid-off miners looked on aghast as the recklessness of far-off bankers imperilled the resource revenues that were Africa's economic lifeblood. But China and the rest went on growing. Within a couple of years commodity prices were back to their pre-crisis levels. The boom resumed.

I traversed southern Africa for a year, covering elections, coups and corruption trials, efforts to alleviate poverty and the fortunes of the giant mining companies based in Johannesburg. In 2009 I moved to Lagos to spend two years covering west Africa's tinderbox of nations.

There are plenty of theories as to the causes of the continent's penury and strife, many of which treat the 900 million people and forty-eight countries of black Africa, the region south of the Sahara desert, as a homogenous lump.[3] Colonizers had ruined Africa, some of the theorists contended, its suffering compounded by the diktats of the World Bank and the International Monetary Fund; others considered Africans incapable of governing themselves, excessively 'tribal' and innately given to corruption and violence. Then there were those who thought Africa was largely doing just fine but that journalists seeking sensational stories and charities looking to tug at donors' heartstrings distorted its image. The prescriptions were as various and contradictory as the diagnoses: slash government spending to allow private businesses to flourish; concentrate on reforming the military, promoting 'good governance' or empowering women; bombard the continent with aid; or force open African markets to drag the continent into the global economy.

As the rich world struggled with recession, pundits, investors and development experts began to declare that Africa, by contrast, was on the rise. Commercial indicators suggested that, thanks to an economic revolution driven by the commodity boom, a burgeoning middle class was replacing Africa's propensity for conflict with rampant consumption of mobile phones and expensive whisky. But such cheery analysis was justified only in pockets of the continent. As I travelled in the Niger Delta, the crude-slicked home of Nigeria's oil industry, or the mineral-rich battlefields of eastern Congo, I came to believe that Africa's troves of natural resources were not going to be its salvation; instead, they were its curse.

For more than two decades economists have tried to work out what it is about natural resources that sows havoc. 'Paradoxically,' wrote Macartan Humphreys, Jeffrey Sachs and Joseph Stiglitz of Columbia University in 2007, 'despite the prospects of wealth and opportunity that accompany the discovery and extraction of oil and other natural resources, such endowments all too often impede rather than further balanced and sustainable development.'[4] Analysts at the consultancy McKinsey have calculated that 69 per cent of people in extreme poverty live in countries where oil, gas and minerals play a dominant role in the economy and that average incomes in those countries are overwhelmingly below the global average.[5] The sheer number of people living in what are some of the planet's richest states, as measured by natural resources, is staggering. According to the World Bank, the proportion of the population in extreme poverty, calculated as those living on $1.25 a day and adjusted for what that wretched sum will buy in each country, is 68 per cent in Nigeria and 43 per cent in Angola, respectively Africa's first and second-biggest oil and gas producers. In Zambia and Congo, whose shared border bisects Africa's copper-belt, the extreme poverty rate is 75 per cent and 88 per cent, respectively. By way of comparison, 33 per cent of Indians live in extreme poverty, 12 per cent of Chinese, 0.7 per cent of Mexicans, and 0.1 per cent of Poles.

The phenomenon that economists call the 'resource curse' does not, of course, offer a universal explanation for the existence of war or hunger, in Africa or anywhere else: corruption and ethnic violence have also befallen African countries where the resource industries are a relatively insignificant part of the economy, such as Kenya. Nor is every resource-rich country doomed: just look at Norway. But more often than not, some unpleasant things happen in countries where the extractive industries, as the oil and mining businesses are known, dominate the economy. The rest of the economy becomes distorted, as dollars pour in to buy resources. The revenue that governments receive from their nations' resources is unearned: states simply license foreign companies to pump crude or dig up ores. This kind of income is called 'economic rent' and does not make for good management. It creates a pot of money at the disposal of those who control the state. At extreme levels the contract between rulers and the ruled breaks down because the ruling class does not need to tax the people to fund the government – so it has no need of their consent.

Unbeholden to the people, a resource-fuelled regime tends to spend the national income on things that benefit its own interests: education spending falls as military budgets swell.[6] The resource industry is hard-wired for corruption. Kleptocracy, or government by theft, thrives. Once in power, there is little incentive to depart. An economy based on a central pot of resource revenue is a recipe for 'big man' politics. The world's four longest-serving rulers – Teodoro Obiang Nguema of Equatorial Guinea, José Eduardo dos Santos of Angola, Robert Mugabe of Zimbabwe, and Paul Biya of Cameroon – each preside over an African state rich in oil or minerals. Between them they have ruled for 136 years.

From Russia's oil-fired oligarchs to the conquistadores who plundered Latin America's silver and gold centuries ago, resource rents concentrate wealth and power in the hands of the few. They engender what Said Djinnit, an Algerian politician who, as the UN's top official in west Africa, has served as a mediator in a succession of coups, calls 'a struggle for survival at the highest level'.[7] Survival means capturing that pot of rent. Often it means others must die.

The resource curse is not unique to Africa, but it is at its most virulent on the continent that is at once the world's poorest and, arguably, its richest.

Africa accounts for 13 per cent of the world's population and just 2 per cent of its cumulative gross domestic product, but it is the repository of 15 per cent of the planet's crude oil reserves, 40 per cent of its gold and 80 per cent of its platinum – and that is probably an underestimate, given that the continent has been less thoroughly prospected than others.[8] The richest diamond mines are in Africa, as are significant deposits of uranium, copper, iron ore, bauxite (the ore used to make aluminium), and practically every other fruit of volcanic geology. By one calculation Africa holds about a third of the world's hydrocarbon and mineral resources.[9]

Outsiders often think of Africa as a great drain of philanthropy, a continent that guzzles aid to no avail and contributes little to the global economy in return. But look more closely at the resource industry, and the relationship between Africa and the rest of the world looks rather different. In 2010 fuel and mineral exports from Africa were worth $333 billion, more than seven times the value of the aid that went in the opposite direction (and that is before you factor in the vast sums spirited out of the continent through corruption and tax fiddles).[10] Yet the disparity between life in the places where those resources are found and the places where they are consumed gives an indication of where the benefits of the oil and mining trade accrue – and why most Africans still barely scrape by. For every woman who dies in childbirth in France, a hundred die in the desert nation of Niger, a prime source of the uranium that fuels France's nuclear-powered economy. The average Finn or South Korean can expect to live to eighty, nurtured by economies among whose most valuable companies are, respectively, Nokia and Samsung, the world's top two mobile phone manufacturers. By contrast, if you happen to be born in the Democratic Republic of Congo, home to some of the planet's richest deposits of the minerals that are crucial to the manufacture of mobile phone batteries, you'll be lucky to make it past fifty.

Physical cargoes of African oil and ore go hither and thither, mainly to North America, Europe and, increasingly, China, but by and large the continent's natural resources flow to a global market in which traders based in London, New York and Hong Kong set prices. If South Africa exports less gold, Nigeria less oil, or Congo less copper, the price goes up for everyone. Trade routes change: the increasing production of shale gas in the United States has reduced imports of Nigerian oil in recent years, for example, with the crude heading to Asia instead. But based on the proportion of total worldwide supply it accounts for, if you fill up your car fourteen times, one of those tanks will have been refined from African crude.[11] Likewise, there is a sliver of tantalum from the badlands of eastern Congo in one in five mobile phones.

Africa is not only disproportionately rich in natural resources; it is also disproportionately dependent on them. The International Monetary Fund defines a 'resource-rich' country – a country that is at risk of succumbing to the resource curse – as one that depends on natural resources for more than a quarter of its exports. At least twenty African countries fall into this category.[12] Resources account for 11 per cent of European exports, 12 per cent of Asia's, 15 per cent of North America's, 42 per cent of Latin America's, and 66 per cent of Africa's – slightly more than in the former Soviet states and slightly less than the Middle East.[13] Oil and gas account for 97 per cent of Nigeria's exports and 98 per cent of Angola's, where diamonds make up much of the remainder.[14] When, in the second half of 2014, commodity prices started to fall, Africa's resource states were reminded of that dependency: the boom had led to a splurge of spending and borrowing, and the prospect of a sharp fall in resource rents made the budgets of Nigeria, Angola and elsewhere look decidedly precarious.

The resource curse is not merely some unfortunate economic phenomenon, the product of an intangible force; rather, what is happening in Africa's resource states is systematic looting. Like its victims, its beneficiaries have names. The plunder of southern Africa began in the nineteenth century, when expeditions of frontiersmen, imperial envoys, miners, merchants and mercenaries pushed from the coast into the interior, their appetite for mineral riches whetted by the diamonds and gold around the outpost they had founded at Johannesburg. Along Africa's Atlantic seaboard traders were already departing with slaves, gold and palm oil. By the middle of the twentieth century crude oil was flowing from Nigeria. As European colonialists departed and African states won their sovereignty, the corporate behemoths of the resource industry retained their interests. For all the technological advances that have defined the start of the new millennium – and despite the dawning realization of the damage that fossil fuels are inflicting on the planet – the basic commodities that lie in abundance in Africa remain the primary ingredients of the global economy.

The captains of the oil and mining industries, which comprise many of the richest multinational corporations, do not like to think of themselves as part of the problem. Some consider themselves part of the solution. 'Half the world's GDP is underpinned by resources,' Andrew Mackenzie, the chief executive of the world's biggest mining company, BHP Billiton, told a dinner for five hundred luminaries of the industry at Lord's cricket ground in London in 2013. 'I would argue: all of it is,' he went on. 'That is the noble purpose of our trade: to supply the economic growth that helps lift millions, if not billions, out of poverty.'[15]

To mine is not necessarily to loot; there are miners, oilmen and entire companies whose ethos and conduct run counter to the looters'. Many of the hundreds of resource executives, geologists and financiers I have met believe they are indeed serving a noble cause – and plenty of them can make a justifiable case that, without their efforts, things would be much worse. The same goes for those African politicians and civil servants striving to harness natural resources to lift their compatriots from destitution. Yet the machinery that is looting Africa is more powerful than all of them.

That looting machine has been modernized. Where once treaties signed at gunpoint dispossessed Africa's inhabitants of their land, gold and diamonds, today phalanxes of lawyers representing oil and mineral companies with annual revenues in the hundreds of billions of dollars impose miserly terms on African governments and employ tax dodges to bleed profit from destitute nations. In the place of the old empires are hidden networks of multinationals, middlemen and African potentates. These networks fuse state and corporate power. They are aligned to no nation and belong instead to the transnational elites that have flourished in the era of globalization. Above all, they serve their own enrichment.

» 1 «

Futungo, Inc.

LITTLE BUT FEAR and sewage flows down the precipitous slope that separates Angola's presidential complex from the waterside slum below. Swelled by refugees who fled a civil war that raged on and off for three decades in the interior, Chicala sprawls out from the main coast road in Luanda, the capital. Periodically the ocean sends a storm tearing through the rickety dwellings. Boatmen ply the inlets, their passengers inured to the stench emanating from the waters.

This is not the face that Angola prefers to present to the world. Since the end of the civil war in 2002 this nation of 20 million people has notched up some of the fastest rates of economic growth recorded anywhere, at times even outstripping China. Minefields have given way to new roads and railways, part of a multibillion-dollar endeavour to rebuild a country that one of the worst proxy conflicts of the Cold War had shattered. Today Angola boasts sub-Saharan Africa's third-biggest economy, after Nigeria and South Africa. Luanda consistently ranks at the top of surveys of the world's most expensive cities for expatriates, ahead of Singapore, Tokyo and Zurich. In glistening five-star hotels like the one beside Chicala, an unspectacular sandwich costs $30. The monthly rent for a top-end unfurnished three-bedroom house is $15,000.[1] Luxury car dealerships do a brisk trade servicing the SUVs of those whose income has risen faster than the potholes of the clogged thoroughfares can be filled. At Ilha de Luanda, the glamorous beachside strip of bars and restaurants a short boat-ride from Chicala, the elite's offspring go ashore from their yachts to replenish their stocks of $2,000-a-bottle Dom Pérignon.

The railways, the hotels, the growth rates and the champagne all flow from the oil that lies under Angola's soils and seabed. So does the fear.

In 1966 Gulf Oil, a US oil company that ranked among the so-called seven sisters that then dominated the industry, discovered prodigious reserves of crude in Cabinda, an enclave separated from the rest of Angola by a sliver of its neighbour, Congo. When civil war broke out following independence from Portugal in 1975, oil revenues sustained the Communist government of the ruling Movimento Popular de Libertação de Angola (the People's Movement for the Liberation of Angola, or MPLA) against the Western-backed rebels of Unita. Vast new oil finds off the coast in the 1990s raised the stakes both for the warring factions and their foreign allies. Although the Berlin Wall fell in 1989, peace came to Angola only in 2002, with the death of Jonas Savimbi, Unita's leader. By then some five hundred thousand people had died.

The MPLA found that the oil-fired machine it had built to power its war effort could be put to other uses. 'When the MPLA dropped its Marxist garb at the beginning of the 1990s,' writes Ricardo Soares de Oliveira, an authority on Angola, 'the ruling elite enthusiastically converted to crony capitalism.'[2] The court of the president – a few hundred families known as the Futungo, after Futungo de Belas, the old presidential palace – embarked on 'the privatization of power'.

Melding political and economic power like many a postcolonial elite, generals, MPLA bigwigs and the family of José Eduardo dos Santos, the party's Soviet-trained leader who assumed the presidency in 1979, took personal ownership of Angola's riches. Isabel dos Santos, the president's daughter, amassed interests from banking to television in Angola and Portugal. In January 2013 *Forbes* magazine named her Africa's first female billionaire.

The task of turning Angola's oil industry from a war chest into a machine for enriching Angola's elite in peacetime fell to a stout, full-faced man with a winning grin and a neat moustache called Manuel Vicente. Blessed with what one associate calls 'a head like a computer for numbers', as a young man he had tutored schoolchildren to supplement his meagre income and support his family. After a stint as an apprentice fitter, he studied electrical engineering. Though he had been raised by a lowly Luanda shoemaker and his washerwoman wife, Vicente ended up in the fold of dos Santos's sister, thereby securing a family tie to the president. While other MPLA cadres studied in Baku or Moscow and returned to Angola to fight the bush war against Unita, Vicente honed his English and his knowledge of the oil industry at Imperial College in London. Back home he began his rise through the oil hierarchy. In 1999, as the war entered its endgame, dos Santos appointed him to run Sonangol, the Angolan state oil company that serves, in the words of Paula Cristina Roque, an Angola expert, as the 'chief economic motor' of a 'shadow government controlled and manipulated by the presidency'.[3]

Vicente built Sonangol into a formidable operation. He drove hard bargains with the oil majors that have spent tens of billions of dollars developing Angola's offshore oilfields, among them BP of the UK and Chevron and ExxonMobil of the United States. Despite the tough negotiations, Angola dazzled the majors and their executives respected Vicente. 'Angola is for us a land of success,' said Jacques Marraud des Grottes, head of African exploration and production for Total of France, which pumped more of the country's crude than anyone else.[4]

On Vicente's watch oil production almost tripled, approaching 2 million barrels a day – more than one in every fifty barrels pumped worldwide. Angola vied with Nigeria for the crown of Africa's top oil exporter and became China's second-biggest supplier, after Saudi Arabia, while also shipping significant quantities to Europe and the United States. Sonangol awarded itself stakes in oil ventures operated by foreign companies and used the revenues to push its tentacles into every corner of the domestic economy: property, health care, banking, aviation. It even has a professional football team. The foyer of the ultramodern tower in central Luanda that houses its headquarters is lined with marble, with comfortable seats for the droves of emissaries from West and East who come to seek crude and contracts. Few gain access to the highest floors of a company likened by one foreigner who has worked with it to 'the Kremlin without the smiles'. In 2011 Sonangol's $34 billion in revenues rivalled those of Amazon and Coca-Cola.

Oil accounts for 98 per cent of Angola's exports and about three-quarters of the government's income. It is also the lifeblood of the Futungo. When the International Monetary Fund examined Angola's national accounts in 2011, it found that between 2007 and 2010 $32 billion had gone missing, a sum greater than the gross domestic product of each of forty-three African countries and equivalent to one in every four dollars that the Angolan economy generates annually.[5] Most of the missing money could be traced to off-the-books spending by Sonangol; $4.2 billion was completely unaccounted for.

Having expanded the Futungo's looting machine, Manuel Vicente graduated to the inner sanctum. Already a member of the MPLA's politburo, he briefly served in a special post in charge of economic coordination before his appointment as dos Santos's vice president, all the while retaining his role as Angola's Mr Oil. He left Sonangol's downtown headquarters for the acacia-shaded villas of the *cidade alta*, the hilltop enclave built by Portuguese colonizers that serves today as the nerve centre of the Futungo.

Like its Chinese counterparts, the Futungo embraced capitalism without relaxing its grip on political power. It was not until 2012, after thirty-three years as president, that dos Santos won a mandate from the electorate – and only then after stacking the polls in his favour. Critics and protesters have been jailed, beaten, tortured and executed.[6] Although Angola is not a police state, the fear is palpable. An intelligence chief is purged, an airplane malfunctions, some activists are ambushed, and everyone realizes that they are potential targets. Security agents stand on corners, letting it be known that they are watching. No one wants to speak on the phone because they assume others are listening.

On the morning of Friday, 10 February 2012, the oil industry was buzzing with excitement. Cobalt International Energy, a Texan exploration company, had announced a sensational set of drilling results. At a depth beneath the Angolan seabed equivalent to half the height of Mount Everest, Cobalt had struck what it called a 'world-class' reservoir of oil. The find had opened up one of the most promising new oil frontiers, with Cobalt perfectly placed either to pump the crude itself or sell up to one of the majors and earn a handsome profit for its owners. When the New York stock market opened, Cobalt's shares rocketed. At one stage they were up 38 per cent, a huge movement in a market where stocks rarely move by more than a couple of percentage points. By the end of the day the company's market value stood at $13.3 billion, $4 billion more than the previous evening.

For Joe Bryant, Cobalt's founding chairman and chief executive, a punt based on prehistoric geology appeared to have paid off spectacularly. A hundred million years ago, before tectonic shifts tore them apart, the Americas and Africa had been a single landmass – the two shores of the southern Atlantic resemble one another closely. In 2006 oil companies had pierced the thick layer of salt under the Brazilian seabed and found a load of crude. An analogous salt layer stretched out from Angola. Bryant and his geologists wondered whether the same treasure might lie beneath the Angolan salt layer.

Bryant had worked as the head of BP's lucrative operations in Angola, where he cultivated the Futungo. 'Joe Bryant made himself an inner-circle oilman very quickly,' a well-connected Angola expert told me. French executives were known to be 'haughty', but Bryant made friends in Luanda. 'He knows how to get on with them, how to speak with them,' the expert said. In 2005 Bryant decided to strike out on his own and founded Cobalt, taking BP's head of exploration with him and setting up an office in Houston, the capital of the US oil industry. 'We were literally going from my garage to competing with the biggest companies in the world,' Bryant recalled.[7]

Bryant needed backers with deep pockets. He found them on Wall Street. Traders at Goldman Sachs had long played the commodities markets; Goldman's razor-sharp bankers oversaw mergers and acquisitions between resources groups. Now, in Cobalt, it would have its own oil company. Goldman and two of the wealthiest US private equity funds, Carlyle and Riverstone, together put up $500 million to launch Cobalt.

In July 2008, as Cobalt was negotiating exploration rights to put its theory about the potential of Angola's 'presalt' oil frontier to the test, the Angolans made a stipulation. Cobalt would have to take two little-known local companies as junior partners in the venture, each with a minority stake. Ostensibly the demand was part of the regime's avowed goal of helping Angolans to gain a foothold in an industry that provides just 1 per cent of jobs despite generating almost all the country's export revenue. Accordingly, in 2010 Cobalt signed a contract in which it held a 40 per cent stake in the venture and would be the operator. Sonangol, the state oil company, had 20 per cent. The two local private companies, Nazaki Oil and Gáz and Alper Oil, were given 30 per cent and 10 per cent respectively. Exploration began in earnest. Even before the jaw-dropping find Cobalt's geologists had christened their Angolan prospect 'Gold Dust'.[8] At the height of the rally in Cobalt stock after it unveiled its Angolan find, Goldman Sachs's shares in the company were worth $2.7 billion. Cobalt moved across Houston to shimmering new headquarters close to the majors' offices. One visitor to Joe Bryant's office at the Cobalt Center noted the stunning view over the city. 'Cobalt,' remarked a local realtor, 'is going to be a huge Houston success story.'[9]

There was just one snag. What Cobalt had not revealed – indeed, what the company maintains it did not know – was that three of the most powerful men in Angola owned secret stakes in its partner, Nazaki Oil and Gáz. One of them was Manuel Vicente. As the boss of Sonangol at the time of Cobalt's deal, he oversaw the award of oil concessions and the terms of the contracts. The other two concealed owners of Nazaki were scarcely less influential. Leopoldino Fragoso do Nascimento, a former general known as Dino, has interests from telecoms to oil trading. In 2010 he was appointed adviser to Nazaki's third powerful owner, General Manuel Hélder Vieira Dias Júnior, better known as Kopelipa. One veteran of Futungo politics who has clashed with Kopelipa told me that, should the day of Kopelipa's downfall ever come, 'the people in the streets will tear him to pieces for what he has done in the past'. As the head of the military bureau in the presidency, he presides over security services that keep the Futungo protected by whatever means necessary. Some even dare to call him 'o chefe do boss' – the boss of the boss.[10] During the war he served as intelligence chief and coordinated the MPLA's arms purchases.[11] More recently he has emerged as the foremost of the 'business generals', the senior figures in the security establishment who have translated their influence into stakes in diamonds, oil, and any other sector that looks lucrative. Between them this trio formed the core of the Futungo's commercial enterprise.

A long-neglected 1977 statute prohibits American companies from participating in the privatization of power in far-off lands. Updated in 1998, the

Foreign Corrupt Practices Act makes it a crime for a company that has operations in the United States to pay or offer money or anything of value to foreign officials to win business. It covers both companies themselves and their officers. For years after it was passed the FCPA was more of a laudable ideal than a law with teeth. However, from the late 2000s the agencies that were supposed to enforce it – the Department of Justice, which brings criminal cases, and the Securities and Exchange Commission, the stock market regulator, which handles civil cases – started to do so with gusto. They went after some big names, including BAE Systems, Royal Dutch Shell, and a former subsidiary of Halliburton called Kellogg Brown & Root. All three admitted FCPA or FCPA-related infringements, and the cases resulted in fines and profit disgorgements totalling more than a billion dollars – though such amounts scarcely dent the profits of companies this big.

Oil and mining companies have been the subject of more cases under the FCPA and similar laws passed elsewhere than any other sector.[12] Indeed, the Halliburton and Shell settlements both concerned bribery in Nigeria. Companies want rights to specific geographical areas under the most favourable terms possible. For the inhabitants of sub-Saharan Africa's resource states, capturing some of the rent that resource companies pay the state in exchange for lucrative territory – or capturing a position as a gatekeeper to that territory – is by far the most direct route to riches.

Delivering a suitcase stuffed with cash is only the simplest way to enrich local officials via oil and mining ventures run by foreign companies. A more sophisticated technique involves local companies, often with scant background in the resource industries. These companies are awarded a stake at the beginning of an oil and or mining project alongside the foreign corporations that will do the digging and the drilling. Sometimes genuine local businessmen own such companies. Sometimes, though, they are merely front companies whose owners are the very officials who influence or control the granting of rights to oil and mining prospects and who are seeking to turn that influence into a share of the profits. In the latter case the foreign oil or mining company risks falling foul of anticorruption laws at home. But often front companies' ultimate owners are concealed behind layers of corporate secrecy. One reason why foreign resources companies conduct what is known as 'due diligence' before embarking on investments abroad is to seek to establish who really owns their local partners. In some cases due diligence investigations amount, in the words of a former top banker, to 'manufacturing deniability'. In others the due diligence work raises so many red flags about a prospective deal that a company will simply abandon it. Frequently the evidence that a due diligence investigation amasses about corruption risks is inconclusive. Then it is up to the company to decide whether to proceed.

In 2007, as its Angolan ambitions started to take shape, Cobalt retained Vinson & Elkins and O'Melveny & Myers, two venerable American law firms, to conduct its due diligence. Corporate records are not easy to obtain in Angola, even though any company is supposed to be allowed access to its partners' records. I was able to get hold of Nazaki's registration documents, and its influential trio of owners appear nowhere on them. But there were some clues. One document names a man called José Domingos Manuel as one of Nazaki's seven shareholders and the company's designated manager. His name also appears alongside those of Vicente, Kopelipa and Dino on the shareholder list for a separate oil venture.[13] That might have raised a red flag for any company considering going into business with Nazaki: it demonstrated a clear link between one Nazaki shareholder and three of the most powerful men in the Futungo. (José Domingos Manuel, I was told by two people who know the Futungo well, had been a senior officer in the military and was a known associate of Kopelipa.) There was another red flag: six of Nazaki's seven shareholders were named individuals, but the seventh was a company called Grupo Aquattro Internacional. Aquattro's own registration documents do not name its own shareholders. But they are Vicente, Kopelipa and Dino.

In 2010, two years after the Angolan authorities had first told Cobalt that they wanted it to make Nazaki its partner, a crusading Angolan anticorruption activist called Rafael Marques de Morais published a report claiming that Vicente, Kopelipa and Dino were the true owners of Aquattro and, thus, of Nazaki.[14] 'Their dealings acknowledge no distinction between public and private affairs,' he wrote. Nazaki was just one cog in a system of plunder, which meant that 'the spoils of power in Angola are shared by the few, while the many remain poor.'[15]

At least one due-diligence investigator was aware of what Cobalt says it was unable to establish. In the first half of 2010 an investigator – we shall call him Jones – exchanged a series of memos with Control Risks, one of the biggest companies in corporate intelligence. Control Risks, the correspondence shows, had launched 'Project Benihana', an endeavour apparently codenamed after a Florida-based chain of Japanese restaurants, to look into Nazaki. Jones, a seasoned Angola hand, warned his contact at Control Risks that oil concessions in Angola were only ever granted if the MPLA and the business elite stood to benefit. He went on to name Kopelipa as one of the men behind Nazaki. No client is named in the correspondence. (In most such cases the freelance investigators are not told on whose behalf they are ultimately working.) Both Cobalt and Control Risks refused to say whether the Texan group was the client in this case. But what is clear is that the warnings were there to be found. At least one other due-diligence investigation I am aware of also got wind of Nazaki's Futungo connections.[16]

By its own account Cobalt went ahead with a deal in a country that was, in 2010, ranked at 168 out of 178 countries in Transparency International's annual corruption perceptions index, without knowing the true identity of its partner, a company with no track record in the industry and registered to an address on a Luanda backstreet that I found impossible to locate when I went looking for it in 2012.

When US authorities informed Cobalt that they had launched a formal investigation into its Angolan operations, the company maintained that everything was above board. With none of the fanfare that accompanied its cork-popping announcement of its big discovery earlier the same month off the Atlantic coast, Cobalt disclosed the investigation in its annual statement to shareholders. 'Nazaki has repeatedly denied the allegations in writing,' Cobalt told its shareholders, going on to say that it had 'conducted an extensive investigation into these allegations and believe that our activities in Angola have complied with all laws, including the FCPA.' Two months later, when I wrote to Joe Bryant to ask him about the allegations, Cobalt's lawyer replied and went further: Cobalt's 'extensive and ongoing' due diligence 'has not found any credible support for [the] central allegation that Angolan government officials, and specifically [Vicente, Kopelipa and

Dino] . . . have any ownership in Nazaki.' Referring to its massive discovery a few weeks earlier, Cobalt's lawyer added, 'Success naturally brings with it many challenges. One of those challenges is responding to unfounded allegations.'

The problem for Cobalt was that the allegations were not unfounded. I had also written to Vicente, Kopelipa and Dino, laying out the evidence that they owned stakes in Nazaki, which I had gathered from documents and interviews. Vicente and Kopelipa wrote near-identical letters back, confirming that they and Dino did indeed own Aquattro and thus held secret stakes in Nazaki but insisting that there was nothing wrong with that. They had held their Nazaki stakes, 'always respecting all Angolan legislation applicable to such activities, not having committed any crime of abuse of power and/or trafficking of influence to obtain illicit shareholder advantages'. The holdings had, in any case, been 'recently dissolved'. If US law led Cobalt to pull out of Angola, Kopelipa and Vicente went on, others would be keen to take its place.[17]

In Manuel Vicente's offices in Luanda's hilltop presidential complex the only sound was the purr of the air-conditioning unit that kept the rooms at a comfortable 70 degrees Fahrenheit and the taps of a hammer as labourers conducted some early-morning maintenance outside. A Mercedes and a Land Cruiser stood ready to part the traffic if the minister needed to venture beyond the tall red-brown wall surrounding the compound. The sole adornment on the beige walls was a portrait of dos Santos in a gold frame.

Vicente swept in, wearing a smart suit and looking fresh from his morning jog. If he was annoyed that I had named him as the beneficiary of a questionable oil deal two months earlier, he didn't show it. Indeed, as Vicente styled it, there was nothing to be embarrassed about. If, while he was the head of Sonangol, he had knowingly owned a stake in the company assigned to be a foreign group's local partner, that would have been 'a conflict of interests', he acknowledged.[18] But Vicente, a man with a reputation for ruthless competence and a commanding knowledge of Angola's oil industry, claimed he had not known that Aquattro, the investment company he shared with Kopelipa and Dino, had owned a stake in Nazaki, Cobalt's local partner. When 'all this news came,' revealing that he did indeed own a stake in Nazaki, 'we decided to quit,' he said. His interest in Nazaki had been 'liquidated' the previous year, he said. 'Today I'm not director and direct beneficiary of Nazaki.'

Vicente's position was essentially the same as Cobalt's: if there was anything untoward in the oil deal, they were ignorant of it. Vicente told me that he knew Joe Bryant 'very well'. Their relationship had stretched back years beyond the formation of Cobalt to when Bryant worked for Amoco, an American oil company that merged with BP in 1998. That relationship, it seemed to me, might have provided a simple way to check whether Vicente and his friends secretly owned stakes in Nazaki. Bryant could just have asked Vicente whether the rumours were true. I asked Vicente: Did you and Bryant ever discuss the matter? 'No,' he said.

Alongside their personal stakes in the oil business, the members of the Futungo ensure that the oil revenues that accrue to the Angolan state are deployed to serve the regime's purposes. Angola's 2013 budget allocated 18 per cent of public spending to defence and public order, 5 per cent to health, and 8 per cent to education. That means the government spent 1.4 times as much on defence as it did on health and schools combined. By comparison, the UK spent four times as much on health and education as on defence. Angola spends a greater share of its budget on the military than South Africa's apartheid government did during the 1980s, when it was seeking to crush mounting resistance at home and was fomenting conflict in its neighbours.[19]

Generous fuel subsidies are portrayed as a salve for the poor, but in truth they mainly benefit only those wealthy enough to afford a car and politically connected enough to win a fuel-import licence. Angola's government has ploughed petrodollars into contracts for roads, housing, railways and bridges at a rate of $15 billion a year in the decade to 2012, a huge sum for a country of 20 million people. Roads are getting better, railways are slowly snaking into the interior, but the construction blitz has also proved a bonanza for embezzlers: kickbacks are estimated to account for more than a quarter of the final costs of government construction contracts.[20] And much of the funding is in the form of oil-backed credit from China, much of which is marshalled by a special office that General Kopelipa has run for years. 'The country is getting a new face,' says Elias Isaac, one of Angola's most prominent anticorruption campaigners. 'But is it getting a new soul?'[21]

Manuel Vicente was keen to correct the impression that Angola's rulers have abdicated their duties toward their citizens. 'Just to assure you, the government is really serious, engaged in combating, in fighting the poverty,' he told me.[22] 'We are serious people, we know very well our job, and we know very well our responsibility.' Talking with him, I had no doubt that there was some part of Vicente that wanted to better the lot of his compatriots, or at least to be seen to be trying to do so. 'I'm a Christian guy,' he said. 'It doesn't work if you are okay and the people around have nothing to eat. You don't feel comfortable.'

There are two solutions to that problem: share some food or dump the hungry out of sight. The Futungo's record suggests it favours the latter.

António Tomás Ana has lived in Chicala since 1977, before new arrivals fleeing the civil war in the interior turned what had been a sleepy fishing settlement into the profusion of humanity it is today, sandwiched between the ocean and the slopes rising up to the presidential complex. Better known as Etona, he is one of Angola's foremost artists. At an open-air workshop walled with breezeblocks, his assistants chip away at acacia trunks with chisels and mallets. One of his trademark sinewy wooden sculptures graces the lobby at Sonangol headquarters.

Among Etona's sixty-five thousand neighbours in Chicala are military officers and a professional photographer who brings in $5,000 a month, which does not go far in ultra-costly Luanda but has allowed him to build up the corrugated-iron shack he bought twenty-five years ago into the angular but solid edifice around which his grandchildren gallivant today. In June 2012 that house, like Etona's workshop and the community library he is building, were, along with the rest of Chicala, scheduled to be flattened – and not, this time, by the ocean.

Given the choice, few people would choose to live with Chicala's meagre amenities and opportunities. The ruling party promised electricity during the 2008 election campaign, but little arrived, and not much had come of the latest pledge, made in the run-up to the 2012 polls, to provide piped water. But places like Chicala are communities, with their own ways and their own comradeship. An estimated three in every four of Luanda's inhabitants, out of a total population of between 5 and 8 million, live in slums known as *musseques*. Although conditions in some, like the precarious settlement on top of a rubbish dump, are dire, Chicala and other central musseques have their advantages. Work, formal or informal, is close at hand in Luanda's commercial districts.

Etona spends a lot of time thinking about the betterment of a slum he could easily have afforded to leave. 'Regeneration is not about roads and sidewalks – it's in the mind,' he told me when we met at his workshop, his red shirt pristine despite the afternoon heat.[23] 'This,' he said, waving an arm at the bustling slum, where nearby youngsters were furiously duelling at table football, 'this is also part of the culture, part of the country.' But Chicala's days were numbered. Its inhabitants were to be relocated, whether they liked it or not, to new settlements on the outskirts of Luanda. A new luxury hotel and the gleaming offices of an American oil company had risen on the fringes of Chicala, harbingers of what was to take the neighbourhood's place. A beach that once buzzed with fish restaurants and bars had been fenced off, ready for the developers.

The Chicala residents I spoke to regarded the authorities' promises of a better life elsewhere with deep suspicion. About three thousand had already been shipped off, some rounded up by police and packed with their belongings into trucks, any objections ignored. The government has been willing to use force to cleanse the slums, deploying troops by helicopter to conduct dawn evictions.[24] But Etona, for one, intended to resist when his turn came. 'If we don't speak out, we will be carried off to Zango.'

Zango lies just over 20 kilometres south of central Luanda, where the capital's sprawl thins out, giving way to the ochre scrub of the bush. Like a matching settlement to the north, it is supposed to represent a new beginning for Angola's slum-dwellers. To listen to officials, Zango is the promised land. 'We are moving them to more dignified accommodation,' Rosa Palavera, the head of the poverty reduction unit in the presidency, told me.[25] 'There are no basic services [in Chicala]. There is crime.'

Even if one overlooks the official neglect that lies behind the lack of amenities in Chicala, Zango is hardly preferable. Those who moved to Zango were lucky if they found basic services merely on a par with those they had left behind.[26] Sometimes the new houses were even smaller than the old ones. In aerial photographs the new settlements looked like prison camps, with their squat dwellings arranged in unvarying rows. Shacks that were far more rickety than anything in Chicala had sprung up too. Those who tried to make a go of it by commuting back from Zango into the city each departed well before dawn and returned at midnight, scarcely leaving enough time to sleep, let alone see their children. Other new arrivals simply went straight back to Chicala, a daring move given that the slum lies within the purview of the military bureau run by General Kopelipa, the feared security chief.

On the drive from Zango back toward the centre of Luanda, the road crosses the invisible frontier that separates the majority of Angolans from the enclave of plenty that the petro-economy has created.

The gleaming new settlement at Kilamba was constructed from scratch by a Chinese company at a cost of $3.5 billion. The guards on duty at the gates adopted an intimidating strut as we drove toward them down the long, curving driveway. They let my companions and me through in exchange for the price of a bottle of water. Inside the atmosphere was eerie, reminiscent of one of those disaster movies in which some catastrophe has removed all trace of life. Nothing stirred in the dry heat. Row after parallel row of gleaming, pastel-coloured apartment blocks between five and ten storeys high stretched to a vanishing point at the horizon, tracked by manicured grass verges and pylons carrying electricity lines. The roads were like silk, the best in Angola. Outside the most affluent parts of South Africa, particularly the gated communities known to their more poetic detractors as 'yuppie kennels', I had seen nothing in Africa that looked anything like Kilamba.

The newly completed units were for sale for between $120,000 and $300,000 apiece to those rich enough to escape the crush of central Luanda. The first residents of Kilamba's twenty thousand apartments were said to have moved in, but there was no sign of them. About half of Angola's population live below the international poverty line of $1.25 a day; it would take them each about 260 years to earn enough to buy the cheapest flat in

Kilamba.[27] The prices came down after an official visit by the president, but nonetheless only the wealthiest Angolans could afford to live there.

Teams of Chinese labourers in blue overalls and hard hats trundled into view in pickup trucks. Like other Chinese construction projects in Africa, Kilamba was built with Chinese finance and Chinese labour, and it formed part of a bigger bargain that ensured Chinese access to natural resources – in this case, Angola's oil. The Chinese and Angolan flags fluttered above Kilamba's entrance. This was a flagship project for China's undertaking in Africa: Xi Jinping toured the site while it was under construction in 2010, three years before he ascended from the Chinese vice presidency to the presidency. A vast billboard proclaimed that Citic, the Chinese state-owned conglomerate whose operations span banking, resources and construction, had built the new town. Oversight of the construction had been assigned to Sonangol, which subcontracted the management of the sales of apartments to a company called Delta Imobiliária. Delta was said to belong to the private business empire of Manuel Vicente and General Kopelipa. Both men were perfectly placed to use the power of the public office to dispense personal gain for themselves, just as they had been assigned concealed stakes in Cobalt's oil venture. Kilamba was, in the words of the Angolan campaigner Rafael Marques de Morais, 'a veritable model for African corruption'.[28]

Hexplosivo Mental raps with intensity – brow furrowed, left hand gripping the microphone, right hand chopping through the air. Like Public Enemy and other exponents of protest rap before him, he makes it his business to attack the abuses of the mighty. A rangy figure in a hoodie, he gives loud and lyrical voice to dissent in Angola that had long been mostly whispered, exhorting a counterpunch against the ruling class's monopoly on wealth and power with tracks like 'How It Feels to Be Poor', 'Reaction of the Masses', and 'Be Free'.

One Tuesday in May 2012 a group of ten young Angolans gathered at the Luanda home of one of a new generation of politically conscious rappers. Hexplosivo Mental was among them. They had been involved in organizing the small but concerted demonstrations that had rattled the regime. In the vanguard of protest against the Futungo's power, the group had had brushes with the authorities before, notably when the police dispersed their demos.

This was not the first time the house had been raided. But the band of fifteen men who turned up at just after ten that night wanted to teach the dissidents a more serious lesson.[29] Elections at which dos Santos planned to ensure a thumping victory were three months away, and the deployment of oil money alone would not be enough to neutralize public displays of opposition to his rule. Bursting through the door, the men bore down upon their victims with iron bars and machetes, breaking arms, fracturing skulls and spilling blood. Their work done, they zoomed away in Land Cruisers. One account of the attack alleged that the vehicles belonged to the police – evidence that the assailants were part of one of the pro-regime militias whose task was to instil fear ahead of the polls.

No one died that night, but when I spoke to Hexplosivo Mental weeks later, his badly injured arm was still being treated. We arranged to meet discreetly at a busy roundabout in Luanda. I waited thirty minutes or so before he called to say he had had to go back to the hospital. When he spoke later by phone the young rapper put it simply: 'Before, we did not know how to protest. Now we are growing.'

There were some serious anti-government demonstrations in the run-up to the elections, but if Hexplosivo Mental and his comrades hoped to mount a challenge to an entrenched regime on the scale of the Arab Spring revolutions that had erupted far to the north, they did so in vain. The amount of official funding available to political parties was slashed from $1.2 million in the legislative elections of 2008 to $97,000. Meanwhile, the MPLA was said to have spent $75 million on its campaign.[30]

The MPLA has genuine support, especially in the coastal cities that were its bastion during the war and among those Angolans so traumatized by the conflict that they see a vote for any incumbent, no matter how venal, as the option that carries the smallest risk of a return to hostilities. The regime leaves little to chance, dominating the media, appointing its stooges to run the institutions that conduct elections, co-opting opposition politicians, and intimidating opponents. Kopelipa presided over an electoral apparatus that left 3.6 million people unable to cast their ballots – almost as many votes as the MPLA received.[31] The MPLA's share of the vote fell nine points compared with the 2008 election, but it still recorded a landslide victory, with 72 per cent. Under a new system the first name on the winning party's list would become president. More than three decades after he took power, dos Santos could claim he had a mandate to rule, despite the findings of a reputable opinion poll that showed he enjoyed the approval of just 16 per cent of Angolans.[32]

In August 2014, three years after the US authorities had begun their corruption investigation into its Angolan deal, Cobalt issued a statement revealing that the Securities and Exchange Commission had given notice that it might launch a civil case against the company.[33] 'The company has fully co-operated with the SEC in this matter and intends to continue to do so,' Cobalt announced. Joe Bryant called the SEC's decision 'erroneous' and said Cobalt would continue to develop its Angolan prospects. At the time of writing no proceedings have been brought, and Cobalt continues to deny wrongdoing, as it has throughout. Cobalt's share price, which took a billion-dollar hit after news of its secret Angolan partners emerged and declined even further after some mediocre drilling results, fell another 10 per cent when the SEC's warning emerged.

Cobalt's founders have already turned a tidy profit. Between February 2012, when Cobalt revealed that it was under formal investigation, and that April, when Kopelipa and Vicente confirmed to me that they and Dino held stakes in Nazaki, Joe Bryant sold 860,000 of his shares in the company for $24 million. Between the start of the corruption investigation and the end of 2013 – during which period Cobalt also struck oil in the Gulf of Mexico – Goldman Sachs, a joint Riverstone-Carlyle fund, and First Reserve, another big American private equity firm, each made sales of Cobalt stock worth a net $1 billion.[34]

I tried to find out who had taken over the stake in Nazaki that, according to Vicente, he, Kopelipa, and Dino had 'liquidated' as well as whether their business associates were still shareholders, but neither the trio nor the company itself would tell me. In February 2013 Nazaki transferred half its interest to Sonangol, the state oil company. The official journal did not disclose the size of any fee that Sonangol paid for the stake, but bankers' valuations indicated it was worth about $1.3 billion, at least fourteen times the amount Nazaki would have been expected to pay in development costs up to that point.[35] If any fee was paid, it represented a transfer of funds from the coffers of a state where the vast majority live in penury to a private company linked to the Futungo. Then, in 2014, three weeks after Cobalt disclosed that it was facing possible proceedings by the SEC, the company announced it had severed ties with Nazaki and with Alper, whose ownership remains undisclosed. Both companies transferred their stakes in Cobalt's venture to Sonangol. Again, none of the parties involved revealed what, if any, fees were paid.[36]

Cobalt is just one among dozens of companies vying for Angolan crude, and Nazaki was but a single cog in the Futungo's machine for turning its control over the state into private gain.

Just before Christmas 2011, as Manuel Vicente was preparing to hand over the reins of Sonangol to his successor and with the expenses of the following year's election looming, seven international oil companies snapped up operating rights to eleven new blocks in the Atlantic. The acreage was in the 'presalt' zone, where Cobalt was already exploring. As in previous bidding rounds in Angola and elsewhere, the companies agreed to pay signature bonuses. These are upfront payments that oil companies make to governments when they win rights to explore a block, often through auctions. The payments are perfectly legal, though frequently the amounts paid are not disclosed. If they were delivered on the sly to officials, such payments would be called bribes; instead, they are deposited in the leaky treasuries of oil states.

Any Angolans curious to know how much their government had brought in from the auction would be disappointed. Mindful that in 2001 BP had been threatened with ejection after it announced plans to publish some details of its Angolan contracts, the oil companies kept the terms of the bonuses safely shrouded. Norway's Statoil made something resembling a disclosure. It said its total 'financial commitment' for two oil blocks, where it would be the operator of the project, and working interests in three other blocks came to $1.4 billion, 'including signature bonuses and a minimum work commitment'. The regime's overall take from the whole bidding round would have been a multiple of that figure.

Both the Futungo's business ventures and the state institutions' activities are kept within a fortress of secrecy, so much so that Edward George, an Angola specialist who has studied dos Santos's rule for many years, calls the regime a 'cryptocracy' – a system of government in which the levers of power are hidden.

When I met Isaías Samakuva at a London hotel one afternoon in early 2014 he had been the leader of Unita, today Angola's main opposition political party, for more than a decade. Samakuva has spent his life fighting a losing battle, but he remains eloquent and composed. He had been posted in London as Unita's representative in the 1980s and had come back to see family and try to lobby against what he saw as Western powers' readiness to cosy up to dos Santos in order to safeguard their companies' access to Angolan oil. 'The international community itself protects these guys,' Samakuva told me, sipping a cup of tea.[37] 'Their money is not actually in Angola. They deal with the banks in Portugal, in Britain, in Brazil, the United States. The only explanation that we can find is that they have the blessing of the international community.'

The eruptions of the Arab Spring were giving dos Santos the pretext to tighten security still further, Samakuva went on. 'Dos Santos is so entrenched in power that he won't allow what happened in Egypt.' Samakuva added, 'We have to have real peace, not just for them and their interests.'

Samakuva does not doubt that the key to the Futungo's survival lies in the shadowy structures of the oil industry. 'There's no separation between private and state,' he said. 'There's no transparency. No one knows what is the property of Mr dos Santos and his family.' I asked him about one particular company. 'I think it is the key to all the support that is given to Mr dos Santos, to his rule.' How can one company provide such vital support, I asked. 'We can only speculate. Everything is in the dark.'

The company Samakuva was talking about operates from the golden Luanda One tower. It is the sister company to China International Fund, whose flag flies above the entrance and which has raised billions for infrastructure projects under undisclosed terms, among them an expansion of Kilamba.[38] Cobalt, Nazaki and other oil groups have offices on the lower levels, but the top floors are reserved for the company that Samakuva had in mind – China Sonangol. Since 2004 China Sonangol has amassed stakes in a dozen Angolan oil ventures, including some of the most prolific, as well as a slice of the country's richest diamond mine. Sonangol, the state oil company that is the Futungo's financial engine, owns 30 per cent of China Sonangol. The remainder belongs to the band of Hong Kong-based investors that is known as the Queensway Group and is fronted by a bearded, bespectacled Chinese man called Sam Pa.

'It Is Forbidden to Piss in the Park'

IT IS HARD to imagine a place more beautiful than the east of the Democratic Republic of Congo. The valleys are a higher order of green, dense with the generous, curving leaves of banana plants and the smaller, jagged ones of cassava shrubs. The hillsides are a vertiginous patchwork of plots. Just before dusk each day the valleys fill with a spectral mist, as though Earth itself had exhaled. The slopes drop down to Lake Kivu, one of the smaller of central Africa's great lakes but still large enough to cover Luxembourg. On some days the waters lap serenely; on others, when the wind gets up, the lake turns slate-grey and froths. At the northern shore stand the Virunga, Lake Kivu's crown of volcanoes.

Beneath the beauty there is danger. From time to time the volcanoes tip lava onto the towns below. Cholera bacteria lie in wait in Lake Kivu's shallows. Deeper and more menacing still are the methane and carbon dioxide dissolved in the water, enough to send an asphyxiating cloud over the heavily populated settlements on the shores should a tectonic spasm upset the lake's chemical balance.

But there is something else that lies under eastern Congo: minerals as rich as the hillsides are lush. Here there are ores bearing gold, tin and tungsten – and another known as columbite-tantalite, or coltan for short. Coltan contains a metal whose name tantalum is derived from that of the Greek mythological figure Tantalus. Although the Greek gods favoured him, he was 'not able to digest his great prosperity, and for his greed he gained overpowering ruin'.[1] His eternal punishment was to stand up to his chin in water that, when he tried to drink, receded, and beneath trees whose branches would be blown out of reach when he tried to pluck their fruit. His story is a parable not just for the East but for the whole of a country the size of western Europe that groans with natural riches but whose people are tormented by penury. The Congolese are consistently rated as the planet's poorest people, significantly worse off than other destitute Africans. In the decade from 2000, the Congolese were the only nationality whose gross domestic product per capita, a rough measure of average incomes, was less than a dollar a day.[2]

Tantalum's extremely high melting point and conductivity mean that electronic components made from it can be much smaller than those made from other metals. It is because tantalum capacitors can be small that the designers of electronic gadgets have been able to make them ever more compact and, over the past couple of decades, ubiquitous.

Congo is not the only repository of tantalum-bearing ores. Campaigners and reporters perennially declare that eastern Congo holds 80 per cent of known stocks, but the figure is without foundation. Based on what sketchy data there are, Michael Nest, the author of a study of coltan, calculates that Congo and surrounding countries have about 10 per cent of known reserves of tantalum-bearing ores.[3] The real figures might be much higher, given that reserves elsewhere have been much more comprehensively assessed. Nonetheless, Congo still ranks as the second-most important producer of tantalum ores, after Australia, accounting for what Nest estimates to be 20 per cent of annual supplies. Depending on the vagaries of supply chains, if you have a PlayStation or a pacemaker, an iPod, a laptop or a mobile phone, there is roughly a one-in-five chance that a tiny piece of eastern Congo is pulsing within it.

The insatiable demand for consumer electronics has exacted a terrible price. The coltan trade has helped fund local militias and foreign armies that have terrorized eastern Congo for two decades, turning what should be a paradise into a crucible of war.

Edouard Mwangachuchu Hizi avoided the brutal end that befell many of his fellow Congolese Tutsi as the aftermath of the Rwandan genocide of

1994 spilled across the border, but he suffered nonetheless. The son of a well-to-do cattle farmer, Mwangachuchu was in his early forties and working as a financial adviser to the local government in Goma, the lakeside capital of eastern Congo's North Kivu province, when extremist Hutus on the other side of the water in Rwanda embarked on what is reckoned to be the fastest mass extermination in history, butchering eight hundred thousand Tutsi and moderate Hutus in one hundred days. Two million people fled, many of them into eastern Congo, where analogous ethnic tensions were already simmering.

On his way to work one day in 1995 a mob dragged Mwangachuchu from his jeep.[4] He was choked with his tie and stripped. The mob dumped him at the border with Rwanda, where Tutsi rebels had seized control from the Hutu-led government following the genocide. His herds slaughtered, Mwangachuchu found himself among the flotsam of war, albeit more fortunate than those consigned to the squalid refugee camps beside Lake Kivu. He was granted asylum in the United States in 1996, along with his wife and six children.

Mwangachuchu watched from afar as the Hutu *génocidaires* licked their wounds in eastern Congo and began to launch raids against the new Tutsi-led authorities in Rwanda. He looked on from Maryland as Paul Kagame, the steely guerrilla who had become Rwanda's leader, and his regional allies plucked an obscure Congolese Marxist rebel called Laurent-Désiré Kabila from exile in Tanzania to head a rebel alliance that swept through eastern Congo. The rebels perpetrated revenge massacres against Rwandan Hutu refugees and génocidaires as they went and then pushed on westward across a country the size of western Europe, all the way to Kinshasa, Congo's capital. They toppled Mobutu Sese Seko, the decrepit kleptocrat, and installed Kabila as president in 1997. But Kabila barely had time to change the country's name from Zaïre to the Democratic Republic of Congo before his alliance with his most powerful backer, Rwanda, started to fray. A little over a year after he took power, after Kabila had begun to enlist Hutu génocidaires to counter what he perceived as a Tutsi threat to his incipient rule, the alliance snapped. Half a dozen African armies and a score of rebel groups plunged Congo into five more years of war, during which millions died.

When Mwangachuchu went home in 1998, the dynamics of eastern

Congo were shifting once again. Anti-Kabila rebels supported by Rwanda's Tutsi-led government had taken control of the East. No one in this ethnic cauldron is ever safe, but the latest realignment favoured Congolese Tutsis like Mwangachuchu. He set about reclaiming his ancestral lands at Bibatama, 50 kilometres northwest of Goma. Mwangachuchu knew that the territory contained something still more precious than fertile pastures for grazing cattle – the rocks beneath were rich with coltan.[5]

Investors from Congo's old colonial master, Belgium, had mined the area around Mwangachuchu's lands, but their joint venture with the government had collapsed in the mid-1990s. Invading Rwandan forces and their allies looted thousands of tons of coltan and cassiterite, the tin-bearing ore, from the company's stockpiles, UN investigators found.[6] When Mwangachuchu arrived home, artisanal miners around his mountain hometown were hacking away at the rock with picks and shovels. The cassiterite would fetch a few dollars per kilo. But far-off developments in global markets were about to spur the coltan trade – and pour cash into eastern Congo's war.

The boom in mobile phones as well as in the rest of consumer electronics and games consoles caused voracious demand for tantalum. The two biggest companies that processed tantalum, Cabot of the United States and H. C. Starck of Germany, foresaw prolonged high demand. They signed long-term contracts, locking in their supply of tantalum ores.[7] That created a shortage on the open market and sparked a scramble to find new supply sources. In the course of 2000, prices for tantalum ores rose tenfold. Congo was ripe for the picking.

Thousands of eastern Congolese rushed into coltan mining. Many exchanged a farmer's machete for a miner's pick. Militias press-ganged others into mining. Livestock had long been the East's most prized commodity, but now, suddenly, it was coltan. In 1999 North Kivu officially exported five tonnes of coltan; in 2001 it exported ninety tonnes. Even after the flood of Congolese supply brought the world price back down, coltan remained more lucrative than other ores.

Coltan was not the sole catalyst of the conflict – far from it. Congo was seething before the boom and would have seethed even if coltan had never been found. But the surging coltan trade magnified eastern Congo's minerals' potential to sustain the myriad factions that were using the hostilities to make money. 'Thanks to economic networks that had been established in 1998 and 1999 during the first years of the Congo war, minerals traders and military officials were perfectly placed to funnel [coltan] out of the country,' writes Nest.[8]

Mwangachuchu started mining his land in 2001, employing about a thousand men. An amiable man with an oval face and soft features, he breaks bread with his workers and sometimes even works the mines himself, people who know him told me. Mwangachuchu Hizi International (MHI), the business he founded with his partner, a doctor from Baltimore named Robert Sussman, swiftly came to account for a large chunk of North Kivu's coltan output. 'We are proud of what we are doing in Congo,' Sussman said at the time. 'We want the world to understand that if it's done right, coltan can be good for this country.'[9] But UN investigators and western campaigners were starting to draw attention to the role Congo's mineral trade played in funding the war. The airline that had been transporting MHI's ore to Europe severed ties with the company. 'We don't understand why they are doing this,' Mwangachuchu told a reporter. 'The Congolese have a right to make business in their own country.'[10]

Other foreign businesspeople were less concerned about doing business in a war zone, which is what eastern Congo remained even after the formal end of hostilities in 2003. Estimates I have heard of the proportion of Congolese mineral production that is smuggled out of the country range from 30 to 80 per cent. Perhaps half of the coltan that for years Rwanda exported as its own was actually Congolese.[11]

Militias and the Congolese army directly control some mining operations and extract taxes and protection money from others. Corrupt officials facilitate the trade. The *comptoirs*, or trading houses, of Goma on the border with Rwanda orchestrate the flow of both officially declared mineral exports and smuggled cargoes. Other illicit routes run directly from mines across the Rwandan and Ugandan borders. UN investigators have documented European and Asian companies purchasing pillaged Congolese minerals. Once the ores are out of the country, it is a simple step to refine them and then sell the gold, tin, or tantalum to manufacturers. The road may be circuitous, but it leads from the heart of Congo's war to anywhere mobile phones and laptops can be found.

In the absence of anything resembling a functioning state, an ever-shifting array of armed groups continues to profit from lawlessness, burrowing for minerals and preying on a population that, like Tantalus, is condemned to suffer in the midst of plenty. In 2007 Mwangachuchu fell out with Robert Sussman, the co-founder of his mining business, a dispute that would lead a Maryland court to order the Congolese to pay the American $2 million. Mwangachuchu pressed on alone. His lands went on yielding up their precious ore. And he began to cultivate a new partner: the Congrès National pour la Défense du Peuple (National Congress for the Defence of the People), a militia that largely does the opposite of what its name suggests.

The relentless conflict in eastern Congo has prevented the development of large-scale industrial mining there. Almost all mining is done by hand. The East's minerals have fuelled the war, but the value of its output is tiny compared with the immense mines to the south.

Congo's Katanga province, sandwiched between Angola and Zambia, holds about half of the world's stocks of cobalt.[12] The metal is mostly used to make the ultra-strong superalloys that are integral to turbines and jet engines. It is mined as a by-product of copper, a crucial ingredient of human civilization, from its first uses in ancient coins to the wiring in electricity networks. The African copperbelt stretches from northern Zambia into Katanga and holds some of the planet's richest copper stocks. In Katanga vast whorls of red earth and rock have been cut into the forest, open pit mines that descend in steps like amphitheatres.

Katanga has endured secessionist conflict and suffered heavy fighting during the war. But, lying much further from the border with Rwanda, the principal foreign protagonist in the rolling conflicts, Katanga has known more stability than the East. Mining multinationals from Canada, the United States, Europe, Australia, South Africa and China have operations in Katanga; the region's mining output dwarfs the rest of Congo's economy. Congo's rulers have built a shadow state on the foundations of Katanga's minerals, resembling the one that Angola's Futungo has fashioned from crude oil.

Augustin Katumba Mwanke grew up in Katanga idolizing the executives who ran Gécamines, the national copper-mining company. As Congo crumbled in the dying years of Mobutu's rule, a combination of fierce intelligence, luck and determination carried him to South Africa, then brimming with possibility after the end of apartheid. He worked for mining companies before landing a job at a subsidiary of HSBC. In April 1997, when Laurent Kabila's forces captured Katanga on their advance across Congo, the bank grew nervous that the rebels might not honour a loan it had made to Gécamines. A delegation was dispatched to Congo for talks with the rebels. Katumba was added to the party in the hope that a Congolese face might help the bank's cause.[13]

'When they came I saw a young man who looked very bright,' Mawapanga Mwana Nanga, then the rebels' finance chief, told me years later.[14] An agronomist who had trained in Kentucky, Mawapanga was on the lookout for talented recruits as he prepared to inherit a ransacked treasury. He took a shine to Katumba. 'I told him, "You should come back. The country needs people like you." We were just joking. I said, "I can give you a job, but I can't pay you yet."' The lighthearted exchange contained a serious offer. Mawapanga exhorted Katumba to have the bank second him to what was about to become Congo's new government. Katumba craved influence but had foreseen a career in international business, not the chaos of Congolese government. Nonetheless, aged thirty-three, he headed home to take up Mawapanga's invitation. His transformation into one of Africa's most powerful men had begun.

As the rebels struggled to start governing after deposing Mobutu, Katumba impressed as an adviser in the finance ministry. He had been back in Congo less than a year when his phone rang. 'Hello, may I speak with Katumba?' said the voice on the line.

'Yes, this is he.'

'This is Kabila.'

Katumba had a friend with the same name and asked him what he wanted.

'No,' said the voice. 'This is Laurent-Désiré Kabila.'[15]

The president, a fellow Katangan, told Katumba he wanted to meet him. A few weeks later Katumba stood before the corpulent guerrilla at the presidential palace. Following some brisk questioning about the young man's background, the president said, 'I want to name you governor of Katanga.' According to his memoir, a stunned Katumba protested that he was utterly unqualified for what was one of the most influential positions in Congolese politics. But he could hardly refuse. The appointment was made public that evening. 'Katanga is as big as France,' Mawapanga, the finance minister, told his protégé. 'If you can manage that, the sky's the limit.' He might have added that Katumba was being handed the keys to one of the world's greatest vaults of minerals.

Kabila's rebels-turned-rulers needed to generate money from Congo's dilapidated mining industry for the twin purposes of resisting an invasion by their erstwhile Rwandan backers and making sure that they used what might prove a brief stint in power to bolster their personal finances. Oscar Mudiay, a senior civil servant in Kabila's government, told me that the president received a minimum of $4 million each week delivered in suitcases by state-owned and private mining companies.[16] Kabila's government soon signed a flurry of mining and oil deals, with scant regard for due process. The regional coalition that had swept him to power had split into pro-Kabila and pro-Rwanda alliances, and Kabila needed to keep his foreign allies, principally Zimbabwe and Angola, sweet. One beneficiary of the deal-making was Sonangol, the Angolan state oil company controlled by the Futungo, with which the Congolese state formed a partnership.[17] As governor of Katanga province, Katumba was perfectly placed to build his influence over the mining industry. 'He was more intelligent than the others and got close to Gécamines,' Oscar Mudiay recalled.

As he built a base for himself in Congo's mining heartland, Katumba became a member of Kabila's inner circle. He befriended the president's son while they travelled together on sensitive diplomatic missions. Monosyllabic and withdrawn, Joseph Kabila had been thrown into the military when his father became the figurehead of the rebellion against Mobutu. He was prematurely promoted to general and, in name at least, appointed head of the army. In December 2000 Rwandan troops and anti-Kabila forces routed the Congolese army and its foreign allies at Pweto, Katumba's hometown in Katanga. The Rwandans seized a valuable cache of arms, but there was another prize within their reach: Joseph Kabila was on the battlefield. As the Congolese army melted into frantic retreat and the high command took to its heels, Katumba received a call from the president: 'Kiddo, find Joseph, my son.'[18]

Katumba raced to reach Joseph by phone and discovered he was alive and still free. Such were the straits of the government campaign that Katumba, according to his memoir, personally had to find fuel and take it to the airport for a plane to evacuate the president's son.[19] This was the moment that formed an unbreakable bond between Katumba and the younger Kabila.

Four weeks later one of Laurent Kabila's bodyguards, an easterner who had been among the cohort of child soldiers in Kabila's rebel army, approached the president and shot him three times at close range, for reasons that have been the subject of competing conspiracy theories ever since. In disarray, his senior officials decided to create a dynasty on the spot and summoned Joseph to Kinshasa to inherit the presidency. Mawapanga Mwana Nanga, the former finance minister who had brought Katumba back to Congo, was involved in the tense efforts to hold the government together after the assassination. 'Joseph was a general – he did not know politics,' Mawapanga told me. 'So he called Katumba to come back and be his right-hand man and show him how to navigate the political waters.'

In four years Katumba had gone from a junior post in a Johannesburg bank to the side of Congo's new president. He was appointed minister of the presidency and state portfolio, in charge of state-owned companies. In 2002 UN investigators appointed to study the illegal exploitation of Congo's resources named him as one of the key figures in an 'elite network' of Congolese and Zimbabwean officials, foreign businessmen and organized criminals who were orchestrating the plunder of Congolese minerals under cover of war.[20] 'This network has transferred ownership of at least \$5 billion of assets from the state mining sector to private companies under its control in the past three years with no compensation or benefit for the state treasury of the Democratic Republic of the Congo,' the UN team wrote.

When the UN investigators recommended Katumba be placed under UN sanctions, he was shuffled out of his official post in Kabila's government – and moved into the shadow state. He became the leading exponent of a system that *Africa Confidential*, the most comprehensive publication in English on the continent's affairs, encapsulated: 'Exercising power, from the late President Mobutu Sese Seko to the Kabila dynasty, has relied on access to secret untraceable funds to reward supporters, buy elections and run vast patronage networks. This parallel state coexists with formal structures and their nominal commitment to transparency and the rule of law.'[21]

I have heard people compare Katumba to Rasputin, Karl Rove and the grand viziers of the Ottoman Empire. Diplomats rarely met him. In photographs his eyes look penetrating, his face set in a permanent semifrown of calculation. One foreigner who found himself in the same room as Katumba described an impressive man, shrewd and gentlemanly, with a fondness for his own jokes. 'He never spoke much,' said Oscar Mudiay, the official who served under Laurent Kabila. 'Just a glance.'

Katumba was like an elder brother to the young president. 'Joseph Kabila put his total faith in Katumba,' Olivier Kamitatu, an opposition politician who served for five years as planning minister in Kabila's government, told me.[22] 'He was hugely intelligent. He knew how to run the political networks and the business networks. The state today is the property of certain individuals. Katumba's work was to create a parallel state.'

On 15 October 2004, the residents of the Katangan mining town of Kilwa discovered what it meant to fall foul of Katumba's looting machine. The previous day Alain Kazadi Makalayi, a twenty-year-old fisherman with delusions of grandeur, had arrived in Kilwa at the head of half a dozen ramshackle separatists and proclaimed the independence of Katanga.[23] His call to arms attracted fewer than a hundred young followers. Realizing that a rebellion that could not even organize a radio broadcast was unlikely to last long and that the national army could not be far off, most of Kilwa's inhabitants ran away.

The separatists posed a negligible threat, but they had dared to challenge the interests of the shadow state. Dikulushi, the copper mine that lay 50 kilometres outside the town, was linked to Katumba.

Anvil Mining, a small Australian outfit, had won the rights to mine the area in 1998 and began producing copper in 2002. According to a subsequent inquiry by the Congolese Parliament, the company was granted a twenty-year exemption from paying any taxes whatsoever.[24] Katumba was a founding board member of Anvil's local subsidiary, and his name appeared on the minutes of three board meetings between 2001 and 2004.[25]

Bill Turner, Anvil's chief executive, denied that Katumba held any shares in the company; he said Katumba sat on the board as the government's representative. But Turner admitted to a reporter from Australia's ABC television that, as well as a few thousand dollars in director's fees, the company paid some $50,000 a year to rent a compound Katumba owned in Lubumbashi, Katanga's capital, for its headquarters.

After the young separatist convened a public meeting in Kilwa's marketplace to proclaim his rebellion and declare that the days of Joseph Kabila and Katumba 'pocketing money from the mines' were over, the president ordered the regional military commander to retake the town within forty-eight hours.[26] Troops had orders to 'shoot anything that moved', according to a UN inquiry into what followed.[27]

The soldiers arrived on Anvil Mining's aircraft and made use of the company's vehicles. They encountered scant resistance and suffered no casualties putting down the inept rebellion. Once the fighting was over they taught Kilwa a lesson.

Soldiers went from house to house, dispensing vengeance. At least one hundred people were killed. Some were forced to kneel beside a mass grave before being executed one by one. Among the dead were both insurgents and civilians, including a teenager whose killers made off with his bicycle. Kazadi, the hapless separatist leader, was said to have died of his wounds in the hospital. Soldiers who ransacked homes and shops carried their loot away in Anvil vehicles, which were also used to transport corpses, according to the UN investigation, claims the company denied.[28]

A decade later, in 2014, I asked Bill Turner about Anvil's role in the Kilwa massacre. 'Anvil were of course aware of the rebellion and the suppression of the rebellion in Kilwa in October 2004, having provided logistics to the DRC Military, under force of law,' he told me, declining to elaborate on what those logistics were. But Turner told me he had not been aware of 'allegations of war crimes or atrocities' until an ABC reporter asked him about them in an interview seven months after the massacre. (He added that the interview was edited with the aim of 'portraying Anvil and me in the worst possible light'.) 'There have been multiple government enquiries in a number of countries, including a detailed Australian Federal Police investigation in Australia into those allegations,' Turner continued in a letter responding to my questions. 'None of those enquiries has found that there is any substance whatsoever to the allegations. In addition, there has been litigation instigated in the Democratic Republic of Congo, Western Australia and Canada, which has at least touched on the matters raised by you. In none of those cases have there been findings against Anvil.'[29]

The survivors' representatives fought for years to hold those responsible for the Kilwa massacre to account, but they got nowhere. Katumba was untouchable. In 2009 a US diplomatic cable described him as 'a kind of shady, even nefarious figure within Kabila's inner circle, [who] is believed to manage much of Kabila's personal fortune'.[30] The cable was transmitting news that Katumba had stepped down from his latest formal position, heading Kabila's majority in the national assembly. But it predicted – accurately – that his influence would remain.

In 2006 and 2007 two rebel groups and the Congolese army fought for control over Edouard Mwangachuchu's coltan mine at Bibatama.[31] The group that won out was arguably the most formidable rebel force in eastern Congo – quite an accolade, given the ferocity of the fighting that continued to erupt regularly despite the formal end of the war in 2003.

Known by its French acronym, CNDP, the Congress for the Defence of the People was the creation of Laurent Nkunda, a Tutsi renegade general and Seventh-Day Adventist pastor from North Kivu. Nkunda had fought with Rwanda against Laurent Kabila before joining the Congolese national army when it incorporated various warring factions under the 2003 peace deal. He rose to general before returning to the cause of rebellion – this time, his own.

The hills and forests around Nkunda's hometown in North Kivu became his fiefdom, as the forces at his command swelled to eight thousand men (and children).[32] A student of psychology, for a time he outwitted everyone, navigating with cunning the treacherous terrain in which Rwanda and Kinshasa jostled for influence with UN peacekeepers, arms dealers, local politicians and eastern Congo's constellation of paramilitary groups.

For all Nkunda's rhetoric – he spoke to a *Financial Times* reporter in 2008 of 'a cry for peace and freedom' – his operation was, in large measure and like many of its rivals, a money-making venture.[33] Eastern Congo's militias – not to mention the army itself – have many ways to bring in revenue, from taxing commercial traffic to ranching and trading in charcoal. But the mining trade is particularly lucrative and has the advantage of bringing in foreign currency that can buy arms.

The business arrangements of eastern Congo's clandestine mineral trade reveal something else, something that undercuts the crass notion that the primitive hatreds of African tribes are the sole driver of the conflict. The two most important militias, the CNDP and the Forces Démocratiques de Libération du Rwanda (FDLR), are sworn enemies. The former's stated reason to exist is to defend the Tutsis of eastern Congo from the latter, a cohort formed by the Hutu extremists who perpetrated the Rwandan genocide. Both also serve as proxies: Joseph Kabila has supported the FDLR to counter the influence that Paul Kagame's Tutsi-led government in Rwanda exercises through the CNDP.

But as one easterner who has worked in both mining and intelligence told me, 'Formally the groups are all enemies. But when it comes to making money and mining, they cooperate pretty well. War changes, but business goes on. The actors change, but the system stays – the links between the armed groups and the mines. The conflict goes on because it has its own financing: the mines and the weapons. It has its own economy.'[34]

On a Sunday afternoon in Goma I drank a beer beside a pool at a hotel with Colonel Olivier Hamuli. He is the spokesman of the Congolese armed forces and journalists regard him as one of the more accurate sources of information on the fighting, even if he avoids discussing the military's own role in plunder and atrocities. An easterner, his convivial demeanour cannot mask the eyes of a man who has seen too much. When we met he was fielding call after call about clashes between Tutsi rebels and the army. The rebels had advanced to take strategic positions on the edge of Goma; the army and UN peacekeepers were preparing helicopter gunships for a counterattack.

'The CNDP, the FDLR, they say they are fighting against bad governance. They are just mining. Even the FDLR, they are not trying to challenge the Rwandan government – they are here to mine. This is the problem of the war in the east,' the colonel said.[35] 'It's a war of economic opportunity. It's not just Rwanda that benefits; it's businessmen in the United States, Australia too.' He brandished one of his incessantly buzzing mobile phones. 'Smuggling goes on. Mobile phones are still being made. They need the raw materials one way or another.'

According to the UN panel of experts that tries to keep track of the links between eastern Congo's conflict and the mineral trade, after Nkunda won the battle for the territory that contained Mwangachuchu's mining operations, the warlord permitted the businessman to retain control of his mines in return for a cut of the coltan.[36] Mwangachuchu told the UN team he paid 20 cents per kilo of coltan exported from his mines at checkpoints he suspected were run by the CNDP.[37] That levy alone would have channelled thousands of dollars a year into the militia's war chest. Altogether eastern Congo's militias are estimated to have raked in something to the tune of $185 million in revenues from the trade in coltan and other minerals in 2008.[38] The UN team also reported Mwangachuchu's excuse for funding the militia: he told the team he had 'no choice but to accept the presence of CNDP and carry on working at Bibatama, as he needs money to pay $16,000 in taxes to the government.'

To his supporters, Mwangachuchu is a well-meaning employer (of both Tutsis and other ethnicities) assailed by grasping militiamen. His supporters, none of whom wanted to be named when they spoke to me, described a legitimate businessman striving to introduce modern mining techniques in the face of turmoil and wrongheaded foreign interventions. Some well-informed Congolese observers are less inclined to give him the benefit of the doubt. One night in a Goma bar a senior army officer fumed with anger when I asked him about Mwangachuchu and other mining barons of North Kivu. He damned them all as war profiteers who preferred to pay a few dollars to rebel-run rackets than have a functioning state tax them properly. When I asked the easterner who has worked both on mining policy and in Congolese intelligence about Mwangachuchu's claim that he had been forcibly taxed by the CNDP, he shot back, 'It's not a question of taxes. Mwangachuchu and the armed groups are the same thing.'

It is hard to see how Mwangachuchu could have established himself as a leading Tutsi businessman in the East without becoming intertwined with the armed groups. As well as seeking prosperity, Tutsis in eastern Congo have faced near-constant threats to their survival, most terrifyingly from the Rwandan Hutu génocidaires who roam the hills.

In 2011 Mwangachuchu stood as a candidate for CNDP's political wing in the national assembly – and its foot soldiers helped guarantee his victory. They had been absorbed into the lawless ranks of Congo's army under a shaky peace deal but retained their mining rackets and their loyalties.[39] 'The CNDP guys used every trick in the book to make sure he got through,' said a foreign election observer who watched former CNDP rebels filling out ballot papers for Mwangachuchu after the polls had closed.[40] Ex-CNDP fighters in the national army were observed brazenly intimidating voters in North Kivu, some of the most egregious abuses in a deeply flawed national election that secured Kabila a fresh term.[41] According to a report to the Security Council by a UN group of experts, to ensure the support of the CNDP's fighters, Mwangachuchu had paid off Bosco Ntaganda. Known as 'The Terminator', Ntaganda had replaced the deposed Laurent Nkunda three years earlier as the CNDP boss and brought his boys into the army even though he was wanted by the International Criminal Court for war crimes including murder, rape, conscripting child soldiers, and ethnic persecution.[42] Despite overwhelming evidence of foul play and months of legal wrangling, Mwangachuchu's election stood. Even before his victory was secure, Ntaganda named him president of the CNDP's political party.

Mwangachuchu's leadership was short-lived. A few months after the 2011 election Kabila's government sought to strengthen its writ in the East by relocating the former CNDP militiamen who had been brought into the national army to postings elsewhere in the country, far from the East's coltan, gold and tin mines. But the militiamen were not about to give that up without a fight. Several hundred mutinied under a new acronym, M23, short for March 23, the date of the 2009 deal that had brought them into the army. Rwanda, deeply involved in both eastern Congo's military and mining networks, again provided covert support to the mainly Tutsi rebels as they advanced on Goma.[43]

In early May 2012 General James Kabarebe, the redoubtable Rwandan defence minister who had masterminded its military campaigns in Congo and surreptitiously commanded M23, called Mwangachuchu. He ordered him to support the rebels and pull the CNDP political party out of its alliance with Kabila.[44] Mwangachuchu refused. Perhaps he feared that crossing Kabila would imperil his mining interests; perhaps he sensed that the new rebellion was doomed. A furious Kabarebe told Mwangachuchu that 'a lightning bolt will strike you'. Within days he had been ousted as president of the CNDP's political party.

But Mwangachuchu had chosen wisely. Western powers that had long turned a blind eye to Rwanda's meddling in Congo ran out of patience and suspended aid. Bosco Ntaganda, the Tutsi warlord who had joined the mutiny, found himself under such mortal threat that he chose to take his chances in The Hague and turned himself in at the US embassy in Rwanda, from where he was sent to face justice at the International Criminal Court. At negotiations in Uganda between Kabila's government and the M23 rebels, Mwangachuchu was part of the government delegation. The talks came to little, and in late 2013 Congolese forces, backed by a new UN force with a mandate to smash the rebel groups, routed the M23 rebels.

I asked Mwangachuchu to give me his own account. He declined. When I e-mailed him a list of questions, it was his lawyer who replied. Mwangachuchu, the lawyer wrote, 'reminds you that there is a war on in this part of the country and he cannot afford at this stage to answer your questions.' Mwangachuchu can claim to have played peacemaker – but only when it suits him. 'He's not a fighter; he's a businessman,' a former minister in Kabila's government told me. 'His loyalties are not so strong – except to his business.'

Our two-jeep convoy slowed as it approached a roadblock deep in the tropical forests of one of eastern Congo's national parks. Manning the roadblock were soldiers from the Congolese army, theoretically the institution that should safeguard the state's monopoly on the use of force but, in practice, chiefly just another predator on civilians. As my Congolese companions negotiated nervously with the soldiers, I stepped away to take advantage of a break in a very long drive and relieve myself, only to sense someone rushing toward me. Hurriedly zipping up my fly, I turned to see a fast-approaching soldier brandishing his AK47. With a voice that signified a grave transgression, he declared, 'It is forbidden to piss in the park.' Human urine, the soldier asserted, posed a threat to eastern Congo's gorillas. I thought it best not to retort that the poor creatures had been poached close to extinction by, among others, the army, nor that the park attracted far more militiamen than gorilla-watching tourists.

My crime, it transpired, carried a financial penalty. My companions took the soldier aside, and the matter was settled. Perhaps they talked him down, using the presence of a foreign journalist as leverage. Perhaps they slipped him a few dollars. As we drove away it occurred to me that we had witnessed the Congolese state in microcosm. The soldier was following the example set by Kabila, Katumba, Mwangachuchu and Nkunda: capture a piece of territory, be it a remote intersection of potholed road, a vast copper concession, or the presidency itself; protect your claim with a gun, a threat, a semblance of law, or a shibboleth; and extract rent from it. The political economy of the roadblock has taken hold. The more the state crumbles, the greater the need for each individual to make ends meet however they can; the greater the looting, the more the authority of the state withers.

Leaving the roadblock behind, we bounced along the pitted tracks that lead into the interior of South Kivu province. It was late 2010, and a joint offensive against Hutu rebels by Congolese and Rwandan forces and their allied militias had driven masses of civilians from their farmsteads. Kwashiorkor, or severe acute malnutrition in children, was rife.

The lone hospital in Bunyakiri serves 160,000 people. It has no ambulance and no electricity, making it almost impossible after nightfall to find a vein for an injection. The rusting metal of its roof is scarcely less rickety than the surrounding mud huts. When I visited, medicine was in short supply, the army having recently ransacked the hospital. There was no mobile phone reception, an irony in a part of the world whose tantalum is crucial in making the devices.

The hospital's pediatric ward had fourteen beds. At least two mothers sat on each, cradling their babies. On one, Bora Sifa regarded her surroundings warily. Two years earlier a raiding party from the FDLR, the militia formed by the perpetrators of the Rwandan genocide, had descended on her village in search of loot to supplement the income from their mining operations. The raiders ordered Bora's husband to gather up what they wanted. 'They forced him to carry all the things away into the forest,' Bora told me. 'Then they killed him.'

Bora fled and a stranger in another village took her in, allowing her and her children to live in an outhouse. Now twenty, she made about a dollar a day helping to cultivate cassava, a root crop that fills empty bellies but has little nutritional value. Five days ago she had brought her son, Chance, to the hospital. 'He wasn't growing,' Bora said. 'I wasn't making enough milk.' Like many malnourished children, Chance's features had aged prematurely. His eyes were sunken, his hair receding.

At any given moment since the start of Congo's great war in 1998, between 1 million and 3.5 million Congolese have been adrift like Bora. The vast majority are in the East, driven from mining areas or the shifting frontlines of multiple interwoven conflicts. In 2013 2.6 million of Congo's 66 million people were 'internally displaced', as refugees who have remained in their country are known in the jargon of human catastrophe, making up one in ten of the worldwide tally.[45] Many end up in flimsy bivouacs fashioned from tarpaulins bearing the brands of assorted relief agencies; others appeal to the solidarity of their fellow Congolese, which persists despite the myriad fissures that war, desperation and ethnicity have opened between them. That solidarity can only do so much in a country where two-thirds lack sufficient food. Uprooted, Congo's wandering millions starve.

With the help of the hospital's tireless doctor and a French charity, Chance was recovering.[46] Few others shared his fortune. Further up the road I visited a hilltop clinic beside a school in the town of Hombo Sud. One by one, dozens of emaciated children were being dangled from weighing scales and checked for telltale signs of severe malnutrition: oedema (a buildup of fluids in the legs) and arms with a circumference of less than 10.5 centimetres.

Anna Rebecca Susa, a bundle of spindles in a pink skirt emblazoned with the word 'Princess', was dangerously underweight. The special measuring tape showed red when a medic pulled it tight round her arm. Her belly was swollen beneath fleshless ribs, her hair reduced to a faint frizz. At five, she could not understand what was happening to her, but her big eyes were full of anxiety, as though she could sense that her body was failing. She could not keep down a sachet of the peanut paste that can do wonders for malnourished children and was sent home with more in the hope her stomach would settle. Her father, Lavie, invited me back to his home, an outhouse belonging to a distant relative where Lavie, his wife, and their four children had lived since they fled rebel attacks on their home village two years previously.

The signature falsetto guitar of Congolese music drifted over the jagged rooftops of the tiny metal shacks sprayed across the slopes. Lavie's wife, whose wedding ring he had fashioned from a plastic bottle top, was out foraging for leaves. Anna fell asleep on the shack's lone bed. Her younger brother, Espoir, tottered around, oblivious to his sister's plight.

A few weeks later I got in touch with the clinic's medics to ask after Anna. When she had kept throwing up the peanut paste, the French charity had driven her to the hospital at Bunyakiri. By then there was little anyone could do. Her immune system destroyed by malnutrition, she died of an infection.

The heavens opened the day they buried Augustin Katumba Mwanke. The Congolese establishment sheltered under marquees in Kinshasa before the coffin that sported an enormous floral garland.[47] In a black suit and black shirt Joseph Kabila arrived amid a phalanx of bodyguards manoeuvring to keep an umbrella over his head. It was a rare public appearance for a reclusive president said to have spent his early years in office in the company of video games. His face was expressionless. Barely two months had passed since he had rigged his way to victory in the presidential election, securing a second five-year term. Now the mastermind behind both his power and his wealth was gone. The previous day, 12 February 2012, the American pilot of the jet carrying a group of Kabila's senior officials to Bukavu by Lake Kivu had misjudged the landing. Katumba's last moments came as the aircraft veered off the runway and smashed into a grassy embankment. He was forty-eight.

One other guest at the funeral stood out. He was the lone white face in the front row. Kabila clasped his hand. The burly, bearded man in a yarmulke, the Jewish skullcap, was Dan Gertler. He was the all-important intersection between the shadow state that controlled access to Congo's minerals and the multinational mining companies that coveted them.

The grandson of one of the founders of Israel's diamond exchange, in his early twenties Gertler set forth to seek his own fortune. He went to

Angola, then still deep in civil war and a rich source of diamonds. But another Israeli, Lev Leviev, had already staked a strong claim there. Gertler arrived in Congo in 1997, days after Laurent Kabila had overthrown Mobutu. An ultra-orthodox Jew, he was introduced by a rabbi to Joseph Kabila, newly installed as the head of the Congolese army.[48] The younger Kabila and Gertler had much in common. Each stood in the shadow of his elders, carrying a heavy burden on young shoulders into the cauldron of Congolese warfare and politics. They became firm friends.

Gertler soon discovered the value of his friendship with the president's son. Kabila Sr was in urgent need of funds to arm his forces against Rwandan and Ugandan invaders and to butter up his allies for the fight.[49] When Joseph took his new friend to meet his father, the president told the young Israeli that if he could raise $20 million without delay, he could have a monopoly to buy every diamond mined in Congo. Gertler cobbled together the cash and was granted the monopoly.

Not for the last time, an arrangement that suited Gertler and the Kabila clan hardly served the interests of the Congolese people. 'It wasn't a good deal for us,' Mawapanga Mwana Nanga, then the finance minister, told me. 'We should have opened the market to the highest bidder.'[50] UN investigators declared that Gertler's diamond monopoly had been a 'nightmare' for Congo's government and a 'disaster' for the local diamond trade, encouraging smuggling and costing the treasury tax revenue.[51] It could not last. After Joseph Kabila succeeded his assassinated father in 2001, the monopoly was cancelled under pressure from foreign donors.[52]

Gertler was not deterred. He re-established a commanding position in the Congolese diamond trade by arranging to buy stones from the state-owned diamond miner and began to turn his attention to the far bigger prize: the copper and cobalt of Katanga, where production and prices would rise dramatically as Asian demand for base metals soared. His most important asset – his bond with the new president – was intact. 'Gertler showed that he could help the family and, in return, they said, "We can do business with you,"' a diplomat who spent years watching Gertler's exploits in Congo told me. 'Kabila can only keep himself in power with the help of people like Gertler: it's like an insurance mechanism – someone who can get you money and stuff when you need it.'

Over the years that followed, Gertler cultivated Katumba too, even inviting him to a party on a yacht in the Red Sea that included a performance by
Uri Geller, the Israeli illusionist and self-proclaimed psychic.[53] In a reverie
of gratitude to Gertler, in the final pages of his posthumously published
memoir Katumba wrote that 'in spite of all our seeming differences, I am
proud to be the brother you never had.'[54]

The trio of Kabila, Katumba and Gertler was unassailable. 'It's like an
exclusive golf club,' one of Kabila's former ministers told me. 'If you go
and say, "The founders are cheating," they're going to say: "And who the
hell are you?"'[55] Gertler's role in this exclusive club was manifold. 'It's an
amalgam – business, political assistance, finance,' said Olivier Kamitatu,
who became an opposition legislator after his five-year stint as Kabila's
planning minister.[56] Gertler's particular contribution was to build a tan-
gled corporate web through which companies linked to him have made
sensational profits through sell-offs of some of Congo's most valuable mining assets. 'The line between the interests of the state and the personal interests of the president is not clear,' Kamitatu told me. 'That is the presence
of Gertler.'

Since he first rode to Laurent Kabila's rescue with $20 million to fund
the war effort, Gertler has proved himself invaluable to Congo's rulers. Katumba wrote in his memoir that Gertler's 'inexhaustible generosity, and the
extreme efficiency of his assistance, have been decisive for us in the most
crucial moments.'[57] Deals in which he was involved are said to have helped
finance Joseph Kabila's 2006 election campaign.[58] Kamitatu told me that
Gertler had helped Kabila win that election and said he had also come up
with cash for the military campaign against Laurent Nkunda's rebels in
the East. I asked Gertler's representatives whether he had assisted Kabila
at these moments and during the 2011 elections. They did not respond.
Gertler has, however, denied that he has underpaid for Congolese mining assets. 'The lies are screaming to the heavens,' he told a reporter from
Bloomberg in 2012.[59]

Kamitatu, who is the son of one of Congo's independence leaders and
trained in business before a political career that began as a senior figure a
rebel group during the war, sees the shadow state as the root of his nation's
failure to escape poverty. 'You can't develop the country through parallel

institutions. Every infrastructure project you undertake is not done through a strategic vision but with a view to the personal financial results,' he told me as we sat at his house in Kinshasa in 2013. Politics and private business have fused, Kamitatu believed. Winning a presidential election costs tens of millions of dollars, and the only people with that kind of money are the foreign mining houses. 'I am extremely worried about a political system where the voters are starving and the politicians buy votes with money from natural resource companies,' Kamitatu said. 'Is that democracy?'

Dan Gertler's Congolese mining deals have made him a billionaire. Many of the transactions in which he has played a part are fiendishly complicated, involving multiple interlinked sales conducted through offshore vehicles registered in tax havens where all but the most basic company information is secret. Nonetheless, a pattern emerges. A copper or cobalt mine owned by the Congolese state or rights to a virgin deposit are sold, sometimes in complete secrecy, to a company controlled by or linked to Gertler's offshore network for a price far below what it is worth. Then all or part of that asset is sold at a profit to a big foreign mining company, among them some of the biggest groups on the London Stock Exchange.

Gertler did not invent complexity in mining deals. Webs of subsidiaries and offshore holding companies are common in the resource industries, either to dodge taxation or to shield the beneficiaries from scrutiny. But even by the industry's bewildering standards, the structure of Gertler's Congo deals is labyrinthine. The sale of SMKK was typical.[60]

SMKK was founded in 1999 as a joint venture between Gécamines, Congo's state-owned mining company, and a small mining company from Canada.[61] SMKK held rights to a tract of land in the heart of the copper-belt. It sits beside some of the planet's most prodigious copper mines, making it a fair bet that the area the company's permits cover contains plentiful ore. Indeed, Gécamines had mined the site in the 1980s before Mobutu's looting drove the company into collapse.[62] After a string of complicated transactions beginning in November 2007, involving a former England cricketer, a white crony of Robert Mugabe, and assorted offshore vehicles, 50 per cent of SMKK ended up in the hands of Eurasian Natural

Resources Corporation (ENRC), whose oligarch owners had raised a few eyebrows in the City of London in 2007 when they obtained a London Stock Exchange listing for a company they had built from privatized mines in Kazakhstan.[63] The Congolese state, through Gécamines, still owned the remaining 50 per cent of SMKK.

Toward the end of 2009 ENRC bought an option, only made public months later, to purchase the 50 per cent it did not already own. The strange thing was that ENRC did not buy that option from the owner of the stake, state-owned Gécamines, but from a hitherto unknown company called Emerald Star Enterprises Limited.[64] Emerald Star was incorporated in the British Virgin Islands, one of the most popular secrecy jurisdictions, shortly before it struck this agreement with ENRC, which suggests that it was set up for that specific purpose.[65] There is nothing in Emerald Star's registration documents to show who owns it. But other documents related to the deal would later reveal the identity of its principal owner, Dan Gertler's family trust.[66]

At this stage all Gertler had was a deal to sell to ENRC a stake in SMKK that he did not yet own. That was soon rectified. On 1 February 2010, Gertler's Emerald Star signed an agreement with Gécamines to buy the Congolese state's 50 per cent share in SMKK for $15 million.[67] ENRC duly exercised its option to buy the stake by buying Emerald Star for another $50 million on top of the $25 million it had paid for the option. The interwoven deals were done and dusted by June 2010.[68] All the corporate chicanery masked a simple fact: the Congolese state had sold rights to a juicy copper prospect for $15 million to a private company, which immediately sold the same rights on for $75 million – a $60 million loss for the state and a $60 million profit for Gertler.

The Congolese people were not the only losers in the SMKK deal. ENRC's would seem to have suffered too. When it bought the first 50 per cent of SMKK, ENRC had also acquired a right of first refusal should Gécamines decide to sell the other half.[69] That meant that ENRC could have bought the stake when it was offered to Dan Gertler's company for $15 million. Instead, it paid $75 million a few months later, once the stake had first passed to Gertler's offshore vehicle. ENRC has not disclosed the terms of its right of first refusal and did not reply to my questions about it. Perhaps there was some stipulation in it that meant buying the stake directly from Gécamines would have been more expensive for ENRC than buying it via Gertler. But based on the details that have emerged, it is hard to see how the oligarch founders of ENRC thought the SMKK manoeuvre was in the best interests of the rest of the investors who had bought shares in the company when it floated in London.

ENRC was a member of the FTSE 100, the prestigious list of the UK's biggest listed companies, in which pension funds invest savers' money. Investors who bought shares when ENRC listed some of its stock in December 2007 paid £5.40 a share, raising £1.4 billion for the company. Over the six years that followed, ENRC's boardroom was a scene of unceasing turbulence, as the oligarch founders continued to exert their influence over a company that was supposedly subject to British governance rules for listed corporations.[70] ENRC snapped up assets in Africa, including SMKK, and struck other deals with Gertler in Congo. The Serious Fraud Office was in the middle of an investigation (still active at the time of writing) into ENRC's activities in Africa and Kazakhstan – and its share price was sliding precipitously downward – when the oligarchs announced that they planned, with the help of the Kazakh government, to buy back the stock they had listed in London, thereby taking the company private again.[71] The offer was valued at £2.28 a share – less than half of what investors who bought in at the start had paid for them.[72]

If some British pension funds and stock-market dabblers felt burned by their investments in ENRC, their losses were relatively easy to bear compared with those that Gertler's sweetheart deals have inflicted on Congo. The best estimate, calculated by Kofi Annan's Africa Progress Panel, puts the losses to the Congolese state from SMKK and four other such deals at $1.36 billion between 2010 and 2012.[73] Based on that estimate, Congo lost more money from these deals alone than it received in humanitarian aid over the same period.[74] So porous is Congo's treasury that there is no guarantee that, had they ended up there, these revenues would have been spent on schools and hospitals and other worthwhile endeavours; indeed, government income from resource rent has a tendency to add to misrule, absolving rulers of the need to convince electorates to pay taxes. But no state can fulfil its basic duties if it is broke. Between 2007 and 2012 just 2.5 per cent of the $41 billion that the mining industry generated in Congo flowed into the country's meagre budget.[75] Meanwhile, the shadow state flourishes.

Since at least 1885, when Congo became the personal possession of Belgium's King Leopold II, outsiders have been complicit in the plunder of Congo's natural wealth. King Leopold turned the country into a commercial enterprise, producing first ivory then rubber at the cost of millions of Congolese lives. In 1908 Leopold yielded personal ownership of Congo to the Belgian state, which, keen to retain influence over the mineral seams of Katanga following independence in 1960, encouraged the region's secessionists, helping to bring down the liberation leader Patrice Lumumba in a CIA-sponsored coup that ushered in Mobutu, who became one of the century's most rapacious kleptocrats.[76] Richard Nixon, Ronald Reagan and George H. W. Bush welcomed him warmly to Washington. Only once his usefulness expired after the end of the Cold War did the United States abandon Mobutu to flee from Laurent Kabila's advancing rebels.

In the era of globalization the foreign protagonists in Congo's looting machine are not monarchs or imperial states but rather tycoons and multinationals. As well as the likes of Dan Gertler, there are the companies that do business with him. ENRC is one. Another is Glencore, the giant commodity trading house based in the Swiss town of Zug, which listed its shares on the London Stock Exchange in 2011, immediately becoming one of the UK's biggest listed companies. In 2010 and 2011 Glencore was involved in transactions in which, according to calculations by Kofi Annan's Africa Progress Panel, the Congolese state sold mining assets to companies connected to Gertler for hundreds of millions of dollars less than they were worth.[77] (Both ENRC and Glencore insist there has been nothing improper in their Congolese dealings.[78])

From multibillion-dollar copper deals in Katanga to smuggling rackets shifting coltan out of the East, Congo's looting machine extends from the locals who control access to the mining areas, via middlemen to traders, global markets and consumers. During the war UN investigators described companies trading minerals as 'the engine of the conflict'.[79] A senior Congolese army officer remembered Viktor Bout, a notorious KGB agent turned arms dealer who was implicated in the illicit coltan trade – and whose exploits inspired the 2005 film *Lord of War* – dropping in to do business.[80] 'He did terrible things here,' the officer told me.[81] The trade in minerals from eastern Congo spans the globe. In 2012, according to official records, North Kivu's declared exports of raw minerals went to Dubai, China, Hong Kong, Switzerland, Panama and Singapore.

When Wall Street nearly imploded in 2008, triggering economic havoc far beyond Manhattan, the world was reminded of the extent of the damage that a complex cross-border network combining financial, economic and political power can do. The reforming legislation in the aftermath of the crisis dealt mostly with the financial quackery that had grown rife in US banks. But toward the end of the 848-page Dodd–Frank Act of 2010 was an item that had nothing to do with subprime mortgages or liquidity ratios. 'It is the sense of Congress that the exploitation and trade of conflict minerals originating in the Democratic Republic of the Congo is helping to finance conflict characterized by extreme levels of violence in the eastern Democratic Republic of the Congo,' read a clause in the Act that responded to years of pressure from campaigners. In the future companies using coltan and other resources from Congo in their products would have to submit to US regulators a report on their supply chain, signed off by an independent auditor, demonstrating that they were not funding armed groups. Some six thousand companies would be affected, among them Apple, Ford and Boeing.[82]

Few could fault the sentiment. But the legislation was drafted in Congress, not Congo. It backfired. For one thing, the definition of 'armed groups' left out the Congolese army, which has been responsible for looting and wanton violence. Then there was the practical difficulty of tracking supply chains in a war zone. When the Dodd–Frank Act passed, many buyers of Congolese minerals simply took their business elsewhere, reinforcing a temporary ban on mineral exports imposed by Joseph Kabila in response to pressure to curtail the turmoil in the East.

A score of 'conflict-free' certification schemes have sprung up, some connected to Dodd–Frank, some to Congolese initiatives, and some to industry efforts to wipe the stigma from their products. In April 2013 an independent German auditor who had spent five days at Edouard Mwangachuchu's coltan mines concluded that 'with the evidence presented there was no indication that there are armed groups involved in mining'.[83] The bigger militias had pulled back from Mwangachuchu's corner of North

Kivu; M23, the most threatening armed group of the day, was camped close to the Ugandan border, away from the main mining areas.

I wanted to see for myself whether the link between eastern Congo's minerals and its conflict was loosening. I asked to visit Mwangachuchu's mines. He was out of town, and his company declined to grant me access. But I knew that a cooperative of informal miners was also mining the area, the subject of years of dispute with Mwangachuchu. On the three-hour drive from Goma we passed a settlement nestled in a bend in a valley that had served as the base for Laurent Nkunda's CNDP rebels. Further along was a camp for refugees displaced by the M23 conflict. At the metal barriers marking the entrance to each village, young men flagged us down and suggested they might be due payment. Children, no older than five, had imitated their elders and crafted a makeshift roadblock of rocks and half a yellow water-canteen. They scampered from the road as approaching vehicles failed to slow.

Another refugee camp marked the start of Rubaya, the mining town at the foot of the hills that Mwangachuchu and the informal miners exploit. Toddlers with bloated bellies, the signature of malnutrition, tottered at the road's verge. The town itself boasted more robust dwellings than the makeshift tents of the displaced. Mining money had even allowed the construction of a few sturdy wooden houses. Rows of cassava tubers lay whitening in the sun. The whole town sounded as though it were wailing, so numerous were its infants, a chorus pierced by the occasional squawk of a cockerel. A tattered Congolese flag flapped from a skinny tree trunk.

After an hour waiting to pay our respects to the town administrator – during which, a local activist whispered in my ear, the mining bosses were checking that there were not too many children at work for their visitor to see – my Congolese companions and I began our ascent to the summit. Red dust devils swirled around us as we climbed. A local man who worked to get children out of the mines pointed across a valley to the village where he had been one of the few survivors of a revenge massacre of Hutus by Rwandan invaders in 1997.

Porters with white sacks on their heads cascaded down the unpaved paths from the peak, throwing up clouds of red-brown dust. Each sack contained up to 25 kilograms of rock hewn from the mountain. The porters' haste was a matter of economics: they were paid 1,000 Congolese francs per trip (about $1) and had to wash and sift their cargo in the stream at the bottom before it began the long trip toward the border or the buying houses of Goma.

Most of the incipient certification schemes for Congolese minerals work by tagging sacks of ore as they emerge from the mine to certify their provenance, imitating the Kimberley Process, which was designed to stem the flow of 'blood diamonds'. The idea is to prevent belligerents getting around embargoes by passing off their minerals as originating from another mine or smuggling them across borders to allow Congolese coltan to be branded as Rwandan or Angolan diamonds as Zambian. But on this hillside there was not a tag in sight. One local, a peace campaigner who had come along for the climb and who kept his distance from the mining bosses leading the ascent, told me that some of the coltan extracted here was crossing the nearby border into Uganda clandestinely. That took it right through the territory of M23 rebels.

The slope grew steeper. The earth underfoot gave way like a sand dune. Finally a peak of jagged rock emerged, a giant fossilized sponge of warrens that the miners had dug by hand. About two thousand miners, all in Wellington boots, many bearing spades and picks, swarmed among the pits and trenches, some delving as deep as 15 metres into the ground with only rudimentary props to keep the sides from burying them alive. Some looked decidedly younger than eighteen. One was clearly baffled by the white-skinned visitor whose hair was longer than the standard Congolese buzz cut. 'He has the voice of a man,' the young miner intoned with consternation to one of my companions, 'but the hair of a woman.'

On the next hill over we could make out Mwangachuchu's mine. All this territory lay under his concession, but the informal miners had enough political clout to carry on regardless of his protests, in part thanks to ethnic manoeuvring by the cooperative's Hutu leadership against the Tutsi Mwangachuchu. The cooperative had resisted Mwangachuchu's repeated attempts to turf them off his land, challenging the validity of his claim. Mwangachuchu has countered by trying to oblige the informal miners to sell all their production through his company, without which it would be impossible for him to prove that minerals from the concession were not funding militias.

The chief miner, Bazinga Kabano, a well-dressed man with a long walking cane and a penchant for bellowing at his subordinates, told me that when the CNDP controlled the area the miners' association used to pay the rebels a $50 fee to be allowed to dig. But he was keen to paint his industry not as an engine of war but as a path to betterment. He explained that some of the miners graduated to be *négociants*, the intermediaries who buy coltan at the mine and sell it on to the comptoirs that export it. Surveying the teeming hilltop, he declared, 'We are helping them to live their dreams.'

I wandered off to talk to some miners out of earshot of the boss. Kafanya Salongo bore a passing resemblance to a meerkat as his blinking head popped out of a hole in the ground. He was short, slim and strong, ideal for a human burrower. He churned out one hundred sacks worth of rock a day, and that brought in $9. From that he had to find the $25 each miner must pay the bosses every month for the privilege of digging. 'It's not enough for the family,' he told me. 'I can afford some food and some medicine, but that's it.' At thirty-two, he had a wife and two sons. He laughed in the face of danger. 'Yeah, it looks dangerous, but we know how to construct the shafts, so it's fine.'

It is easy to scoff at the boss's notion that these miners are digging toward their dreams. The work is gruelling and perilous. The official statistics recorded twenty deaths in mining accidents in North Kivu in 2012, six of them at an adjacent mine worked by the cooperative. The authorities noted that it is 'very possible' that not all deaths were reported. But by local standards the miners' wages amount to big bucks. Some splash their pay on booze and hookers; some build better houses.

Kabila's mining ban and the boycott prompted by the Dodd–Frank Act pitched thousands of eastern Congolese miners out of work. The World Bank has estimated that 16 per cent of Congo's population is directly or indirectly engaged in informal mining, which accounts for all but a fraction of the industry as measured by employment;[84] in North Kivu in 2006 mining revenue provided an estimated two-thirds of state income.[85] But revenues to the provincial government's coffers fell by three-quarters in the four years before 2012, in part because of what officials called the 'global criminalization of the mining sector' of eastern Congo. The state's loss is the smugglers' gain: when the official routes are closed, the clandestine trade picks up the slack.

By the middle of 2013 Kabila's ban had been partially relaxed, and previously blacklisted comptoirs in Goma had reopened. A dozen mines in North Kivu that the government deemed to be unconnected to armed groups had been 'green-lighted' to export. But Emmanuel Ndimubanzi, the head of North Kivu's mining division, told me that not a single mine was tagging its output so that buyers could identify the mine at which it had originated. 'Tagging is very expensive,' he said. 'We don't have the partners to pay for it.' In what might have been a line from *Catch-22*, he added, 'Certification can only happen with better security.'

Regional initiatives are increasingly tracking shipments of coltan and other ores, even if North Kivu is lagging behind. Some campaigners have welcomed what appears to be a significant reduction in the documented connections between militias and mining sites as a result of certification efforts and a UN-backed offensive against the armed groups.[86] Gradually Western-based electronics groups are drawing up lists of approved smelters that can demonstrate that their metals come from mines that do not benefit Congolese militias, although the campaign group Global Witness warned in 2014 that the first supply-chain reports, which US companies buying Congolese minerals are now required to submit to regulators, 'lack substance'.[87] The German Federal Institute for Geosciences and Natural Resources has developed 'fingerprinting' technology that can trace a shipment of ore back to the mine from which it was extracted. This technology could, if comprehensively applied, prevent the entry into the international market of minerals from militia-controlled mines, provided that it were matched with an intelligence-gathering programme to keep tabs on all the militias' mining operations.

It appears unlikely that the certification schemes will ever reliably cover the whole of eastern Congo's mining trade. Clean miners have been squeezed, as the retreat of Western buyers has let Chinese comptoirs gain a near-monopoly on Congolese coltan, allowing them to dictate prices. The efforts to impose some control on the mineral trade might trim the income of the armed groups, but it does so at the cost of weakening the already precarious livelihoods of eastern Congo's diggers and porters and their dependents. In a land ruled by the law of the roadblock, such initiatives can look quixotic. As Aloys Tegera of Goma's Pole Institute, one of eastern Congo's most astute commentators, writes, 'Without a Congolese state capable of playing its role in controlling and running affairs, how can the minerals of Kivu be de-criminalised?'[88]

In the run-up to the 2011 elections and during the months that followed, the SMKK transactions and other similar ones effectively transferred hundreds of millions of dollars from the state to a close personal friend of a president. Dan Gertler has doubled as an emissary for the president, conducting diplomatic missions to Washington and Rwanda. 'The truth is, during our very difficult times, there were investors who came and left and others who braved the hurricane,' Kabila has said of Gertler.[89] 'He's one of those.' Kabila might have added that some of those who left did so when their assets were confiscated – and, in some cases, handed to Gertler.[90]

Gertler maintains that, far from being a predator, he is among Congo's greatest benefactors. He and his representatives point out, with some justification, that unlike the most egregious asset-flippers, who do nothing beyond using bribes and connections to win mining rights before selling them on, Gertler's operations in Congo actually produce minerals, and lots of them. His company, the Fleurette Group, says it has invested $1.5 billion 'in the acquisition and development of mining and other assets in the DRC', that it supports twenty thousand Congolese jobs, and that it ranks among the country's biggest taxpayers and philanthropists.[91] Gertler himself has said his work in Congo is worthy of a Nobel Prize.[92]

Katumba's death sent a tremor through Kabila's regime. Would-be investors whose only contract was an understanding they had reached with Katumba evaporated after the plane crash. But the president and Gertler, brothers in spirit, have maintained the shadow government that Katumba helped to construct. Gertler has branched out into oil, prospecting promising new sites at Lake Albert. As for Kabila, he must now decide whether to run in the next elections, due in 2016. To do so he would need to induce the national assembly to change the constitution and remove the two-term limit for presidents, then conduct what one election monitor at the 2011 polls told me would need to be 'a huge rigging operation' to overcome the electorate's outrage. To pull off such an expensive task, Kabila would need to ratchet up the looting machine once again.

» 3 «

Incubators of Poverty

THE CHIEF OF the border post let out another long sigh. '*On attend*.' The wait had already lasted hours. Not for the first time I was at the mercy of a temperamental fax machine. I was trying to cross the Nigerian border with its northern neighbour, Niger, where the official language changes from English to French. Someone in the visa section of Niger's embassy in Nigeria had neglected to send some document or other to headquarters to authorize my visa, and faxing it over was proving complicated. I sat on the stoop of the border post, looking out over the scorched terrain that leads up to the Sahara. Goats, the hungry and the maimed shuffled between breezeblock structures, lashed by the swirling dust. Periodically the chief of the border post would make a call on his mobile phone to check whether I should be allowed to pass. Then he would resume his contemplative silence, speaking only to bemoan 'this interminable heat'. The sun was melting the horizon to a shimmer. '*On attend*.'

Whiling away the morning beside the taciturn border chief offered me an opportunity to observe one of the few effective institutions in this part of the world: the smuggling racket.[1] Dozens of trucks were queuing to cross from Niger into Nigeria. Their contents seemed harmless enough: many contained textiles and clothing bound for the markets of Kano and Kaduna, northern Nigeria's two main cities.

Weapons and unwilling human traffic cross Nigeria's northern border covertly. But the flow of counterfeit Chinese-made textiles has grown so voluminous that it would be impossible to keep it secret even if secrecy were required to ensure its safe passage. All the same, most of the shipments go through under cover of darkness. Those who control the trade engage in highly organized 'settling', or bribing, of the border officials, smoothing the textiles' transit.

The Nigerian stretch is just the final leg of a 10,000-kilometre journey. It begins in Chinese factories, churning out imitations of the textiles that Nigerians previously produced for themselves, with their signature prime colours and waxiness to the touch. By the boatload they arrive in west Africa's ports, chiefly Cotonou, Benin's biggest city, a tiny country beside Nigeria that has, like Montenegro in Europe or Paraguay in South America, become a state whose major economic activity is the trans-shipment of contraband. At the ports the counterfeit consignments are loaded onto trucks and either driven straight over the land border between Benin and western Nigeria or up through Niger and round to the border post with its taciturn chief. The trade is estimated to be worth about $2 billion a year, equivalent to about a fifth of all annual recorded imports of textiles, clothing, fabric and yarn into the whole of sub-Saharan Africa.[2]

Smuggling is a long-established profession here. Before colonial cartographers imposed the frontier, today's smuggling routes were the byways of legitimate commerce. The border marks a delineation of what used to be British and French territory in west Africa, but no natural division of language or ethnicity exists. People on both sides speak Hausa, a tongue in which the word for smuggling, *sumoga*, strikes a less pejorative note than its English equivalent. The textile-smuggling bosses are the oligarchs of the northern borderlands. For those in their pay, they can be generous benefactors.

Not being a roll of fake west African fabric, I was not a priority for processing. Eventually the border chief's phone rang. Off we trundled, past trucks with 'Chine' daubed on the side, a brazen reference to their cargo's origin. Another name went unrecorded, that of the trucks' proprietor. Few dare to speak it openly here. But further to the south, where the truckloads of counterfeit textiles have helped to wreak economic destruction, I had heard it whispered a year earlier.

A country of 170 million people – home to one in six Africans, three main ethnic groups subdivided into hundreds more speaking five hundred

languages and bolted together on the whim of British colonial adminis-
trators; split between a north that largely follows Allah and a south more
partial to the Christian God and animist deities; hollowed out by corruption that has fattened a ruling class of stupendous wealth while most of the
rest lack the means to fill their stomachs, treat their ailments, or educate
their children; humiliated by a reputation for contributing little to human
endeavour but venal politicians and ingenious scams – Nigeria has paid
quite a price for the dubious honour of being the continent's biggest oil
producer.

The crude began to flow in 1956, four years before independence from
Britain. Almost immediately it started to ruin Nigeria. Two-thirds of the
newfound oil reserves lay within the territory that secessionists claimed
for themselves when they declared the Republic of Biafra in 1967, raising the stakes in the standoff between the ethnic blocs vying for power in
the young nation. Between five hundred thousand and 2 million Nigerians
died in the civil war that ensued, many from starvation. Nigeria remained
whole, but any hope that it might rise as a black star to lead an independent
Africa dissipated as dictator followed ruinous dictator. Instead, it became
a petro-state, where oil accounts for four in every five dollars of government revenue and capturing a share of the resource rent is a life-and-death
struggle.

The Niger Delta, the maze of creeks where the River Niger reaches the sea
at Nigeria's southern edge, proved to be a prodigious font of crude. Along
with the offshore discoveries that followed, it made Nigeria a major supplier
of oil to the United States and the fourth-biggest source of European oil imports. Few countries can claim to be so vital a source of the basic ingredient
of the world's oil-fired economy. Nigeria's stocks of natural gas, estimated
to be the eighth-largest on the planet, have scarcely been tapped, but they
already account for one in every twenty cubic feet that the European Union
imports.

The insidious effects of oil have permeated outward from the brutalized,
despoiled and destitute Niger Delta. I had been living in Nigeria for less
than two weeks when I arrived in Kaduna. The city is the gateway between
the Christian south and the northern half of the country, an expanse that
stretches up to the border with Niger and used to form part of an Islamic

caliphate that the jihad of Usman dan Fodio founded two hundred years ago. Kaduna lies in the turbulent Middle Belt, prone to spasms of communal violence when patronage politics, dressed in the garb of religion or ethnicity, turns bloody.

On a stifling Sunday morning a friend took me around Kaduna's central market, a teeming grid of wooden booths. Many of the stalls were selling clothes. Some bore the misspellings that are counterfeiters' inadvertent trademark: 'Clavin Klein' read one shirt label. Others carried the equivalent of the *appellation d'origine contrôlée* badges that French vineyards and cheese makers append to their produce. 'Made in Nigeria' the labels declared. But they were fake too. Aike, a young trader from the East, told me he stocked up on bogus labels when he went north to Kano to replenish his supplies of lace. 'Mostly everything is made in China,' explained another trader selling jeans.

At Raymond Okwuanyinu's stall I found rolls and rolls of the coloured fabric that is used for fashioning a popular style of billowing trousers. Here there was no attempt at subterfuge. Raymond told me it was a matter of simple economics. Nigeria may be the largest source of African energy exports, but it generates only enough electricity to power one toaster for every forty-four of its own people. Billions of dollars assigned to fix the rundown power stations and the dilapidated grid have been squandered or pilfered. A privatization drive in recent years has raised some tentative hope of improvement, but for now Nigeria produces only half as much electricity as North Korea. Even those lucky enough to be connected to a functioning cable face the maddening task of negotiating with what used to be called the National Electric Power Authority, or NEPA (but known as Never Expect Power Anytime). It was rebranded as the Power Holding Company of Nigeria, or PHCN (Please Have Candles Nearby or, simply, Problem Has Changed Name). Most must make do with spluttering diesel generators. In a country where 62 per cent of people live on less than $1.25 a day, running a generator costs about twice as much as the average Briton pays for electricity.[3]

The crippling cost of electricity makes Nigerian textiles expensive to produce. Raymond, the Kaduna trader, told me he could sell trousers made from Chinese fabric at two-thirds the price of those made from Nigerian fabric and still turn a profit. Hillary Umunna, a few stalls over, concurred. The government's attempt to support the Nigerian textile sector by banning imports was futile, Hillary opined, his tailor's tape-measure draped around his shoulders. 'These things now,' he said, gesturing at his wares, 'they say it is contraband. They can't produce it, but they ban it. So we have to smuggle.'

The cheaper price of smuggled garments relative to locally produced ones was good news, superficially at least, for the traders' hard-pressed customers but less so for the employees of Nigeria's textile industry. 'It is a pitiable situation,' said Hillary, apparently oblivious to his and his colleagues' role in their compatriots' downfall. 'All the [textile factories] we have here have shut down. The workers are now on the streets.'

In the mid-1980s Nigeria had 175 textile mills. Over the quarter-century that followed, all but 25 shut down. Many of those that have struggled on do so only at a fraction of their capacity. Of the 350,000 people the industry employed in its heyday, making it comfortably Nigeria's most important manufacturing sector, all but 25,000 have lost their jobs.[4] Imports comprise 85 per cent of the market, despite the fact that importing textiles is illegal. The World Bank has estimated that textiles smuggled into Nigeria through Benin are worth $2.2 billion a year, compared with local Nigerian production that has shrivelled to $40 million annually.[5] A team of experts working for the United Nations concluded in 2009, 'The Nigerian textile industry is on the verge of a total collapse.'[6] Given the power crisis, the near-impassable state of Nigeria's roads and the deluge of counterfeit clothes, it is a wonder that the industry kept going as long as it did.

The knock-on effects of this collapse are hard to quantify, but they ripple far into the Nigerian economy, especially in the North. About half of the million farmers who used to grow cotton to supply textile mills no longer do so, although some have switched to other crops. Formal jobs in Nigeria are scarce and precious. Each textile employee supports maybe half a dozen relatives. It is safe to say that the destruction of the Nigerian textile industry has blighted millions of lives.

After I left Kaduna's market my friend took me to meet some of those who had felt the industry's collapse hardest. Sitting around on rickety desks in the half-light of a classroom beside the church where some of

Kaduna's Christians were loudly asking a higher power for succour, nine redundant textile workers poured forth their woes. Tens of thousands of textile jobs had disappeared in Kaduna alone, the mill hands told me. I had seen the factory where some of them used to work. The gates of the United Nigerian Textiles plant were firmly shuttered. Jagged glass topped the high walls, and a lone security guard kept watch, protecting the machinery within on the minuscule chance that it would someday whir into action again.* No other living thing came or went, save for the yellow-headed lizards scuttling among the undergrowth.

Father Matthew Hassan Kukah looked pained as he recalled the day when the factory, Kaduna's last, had closed its doors the previous year. The hymns from his Sunday service had subsided. Like Archbishop Desmond Tutu in South Africa, Kukah is a figure of moral authority in Nigeria – and shares with Tutu a subversive sense of humour in the face of adversity. Kukah's voice needles the mighty as few others can. The demise of Kaduna's textile industry had drained the life from the city, he told me, sitting in a sweltering office above his sacristy and dressed in a simple black vestment. 'We've gone backward twenty years,' he said. 'Back in the seventies there were textiles, people were energetic. But that generation was not able to produce the young, upwardly mobile elite. That's what their children should have been.' Kaduna's impoverished inhabitants had retreated into their ethnic and religious identities. 'Kaduna is now a tale of two cities,' said the priest. 'This side of the river is Christians; the other is Muslims.'

Kaduna's decline was only one symptom of Nigeria's descent into privation, Kukah went on. The national political class had abandoned civic duty to line its own pockets instead. The social fabric had been rent. 'As a result of the collapse of the state, everybody, from the president down, is trying to find his own power, his own security. People are falling back on vigilante groups.' Violence had become the tenor of life. 'Everywhere in the world the ghettoes are combustible. The North is an incubator of poverty.'

The former mill hands among Kukah's congregation and Kaduna's Muslims shared in that poverty: buying food, let alone paying school fees that even the dilapidated state-run schools charge, was a daily trial. The

---

*The United Nigerian Textiles plant did reopen years later, but only at a fraction of its capacity. The industry as a whole continued its decline.

mill hands told me they had tried to hold a demonstration outside the state governor's house, but the police had blocked them. The federal government had repeatedly promised to bail out the industry, yet little assistance had been forthcoming. The more clear-eyed workers realized that, in any case, the game was up. Even if they could get the factories running again, Chinese contraband had so thoroughly captured the market that it would be impossible for the Nigerian operations to compete. And there was something that had accelerated the mill hands' consignment to the trash can of globalization. Shuffling their feet and looking warily around for anyone who might be eavesdropping, the men murmured a single word: 'Mangal.'

Alhaji Dahiru Mangal is a businessman whose fortune is thought to run to billions, a confidant of presidents, a devout Muslim, and a philanthropist whose airline transports Nigerian pilgrims to the annual hajj in Mecca. He also ranks among west Africa's pre-eminent smugglers.

Growing up in Katsina, the last outpost before Nigeria's frontier with Niger, Mangal received little formal education. More cosmopolitan Nigerian businessmen speak of him with a mixture of snobbery, envy and fear. He got his start as a teenager in the 1980s, following his father into the import-export business, and he swiftly made the cross-border freight routes his own.[7] 'He is shrewd,' a northern leader who knows him told me. 'He knows how to make money.'

In the shadier corners of the workshop of the world Mangal found the perfect business partners. 'The Chinese attacked at the heart of the industry: the wax-print and African-print segment,' a consultant who has spent years investigating – and trying to reverse – the slow death of Nigerian textiles explained to me. During the 1990s Chinese factories began copying west African designs and opening their own distribution branches in the region. 'This is 100 percent illicit – but the locals do the smuggling,' the consultant went on. There are, he said, sixteen factories in China dedicated to churning out textiles with a 'Made in Nigeria' badge sewn into them. For a time the Chinese material was of a much lower quality than Nigerian originals, but that gap narrowed as Chinese standards rose. The Chinese began to take control of the market, in league with Nigerian vendors. Mangal acts as the facilitator, the conduit between manufacturer and distributor, managing a shadow economy that includes the border authorities and his political allies. Like many others who profit from the resource curse, he plies the hidden byways of the globalized economy.

Mangal's network of warehouses and agents stretches to Dubai, the Gulf emirate where much clandestine African business is done, and beyond into China and India. 'You put it in his warehouse, and he will smuggle,' a top northern banker told me. 'He controls the import of everything that requires duty or is contraband.'

From his base in Katsina Mangal arranges the import of food, fuel, and anything his wealthy Nigerian clients might desire. But the staple of his operation is the textiles that have helped kill off the local industry. He is said to charge a flat fee of 2 million naira (about $13,000) per cargo, plus the cost of goods.[8] In 2008 Mangal was estimated to be bringing about a hundred 40-foot shipping containers across the frontier each month.[9]

Mangal's fortunes have risen and fallen with Nigeria's procession of dictators. When democracy – and, notionally, the rule of law – returned in 1999, he needed allies in the new order. He found one in Umaru Yar'Adua. The People's Democratic Party, the affiliation comprising most of Nigeria's political elites that would dominate the new dispensation, had chosen Yar'Adua to be the governor of Mangal's home state, Katsina. Several northern leaders, businessmen and government insiders told me Mangal was one of the most generous funders of Yar'Adua's two successful gubernatorial campaigns, in 1999 and 2003.

The master smuggler's political largesse did not make him entirely immune, however. Around 2005 Olusegun Obasanjo, the former military ruler then embarking on his second term as elected president, decided to do something about smuggling and the damage it was causing to the textile industry. Obasanjo was told, according to a consultant who was involved in lobbying the president, that Mangal was 'the kingpin'. Obasanjo dispatched Nasir El-Rufai, a northern-born minister with a reputation as a reformer, to try to get Mangal to clean up his act.[10] El-Rufai told me he reached an agreement with Yar'Adua, the beneficiary of Mangal's generous campaign funding and his political protector, and the smuggler would endeavour to transform himself into a legitimate businessman.

El-Rufai recalled that Mangal asked him, 'Why does Obasanjo call me a smuggler? I just do logistics. I don't buy any of the goods that are smuggled. I'm just providing a service.' Mangal told El-Rufai that he had a fleet of six hundred trucks plying the trade routes. He promised to switch into refined petroleum products, another time-honoured money spinner for Nigeria's politically connected trading barons. But the illicit textile trade continued, and Mangal's operations remained under scrutiny. Nigeria's Economic and Financial Crimes Commission, traditionally nothing more than a vehicle for settling political scores, had gained some teeth and a degree of independence under an energetic fraud-buster called Nuhu Ribadu. It began to take an interest in Mangal.[11] But then the gods of Nigeria's petro-politics smiled on the smuggler once again.

When Obasanjo's attempts to change the constitution to allow himself a third term as president were thwarted, he sought to maintain his influence from behind the scenes by plucking Yar'Adua from the obscurity of Katsina to be the People's Democratic Party candidate in the 2007 presidential elections – tantamount, given the party's dominance, to handing him the keys to the presidential palace. Mangal contributed to Yar'Adua's presidential campaign, along with other backers who had also attracted the attention of the anticorruption squad. Not long after Yar'Adua took office they got their payback. Ribadu was forced out, and the anticorruption unit's teeth were pulled. 'The moment Yar'Adua became president [Mangal] had a blank cheque,' El-Rufai, whom Yar'Adua also cast into the wilderness, told me. It was another death knell for the north's textile industry.

Mangal and the rest of northern Nigeria's crime lords can trace their hegemony – and the abandoned textile workers their strife – to the discovery of oil in the Niger Delta.

In 1959, three years after Royal Dutch Shell struck oil in commercial quantities in the Delta, the company sank another well by the village of Slochteren in the northern Netherlands, in partnership with Exxon of the United States. They discovered the biggest gas field in Europe. A gas bonanza followed. It was not long, however, before the Dutch began to wonder whether the discovery had truly been a blessing. People outside the energy industry started losing their jobs.[12] Other sectors of the economy slumped, following a pattern that *The Economist* would, in 1977, diagnose as 'Dutch Disease'.

What happened in the Netherlands was not an isolated outbreak, even if a prosperous European country was better placed than many to withstand it. Dutch Disease is a pandemic whose symptoms, in many cases, include poverty and oppression.

The disease enters a country through its currency. The dollars that pay for exported hydrocarbons, minerals, ores and gems push up the value of the local currency. Imports become cheaper relative to locally made products, undercutting homegrown enterprises. Arable land lies fallow as local farmers find that imported fare has displaced their produce. For countries that have started to industrialize, the process goes into reverse; those that aspire to industrialize are stymied. Processing natural commodities can multiply their value four hundredfold, but, lacking industrial capacity, Africa's resource states watch their oil and minerals sail away in raw form for that value to accrue elsewhere.[13]

A cycle of economic addiction sets in: the decay of the other parts of the economy increases the dependency on natural resources. Opportunity becomes confined to the resources business, but only for the few: whereas mines and oil fields require vast sums of capital, they employ tiny workforces compared with farming or manufacturing. As oil or mining suck the life from the rest of the economy, infrastructure that could foster broader opportunities – electricity grids, roads, schools – is neglected.

In Africa Dutch Disease is chronic and debilitating. Instead of broad economies with an industrial base to provide mass employment, poverty breeds and the resource sector becomes an enclave of plenty for those who control it. Measured as a share of the overall output of the combined African economy, manufacturing has fallen from 15 per cent in 1990 to 11 per cent in 2008.[14] Telecoms and financial services have boomed, but the path to industrialization is blocked off. During the very years when Brazil, India, China and the other 'emerging markets' were transforming their economies, Africa's resource states remained tethered to the bottom of the industrial supply chain. Africa's share of global manufacturing stood in 2011 exactly where it stood in 2000: at 1 per cent.[15]

There are pockets of Africa where manufacturing has taken hold, notably in South Africa, where platinum is used to make catalytic converters, and in Botswana, where a nascent cutting and polishing industry is retaining some of the value-addition process for diamonds. But far more common are sights like the defunct General Motors assembly plant that used to hum outside Kinshasa or the uptown Luanda supermarket that boasts eight varieties of tinned peas, none of them home-grown despite Angola boasting enough arable land to cover Germany. The commodity boom of the past decade that has had hedge funds and investment analysts salivating over Africa's economic prospects might even have made matters worse for those outside the resource bubble. While Nigeria was recording annual gross domestic product growth of more than 5 per cent, unemployment increased from 15 per cent in 2005 to 25 per cent in 2011.[16] Youth unemployment was estimated at 60 per cent.

A recalculation of Nigeria's GDP in 2014, to take into account hitherto under-recorded booms in services such as telecoms and banking, made Africa's most populous nation officially its biggest economy, surpassing South Africa. The statistical revisions did nothing to make Nigerians less poor, but it did halve the share of oil in GDP to 14 per cent. 'The new figures show that Nigeria is much more than just an oil enclave,' declared *The Economist*.[17] 'Nigeria now looks like an economy to take seriously.'

But oil has so corrupted Nigeria that, for those trying to make an honest buck, the outlook is dispiriting. Richard Akerele, a veteran British–Nigerian businessman from an old Lagos family whose latest endeavour has been to establish a new line of passenger suites at African airports, is of an almost unassailably cheery disposition. Yet even he is losing hope.

'We have everything here, everything,' Akerele told me. 'But our people are poor and our society is poor.' We were sitting at a waterside bar on one of the islands of uptown Lagos. The sun danced on the waters that separate the wealthy islands from the heaving mass of humanity on the mainland, with its profusion of crammed yellow buses, its cacophony of Afrobeat and generators, its defiantly sharp-suited slum dwellers.

For Akerele's generation there is something deeply poignant about what Nigeria has become. He was right – Nigeria has everything: fertile land, great natural wealth, universities that in the years after independence were the envy of Africa, an abundance of intelligence and ingenuity reflected in the ease with which Nigerian expatriates make headway abroad, Nobel Prize-winning novelists, and savvy businessmen. But oil has sickened Nigeria's heart. Akerele, who worked for a while with Tiny Rowland of Lonrho, one of Africa's most successful and contentious mining tycoons, knows better than most what the resources industry had done to his country and his continent.

One evening, when he and I were the last two still going at 3 A.M. after a merry evening attempting to skewer Nigeria's ills, I asked Akerele what he foresaw for Africa. His expression, usually jovial, fell. 'Africa will be a mine,' he said, 'and Africans will be the drones of the world.'

The electronics market at Alaba proclaims itself to be Africa's biggest. It is a sprawling bazaar located close to the clogged road – known, improbably, as the expressway – that arcs through mainland Lagos where most of the city's 20 million inhabitants live. On sale here are the trappings of a middle-class life: refrigerators and telephones, stereos and televisions. The traders are proud that they have brought the means for a comfortable existence within reach for more of their compatriots, not just the elite who used to be the market's sole customers before Chinese-manufactured cheaper goods arrived. But, just as in the textile markets of the North, the omnipresence of foreign-made wares testifies to Nigeria's near-total failure to develop a strong manufacturing sector of its own.

As I wandered through the stacks of white goods, one of the traders drew me aside. Okolie was fifty-nine. He had spent thirty years selling radios and working out how Nigeria's petro-politics shapes the dynamics of supply and demand.

Business was slow just then, Okolie told me. It was May 2010: Greece was on the brink of defaulting on its debts, and I presumed the reason for the slowdown at Alaba was another symptom of the global economy's travails. I was wrong. 'Money is down,' Okolie explained, 'since the president is sick.'

Umaru Yar'Adua's health had been weak since well before his elevation to the highest office. The state of the presidential kidneys was a favourite topic of conversation among taxi drivers and in the hotel bars where businessmen and politicians gathered. In the final weeks of 2009 Yar'Adua's heart began to fail. He was rushed to Saudi Arabia for treatment, triggering political paralysis.

Alaba market was struggling because the patronage system had ground to a halt. It was a perfect illustration of what Noo Saro-Wiwa, the daughter of the executed Niger Delta activist Ken Saro-Wiwa, has called Nigeria's 'contractocracy'.[18] The beneficiaries of the government contracts that spew Nigeria's oil rent into the patronage system, both the favoured contractors and the officials and politicians they cut in on the deals, would, under normal circumstances, spend some of their dubious earnings in places like Alaba market. But Yar'Adua's long illness and the ensuing power struggle meant that contracts were not getting signed. The outflow of the looting machine had been temporarily blocked. But Okolie was not overly concerned. Soon the contractocracy would resume normal service. The public goods the contracts were supposed to deliver would not materialize – the subsidized fuel would be siphoned off, the potholes would go unfilled, the lights would stay off – but at least the shadow economy would be moving again. 'If the government gives money to the contractors, money will reach us,' Okolie said.

Okolie had grasped a central truth about how resource states work. Demanding their rights from their British colonial rulers, the American revolutionaries declared that there would be no taxation without representation. The inverse is also true: without taxation, there is no representation. Not being funded by the people, the rulers of resource states are not beholden to them.

Taking Africa as a whole, for every six dollars that governments bring in from direct taxation – taxes on personal income and company profits – they bring in ten dollars from taxes on the extraction and export of resources.[19] In Mali gold and other minerals account for 20 per cent of government income; in Chad, an oil producer, resource revenues are more than half the total. In Nigeria the sale of crude oil and natural gas generates about 70 per cent of government revenue; in newborn South Sudan the figure is 98 per cent. Taxes, customs receipts and revenues from the sale of state assets – the things on which industrialized nations rely to fund the state and that require the acquiescence of the population – matter far less than keeping the resource money flowing. Nigeria's GDP recalculation in 2014 showed that, once taxes from the oil industry were stripped out, the government relied on the people for just 4 per cent of its income.[20]

The ability of the rulers of Africa's resource states to govern without recourse to popular consent goes to the heart of the resource curse. The resource business ruptures the social contract between rulers and ruled

– the idea, shaped by political philosophers such as Rousseau and Locke, that a government draws its legitimacy from the consensual sacrifice of certain freedoms by the people in exchange for those vested with authority upholding the common interest. Instead of calling their rulers to account, the citizens of resource states are reduced to angling for a share of the loot. This creates an ideal fiscal system for supporting autocrats, from the Saudi royal family to the strongmen of the Caspian states. And data collected by Paul Collier, a professor at Oxford University who has spent his career studying the causes of African poverty, suggest a still more insidious effect. 'The heart of the resource curse,' Collier writes, 'is that it makes democracy malfunction.'[21]

Collier estimated that once natural resource rents exceed about 8 per cent of GDP, the economy of a country that stages competitive elections typically grows 3 percentage points more slowly than an equivalent autocracy's economy. Collier's research suggests that, in countries where a significant share of national income comes from natural resource industries, the purpose of elections is subverted. Normally electoral competition is healthy, ensuring some accountability for elected officials. Political parties can be turfed out of office. In the resource states that go through the motions of democracy, however, the rules governing both how power is won and how it is used are turned on their head. Greater ethnic diversity makes things worse, generating greater demands on the patronage system. 'Where patronage politics is not feasible, the people attracted to politics are more likely to be interested in issues of public service provision,' Collier writes. 'Of course, for societies where patronage is feasible, this works in reverse: democratic politics then tends to attract crooks rather than altruists.' Collier has a name for this law of resource-state politics: 'the survival of the fattest'.

Maintaining power through patronage is expensive. But self-enrichment is part of the prize. And all that stolen money has to go somewhere. Some of it is used to pay off patronage networks. Some of it buys elections. Much of it goes overseas: according to a US Senate report, kleptocrats from African resource states have used banks, including HSBC, Citibank and Riggs, to squirrel away millions of plundered dollars in the United States alone, often concealing the origin of their wealth by shifting funds through secretive offshore tax havens.[22] But some of it needs to be laundered at home.

An hour or two through Lagos's suffocated thoroughfares from the electronics market at Alaba, on a leafy avenue close to the financial district, Bismarck Rewane oversees an office full of phenomenally bright young Nigerians trying to fathom the mysteries of the world's twenty-sixth-largest economy. Slick-haired and loudly pinstriped, Rewane is one of Nigeria's shrewdest financiers and a trenchant critic of the misrule that has turned a country of immense potential into the sorry mess that it is. Some of the distortions that trouble him are glaring: the effects of oil on inflation, the exchange rate and the financial system. But one of the biggest is almost undetectable: the effect of stolen money being injected back into the economy.

'Money is trapped in the hands of those who need it for maintaining power through patronage,' Rewane told me. 'It can't be invested openly because it has to be hidden.' The effects of all this clandestine money sloshing through an underdeveloped economy are almost impossible to gauge. Because money launderers are seeking primarily to turn dirty cash into other assets as quickly as possible rather than to turn a profit or invest prudently, they are happy to pay more than a fair price for goods and services. That distorts everything, from banking to real estate. It furthers the accumulation of a country's prime economic assets in the hands of the minority, just as Sonangol, the Angolan state-owned oil company that is the engine of the Futungo's looting machine, has expanded into property, finance and aviation. Then there is the dirty money that is simply parked in bank accounts or basements rather than stimulating the economy by circulating. When I asked Rewane how much money he thought was trapped, he laughed. 'That's the million-dollar question.' I asked him what the consequence of all this skulduggery was for the Nigerian economy as a whole. 'When you have an imperfect economy where all money is dirty money, you will just have a completely dysfunctional economic arrangement.'

Where legitimate business cannot thrive, crime flourishes. Mafias from New York to Naples work by creating scarcity and controlling supply. Northern Nigeria's Mafiosi are no different. Dahiru Mangal might not have been responsible for the collapse of the electricity network and the crumbling roads that crippled the Nigerian textile industry – Dutch Disease and oil-fuelled corruption took care of that. Neither is he the sole corrupter of the Nigerian customs service – Shell has admitted paying bungs worth $2 million between 2004 and 2006 to Nigerian customs officials to smooth the importation of materials for Bonga, its giant offshore oilfield, part of a wider scheme in which the Swiss group Panalpina showered bribes on Nigerian officials, some on behalf of Shell, booking them as 'evacuations', 'special handling', and 'prereleases'.[23] But Mangal has scavenged the terrain laid waste by Dutch Disease, further weakening northern Nigeria's chances of recovery.

From the early 1970s to the mid-1980s, during the period when two oil shocks drove up the price of crude from $3 to $38 a barrel, Nigeria's currency appreciated dramatically.[24] The shift in the real naira exchange rate against the dollar sent a chill wind through the incipient industrial base. 'This is what killed industries and agriculture, in conjunction with the power crisis,' Nasir El-Rufai, the former minister, told me. 'As industries were collapsing, people like Mangal saw the opportunity.'

As a political economy took hold that was based on embezzlement and manipulating public office for private gain, government contracts for the upkeep of public goods that support industrialization – a functioning electricity system chief among them – were diverted to the cronies of the rulers of the day. The pattern was the same as in Angola or Congo: the more the non-oil economy withered, the greater the impulse to embezzle, perpetuating the cycle of looting. The deterioration of northern Nigeria's textile industry created new demand for imported clothes and fabrics, strengthening Mangal's stranglehold on the market and throttling the indigenous industry's chances of resuscitation.

The sheer scale of Mangal's smuggling operation gave him sway over Nigeria's northern borderlands, and many of the North's senior politicians were, I was told, in his pocket. 'So many people are benefiting from the [customs] service the way it is and they want to keep it like this,' Yakubu Dogara, a northern member of Nigeria's national assembly who had chaired an inquiry into the customs service, told me.[25] I asked him about Mangal's role, suggesting he was at the centre of the smuggling operation. 'Some of the perpetrators are well known,' Dogara said. 'Even the customs know them. But they are not empowered to go after them.' He paused. 'The person you have just mentioned is untouchable, untouchable.'

By funding Umaru Yar'Adua's election campaigns, Mangal had ensured he had a protector at the top of the rentier class that uses Nigeria's oil to maintain its hegemony. He had also made himself an important bene-ficiary of the People's Democratic Party more broadly, securing a hedge against the ceaseless infighting. Mangal became Yar'Adua's equivalent of Andy Uba. Uba, a Nigerian expatriate in the United States, had ingrati-ated himself with Olusegun Obasanjo as he came to power in 1999 and served as gatekeeper to the president, becoming a notorious presence in backroom oil deals. Mangal, like Uba before him, earned the moniker 'Mr Fix It'. According to a northern businessman quoted in a US diplomatic cable, Mangal took care of 'anything filthy that Yar'Adua needs done'.[26] Yar'Adua had grown up in the left-leaning current of northern Nigerian political thought, but he was sickly and either unable or unwilling to break the rule of Nigerian petro-politics, which equates high office with theft. He once described himself as the resident of 'a gilded cage', an apparent reference to the grasping coterie that surrounded him.[27]

No sooner had Yar'Adua left the country for a Saudi Arabian hospital than the barons of Nigerian politics began to manoeuvre for position in the event he should never return. Within weeks Nigeria was in a full-blown crisis. An eruption of communal violence in Jos – a city, like Kaduna, in the combustible Middle Belt – added to the sense that Africa's oil-fired jugger-naut was hurtling toward disaster with no one at the controls. Militants in the Niger Delta abandoned a cease-fire and resumed a bombing campaign. Goodluck Jonathan, the vice president, was theoretically in charge, but he held little sway. The members of Yar'Adua's inner circle, dubbed 'the ca-bal', clung to power. For the first tense months of 2010, they held Nigeria to ransom.

The cabal included a handful of Yar'Adua's trusted northern aides and two men whose presence illustrated the extent to which organized crime had infiltrated the highest levels of power: James Ibori and Dahiru Mangal. Ibori had come up through the ranks of the Niger Delta's politics-by-AK47 to secure the governorship of Delta state, one of the oil region's three main states. An imposing man with an unnerving gaze, he amassed an enormous fortune, a fleet of top-end cars, luxury homes, and a $20 million private jet.[28] Although his attempt to secure the People's Democratic Party's vice presidential nomination in 2007 narrowly failed, he was said to have been a principal funder of Yar'Adua's presidential campaign, along with Mangal.

Well aware that even healthy Nigerian presidents have had their stints in office curtailed by putsches and assassinations, Yar'Adua's court had hoarded the profits of power greedily, failing to dispense enough of the patronage that keeps rivals at bay. And when Yar'Adua was forced to go abroad – the Nigerian health system, like every other purveyor of public goods, having been left to rot – the cabal's refusal to yield power began to imperil a larger project. As rumours of coup plots swirled, the kingmakers of the ruling party knew that it would only take one junior officer to decide that the civilians could no longer be trusted to govern, and control of the looting machine would be snatched from them. When the cabal staged a last-ditch attempt to pretend that Yar'Adua might recover by spiriting him back into the country in the dead of night and deployed troops onto the streets of the capital, Abuja, the stunt prompted an unusually blunt public warning from the United States, a major importer of Nigerian oil. 'We hope that President Yar'Adua's return to Nigeria is not an effort by his senior advisers to upset Nigeria's stability,' said Johnnie Carson, assistant secretary of state.[29] It was, but it failed.

Fearing calamity on a scale they could not control – and rightly suspecting that Goodluck Jonathan would need to put the looting machine into overdrive and distribute the proceeds widely to compensate for his lack of authority – the big beasts of the ruling class lined up behind him. Jonathan was named acting president and, when Yar'Adua finally died, sworn in as president.

Most of Yar'Adua's allies were swiftly dislodged; their impunity evaporated. For James Ibori, the game was up. He fled to Dubai, where he was detained and extradited to face trial in London, a rare example of the British authorities going after the foreign loot stashed in the UK capital's property market. Ibori pleaded guilty to money laundering and fraud and, in April 2012, was sentenced to thirteen years in prison.

Mangal escaped such a fate. Unlike Ibori, he was not dependent on political favour and intimidation alone. He had Dutch Disease on his side, not to mention a battalion of Chinese counterfeiters, Nigerian textile distributors and bent customs officials. Goodluck Jonathan had enough rivals among the Machiavellian state governors and schismatic rebels within his own party that he knew better than to start picking fights with a smuggler who had proved himself a generous benefactor to the PDP in the past. Yar'Adua's untimely death and Jonathan's ascent had broken an unwritten rent-sharing rule within the party that rotates power between northerners and southerners, and the new southern president had little to gain by antagonizing an influential northerner.

Even if the day comes when Mangal's smuggling empire topples, it would be a monumental task to salvage what remains of northern Nigeria's textile industry, let alone return it to its former glory. It is the structure of an economy in thrall to oil, more than any one crime lord, that condemned those mill hands to penury. The headline GDP numbers declare that Nigeria is booming, but the North is disintegrating. For the likes of Boko Haram, the northern Islamist terrorists linked to al-Qaeda who have proved more than a match for the security forces, the corruption of the state and the lack of economic opportunity serve as recruiting sergeants.

The economic distortions of resource dependency create the conditions in which repressive regimes and their allies can thrive. Mangal's operation is just one example of the kind of networks that emerge to profit from the enclave economies of Africa's resource states. These networks vary by country, creed and commodity, but they have some traits in common. They fuse private interests with public office; they operate in the underbelly of globalization, where criminal enterprises and international trade overlap; and they depend on the power of the oil and mining industries to create narrow economies in which access to wealth is concentrated in the hands of small, repressive ruling classes and those who bribe their way to favour.

Some of these networks date back decades, to before African independence. Others have formed more recently. One in particular was born out of the greatest upheaval in Africa since the end of the Cold War, perhaps even since independence: China's quest for the continent's natural resources.

» 4 «

Guanxi

A S THE TWENTIETH CENTURY drew to a close, two decades of rapid economic growth were returning China, home to a fifth of humanity, to the ranks of the great powers. As they balanced the cautious introduction of something resembling a market economy with unstinting political control, China's Communist rulers, led by President Jiang Zemin, decided that this was the moment to 'go out'. Chinese state-owned companies were instructed to surge forth into the world. China's economy was opening, and domestic companies would face foreign competition once China joined the World Trade Organization. China was hungry for new markets in which to sell the prodigious output of its factories, jobs overseas for its brimming workforce, contracts for its construction groups – and natural resources to feed the economy back home. Between the early 1990s and 2010 China's share of world consumption of refined metals went from 5 per cent to 45 per cent, and oil consumption increased fivefold over the same period to a level second only to the United States.[1] China's economy was eight times bigger in 2012 than it was in 2000, and demand for commodities rapidly outstripped China's own resources.

When it came to navigating the resource industries, government-run enterprises based in Beijing were no match for Western groups that had been planting imperial flags in oil fields and mineral seams since colonial days. Middlemen were required – especially middlemen who could open the doors to the dictators and kleptocrats who controlled the riches of the soils and seabeds of Africa, home to some of the greatest untapped reserves of raw materials.

To capitalize, a would-be middleman needed stocks of an intangible commodity that is highly prized in China. There is no direct translation that captures the meaning of the Mandarin word 关系, or *guanxi*. It connotes something like the Western ideas of connections or relationships or network, only far more pervasive. To have good guanxi is to have cultivated the personal ties that, though unwritten, carry as much force as any contract. At one level guanxi is a homespun maxim of etiquette: one good turn deserves another. Not to return a favour is a grave social transgression. The bonds extend beyond family to anyone who might be in a position to provide advancement. Like karma or air miles, guanxi is accumulated. When applied to politics and business guanxi can become indistinguishable from corruption or nepotism. Some of the recent slew of corruption scandals involving foreign multinationals in China, such as the slush fund allegedly run by GlaxoSmithKline to bribe doctors and officials and J.P. Morgan Chase's alleged practice of giving jobs to relatives of the Chinese elite (currently under investigation by the American, British and Hong Kong authorities), might be regarded as the overzealous pursuit of guanxi. When the Chinese caravan embarked for Africa, one ambitious but obscure man in his mid-forties had amassed enough guanxi to hitch a ride.

Sam Pa has many names and many pasts. According to the US Treasury, which would put seven of his names on a sanctions list fifty-six years later, he was born on 28 February 1958.[2] There is no authoritative version of Pa's life, only fragments, some of them conflicting, many unverified. Some accounts place his birth in Guangdong, the Chinese province that abuts the South China Sea, possibly in the port city of Shantou. When he was still young his family relocated to Hong Kong, a short move but one that crossed the frontier between Mao Zedong's People's Republic of China and one of the last outposts of the British empire.

From his start in Hong Kong, Pa travelled far and wide. Today he holds dual, possibly triple citizenship: Chinese and Angolan, as well as, according to the US Treasury, and perhaps on account of his roots in Hong Kong, British.[3] He speaks English and, one of his business associates told me, Russian. He is a compact man, short with a middling build. His cheeks are rounded, his black hair is receding, and his chin and upper lip are occasionally decorated with a goatee beard. The fixed gaze of his eyes through rectangular spectacles and the thin smile he wears in photographs hint at steel within. He has an explosive temper but can be charming. 'He's a very serious and intense individual at times,' said Mahmoud Thiam, who met Pa as minister of mines in the west African state of Guinea.[4] 'He has a very ideological view about the role China should play in the world. But he can joke and be personable.'

Hong Kong company records from the mid-1990s show Pa with a Beijing address as a director of a company called Berlin Limited, which had some Panamanian shareholders. In the late 1990s and early 2000s Pa and his companies were repeatedly sued over unpaid debts.[5] Another company filing describes him as a commercial engineer. But Sam Pa was more than just a businessman trying to make his way – he was also a spy.

A contact of mine, who has for many years been close to African intelligence agencies and arms dealers and whom I will call Ariel, first encountered Sam Pa around the late 1980s. 'All his life he's worked in Chinese intelligence,' Ariel told me. When Ariel met Pa he was based in the intelligence section of a Chinese embassy. He was young, ambitious, and capable. 'He's very serious,' Ariel said. 'He knows what he's doing.' Ariel told me that Pa was seeking to cultivate high-level contacts in Africa, where liberation movements, guerrilla armies and despots were vying for power during the Cold War.

Even the most dedicated analysts of China's intelligence agencies acknowledge that outsiders understand their workings far less than they understand, say, the CIA or MI6.[6] Since 1983, when the intelligence arm of the Communist Party of China was absorbed into the newly formed Ministry of State Security, the MSS has been China's main civilian intelligence agency, the nearest equivalent to the CIA, focused above all on ferreting out foreign links to domestic threats to Communist rule. Like other Chinese institutions, including the Ministry of Public Security, which handles domestic intelligence and policing, the MSS is answerable both to the formal government and to the overarching power, the Party itself. Its military counterpart is the Second Department of the People's Liberation Army's General Staff Department, better known as 2PLA. This unit employs many of the same tactics as the MSS and intelligence agencies the world over – running agents abroad, intercepting foreign communications, and conducting covert missions – but it reports to the Chinese military, the Party's guarantor of power.

Sam Pa's precise place in the constellation of Chinese espionage is not clear. Chinese agents abroad have been exposed from time to time, and there has been an outcry in recent years over Chinese theft of Western technology and the audacity of Chinese hacking units, but the broader activities of China's intelligence agencies remain veiled. I have been unable to verify many of the details of Pa's career in espionage that have been related to me. By some accounts he worked as an asset for Chinese intelligence in the 1990s within the inner circle of Cambodia's Communist ruler, Hun Sen, helping to repair relations between him and Beijing, which had supported the man Hun Sen overthrew, the genocidal tyrant Pol Pot. What is clear is that Pa mastered what many of his colleagues in the Chinese security services also attempted: translating connections made in the world of espionage into business opportunities.

When Deng Xiaoping ousted the Maoists and began reforming China's economy in 1978, he encouraged the military to bring in its own revenues through business, freeing up the national budget to fund development projects. By the end of the following decade the PLA's network of twenty thousand companies had interests ranging from pharmaceuticals to manufacturing weapons and smuggling commodities. 'The profits were meant to fund improved living conditions for ordinary soldiers,' writes Richard McGregor, a former *Financial Times* bureau chief in Beijing.[7] 'In reality, much of the money went into the pockets of venal generals and their relatives and cronies.' Those with influence over the PLA's two arms companies, Norinco and China Poly, could make fortunes from exporting weaponry. 'Lots of people from this time started to mix military matters with private business and grew fat – often literally,' Nigel Inkster, a China specialist who spent thirty-one years in MI6, told me.[8]

Pa's career in intelligence was intertwined with the trade in Chinese weapons. 'Sam is a big player in arms in Africa,' said Ariel, who told me that Sam had worked with Norinco. 'Sam's contacts [in Africa] were made during the freedom movements, and now they are diversified into business,' Ariel went on. 'It's a closed club. The world of weapons is a tiny world – everybody knows everybody. You make money for the club, and you make money for yourself. Once you get very high you are allowed to have your own private businesses. Oil, diamonds and weapons go together.' As globalization replaced ideology as the dominant force in geopolitics, the mission of foreign spooks in Africa evolved. 'Today intelligence is not for starting wars,' Ariel said. 'Today intelligence is for natural resources.'

Sam Pa was not the first foreigner in Africa to use espionage and arms dealing as a gateway to Africa's subterranean treasure. Viktor Bout took weapons into eastern Congo and coltan out.[9] Simon Mann, an alumnus of Eton and the Scots Guards, went in search of oil revenues in Angola and diamonds in Sierra Leone at the head of a pack of mercenaries and staged a botched attempt at a coup in the tiny petro-state of Equatorial Guinea.[10] Home-grown entrepreneurs have combined arms and resources too: in Nigeria, the ability of a kingpin of the Niger Delta called Henry Okah to supply weapons to the militants who roam the creeks made him a powerful figure in the rackets that feed on stolen crude. But Sam Pa had the advantage of being able to link himself not only to the arms trade but also to a transformation in the world economy.

After twenty-five years of stop–start civil war, by the end of the last century Angola was broke. As his MPLA government bore down on the Unita rebels, José Eduardo dos Santos appealed to the world for funds to rebuild his shattered country. But the Futungo had already acquired a reputation for corruption. Western donors refused to cough up without reassurances that the money would not simply flow into the bank accounts and patronage networks of dos Santos and his circle. Infuriated, the president looked east. China had backed the rebels in the early phases of the Angolan conflict but later switched its allegiance to the MPLA. Dos Santos visited Beijing in 1998, four years before the end of the war, setting in motion talks that would lead to China's first megadeal in Africa.

For his chief emissary to Beijing, dos Santos selected his spymaster. As the head of Angola's external intelligence service, an agency that reported directly to the president, General Fernando Miala was at the heart of the Futungo. A courteous man, he had grown up poor – 'he knows what it is to play football without shoes,' an associate told me – before rising through the military. By the time victory over the rebels of Unita looked assured, Miala had concluded, in the words of his associate, 'We have to make money because we have learned that money is power.'

China had made previous forays into Africa, notably during the Cold War, but the scale of what it now envisaged was unprecedented. The first summit of the Forum on China-Africa Co-operation, held in Beijing in October 2000 to mark the formal start of the Sino-African courtship, was attended by ministers from forty-four African states and addressed by Jiang Zemin, the architect of China's 'go out' policy. The item at the top of the summit's agenda reflected the scope of Beijing's ambition: 'In what way should we work towards the establishment of a new international political and economic order in the 21st century?'[11]

In 2002 Chinese trade with Africa was worth $13 billion a year, half as much as African trade with the United States. A decade later it was worth $180 billion, three times the value of Africa–US trade – although still needing to double again to eclipse African trade with Europe.[12] Two-thirds of China's imports from Africa were oil; the rest was other raw materials, mainly minerals.[13] The fates of the world's most populous nation and the planet's poorest continent have become wedded, with demand in the former helping to determine the economic prospects of the latter via the price of commodities. When China sneezes, Africa catches cold.

China was reshaping Africa's economy through trade, but it was also investing directly. The biggest deals, replicated across the continent's resource states, involved a cheap loan, typically in the single-digit billions of dollars, to fund infrastructure built by Chinese companies and to be repaid in oil or minerals. China's grand bargains came to be known, after their prototype, as 'Angola Mode'. The diplomacy of Fernando Miala and other senior members of the Futungo bore fruit on 2 March 2004, when China signed an agreement to lend Angola $2 billion to fund public works, with repayments to be made in oil.[14] Over the years that followed, the credit line would grow to about $10 billion (like the rest of Angola's finances, the details were closely guarded). Angola became the second-biggest supplier of oil to China, after Saudi Arabia.

In February 2005 Zeng Peiyan, China's vice premier, shook hands with dos Santos in Luanda and hailed Sino-Angolan friendship.[15] Like similar bargains China struck in central Asia and Latin America, the nine 'cooperation agreements' that the two governments signed that day – covering energy, infrastructure, mining, oil exploration, and 'economic and technical assistance' – were billed as mutually beneficial pacts. The rhetoric placed China's agreements with Angola among the founding covenants of a new world order, in which long-downtrodden peoples could unite to ensure their advancement. This was a state-to-state bargain: Chinese finance would fuel Angola to rise from the ashes of war, while Angolan crude was helping a Chinese transformation that was lifting many millions from poverty. But with much less fanfare, another deal had also been forged, not between two nations' governments but rather between two shadow states. It was designed to harness Angola's natural resources to serve the interests of the Futungo and a little-known group of private investors from Hong Kong.

Sam Pa operates in the borderlands of the global economy, where state power and multinational business intersect. When China went to Africa, his horizons widened to contain vast new frontiers, groaning with oil, diamonds and minerals. To stake his claim, Pa needed to deploy his guanxi, both in Beijing and Luanda – or, at least, he needed to be able to give off the impression that he enjoyed the blessing of some of the most powerful men and women in both cities.

During his years in intelligence and arms-dealing Pa had built a network of contacts in Africa, including Angola. When Unita resumed its rebel campaign after the aborted elections of 1992, the MPLA rearmed massively for a final push for victory. Between 1996 and 2000 Angola bought a quarter of all arms sold to sub-Saharan Africa, excluding South Africa.[16] The Futungo arranged arms shipments through French intermediaries in what became the 'Angolagate' scandal. China was another ready supplier, although far fewer details of sales of Chinese arms in Angola have emerged.[17] According to Ariel, Sam Pa was involved in brokering sales of Chinese arms to Angola around this time, a claim others also make but for which, like many of the details of the arms business, there is no firm confirmation.

Early in 2003, a few months after dos Santos's forces killed the rebel leader Jonas Savimbi and brought an end to the civil war, Sam Pa turned up at the Lisbon office of Helder Bataglia. Bataglia was born in Portugal, but his family moved to Angola, then still a Portuguese colony, when he was a year old, and he thinks of himself as Angolan. During the war he had established himself as one of the biggest private investors in Angola. With a Portuguese bank, he had founded Escom, a conglomerate that amassed assets worth hundreds of millions of dollars in diamonds, oil, cement and real estate in Angola as well as interests elsewhere in Africa and in Latin America. When Pa was looking to make the leap from spook to business-man, Bataglia was a prime potential partner.

'They came to our office because they said we know a lot about Africa and Latin America, especially the ex-Portuguese colonies,' Bataglia told me years later of his first visit from Sam Pa and his associates.[18] 'They wanted to make a company with us to explore these markets. I said, "Listen, it's fantastic, we would like to help because China is very important to the development of these continents, but we need to know more about you."'

When Pa took Bataglia to Beijing he staged a demonstration of his guanxi, including introductions to people from Sinopec, China's giant state-owned oil company. 'We were received in China very well,' Bataglia recalled. 'In the airport we were received in the protocol area by local au-thorities, guys from Sinopec, everywhere. They say exactly what Sam Pa said to us: "Let's cooperate because we lack experience in this field."' This was Bataglia's first time in China, and he was impressed. He and his col-leagues ate dinner in the grand halls where Chinese officials receive vis-iting dignitaries. 'Of course, I thought Sam worked for the government,' Bataglia recalled. 'His background, I thought, was in the secret services, that he had a mission now to expand China into the world.' When I asked Bataglia whether he was aware of Pa's arms dealing, he said he knew noth-ing of it, although Pa had told him that he had met dos Santos many years earlier. 'Sam told me that ten or fifteen years ago he was in Angola. In that time, to go to Angola, it must be for official purposes.'

Bataglia told me he never quite got the measure of Sam Pa. When I asked him what he had gleaned about Pa's past, he said, 'Until today I still don't understand very well.' He added, 'He's very intense, very well pre-pared. He has a strong mind.' Bataglia agreed to go into business with Pa. Their partner would be Beiya Industrial Group, one of China's sprawling state-owned conglomerates to whose chairman Pa had introduced Bataglia in Beijing. They called the new venture China Beiya Escom and registered it in Hong Kong, where many Chinese companies seeking to do international business form their companies.

The new venture's first targets were in Latin America. Bataglia recalls that he and Pa flew to Caracas with a delegation of Chinese state-owned companies to court Hugo Chávez, the socialist, populist, anti-American firebrand who had won the 1998 presidential elections and embarked on a massive programme of using revenues from Venezuela's oil to fund health care, education and public works. Pa, Bataglia and their entourage wanted infrastructure contracts to be paid for in oil that would flow back to China. 'Our goal was to implement the business they wanted to do, especially railways and construction,' Bataglia told me.

Chávez announced that he had signed a letter of intent with Portugal and China for assorted projects worth $300 million, with Bataglia signing for Portugal and one of Sam Pa's key collaborators signing for China. Venezuela's president styled the agreement as a momentous development in a South American struggle to resist American domination. But little appears to have come of this agreement (though official ties and trade between Caracas and Beijing did subsequently flourish).[19] Across the Atlantic in Angola, however, Sam Pa had another play in the works, which would pay off spectacularly.

If Sam Pa was to capitalize on Africa's incipient embrace of China, he would need to demonstrate to the rulers of Africa's resource states that he enjoyed access to the highest levels of power in Beijing. For all the Communist Party's image of disciplined hegemony, power in today's China is not monolithic but instead spread between competing strongholds in the Party, the security services and the increasingly mighty corporations that are state-owned but are coming to resemble in their strategies and priorities the multinationals of the West, for whom the pursuit of profit trumps national goals. Pa's network would need to reach all of them.

By 2002 Pa had forged an alliance with the woman who would be his principal collaborator. A photograph of Lo Fong-hung shows a petite woman flashing a wide smile and wearing a chunky necklace, with her dark hair in a bob. The details of her past are as fragmented as Pa's, and, as with Pa, it is hard to differentiate between genuine connections and an ability to broadcast an impressive aura of guanxi that may overstate the extent of their relationships. Company filings in Hong Kong show no record of any business ventures in which Lo participated before her alliance with Pa. Mahmoud Thiam, the Guinean minister who would work with Lo and Pa years later, was one of several people who heard that she used to be a translator for Deng Xiaoping.[20] Between them, Pa and Lo had 'extensive business connections in Africa and South America' by the time they came together, according to a court filing years later.[21] It was Lo who signed the Venezuela agreement. When she appeared with Hugo Chávez on *Aló Presidente*, his weekly broadcast, to trumpet the deal, the Venezuelan president told the nation that his guest came from a prestigious military family and was the daughter of a general.[22]

Lo exudes an authority that many foreigners who have met her have found hard to decode. She was one of the first people to whom Sam Pa introduced Helder Bataglia in China. Bataglia, like Chávez, believed she was a general's daughter. 'Lo is very polite and a very important lady down there,' Bataglia told me.[23] 'She's very calm.' Of her double-act with Sam Pa, Mahmoud Thiam recalled, 'Everything indicated that he was the boss. But you got the sense that if he wanted to get rid of Lo, he could not.'

A Western businessman who had dealings with Pa and Lo went for dinner with them and their subordinates in 2009 in a private room on the top floor of a Hong Kong skyscraper with magnificent views over the harbour. 'It's very clear during the dinner that [Lo] is the matriarch,' the businessman told me. 'She is in all black. Sam looks like a guy off the street, with an open collar, like a ladies' undergarment salesman. He didn't act nefarious or powerful. The woman, Lo, acted strange.' There was nothing to indicate whether she was wealthy. 'She didn't give off any impression other than a sense of power. She just sits there and listens. Sometimes things are whispered to her. You absolutely get the sense that she was the power behind the throne, and Sam was just a regular Joe.'

Lo derived a portion of her guanxi from her marriage.[24] Her husband, Wang Xiangfei, is a serious businessman with a background in finance who has sat in some of China's most prestigious boardrooms. He studied economics at the elite Renmin University in Beijing and became an associate professor of finance there. When his wife and Sam Pa began to craft their business venture in 2002, Wang had already spent two decades at China Everbright, an important state-owned financial conglomerate. Wang joined Everbright in 1983, the year it was founded as an early embodiment of Deng Xiaoping's desire for China to take its place on the international commercial stage. It grew to hold assets worth hundreds of billions of dollars, including its own bank. Wang served both at the parent group in China and at its subsidiaries in Hong Kong, holding a succession of senior posts. China Everbright's management reports directly to the State Council, the highest organ of the Chinese government and the most powerful body in the land after the Standing Committee of the Politburo of the Communist Party, and its executives move in the upper echelons of China's interlocking elites. Among Wang's colleagues in Everbright's senior staff was a man who went by the pseudonym Xueming Li. He was the brother of Bo Xilai, the Icarus of recent Chinese politics who soared close to the peak of power before the Beijing establishment purged him.

Pa and Lo picked an auspicious name for the company that would form the keystone of the corporate network they started to build. On 9 July 2003, New Bright International Development Limited was registered in Hong Kong, one of thousands of companies incorporated there each month. Shortly after it was founded New Bright moved its registered address a couple of blocks across the Admiralty business district to Two Pacific Place, a skyscraper in a redevelopment of what had once been a barracks into smart offices and up-market shops at 88 Queensway. The first seed of the syndicate that would come to be known as the Queensway Group had been sown.

New Bright had two shareholders. One, with 30 per cent of the stock, was Lo Fong-hung. The remaining 70 per cent was allotted to another woman, who lacked the credentials of her partner. Whereas Lo exuded regal authority stemming from her apparent connections to the military and Party elites and Wang boasted a glittering CV, Veronica Fung had only one discernible connection of note – to Sam Pa.

Veronica Fung's sole recorded business venture before 2003 that I was able to find in searches of company records was a 50 per cent shareholding in an obscure company registered in Hong Kong in 1988 and dissolved in 2001, called Acegain Investments Limited. In the company's annual filing for 1993 Fung gives a Hong Kong address and states her occupation as 'secretary' and her nationality as British, this being four years before the British handover of Hong Kong. There is nothing to indicate what Acegain did as a company, but the filing does reveal the identity of the man who held the other 50 per cent of its shares. His name is recorded as 'Ghiu Ka Leung (Alias: Sam King)'. He also goes by other names, not recorded on this filing, including Xu Jinghua, Tsui King Wah – and Sam Pa.

I have been told that Veronica Fung's relationship with Pa extends beyond business. She has been described as his girlfriend.[25] Pa introduced Helder Bataglia to her in Macau, the former Portuguese outpost and casino hotspot beside Hong Kong, but Bataglia told me that Pa never revealed whether they were a couple nor whether she was the mother of his two children. By some accounts Sam and Veronica are married, although I have never seen a marriage certificate. (When I wrote to the in-house lawyer of China Sonangol, the Queensway Group's joint venture with Angola's national oil company, asking him to clarify whether Fung is a proxy for Pa's business interests, he declined to answer the question.)[26]

Sam Pa's name appears nowhere in the shareholder records of New Bright, nor in those of the dozens of other companies that would follow as the Queensway Group took shape. Officially he has no direct stake in the business he founded, though he does receive hefty payments from it and is afforded senior titles at Queensway Group companies in public statements by the foreign governments with which they do deals.[27] Normally the allocation of shares in a new company is based on the amount of capital its founding investors put into it or to reward some vital service. But there is nothing to indicate that New Bright had any capital of its own. It was created, the events that followed would show, as the vehicle through which its founders would turn their guanxi into profit. Lo had her 30 per cent share of New Bright to reflect her central role; it is hard to see why Veronica Fung was given the majority stake in the company at the apex of its corporate structure if not for her ties to Sam Pa.

Between them, Sam Pa, Lo Fong-hung and her husband Wang Xiangfei had sufficient connections to the Party, the military, the government and business to give them the cover they would need to play the role of middleman in some of China's most important foreign relationships. They just needed one more slice of guanxi: someone who could introduce them to China's government-owned giant of an oil company, Sinopec. In 2002 Pa and Lo approached Wu Yang, a man who, by his own account, was a mover and shaker. The address he gave in company filings matched that of the Ministry of Public Security in Beijing, which is in charge of the police and domestic intelligence service, and was also said to house a reception office for the MSS, the foreign intelligence service.[28] Wu, according to his own testimony quoted a decade later in a Hong Kong court judgment, had been 'active in business circles in the Mainland for some time' and had 'strong and useful connections in official circles and with various large companies', including Sinopec.[29] Wu agreed to make some introductions, for which he would be rewarded with a cut of the deal that resulted.

In late 2003 the competition for Angola's oil was heating up. The war had been over for more than a year. The world's biggest oil companies were vying for access to what was becoming one of the planet's most important energy frontiers, courting the Futungo and spending heavily to pull off the feats of engineering required to send drills into the reservoirs of crude locked deep beneath the seabed. Royal Dutch Shell ranked among the titans of the industry, but it had been slow to gain a foothold in Angola. When it decided to concentrate its investment on Nigeria and put its stake in an Angolan oil prospect up for sale in late 2003, there were plenty of eager bidders. The stake was 50 per cent of Block 18, a concession area three times the size of London off the Angolan coast. BP, which held the other 50 per cent and was the operator of the project, in charge of hiring the rigs and drilling the wells, had already discovered half a dozen oilfields containing about 750 million barrels of crude. It was shaping up to be another Angolan megaproject, involving the largest corporations in global commerce: that year *Forbes* rated Shell and BP as the world's sixth- and seventh-biggest companies by revenue, respectively. An industry analyst predicted in the trade press that the successful bidder was 'highly unlikely to be anyone other than the supermajors', the half-dozen giants of the industry, including Exxon Mobil and Chevron of the United States and Total of France.[30]

But times were changing. New powers were rising, with government-controlled oil companies like Petrobras of Brazil and Petronas of Malaysia that were beginning to jostle the venerable majors. In April 2004 it was reported that ONGC of India had agreed to buy Shell's stake in Block 18 for $600 million.[31] As the weeks went by, however, it emerged that Sonangol, Angola's state oil company, was refusing to waive its right to purchase the stake itself. By the end of the year India had been gazumped by its gargantuan neighbour. Sinopec, the Chinese oil group that was growing into one of the world's biggest companies as it snapped up assets overseas, bought Shell's stake in Block 18.[32] It looked like a simple case of one rising power outmuscling another for oil. But that was not the whole story.

Around the time when Shell had made it known that it wanted to sell its stake in Block 18, a delegation from Luanda travelled to Beijing. The delegation held talks with some of the most powerful people in China, including Zeng Peiyan, the vice premier. Zeng had had an exemplary career in the Communist Party – training as an engineer, serving as a diplomat in the Chinese embassy in Washington, studying at the Central Party School where cadres are groomed for high office, and holding top posts in the Party organs for economic planning, including as deputy director of the commission on the construction of the immense Three Gorges Dam, before graduating to the Politburo in 2002 and the vice premiership in 2003.[33]

The delegation who visited Zeng in late 2003 included Sam Pa, Helder Bataglia and Manuel Vicente, the boss of Sonangol, Angola's state oil company and the Futungo's unofficial treasury.[34] Pa's ability to engineer a meeting with Zeng, an elder statesman, was one of the reasons Bataglia became convinced that his new Chinese business partner enjoyed the support of China's rulers. 'More official than that is not possible,' Bataglia told me. In 2005 Zeng would visit Luanda to unveil China's state-to-state pact with Angola. But first Manuel Vicente and Sam Pa would craft a shadowy alliance that would put the newfound allegiance between China and Angola at the service of the Futungo and the Queensway Group.

When Shell put its stake in Block 18 up for sale, Manuel Vicente saw an opportunity. As the head of Sonangol, Vicente had ambitions to make

Angola's national oil company into an international force like its counter-parts from Malaysia and Brazil. To edge out the Indian bidder that was on the verge of buying Shell's stake, however, Sonangol needed a financial backer. 'We had no money,' Vicente told me, 'and we looked for a partner in China to join us and to get that stake, and that's why we formed this company. They got the loan, we paid Shell. It was, let's say, 800 [million dollars] something. And after that, later on, we called Sinopec, another Chinese company, one of the biggest.'[35]

The partner the Futungo found was Sam Pa and his newly formed Queensway Group. The company they formed was called China Son-angol. China was in the early phases of its thrust into Africa, and it was natural for onlookers to assume that China Sonangol was nothing more than what its name suggested: a partnership between the Chinese state and the Angolan national oil company. But Vicente and Sonangol opted not to deal directly with China's government and its state-owned oil company, Sinopec. Instead, it went into business with an obscure private company registered in Hong Kong, with no assets other than its founders' guanxi.[36]

On its articles of association, the names of China Sonangol's two share-holders are handwritten in a spidery script. The minority shareholder, with 30 per cent, was Sonangol. The holder of the remaining 70 per cent was a holding company owned by the Queensway Group, with Lo Fong-hung as its signatory.[37] China Sonangol was registered as a company in Hong Kong on 27 August 2004. Seven weeks later, on 15 October, a com-pany called Sonangol Sinopec International Limited was incorporated in the Cayman Islands, co-owned by Sinopec, Sonangol, and, although there is nothing in its name to indicate as much, the Queensway Group.[38] It was Sonangol Sinopec International Limited that, by the end of the year, had secured Shell's 50 per cent stake in Block 18, with Sinopec arranging more than a billion dollars in finance for the new venture.[39]

Manuel Vicente and Sam Pa had constructed an enclave within An-gola's oil industry, a corporate bunker within the already opaque walls of Sonangol. Through a network of obscure companies registered in Hong Kong, the Futungo had plugged itself into an offshore mechanism that channelled the political power of Angola's authoritarian rulers into the pri-vate corporate empire that Pa and his fellow founders of the Queensway

Group had begun to assemble. The Futungo was swapping a Cessna for a Concorde, a trawler for a submarine, and it had poured some Chinese guanxi into the engine of its looting machine.

With its new partners, BP pressed on with the development of Block 18's oil fields, and in October 2007 the project began pumping two hundred thousand barrels of oil a day. In 2010 the Queensway Group's stake in Block 18 was valued at just shy of a billion dollars.[40] Its share of the crude was worth about $3.5 million every day.[41] (BP declined to answer questions about its relationship with China Sonangol.)

That was just the beginning. China Sonangol was inserted into a multi-billion-dollar financing deal under which banks lent money to Sonangol, to be repaid from the proceeds of Angolan oil sales to Sinopec, once China Sonangol had taken its cut. Over the years that followed the initial Block 18 deal China Sonangol was awarded stakes in nine more Angolan oil blocks in its own right and three via its partnership with Sinopec, a portfolio of assets in one of the world's fastest-growing oil industries worth billions of dollars. But China Sonangol does not drill wells or pump crude. It is a pipeline for petro-dollars – and a way for the Futungo to use Sam Pa and his associates as a vanguard in Africa's resource states. 'If there is an opportunity for some oil, they call us, taking into account this joint venture we have,' Vicente told me.[42]

Isaías Samakuva, the leader of the Angolan opposition political party into which Unita has evolved since its defeat in the civil war, told me that China Sonangol was 'the key to all the support that is given to Mr dos Santos, to his rule' but that understanding how the Futungo drew wealth and power from the company was impossible because 'everything is in the dark'.[43]

Not quite everything is in the dark. Corporate filings in Hong Kong and elsewhere reveal glimpses of the Queensway Group's corporate labyrinth. But, as in Dan Gertler's deals in Congo, many of the trails vanish behind the thick walls of offshore finance. For example, Manuel Vicente and other senior Angolan officials have been named in company filings alongside founding members of the Queensway Group as directors of a company called Worldpro Development Limited. Its registration documents in

Hong Kong give no indication of the company's purpose and state that it is wholly owned by World Noble Holdings Limited, which is registered in the British Virgin Islands, a Caribbean archipelago where companies can keep their owners secret. Manuel Vicente does not dispute that he served as the corporate president of China Sonangol, but he told me he only did so as the representative of Sonangol's stake in the company, not for any personal benefit. When he switched to his new role in the presidency, his successor as Sonangol boss took over the position in his place.[44]

Unlike, say, the concealed stakes that Vicente and his confreres held in Cobalt International Energy's Angolan oil venture, there is nothing in the reams of company filings that I have scoured to show that anyone in the Futungo directly benefits from a stake in the Queensway Group's companies. Unita's Isaías Samakuva was on to something, though: the extra layers of secrecy their arrangements with the Queensway Group provided are valuable in themselves to the rulers of Angola's 'cryptocracy'. They create new hidden passageways for Sonangol, a company at the centre of a $32 billion hole in Angola's public finances. Crucially, these passageways extend beyond Angola's borders, winding through offshore tax havens and into the global business empire that the Queensway Group would build from its Angolan foundations, stretching from Manhattan to Pyongyang and penetrating other African resource states. A century after King Leopold was declared the private owner of Congo, China Sonangol became a prime vehicle for those, foreign and African alike, who sought to make the continent and its natural riches their personal possessions.

From the beginning scandals of financial impropriety swirled around the Queensway Group and companies to which it was linked. The chairman of Beiya Industrial Group, the Chinese state-owned railway company that had ties to Queensway companies in the early days, was jailed for life for bribery and embezzlement.[45] In an early oil-trading venture in Congo-Brazzaville, another crude producer north of Angola, the Queensway Group went into business with companies connected to the ruling elite and that would be implicated in a scheme to use sham companies to hide oil revenues.[46] Then, in 2007, the Queensway Group's success nearly came to an abrupt end.

To begin with, while China Sonangol was no more than an obscure vehicle buried in a complicated oil deal, the Queensway Group's most prominent face was a company called China International Fund (CIF). Incorporated in Hong Kong in 2003, like its sister company, CIF was frequently mistaken for an arm of the Chinese state, partly because of its name and partly because, in the early years of China's thrust into Africa, it was perfectly natural, if overly simplistic, to assume that every corporation run by Chinese people was subject to the diktats of the Communist regime in Beijing. Again, though, this was not the case. CIF was wholly owned by the founders of the Queensway Group – Lo Fong-hung; Sam Pa's partner, Veronica Fung; and Wu Yang, the Chinese oilman who had made some useful introductions in Beijing.[47]

CIF's primary business is infrastructure. Mimicking the Chinese state's grand pacts in Africa's resource states, the Queensway Group undertakes, through CIF, to build bridges, airports and roads, usually alongside oil and mining deals. In 2005 CIF organized a $2.9 billion loan to fund a plethora of contracts from the Angolan government, including a new airport, a railway, two highways, drainage works in Luanda and a housing project.[48] When I asked Manuel Vicente about China International Fund, he told me it was 'completely separate' from the Chinese government's multibillion-dollar oil-backed loans to pay for public works in Angola. But just as China Sonangol was nothing more than a middleman in the shadowy deals that secured its stakes in Angolan oil blocks, CIF was more of a broker than an actual contractor: much of the work was subcontracted to Chinese state-owned engineering and construction groups.

A special office created in the presidency, the Gabinete de Reconstrução Nacional, or Office of National Reconstruction, marshalled CIF's projects. Initially Fernando Miala, the president's spymaster, had been the key man in the Futungo's relations with the Chinese. When the money began to flow, however, the potentates of the Futungo began a tussle for control over these new, huge flows of cash. Miala was outflanked by General Kopelipa, the security chief and tycoon who would join Manuel Vicente in questionable business deals, including the Cobalt one. Miala's fall was swift. He was dismissed in February 2006 and, when he refused to attend his own demotion from general to lieutenant colonel, arrested on a charge of insubordination, accused of plotting against the president.

At his trial in 2007 Miala broke the Futungo's code of silence and claimed that Chinese funds meant to rebuild Angola were being abused. Adopting an affronted tone, Angola's finance ministry, in a rare public statement, professed itself 'stupefied' at accusations by former intelligence officials of 'anomalies in the handling of the Chinese credit line'. The statement went on to enumerate the Chinese credit lines, public and private, and the various good uses to which they were being put. But it also revealed what had until then only been rumoured: China International Fund was in financial straits.

Through hubris on the part of Sam Pa, disputes with subcontractors, mismanagement by the special Angolan office tasked with overseeing Chinese loans, or, most likely, a combination of the three, CIF's ambitious infrastructure projects ran into the sand. When contractors stopped being paid, construction work ground to a halt. In Beijing there was mounting concern that a chancer from Hong Kong was imperilling China's relationship with an increasingly vital oil supplier. The Ministry of Commerce warned Chinese companies to cut back their dealings with CIF. In May 2007, according to a letter I obtained, the Hong Kong corporate regulator opened an investigation into allegations that Hangxiao Steel, the Chinese steel group to which China International Fund had awarded a $5 billion contract for a housing project in Angola, had engaged in stock market manipulations.[49]

The backdrop to Pa's travails was a series of upheavals in the highest reaches of Chinese power. In 2007 Chinese politics was dominated by jockeying ahead of that October's National Congress of the Communist Party of China, a five-yearly transition that would anoint a new leadership of the Party and the nation. Zeng Peiyan, the vice premier to whom Sam Pa had secured access while he was brokering his first Angolan oil deal, was heading for retirement after the congress. Other big names exited the stage less gracefully. In June Chen Tonghai suddenly resigned as chairman of Sinopec, the state oil group he had helped to make into comfortably China's biggest company by revenues and for which the Queensway

Group had served as the middleman in Angola. Sinopec's official statement said Chen had departed for 'personal reasons', but within months he
had been arrested and accused of 'taking bribes to help others, including
his mistress, make unlawful profits', and leading a 'corrupt life'.[50] He was
later convicted of accepting $29 million in bribes between 1999 and 2007
and handed a suspended death sentence, effectively a life term of imprison-
ment.[51] New faces were in charge in the Party and at Sinopec. As ministries
and regulators grew suspicious of the Queensway Group's activities, the
walls were closing in on Sam Pa. His guanxi was depleting rapidly. But he
had one card left – and it was an ace.

Whatever the misgivings about him in Beijing, Sam Pa had made himself an indispensable part of the Futungo's looting machine. By using
China Sonangol and China International Fund as intermediaries in oil
deals and infrastructure contracts, Angola's rulers had created for themselves a new, secretive vehicle to dabble in the oil trade and spray their
petro-dollars across the globe. When Sinopec sought to disentangle itself
from its joint ventures with Queensway companies in Angola – preferring
to cut out the middleman – the Futungo rebuffed them. Alex Vines, whose
research into the Queensway Group as head of the Africa programme at
the UK's Royal Institute of International Affairs think tank at Chatham
House has included interviews with top Chinese oil executives, told me
that Manuel Vicente had informed China's state-owned oil companies that
if they wanted to do business in Angola, they would have to go through
these joint ventures with Queensway Group companies.[52] 'Sinopec saw it
as a short-term joint venture to get in but then realized they were locked
in,' Vines said. When the US ambassador to Luanda privately asked his
Chinese counterpart to clarify his government's relationship with China
International Fund, Beijing's envoy was keen to emphasize that CIF was
a 'private company' and said his embassy had nothing to do with its dealings with the Angolan authorities.[53] What CIF did enjoy, the ambassador
said, was a 'close relationship' with dos Santos. Sam Pa had become the
gatekeeper to Angolan crude, and China was powerless to circumvent him.

Before long the Queensway Group was, if not back in the fold, at least
once more being tolerated by Beijing. China International Fund's money
troubles eased: in October 2007, in the same announcement in which it

dismissed allegations of mismanagement of Chinese funds, Angola's finance ministry revealed that it had issued $3.5 billion in government bonds to bail out CIF's foundering infrastructure projects.[54] The same month BP started pumping oil from Block 18, with the Queensway Group entitled to three in every twenty dollars of the profits.

There are those who describe the Queensway Group as an angel of Angola's salvation. 'The official Chinese government wanted to do it, and the Angolan government wanted to do it,' said Helder Bataglia, who says he bowed out in 2004 once China, Sam Pa, and the Futungo were on their way to sealing their first deals.[55] Bataglia said it was he who persuaded Sam Pa to focus on Angola and that he was proud of having helped to bring some much-needed investment to his adopted homeland. 'For me it was fantastic because my main objective was to put the two nations together, because at that time no country was prepared to help them rebuild the country.' As for China Sonangol and China International Fund, he waved away concerns about their interests. 'For me, it was a huge success. Of course, I wanted much more, but what they did is very important for the country. I don't have any regrets. I am very proud of what I did. At the end of the war 150,000 people demobilized. They had to find work for them, to invest in reconstruction.'

Bataglia went on, 'For the average Angolan it has changed a lot – look at the roads, the railways, the bridges. There isn't a more independent country in Africa than Angola. After China, they developed relationships all over the world. They are fiercely independent. That is very important for the self-esteem of a nation. The Angolans – they are very proud of what they are doing. Of course there are problems, but there are problems in Portugal, in the United Kingdom. When two countries like Angola and China come together to rebuild a country, a company in the middle is not a good thing for either.'

But there was a company in the middle – the Queensway Group. A decade would pass following Sam Pa's audacious first deals in Angola before a glimpse of the true nature of its bargain with Angola's ruler emerged.

In 2011 Wu Yang, the Beijing mover and shaker who said he had been granted a free stake in the Queensway Group holding company that held its interest in China Sonangol in exchange for helping to fix up the Angolan deal with Sinopec, sued Lo, Veronica Fung and the holding company it-self in Hong Kong. Wu claimed he was owed dividends worth about $40 million but that they had not been paid. He demanded to be able to go through the books of several Queensway Group companies to see where all its money was going. In 2013 a judge in Hong Kong granted him per-mission to do so. The judge's account of Lo's testimony in the case was revealing.

Lo accepted that the Block 18 project, which still yields 180,000 barrels of crude a day, was profitable, the judge wrote, but she said that the profits had been diverted to other uses.[56] 'The thrust of her evidence . . . is that the money received by China Sonangol went to fund projects in Angola undertaken to build goodwill. She does not identify any particular project or explain with whom [the Queensway holding company in question] was trying to curry favour. These projects were loss making and the implica-tion of her evidence is that funding them used up the profits made on the Block 18 Project.' In short, Lo Fong-hung, Sam Pa's principal collaborator in the Queensway Group, had acknowledged to a court that its flagship company was diverting money to 'curry favour' in Angola. Putting it deli-cately, the judge went on, 'I do not understand it to be in dispute that oper-ating a company in Angola in accordance with what would be considered in Hong Kong to be best business and accounting practices would be very difficult and in some respects impossible.'

The legal tussles between Wu Yang and the Queensway Group's found-ers wore on. But by then Sam Pa had reached new heights. After turning his guanxi into the foundations of a corporate empire, he would use his Angolan experience as a model for deals with the repressive rulers of other African resource states.

» 5 «

When Elephants Fight, the Grass Gets Trampled

It was a humid, overcast Sunday afternoon in April 2013, and Frederic Cilins was hungry. 'Let's sit down, grab a bite,' he said to the woman who emerged from a taxi to meet him at Jacksonville International Airport in Florida.[1] According to a transcript of their conversation subsequently published by a government inquiry in Guinea, the pair found a place to eat inside the airport's swish terminal and took their seats – Cilins, a balding Frenchman in his early fifties, and Mamadie Touré, a curvaceous west African twenty years his junior. They made small talk for a few moments, speaking in French. Cilins's daughter had given birth the previous day, he said, making him a grandfather for the first time.

Almost immediately the conversation turned to money. 'I need cash, now,' Touré said. Cilins explained that she could have $20,000 right away and would receive $200,000 more once she arrived in Sierra Leone. He would take care of the plane ticket too. She started to haggle. A waitress came over. Cilins switched to English to order a chicken sandwich for Touré and a Caesar salad for himself. He changed tack. In Sierra Leone, the neighbour to Touré's native Guinea, she could be tranquil, far from the troubles that were closing in on them. But Touré wanted to settle the financial terms of their arrangement. Hadn't Cilins said he would give her $50,000 up front, not $20,000?

'No, no, no,' Cilins said. 'Listen carefully, listen carefully. I told you the deal.' He went over it again. A few thousand dollars was neither here nor there. 'The deal for the documents and for the declaration was what I told you: we destroy all the documents, you get two hundred and then eight hundred, which is yours, whatever happens. Whatever happens, you have one million, which is yours.'

The Frenchman was losing his cool. He had done business in Africa's wild west for years, but this was a particularly delicate conversation. Touré had in her possession half a dozen signed contracts dating from 2006 to 2010, apparently detailing how she would be rewarded in cash and shares if she helped to arrange for a company called BSG Resources (BSGR) to be awarded mining concessions, including rights to Simandou, one of the world's richest virgin deposits of iron ore, located in a remote corner of Guinea.[2] (When the contracts later became public, BSGR said they were forgeries.) The Guinean government of the day had granted the company rights to Simandou in 2008. Two years later Vale, the world's biggest iron ore miner, had agreed to pay $2.5 billion for a share of BSGR's rights, a princely return on the $160 million that BSGR had spent on preliminary development work on its prospects and one of the most spectacular deals in the recent history of African mining.

But now there was a problem. Touré had told Cilins that the FBI had come to see her. The reason for their interest was that she was no ordinary Guinean: she had been the fourth wife of Lansana Conté, the dictator who had granted BSGR its rights days before he died in December 2008. The widowed Touré had moved first to Sierra Leone, then to Florida, where federal agents had paid her a visit after they got wind of possible breaches of the Foreign Corrupt Practices Act and of money-laundering statutes that forbid channelling the proceeds of corruption into the United States.

In a series of phone calls and meetings over the previous weeks Cilins – who had worked as BSGR's intermediary in Guinea but, as the company is at pains to stress, had never been its employee – had sought to cajole Touré into destroying the documents before the FBI got hold of them. He had persuaded her to sign a declaration denying that she had played any role in awarding mining rights to BSGR or received any money from the company. He had encouraged her to leave the country for Sierra Leone. On top of the million dollars he had offered for destroying the documents, Cilins had promised as much as $5 million more if BSGR came through the current Guinean government's review of past mining contracts with its interests intact.

'Do you need anything?' asked the waitress, bringing the pair's order. 'Mayonnaise, mustard?' Cilins sent the waitress away and turned back to Touré. The conversation meandered through family, Guinean politics, the weather in Miami. Cilins ordered a cheesecake for each of them and probed Touré about the FBI agents who had asked her questions. She said she had told them she didn't have any documents, but the agents had threatened to get a subpoena and bring her before the grand jury that had been convened in New York to hear evidence about the corruption allegations. 'It has to be destroyed quickly,' he said. The waitress brought Cilins his change. 'No, thank you very much,' he said.

'Oh, thank you so much,' said the waitress, 'have a great one.'

Touré pressed again for more cash up front. 'I'm not a child,' she snapped. Cilins blew his top. 'I'm tired of this, Mamadie. What do you want to do? You tell me what you want to do. Me, I'm tired. You're reproaching me. I come, I bring you money, I find solutions for you, I do this, that. I'm tired. So you tell me what you want. It's up to you to decide.' He told her it was in her own interests to destroy the documents – not to do so would set off an 'atomic bomb' for her. He berated her for giving copies of them to an acquaintance, who in turn had brought them to the attention of the new Guinean authorities. 'I'm not saying you're a child, but I'm saying you've made some bad decisions,' Cilins said. He paused and excused himself, saying he needed to check the departure boards for his flight.

A man approached. 'Stand up,' he said to Cilins. 'Put your hands behind your back.'

Beny Steinmetz was born into the mining business. The youngest son of Rubin Steinmetz, founder of one of Israel's most successful diamond trading companies, in 1977 he completed his military service and embarked, aged twenty-one, for an apprenticeship in Antwerp. The Belgian port has been the centre of the diamond trade for five centuries and is still the conduit for the vast majority of rough stones that flow in from distant mines to be cut, polished and sold on to jewellers. Lean and handsome, Steinmetz soon started to build a reputation as one of the most formidable figures in the African diamond trade. He bought stones in war-torn Angola.[3] The company he founded with his brother, Steinmetz Diamond Group, became the biggest buyer of rough stones from De Beers, the cartel that dominated the trade. The Steinmetz family diamond empire sponsors Formula One cars and showcases its stones at lavish parties set alongside such aesthetic landmarks as Bangkok's Temple of Dawn and Scarlett Johansson.

As his fortune grew, Steinmetz added metal mines and real estate to his portfolio and relocated from Israel to the lakeside Swiss city of Geneva. In 2011 *Forbes* ranked him at 162 in its rich list, with a net worth of $6 billion, comfortably ahead of Bernie Ecclestone and Richard Branson and almost double that of eBay founder Jeff Skoll. On his personal website an unnamed acquaintance is quoted as saying, 'The phrase "the sky is the limit" isn't applicable to Beny. To him, the sky is merely the beginning.'

Steinmetz was quick to respond to the changes in the mining market around the turn of the century. The demand of fast-growing Asian economies for base metals prompted mining houses to diversify their operations, switching investment from treasures like diamonds to the bulky raw ingredients of electrical wiring and steel. Alongside Dan Gertler, his fellow Israeli mining tycoon who had cultivated the Kabila regime in Congo, Steinmetz made a move on Katanga, the southern Congolese repository of copper and cobalt in quantities unsurpassed elsewhere. A company called Nikanor, in which Steinmetz and Gertler were major shareholders, secured rights to a dilapidated copper mine there. In 2008 Glencore, the giant commodities trader that would strike more Congolese deals involving Gertler, bought in to the group.[4] By then Steinmetz was closing in on a still more coveted prize in another benighted state in francophone Africa.

When Guinea's French colonial rulers departed in 1958 they did so in a fit of post-imperial sabotage. Ahmed Sekou Touré, Guinea's liberation leader, had spurned Charles de Gaulle's offer to join a francophone union in Africa. France granted independence, but at a vindictive price, declining to leave behind even the light bulbs in the government offices. Sekou Touré was undaunted. 'We prefer poverty in freedom to riches in slavery,' he proclaimed.[5]

Poverty did indeed endure, but the people of Guinea knew no freedom. Sekou Touré became the first in a procession of venal and violent autocrats. The newly independent Guinea, like dozens of its African peers, enjoyed only nominal sovereignty. Superpowers and mining houses held sway, adapting their allegiances to suit the prevailing despot.

Guinea avoided the civil wars that ripped apart its neighbours, Sierra Leone and Liberia, where rebels funded by diamond sales lopped off hands. Not that you would know it to look at Conakry, Guinea's seaside capital. The malarial metropolis feels as though it is slowly decomposing into the mulch of the tropical foliage. The interior of the country is as deprived as its scenery is breathtaking. Ill starred and misgoverned, Guinea belongs to the lowest circle of poverty, along with Congo, Niger, Somalia and a handful of others, where all the indicators measuring human well-being are abysmal, well below even the African average. On average, out of every thousand babies born in Switzerland, all but four will at least see their fifth birthday. By the same age, one hundred and four Guinean babies per thousand have died.[6] Along the capital's dank, pitted streets shuffle alarmingly high numbers of those who made it through infancy but whose traumatic start in life left them with cerebral palsy. Guinea's 11 million people are significantly more under-educated and unwell than almost anyone else on the planet.

When Sekou Touré died in 1984, Lansana Conté, a soldier who had served in the French army prior to independence before rising to a senior position in the Guinean military, was perfectly placed to lead the coup that commenced his quarter-century rule. He was part of the generation of leaders – Mobutu in Congo, Bongo in Gabon, and dos Santos in Angola among them – whose decades in power through the 1980s and 1990s finally dashed the high hopes of the post-independence years. They ruled through theft and repression, treating their countries' oil and minerals as their personal property. They cocooned themselves in looting machines. But those looting machines only work if they can be plugged into international markets for oil and minerals. For that, Africa's despots need allies in the resource industry.

For a country no bigger than the UK, Guinea has a disproportionate share of the Earth's metal. 'It's got this huge mineral endowment,' a foreign mining executive in Guinea told me. 'Some of the deposits are fabulous, unlike anything else in the world.' The country sits on the largest recorded reserves of bauxite, the ore that is refined into aluminium, a highly resistant metal that is one of the more vital commodities in the global economy. Alloys of aluminium are everywhere: in kitchen foil, drink cans, pill packets, aircraft. Guinea has for decades ranked among the biggest exporters of bauxite. But it is also home to vast, untouched reserves of the only metal more in demand than aluminium: iron.

Iron ore is used to make steel, the material without which the modern world as we know it would not exist. Annual steel production worldwide is 1.5 billion tonnes, or roughly one tonne for every five people. The biggest steelmakers, among them ArcelorMittal, India's Tata family and Baosteel of China, bestride a global industrial economy that needs steel for ships and bridges, forks and scalpels. So do the largest iron-ore miners: Vale of Brazil and Rio Tinto, the Anglo-Australian mining house that has grown from its nineteenth-century origins digging up copper by the banks of a Spanish river to be the world's second-most valuable mining house, after its great rival, BHP Billiton.

In 1996 executives from Rio Tinto met Lansana Conté's mining minister to talk about exploring Guinea's mountainous eastern territory for iron ore.[7] The following year Rio was granted a permit to prospect along the 110-kilometre Simandou range. In 2002 Rio's geologists discovered a body of such high-quality ore that it had few peers in size and value anywhere. Further exploration established that it contained more than 2.4 billion tons of top-notch iron ore, making it the best untapped deposit in the world. But Simandou lay 435 miles from the coast. Tapping the ore would mean building a railway across difficult terrain and a massive port at the end of it. All told, the mine and the infrastructure would cost something like $20 billion – the biggest investment ever undertaken in African mining.

Conté churned through prime ministers and his security forces slaughtered protesters, but Rio maintained its interests. In 2006, after years of wrangling with Guinea's parliament, the company finally secured the document known as a mining convention for Simandou, the legal rights to start digging. But progress was slow. The Guinean authorities grew frustrated, and other parties began to show an interest. Among them was Beny Steinmetz.

Steinmetz had already carved a swathe through Africa's mining industry, and Guinea's bounty of iron ore was a tempting prospect for BSGR, the mining arm of the family conglomerate that bears his initials. But BSGR faced two obstacles. First, Guinea was unfamiliar territory. Second, Rio Tinto had locked up rights to the choicest deposits. The company needed someone on the ground who could work out how to proceed. It found Frederic Cilins. Cilins had done business across Africa since the early 2000s, including in Congo and Angola. With two partners he had also developed what BSGR would later describe as 'extensive business operations' in Lansana Conté's Guinea.[8]

Cilins started to work as an intermediary for BSGR in Guinea in 2005. According to an interview he gave to an investigator years later, he hung around the Novotel, the hotel in Conakry where anybody who is anybody stays, gathering scraps of information on Rio Tinto.[9] While Rio was charting Simandou's ore bodies, Cilins was mapping Guinea's political contours. As Cilins cultivated his contacts, he edged closer to the heart of power: the presidency.

Like many other Guinean Muslims who could afford to do so, Lansana Conté had multiple wives. He had already taken three brides when, in 2000, he met the beautiful eighteen-year-old daughter of a former colleague from the military. Within the year Mamadie Touré became the president's fourth wife.[10] They did not live together, but he supported her financially and they spent time in one another's company at the house she was given and at the presidential villa, discussing the affairs of state.

Around 2005 the president's young wife received a new visitor, the man with whom she would sit in hushed, tense conversation seven years later at the Jacksonville airport. According to Touré's recollections – an important plank in the evidence published by a subsequent Guinean inquiry – Cilins told her when they met that BSGR wanted to get its hands on iron ore rights.[11] Officials and ministers who helped in the endeavour would get a share of $12 million.[12] According to Touré's version of events, supported by the contracts Cilins was so keen to destroy but that BSGR claimed were fakes, she began to advance the company's cause in exchange for agreements to pay her millions of dollars and award her shares in BSGR's Guinean venture. (BSGR has said that it never made any payments to Touré.)[13] First, Touré took Cilins to meet Lansana Conté at the presidential palace. Not long afterward, in February 2006, BSGR received its first iron ore rights. But the company wanted more – a slice of Simandou.

Perhaps Touré saw nothing untoward in her dealings with Cilins and BSGR. In Conté's Guinea there was no division between politics and business. The country was ranked alongside Iraq, Myanmar and Haiti as the world's most corrupt.[14] That which belonged to the state belonged to

Conté. Guinean life was, by and large, destitute and brief. But Touré had found herself among the small clique of Guineans who could ensure their escape from poverty – those who enjoyed the dictator's favour. She recalled years later in a sworn statement that, when she consulted her husband about $200,000 she said she had been given after one of her meetings with Cilins and other emissaries from BSGR, 'he told me it was my good luck.'[15]

After BSGR won its first rights, it stepped up its efforts. Cilins made way for senior figures from the company itself, Touré recalled. Asher Avidan, who served for twenty-seven years as a senior official in Israel's foreign and defence ministries before joining BSGR as the head of its Guinean subsidiary, showered Touré with gifts, she recalled.[16] On one occasion, Touré says, Avidan showed her to a room in which a million dollars was laid out on a bed for her.[17] When in 2014 I asked BSGR about this and other incidents described in Touré's statement, the company declined to answer my questions.

Alongside gifts that BSGR's emissaries provided to influential Guineans – among them a diamond-encrusted miniature Formula One car, which its representatives later said had been given to the mining ministry, not an individual – the company also played on frustration in Conté's government at the slow pace of Rio Tinto's work at Simandou.[18] In 2008 BSGR's strategy paid off. In July the government stripped Rio Tinto of the rights to the northern half of Simandou on the grounds, disputed by Rio, that the company had missed its deadlines to start mining, making it liable, as is standard in the industry, to cede a portion of its holdings. In December, by ministerial decree, those rights were awarded to BSGR. For Beny Steinmetz and his company the breakthrough had come in the nick of time.

Reportedly a diabetic and a chain smoker, Conté's health was failing. On 22 December 2008, two weeks after BSGR had taken possession of the northern half of Simandou, Conté died. If Guineans dared to hope that deliverance was at hand, they were wrong. After twenty-four years in power, Conté's death left a vacuum, into which the army promptly stepped.

After coming close to disaster in 2007, the following year Sam Pa was back on his feet. The Queensway Group had avoided the fallout from stock market regulators' investigations in Beijing and Hong Kong into the award of a contract for an Angolan project given by China International Fund, its infrastructure arm, to a Chinese steel company. The warnings that the Chinese Ministry of Commerce had issued to Chinese companies about doing business with the Queensway Group had either been rescinded or ignored – restoring a crucial plank in the syndicate's business model of using its access to African rulers to generate deals both for itself and for Chinese state-owned groups.[19]

Pa led a dizzying expansion of the Queensway Group's interests. It snapped up prestigious real estate in Manhattan and pressed on with its courtship of North Korea. But Africa – and Angola in particular – remained the foundation of its empire. To replicate the phenomenally lucrative model it had constructed with Manuel Vicente and the Angolan Futungo, it needed to find other African countries that had both natural wealth and rulers who wielded undiluted power through a shadow state.

Guinea's 'Christmas coup' after Lansana Conté's death in late 2008 brought to power a little-known army captain in his forties. Moussa 'Dadis' Camara had a chiselled jaw, a red beret, and a flair for spectacle. Like many a putschist, he proclaimed himself the man to clean the stables. The ringleaders of the cocaine-trafficking networks that had taken root in the security forces were denounced in public, and Conté's son Ousmane confessed on television to being involved in the drug trade and was thrown in jail. The new government would examine past mining deals. The junta baptized itself the National Council for Democracy and Development.

The young captain was unpredictable, paranoid, and apparently nocturnal. He held meetings in the dead of night and slept by day. Ministers and investors were summoned to his base at a Conakry barracks, where bureaucrats and businessmen in robes and suits mingled with soldiers in fatigues. Dadis received visitors in a room hung with portraits of himself in heroic poses.[20] He would scream in the faces of minions who had earned his ire. Even those castigated in error were too scared to point out that the strongman had mistaken them for someone else. A showman, Dadis delighted in upbraiding, live on television, foreign investors and diplomats he deemed disrespectful. The performances became known as 'The Dadis Show'.

The junta's combustible leader was a stark contrast to the suave, cosmopolitan investment banker who returned to Guinea to assume the powerful position of mining minister. Mahmoud Thiam was not the first member of his family to run the gauntlet of holding government office under a despot: when Thiam was five his father, a former head of Guinea's foreign trade bank, was named as finance minister, only to be caught up days later in one of Sekou Touré's purges. He was arrested, tortured, and killed.[21] His young son was taken into exile and wound up in the United States, where he was granted citizenship. Bright and possessed of a winning charm, he gained an economics degree from Cornell University and went into banking, rising through Wall Street. First with Merrill Lynch, then at the New York office of the Swiss bank UBS, Thiam managed wealthy foreign clients' fortunes and advised finance ministries and companies from Norway to China to South Africa. He made enough money to donate $4,600 to Barack Obama's 2008 presidential campaign.[22]

Thiam was in his mid-forties by the time the new dispensation in Conakry gave him a reason to go home. He surveyed the horizons of Guinea's economy and decided to shake things up. Guinea relied on mining revenues for 85 per cent of its exports, but the government only made a pittance from the country's resources, which were under the control of some of the most powerful figures in the industry. The mining ministry Thiam took over was a warren of crumbling corridors whose occupants, though sometimes brilliant, were scarcely equipped to take on the multinationals' armies of lawyers. But Thiam knew the world of high finance and deal making. He has a smooth bearing, enhanced by his shaven head and dapper suits, and he was prepared to lock horns with the big beasts of the mining business.

Thiam's first target was Rusal, the aluminium giant that mined Guinea's bauxite, and its Russian oligarch owner, Oleg Deripaska. Deripaska had acquired a Guinean bauxite mine and refinery in a 2006 privatization. Thiam claimed that the price Rusal paid had been a fraction of what the assets were worth and that the sale was invalid – allegations that Rusal disputed.[23] When Rusal listed its shares amid much fanfare on the Hong Kong stock exchange, Thiam demanded that part of the proceeds of Rusal's share sale go to settle what Thiam claimed it owed the African nation, which accounted for some 10 per cent of the company's worldwide bauxite production. Once alleged environmental damage was included, the sum Thiam sought exceeded a billion dollars.[24]

Rusal refused to buckle, and the standoff dragged on. (Rusal refused to accede to demands for money, and after Thiam and the junta had left office, the company repaired its relations with Guinea's government, announcing in 2014 that it had begun work on a new bauxite mine.)[25] But this was only one front in Thiam's campaign. Like other senior Guinean officials, he bridled at what he saw as the condescension of the multinationals, particularly the brash Australians from Rio Tinto. Rio had been happy to tout Simandou as a prize asset when it fought off an attempted takeover by BHP Billiton, but Guinea had been waiting more than a decade for Simandou to start yielding its ore.

Thiam ratcheted up the pressure on Rio, threatening to strip it of more of its rights if it failed to acknowledge that the northern half of the deposit, which Conté had transferred to BSGR, had been legitimately confiscated. (Thiam's jousting with Rio would eventually prompt Henry Bellingham, minister for Africa in David Cameron's British government, to write to him and three other senior ministers, lobbying for the company and warning that any further action against London-listed Rio would 'send a negative signal to investors'.)[26] Thiam backed BSGR, arguing that having two separate projects to mine Simandou would ensure that the ore would finally start to flow.

'We could be sitting on those reserves for another fifty years as we have already for fifty years,' Thiam told me.[27] Guinea, he noted drily, was not a publicly traded company: unlike listed mining corporations such as Rio, whose share prices benefited from undeveloped mineral reserves on their books, the country gained nothing when its minerals sat in the ground. 'We only make money if and when we export iron ore. We have the richest and most abundant iron ore on Earth, and we are still one of the poorest countries.'

According to his enemies, Thiam also had less honourable motives. In a 2014 lawsuit Rio Tinto accused him of receiving a $200 million bribe – subsequently revised to $100 million – from Beny Steinmetz to ensure that he protected BSGR's newly won claim to Simandou's northern half.[28] (Thiam called Rio's allegations 'false, libelous, and borderline comical' and described them as an attempt by the company 'to divert attention from their unwillingness to develop Simandou'; BSGR was similarly dismissive:

'Rio Tinto chose to do nothing with its mining rights so the mining rights were taken away. Baseless and bizarre lawsuits like this won't change that fact.')[29]

Simandou was the country's greatest prize, but it was many years away from generating revenues, and the junta's most pressing concern was to bring in some ready money. Immediately after the coup Dadis had pledged that he would organize elections, hand power to civilians, and take his boys back to the barracks. But soon he was letting it be known that he planned to renege on his promise not to stand as a candidate. Guinea's isolation deepened, and free-spending soldiers were rapidly depleting coffers that cuts to aid following the coup had already depleted. 'It was a question of the survival of the economy,' Thiam told me later.[30]

One day in the middle of 2009, a few months into the job, Thiam was having lunch when a fellow minister called, insisting that he abandon his meal and come to the Novotel to meet some potential investors. Upon arriving Thiam was introduced to a Chinese woman he had not met before. She was Lo Fong-hung, Sam Pa's cofounder of the Queensway Group. Thiam was told that the Guinean ambassador to China had organized the delegation's visit. China Sonangol, the Queensway Group's joint venture with Angola's state oil company, was raking in revenues from Angolan crude sales, and Lo got Thiam's attention with some sizable numbers. 'She told me how much money they could deploy,' Thiam recalled. 'I was a little sceptical, but I told them they were welcome to join, if you are as big as you say you are.' Sam Pa turned up and introduced himself too. After the meeting Thiam briefed Dadis on the encounter.

Thiam decided to run some checks on the prospective new investors, whose major dealings to date had been in Angola. He knew Manuel Vicente and Sonangol from his banking days; the two men were good friends.[31] He challenged Pa and Lo: 'If you are so close to Manuel Vicente, come back with him.' Three days later, Thiam recalls, Vicente landed in Conakry on a flight with Pa. Thiam took them to see Dadis. Pa promised the head of Guinea's junta that he would send some money forthwith. Within two weeks about $30 million arrived, Thiam said. 'It was a goodwill gesture to show they were serious and capable.' Thiam told me the money was earmarked to fund improvements to Guinea's water supply and to rent emergency power generators. Even if it was indeed spent on such admirable endeavours, it would have freed up other funds for the junta to deploy or to plunder.

When Thiam went to China shortly after his first meeting with Pa and Lo in Conakry he was, like the Portuguese–Angolan tycoon Helder Bataglia before him, left with the distinct impression that they enjoyed high-level connections to the Beijing authorities. 'If they were not a government entity, they definitely had strong backing and strong ties, given the reception we got in China,' Thiam told me. 'The level of clearances they had to do things that are difficult in China, the facility they had in getting people to see us [and] the military motorcade gave us the impression that they were strongly connected.' Thiam was convinced. With his new-found allies, he set up joint ventures between the Guinean state and Queensway Group – registered not in Guinea but in Singapore, where China International Fund and China Sonangol had established headquarters as their international reach grew – and started to hatch plans for Guinea's minerals.

Thiam was jetting around, cutting deals like the investment banker he was, accumulating allies and enemies and helping to keep the junta from bankruptcy. One Monday in September 2009, nine months into his tenure at the mining ministry, he caught a flight in Qatar. When he disembarked in Paris he heard that Dadis had unleashed havoc.

Torrential rains poured down on Conakry on the morning of 28 September 2009. Among the tens of thousands of Guineans who made their way to the national stadium the mood was a mixture of trepidation and jubilation.[32] The stadium lies halfway along a finger of land that juts out into the Gulf of Guinea, not far from the capital's ramshackle airport. Its previous major spectacle had been June's two-to-one victory for the national soccer team over the visiting Malawians in a World Cup qualifier. Today something more feverish even than the west African passion for football was in the air.

The opposition, comprised of assorted human rights groups, Conté-era ministers and agitators for democracy, had called a mass mobilization to put pressure on Dadis to make good on his pledge to allow free elections and make way for the victor. Despite half a century of consecutive tyrannies under Ahmed Sekou Touré and Lansana Conté, Guineans saw a glimmer of opportunity. The crowds thronged into the national stadium's stands and onto the pitch, chanting, 'Liberté! Liberté!' They danced and sang and prayed, cheering the arrival of opposition leaders. Gendarmes tried to force the demonstrators to disperse outside the stadium, firing tear gas and live rounds that killed at least two, but still the crowd massed inside. The downpour delayed some would-be protesters en route to the stadium – they were the lucky ones.

The chanting protesters were about to be taught a brutal lesson in the remorseless logic of resource states. In lands where the state has been hollowed out, ties of ethnicity form a strong bond in the ceaseless struggle to capture the pot of resource rents. In Guinea Dadis was doubly in a minority. He was a Christian in a Muslim nation. And he and his inner circle belonged to small ethnic groups from the *forestière* region in the southeast of the country. For those who owed ethnic allegiance to Dadis, his coup offered a once-in-a-generation shot at prosperity and power, a chance for a turn at the spout of the global economy that poured millions of dollars into Guinea for its ores. Having seized their moment, Dadis and his clan needed to protect their claim.

The day before their scheduled demonstration at the national stadium opposition leaders received calls from the town of Forecariah, about 70 kilometres southeast of Conakry.[33] They were told that buses full of young men had left the town, bound for the capital. A few weeks earlier residents of Forecariah had noticed some new arrivals. The young men had forestière accents; they came from Dadis country. The gendarmerie academy outside Forecariah had been converted to a new use: training an ethnic militia.

An Associated Press reporter who visited the area saw a dozen white men in black uniforms with 'instructor' written on the back. The ones speaking Afrikaans were presumably members of the rough-and-ready corps of white South African former soldiers who signed up as mercenaries after apartheid and who are now to be found scattered across Africa, guarding mines in Congo or attempting coups in Equatorial Guinea. Others were conversing in Hebrew.

Israel has long exported the prowess of its armed forces. Security firms and mercenaries with ties to the Israeli Defence Forces conduct freelance assignments abroad. One of the highest-profile private security firms to emerge from the Israeli military, Global CST, was founded in 2006 by Israel Ziv, a retired major general who had commanded Israel's paratroops and the military's Gaza division.[34] Global CST's website offers 'tailor-made unique solutions for every single client', but in Colombia, where it won a contract to help the government's campaign against leftist rebels, a US diplomat concluded that 'its proposals seem designed more to support Israeli equipment and services sales than to meet in-country needs'.[35] When Dadis took power in Guinea Ziv saw a man with whom he could do business.

A compatriot who had lived in Conakry for years, Victor Kenan, assisted Ziv's entry to Guinea. A tall, wiry and well-connected diamond dealer who travelled around Conakry in luxury vehicles with tinted windows, Kenan worked as a fixer for Israeli companies coming to Guinea. 'He's a middle-man for many Israeli companies for security – dark ones and good ones,' one of his associates told me. 'Kenan at the time of the military was very strong.' When Dadis decided he wanted to stack the presidential guard with members of his ethnic group and sharpen their combat skills, Kenan was at hand to help arrange matters. Ziv then came to Conakry, and Global CST was awarded a $10 million contract. The precise details of the work the company did in Guinea – and the extent to which it knew the purpose to which its services would ultimately be put – are still not clear, however. By some accounts it provided training for Dadis's ethnic militia. By others it also sold the junta military materiel.[36] 'The contract evolved into training a professional presidential security detail,' Thiam told me. 'The people in charge of the recruitment were close to Dadis and from his ethnic group and loaded the ranks with an overwhelming number of men from their region.'[37]

Dadis's personal army took shape, a combination of the presidential guard and irregulars trained in the bush. The force had a clear enemy. The biggest ethnic group in Guinea, accounting for about 40 per cent of the population and dwarfing Dadis's people, is known in French as the Peul. Its members belong to the broad, largely Islamic, Fulani grouping that stretches across to northern Nigeria. Many of the demonstrators who gathered at the national stadium were Peul, as was Cellou Dalein Diallo, the opposition leader regarded as the favourite to win an election if Dadis agreed to stand aside.

The first sign the protesters had of what was about to befall them was the volley of teargas that announced the presence of a contingent of police, soldiers and militiamen, several hundred strong, who had surrounded the stadium. Just after noon members of the presidential guard, wearing the trademark red berets matching their ruler's, led the way through the main entrance, at the command of Dadis's chief bodyguard.

Packed into the stadium, the unarmed demonstrators were fish in a barrel. Bullets ripped into their bodies. Some were trampled to death in the stampede to escape. Others survived by hiding for hours in the stadium's changing rooms, listening to the screams outside. Dozens of women were raped in public, some dragged away to be kept for days as sex slaves. Between being raped for a first and second time on the pitch, one woman turned to see the red beret who had just violated her friend shoot his victim in the head at point-blank range. At least 156 people were killed, and more than 1,000 injured. Dadis's loyalists, perceiving them as the main threat to his power, singled out the Peul, as well as anyone who shared the lighter skin tone for which the Peul are known.[38] 'We're tired of your tricks,' presidential guards told one young woman as they gang-raped her. 'We're going to finish all the Peul.'[39]

Researchers from Human Rights Watch, who compiled a comprehensive account of the massacre, concluded that the atrocities were 'organized and premeditated'. World powers cast the junta into the wilderness. The Economic Community of West African States (Ecowas) declared an arms embargo, and the European Union imposed sanctions on a few dozen senior members of the junta and its civilian government, including Mahmoud Thiam.

Thiam returned from his trip to Paris to 'a very tense and fragile situation' in Conakry. He recalled that he and a small group of senior ministers and soldiers had to keep a round-the-clock watch on Dadis 'because hawkish and panicking soldiers and officers constantly gave him alarmist false reports of ethnic rebels, mercenaries, and foreign troops invading. If we were not there to diffuse the situation, a civilian massacre could have started at any moment.'[40]

When I called Thiam a few days after the bloodshed at the national stadium he sounded rattled and said he wasn't comfortable discussing the massacre. He was, however, happy to talk about the latest deal he had struck. Guinea might have become an international pariah, but there were still those ready and willing to do business with the junta.

Thiam's talks with Sam Pa and Lo Fong-hung had come to fruition. In the coming days, Thiam told me, the Queensway Group, through China International Fund, would announce joint ventures with the Guinean state that would undertake projects in mining, energy and infrastructure. The whole package would be worth $7 billion, equivalent to one and a half times the size of Guinea's economy. China International Fund was to be paid for the infrastructure projects with revenues from mining concessions the government would grant it. Manuel Vicente's ties to the Queensway Group and to Mahmoud Thiam were rewarded too: China Sonangol, 30 per cent owned by the Angolan state oil group that Vicente headed, would receive rights to two-thirds of Guinea's offshore acreage, where the potential for oil had greatly increased following recent finds in neighbouring waters.

Thiam rattled off a shopping list of laudable programmes to be undertaken: 'lower-income and middle-income housing, an airline, et cetera, et cetera'. But the deal's most notable effect was to throw a lifeline to Dadis's junta, which faced financial asphyxiation through the sanctions that followed the massacre. The agreement, which a top official from a previous government described to me as 'rapid and unorthodox', was signed on 10 October, twelve days after the massacre. A 19 November cable from the US embassy in Paris expressing fears about arms shipments and the South African and Israeli trainers helping Dadis to hone his fighting forces noted 'the significant funds that are available to the junta, including the $100 million-plus "security deposit$$ from the Chinese International Fund (CIF)'.[41]

Thiam confirmed to me later that the Queensway Group had indeed moved $100 million into Guinea in the junta's hour of need: $50 million to be used for the first projects envisioned under its $7 billion deal and another $50 million to be deposited at the central bank to prop up Guinea's quickly dwindling reserves of foreign currency.[42] I got hold of the confidential documents setting out the deal, which revealed that the Queensway Group had agreed to transfer cash to the junta by immediately buying some of Guinea's shares in the Singapore-based joint venture they had formed. It had also provided a $3.3 million loan to fund an audit of the bauxite mining operations of Oleg Deripaska's Rusal, which Thiam would use in his efforts to squeeze some money out of the Russian oligarch, with a stipulation that China Sonangol would get a 2 per cent cut of any proceeds that Rusal agreed to pay Guinea.[43] (Rusal contested Thiam's allegations, and in 2014 an international tribunal ruled in the company's favour.)[44]

Foreign powers heaped opprobrium on Dadis, but the combined effects of terrifying violence at home and resource-industry deal-making abroad were keeping his junta intact. Then, one Thursday evening in December 2009, as his reign approached its first anniversary, Dadis's bodyguard shot him in the head.

Lieutenant Aboubacar Diakité, known as Toumba, had scarcely left Dadis's side since he took power. A fellow young officer, he served as chief bodyguard, aide-de-camp and commander of the red berets, the elite presidential guard whose ranks were swelling with recruits from Dadis's tribe. On the day of the massacre Toumba had led the rampaging troops into the stadium. A witness said Toumba had declared, as he opened fire on the demonstrators, 'I want no survivors. Kill them all. They think we have a democracy here.'[45] In the aftermath of the slaughter at the stadium the prosecutor of the International Criminal Court opened a file on the massacre. A UN commission of investigation arrived in Guinea to piece together what had happened and who was responsible. Toumba began to suspect that Dadis was manoeuvring to put the blame for the atrocities solely on him.[46] On 3 December while he and Dadis were at a barracks on Conakry, Toumba aimed and fired.

The bullet struck Dadis in the head, but the man who had spilt so much blood at the national stadium would be denied another scalp: the injuries were not fatal. Dadis was evacuated for treatment in Morocco and remained in exile. Toumba fled into hiding. The junta's deputy leader, an imposing senior officer, took over and promised to give power back to the people.

If the giant cake reminded any of the luminaries present of Marie Antoinette, they didn't let on. Decked out in the national colours of red, green and gold, the confection had been baked to celebrate the launch of Guinea's flag carrier, a new airline to replace the one that had gone bust a decade earlier. Ministers and businessmen who had gathered in a function room of the Novotel in Conakry chatted and applauded. It was a moment for patriotic self-congratulation. Guinea was still a case study in deprivation, but the ruling class had restored a little pride by resurrecting the national airline. There were speeches and a buffet. The German–Egyptian pilot, an alumnus of Thomas Cook Airlines, who had been brought in as chief executive of Air Guinée International, said a few words. So did the minister of transport. Although the new carrier's fleet of Airbus A320s had been delayed by a few months, the minister explained, miniature replicas had been produced to allow the launch party to go ahead.

Six months after the attempted assassination that had forced Dadis into exile the first competitive elections in Guinea's history were days away, and only civilians would be competing. The frontrunners had all pledged to scrutinize – and perhaps rip up – the business deals the junta had struck. Nonetheless, at the gathering at the Novotel there was a certain confidence among the officials and investors who had thrown in their lot with the men in uniform. Mahmoud Thiam looked assured as he worked the room. So did another man, who preferred to stay on the sidelines: Jack Cheung Chun Fai, the representative of China International Fund, the airline's financial backer.

Like other companies hoping to protect their interests once the military yielded the presidency to an elected leader, the Queensway Group had been hedging its bets. The wife of one of the most fancied candidates in the election, Cellou Dalein Diallo, had been appointed deputy chief executive of Air Guinée International.[47] China International Fund had made a start on other infrastructure projects that were the quid pro quo of its mining rights, commencing the construction of two power plants and shipping in rolling stock for a railway.[48] Even as its designs on Guinea's minerals were taking shape, the group said little in public (much like Jack Cheung, who refused to answer my questions when I approached him at the airline launch). A mining executive at another company with interests in Guinea described China International Fund as a 'ghost'.

Thiam was planning to head back to New York once a civilian president was sworn in. Reclining on a sofa beneath the high ceilings of his

grace-and-favour ministerial apartment, he was content with his tumultuous eighteen months in office. He told me he had set projects in motion
that would turn Guinea into the world's biggest iron ore exporter within a
decade. Added to its status as a major source of bauxite, that would make
Guinea a linchpin of the global industrial economy. Thiam's work was
complete: 'Nothing that we have done is reversible.'[49]

Down below on the streets of Conakry, popular expectations that the
vote would transform Guineans' miserable lot were running preposter-
ously high. 'Everything will change,' Rafiu Diallo, a twenty-one-year-old
selling second-hand shoes by the roadside, told me breathlessly. 'Government will change; life will change. We will sell more shoes; people will
have more money,' he said, vigorously buffing a pair of cheap heels. Diallo confidently predicted that a civilian government would be good for
business, allowing him to increase his daily turnover from its current level
of 25,000 Guinean francs, or about $4. More importantly Guinea's rulers
would henceforth be answerable to Guinea's people, Diallo believed. 'It
will be a government of our will.'

When I met Alpha Condé at a hotel in Paris in November 2013 he was halfway through his term as Guinea's elected president. Condé had spent long
stretches of his adult life in France, including a stint as a law professor at
the Sorbonne, in self-imposed exile from his homeland, where he had agi-
tated first for independence then against successive tyrants. Sekou Touré
sentenced him to death in absentia; after Condé went home Lansana Conté
had slung him in jail. Now seventy-five, he was back in France as president
and squeezing in an interview with me between meetings with French ministers, a sign of Guinea's readmission to the international fold.

Condé had surprising energy for his age. His aides told stories of being
left dripping with sweat trying to keep up with him on walkabouts in Conakry. But the presidency was a heavy burden. Between posing for photographs, he shifted from foot to foot, his expression brightening only when
the conversation turned briefly to football. (France had scraped through to
World Cup qualification that week; Guinea had long since been eliminated.)

Before the presidency Condé had never held government office. His
supporters did not doubt his sincerity but conceded that, at first, he was

out of his depth. His opponents were still questioning his election victory. The shambolic polls had produced no clear winner in the first round, and after long delays, during which rivals' supporters traded blows and allegations of foul play, Condé, a Malinke, came from a long way behind to beat Diallo in the runoff, dashing Peul hopes of victory for their candidate. Foreign election observers gave the vote a cautious blessing, and in December 2010, fifty-two years, two months, and nineteen days after Guinea's declaration of independence, Condé was sworn in.

Condé's task was fraught with peril. The dangers of his efforts to reform a military that had grown accustomed to being above the law became apparent six months into his presidency, when renegade soldiers attacked his private residence with rocket-propelled grenades.[50] He won debt relief from Guinea's international creditors, brought down inflation, and attracted investors, but the poverty of a resource state is not overturned in a couple of years. He had some influential foreign friends – George Soros, the Hungarian-born billionaire hedge-fund manager and philanthropist, and Tony Blair, the former British prime minister, were among his advisers – but at home Guinea's ethnic divisions remained wide, periodically erupting into clashes. Some of the high hopes that the new president would change the way business is done in Guinea, especially in the mining sector, diminished as his term drew on. Condé had pledged to break with the corruption of the past, but new scandals emerged on his watch.[51]

Condé's biggest battle, at least in terms of the sums of money involved and the corporate firepower of those he antagonized, was over Guinea's minerals. Inheriting a country ranked among the world's most corrupt, Condé espoused a philosophy promoted by one of his advisers, George Soros, who was among the most prominent advocates of 'transparency' in the oil and mining industries – the theory that publishing contracts and revenues would reduce corruption and raise the state's accountability. Guinea's $7 billion oil, mining and infrastructure agreement with the Queensway Group was quietly ditched. The president appointed an inquiry to review mining deals struck under past dictatorships. One deal in particular would pitch Condé into a struggle between some of the most powerful forces in the resources business.

In the final months of the junta's rule BSGR had struck a sensational deal. Even by the standards of Beny Steinmetz, it was the deal of a lifetime. BSGR reached an agreement to sell to Vale, the Brazilian group that mines more iron ore than any other company, a 51 per cent share in BSGR's Guinean assets, which included the northern half of the bounteous deposit at Simandou – for $2.5 billion. BSGR had paid nothing for its mining rights (companies typically promise to invest to bring the seams into production and pay taxes on royalties on them rather than paying fees at the outset) and had spent, according to the company's public statements, $160 million on preliminary work on its prospects. Vale paid $500 million up front for its stake, immediately securing for BSGR close to a threefold return on its investment. The balance was due to follow as targets were met. One long-serving expatriate in the Guinean mining game shook his head in envy over a beer in downtown Conakry and declared that Steinmetz had won 'the jackpot'.

Mahmoud Thiam had sanctioned the deal, but Alpha Condé's new government suspected something was awry in the way BSGR had acquired its mining rights in the first place. It instructed Vale and BSGR to suspend work and hired Scott Horton, an experienced lawyer from the US law firm DLA Piper who specialized in investigating corruption and human rights abuses, to look into BSGR's activities. Horton and his team compiled a dossier, including an account of what the investigators thought was a scheme to bribe the old dictator's wife, Mamadie Touré. In October 2012 the chairman of Guinea's inquiry into past mining deals wrote to BSGR, laying out the accusations and inviting the company to respond.

BSGR launched a counterattack. A tussle over a remote stretch of west African mountainside became a war of words – and writs – between some of the most illustrious members of the global elite. BSGR's representatives depicted a nimble, daring company that would have delivered a windfall for the Guinean people had the government not decided to confiscate its assets illicitly. The company had not been corrupt, merely fortunate, it argued. 'It's roulette,' Steinmetz said of the mining business in an interview. Companies that are prepared to gamble and work hard sometimes 'get lucky'.[52]

BSGR maintained that it was the victim of a conspiracy orchestrated by, among others, George Soros, who in addition to being an adviser to Condé, was also a major donor to Revenue Watch, a transparency organization that was assisting Guinea with its mining reforms; Soros also gave money to the anticorruption group Global Witness, which published reports on the bribery allegations. The result, BSGR's representatives claimed, was 'a coordinated but crude smear campaign'.[53] Beny Steinmetz sued the public relations firm FTI Consulting, which had dropped BSGR as a client after the corruption allegations came out, and its chairman for Europe, Middle East and Africa, the British peer Mark Malloch-Brown, accusing him of being in league with Soros, for whom Malloch-Brown had once worked. The case was settled out of court.[54]

BSGR retained the London law firm Mishcon de Reya as well as Powerscourt, a London public relations company founded by Rory Godson, a former business editor of the *Sunday Times*, to take the fight to its critics – with Alpha Condé firmly in their sights. His government, BSGR's representatives said, was 'illegitimate', a 'discredited regime'.[55] The inquiry into past contracts 'defied all notions of due process'. (Mahmoud Thiam called the probe a 'witch hunt' that served only to stymie investment and claimed that private investigators had been going through his bins.) [56] The contracts purporting to set out the bribes to be paid to Mamadie Touré were fakes, BSGR said, and it had been 'the victim of numerous extortion attempts by individuals who were seeking economic gains' involving 'the use of forged documentation, blackmail and harassment'. (When in 2014 I asked BSGR to provide details of the alleged extortion, it declined to do so.) In short, the company said, 'BSGR is confident that its activities and position in Guinea will be fully vindicated.'[57]

Alpha Condé was determined to stay the course. 'It's not easy,' he told me in Paris. 'With fifty years of misrule, of corruption, bad habits have set in. Habits built up over fifty years are not changed in two or three days. Time is also against us: the people are impatient. They want to see something concrete.' I suggested to him that Guinea was being used as a laboratory for transparency in mining, an admirable notion if fully implemented but one that ran counter to the secrecy that companies and resource-rich governments had long cherished. 'That exposes me to a great deal of risk, politically and personally,' Condé replied. 'But in life you have to take risks.'[58]

What Frederic Cilins had not known when he sat down with Mamadie Touré in April 2013 to try to persuade her to destroy the contracts promising her cash and shares for helping BSGR and to catch a plane out of the United States was that the FBI was listening in. When she arrived in

Florida following Lansana Conté's death, the dictator's widow had bought what Americans disparagingly call a 'McMansion', a luxurious residence built with more grandeur than taste.[59] Once Alpha Condé took power, the investigation he launched into how BSGR had won its rights followed the trail to her doorstep. The investigators whom Guinea's new government had hired to conduct the probe shared what they had discovered with US prosecutors, who in early 2013 convened a grand jury and pressed ahead with their own investigation.

When FBI agents confronted Touré, her options were stark: deny everything and face jail if she were convicted or give the FBI what it wanted in the hope of being granted immunity or at least a reduced sentence. When Cilins got in touch Touré agreed for her phone to be tapped; when she went to meet him at Jacksonville airport she was wearing a wire and FBI agents were discreetly watching. When they had heard what they needed to, one of them walked over to the Frenchman and arrested him. He spent the next year in jail and was moved to New York, where the grand jury was sitting to assess the merits of issuing corruption and money laundering indictments connected to BSGR's activities in Guinea. A judge granted him permission to conduct forensic tests on the contracts that his lawyers, like BSGR, claimed were fakes, but then, in March 2014, three weeks before he was due to go on trial, Cilins pleaded guilty to obstruction of justice.[60] In July he was sentenced to two years in prison, including time served. He was fined $75,000, and he forfeited the $20,000 he was carrying when he was arrested.[61]

The investigation into BSGR's Guinean dealings spread across three continents. The company is registered in Guernsey, but its directors and executives operate out of offices in Mayfair and Geneva, where Steinmetz lives. Prosecutors in Switzerland responded to a request for legal cooperation from Guinea and then opened their own investigation. They interviewed Beny Steinmetz twice; Swiss police searched his house and private jet and raided offices connected with BSGR. At the time of writing neither BSGR nor Steinmetz has been charged either in the United States or in Switzerland (or, for that matter, anywhere else). In a one-line statement after Cilins – who, as they emphasized, had worked with BSGR as an intermediary, not an employee – pleaded guilty their representatives said, 'As we have been saying all along, no one at BSGR has done anything wrong.'[62]

Steinmetz's representatives say that he is only formally an adviser to the company that bears his initials and of which, through complex layers of trusts and offshore companies, he is the main financial beneficiary.[63] But, as documents published by Guinea's mining inquiry indicated, Steinmetz played more than an advisory role in Guinea.

In a sworn statement submitted to the Guinean inquiry Mamadie Touré said Steinmetz had attended meetings, including one in June 2007, that she arranged between her husband and other emissaries from BSGR, had discussed her lobbying efforts with her, and had been personally involved in striking the agreements under which she would be given cash and shares as a reward for helping the company.[64] BSGR denounced her account as 'a wholly incredible and unsupported version of events related by a witness who has sought to extort money from BSGR in the past' but declined, when I asked the company for more details, to elaborate on the alleged extortion.[65] In April 2014 a person close to the company, who declined to be named, called to tell me, 'Beny Steinmetz looks forward to proving with passports and other evidence that he never set foot in Guinea until 2008.' That contradicted references in Touré's statement to meetings earlier than 2008. (Steinmetz's representatives declined to elaborate on what he did in Guinea in 2008.)

There were other suggestions of Steinmetz's involvement. During one of Frederic Cilins's taped conversations with Mamadie Touré he said the details of how much money he could offer her to destroy the evidence had been 'given to me directly by Number One, I don't even want to give his name'. When Touré asked who he meant, Cilins whispered, 'Beny.' Cilins said he had been to see Steinmetz before coming to Florida and that Steinmetz had told him, 'Do what you want, but I want you to tell me . . . "It's over. There are no more documents."'[66] In 2014, after Guinea's mining inquiry published its findings, I asked BSGR's representatives about this account of events that Cilins unwittingly gave to the FBI. They declined to answer my questions, as did Cilins's lawyer.

In east Africa they have a saying: 'When elephants fight, the grass gets trampled.' The big beasts of the mining industry as well as its own Big Men have thoroughly trampled Guinea. In April 2014 Alpha Condé's government cancelled BSGR's rights after the two-year inquiry into past mining deals concluded that there was 'precise and consistent evidence establishing with sufficient certainty the existence of corrupt practices' in the way the company had won them.[67] That prompted the elephants to stampede.

Echoing Cobalt International Energy's protestations of ignorance over the Angolan officials' concealed stake in its oil venture, Vale's head office in Rio de Janeiro put out a statement saying that the company had struck its deal with BSGR 'after the completion of extensive due diligence conducted by outside professional advisors and on the basis of representations that BSGR had obtained its mining rights lawfully and without any corrupt or improper promises or payments'.[68] With the rights that Vale held jointly with BSGR annulled, one of the foremost deals in Brazil's thrust into Africa – which, like India's, generated fewer headlines than the Chinese advance but was nonetheless a concerted effort to secure oil, minerals and markets – was in tatters. Vale had paid BSGR the initial $500 million fee for its stake but had withheld the outstanding $2 billion. Nonetheless, factoring in the money it had spent working on the project, Vale had lost $1.1 billion.

While Guinea battled the early stages of an outbreak of the deadly Ebola virus in April 2014 the battle for Simandou moved to courtrooms in far-off lands. Vale declared that it was 'actively considering its legal rights and options' after BSGR had assured it that there had been nothing remiss about the way it had won its rights. BSGR hauled Guinea to international arbitration. And Rio Tinto filed a lawsuit in New York against Vale, Beny Steinmetz, BSGR, Mahmoud Thiam, Frederic Cilins, Mamadie Touré and others, accusing them all of complicity in a conspiracy stretching back to 2008 to 'steal' the northern half of Simandou. Rio said the racket had cost it billions of dollars and demanded damages. BSGR, Steinmetz and Thiam strongly denied the allegations, and Vale stressed that it had been cleared of wrongdoing by Guinea's inquiry.[69]

All the while Guinea's most valuable national asset remained stuck under a mountain, with the railway to carry the ore across the country unlaid and the port to ship it off to the steel mills of the world unbuilt. As billions of dollars changed hands among the titans of the mining industry,

Guinea (annual budget: $1.5 billion) had nothing to show for being the place where the ore actually lay.

Guinea has made some money from Simandou – the $700 million that Rio Tinto paid the government after Alpha Condé took office to settle 'the resolution of all outstanding issues' pertaining to its remaining half of the deposit and to secure exemption from Guinea's mining review 'or any future reviews'.[70] The sum was equivalent to half of the $1.35 billion that Chinalco, one of China's biggest state-owned mining houses, had agreed to pay Rio for a stake in its portion of Simandou a year earlier, while the junta was still in power.[71]

When it settled with Guinea, Rio promised to bring a mine into production by 2015. But the deadline slipped and slipped again. The mining giants appeared more determined to plant their flag in the mountain than to mine it. Vale and Rio already controlled the world's two most important stocks of iron ore – in Brazil and Australia, respectively – and a rush of new ore onto the market from Simandou could bring down prices and make those other projects less lucrative. At the same time, although building a mine and the required infrastructure might cost a forbidding $20 billion, neither of the iron-ore trade's two great rivals wanted to cede control of the mountain to the other. At the time of writing, with iron-ore prices falling, few expected mining to start at Simandou much before the end of the decade, if then.

After Guinea's inquiry found that it was not 'likely' that Vale had participated in corruption, it recommended that only BSGR – not Vale – be banned from bidding when the rights to the northern half of Simandou were made available again.[72] That left both Rio and Vale free to bid, alongside any other mining house that wanted to join the fray. 'This is a battle to the death for control of Simandou, with the clear understanding that the firm that controls it also has a dominant position in the iron industry for a generation to come,' someone close to Alpha Condé's government told me when Rio Tinto filed its lawsuit against Vale. 'This suit can only be understood in the context of that struggle – over the future of Simandou, not really over history.'

Even if Simandou goes into production and starts to generate billions of dollars in government revenue, it is dangerous to assume that a flood of resource rent would be a panacea for Guinea. Elsewhere such rents have proved ruinous. The Guinean government's 2012 economic policy blueprint, agreed with the International Monetary Fund shortly before Guinea's creditors forgave $2.1 billion of debt, warned of 'the adverse impact the rapid development of the mining sector could have on the other sectors of the economy through the "Dutch disease" syndrome'.[73] Harry Snoek, the Guinea mission chief for the IMF – who was, as a Dutchman, well aware of the damage that his country's eponymous economic malady can do – told me, 'Like the rest of the region, it's going to be a major challenge for Guinea to benefit from these resources.'[74]

The elephants of the mining and oil industries have stomped on Africa since long before independence. Since the turn of the century a new beast has entered the arena. It came with a promise to muscle out the old colonial herd, to beat a new trail out of enslavement to natural resources. But if you are grass in the path of powerful creatures, it makes precious little difference which feet are doing the trampling.

» 6 «

A Bridge to Beijing

NIGER'S PRESIDENTIAL PALACE lies on a leafy boulevard in Niamey, the capital of the world's poorest country, not far from where the River Niger snakes beneath bridges trod by nomads and their lolloping camels. By day the desert sun scorches the city. By night the only light on the sandy backstreets comes from gas lamps and fluttering candles. On the morning of 18 February 2010, President Mamadou Tandja received his ministers at the palace for the weekly cabinet meeting. There was much to discuss. Hunger was once again stalking this landlocked nation on the arid southern fringe of the Sahara. But that was not the main reason why the mood in Niger was tense. Tandja, a shepherd's son and former army colonel, had been the first president in Niger's history to have won successive elections, quite a feat in a country with a knack for coups. But of late his attachment to democracy had waned. His term in office should have expired two months earlier, yet he showed no sign of departing.

The first signs that Tandja was heading in the direction of west Africa's pantheon of autocrats had come in late 2008 at a ceremony to lay the foundations for the country's first oil refinery. A band of Tandja supporters staged a demonstration demanding that he extend his rule beyond its constitutional limit. The partisans wore T-shirts bearing the president's face and emblazoned with a single word in Hausa: *tazartché* – continuity. More rallies followed, ostensibly spontaneous and driven by popular sentiment but also attended by senior allies of the president. Tandja declared that the people had spoken. He had work to do, and this was no time to leave office. When Niger's constitutional court ruled that the president was acting illegally, he ignored the justices. When they persisted in opposing him, he dissolved the court. The national assembly objected to his plans for a referendum on a new constitution without term limits, so he dissolved that too and began to rule by decree. An opposition boycott of the referendum, held in August 2009, meant Tandja recorded an overwhelming victory.

International condemnation rained down. The regional bloc, Ecowas, is hardly a club of democrats, but it tends to draw the line at the overt accumulation of untrammelled power. Niger's membership was suspended. Donors cut aid. France led Western powers in their outcry. Bernard Kouchner, the French foreign minister, declared that 'it is necessary to respect and return to the constitutional order.'[1]

Few argued with the sentiment, but France had an ulterior motive for condemning Tandja. He had thumbed his nose at Niger's former colonial master. For decades France had enjoyed a de facto monopoly on the stuff that makes Niger a place of strategic importance – its uranium. France consumes more uranium than any country apart from the United States. Nuclear power stations supply three-quarters of France's electricity. Areva, the French state-owned atomic energy group, held sway over the stretches of northern Niger under which lie some of the planet's richest seams of uranium. Areva mines about a third of its uranium in Niger, with the rest coming from Canada and Kazakhstan. It is the world's biggest nuclear company, and its annual revenues are twice Niger's gross domestic product. But Tandja had taken it on, breaking Areva's monopoly, driving a harder bargain, and handing uranium permits to companies from half a dozen other countries. The relationship soured to the point that Areva was accused of colluding with the Tuareg rebels of the North, and two of its employees were ejected from the country.

To break with France so brazenly, Tandja needed an alternative ally among the world powers. He found one in the country with the fastest-growing nuclear industry: China.

In return for permits to dig for uranium and rights to drill Niger's previously untapped reservoirs of oil, China furnished Tandja with the means to indulge his authoritarian streak. Of the $56 million that Sino-U, China's answer to Areva, paid for its licence to mine uranium in Niger, $47 million was spent on arms to suppress the Tuareg rebels, according to Ali Idrissa, a local anticorruption activist.[2] A far greater sum – $300 million – arrived

The Chicala slum sits between the presidential complex that houses Angola's ruling clique and the Atlantic waters under which lie some of the world's richest oil reserves.

Kilamba, a city for the wealthy carved out of the bush, is a symbol of the enclave of plenty amid penury that Angola's petro-economy has created. 'The country is getting a new face,' says one anti-corruption activist. 'But is it getting a new soul?'

António Tomás Ana, an Angolan artist better known as Etona, is determined
to resist the Angolan government's plans to uproot him and his 65,000 neighbours
in order to make way for luxurious properties to service the oil-fuelled elite.

Rich stocks of oil and minerals are a recipe for Big Man politics. Along with his counterparts in Equatorial Guinea, Zimbabwe and Cameroon, Angola's José Eduardo dos Santos completes a club of the world's four longest-serving rulers, with a combined tally of 136 years in office.

Manuel Vicente, Angola's Mr Oil and a key man in the ruling *Futungo*'s privatisation of power. 'I'm a Christian guy,' he says. 'It doesn't work if you are okay and the people around have nothing to eat. You don't feel comfortable.'

Edouard Mwangachuchu was chased out of eastern Congo in the turmoil that followed the Rwandan genocide. He returned and started mining the mineral that is crucial both in the manufacture of mobile phones and in the funding of the region's constellations of militias.

The Mutanda mine, jointly owned by Glencore and one of Dan Gertler's companies, is carved into the copperbelt, a bounteous repository of copper and cobalt that serves as the treasury of Congo's shadow state.

The sacks of coltan that porters carry down the mountainsides of eastern Congo flow into a conflict economy that underpins decades of strife. But efforts to clean up the trade risk undercutting one of the few livelihoods in a region stalked by hunger.

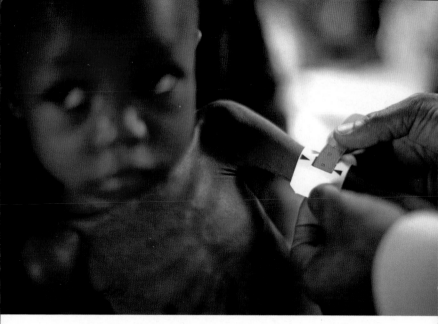

Anna Rebecca Susa succumbed to malnutrition despite the spectacular mineral wealth of the eastern Congolese valleys where she had been born five years earlier.

Mineral-funded militiamen raided Bora Sifa's village and took away her husband. 'They forced him to carry all the things away into the forest. Then they killed him.' She and her children joined Congo's millions of refugees battling hunger.

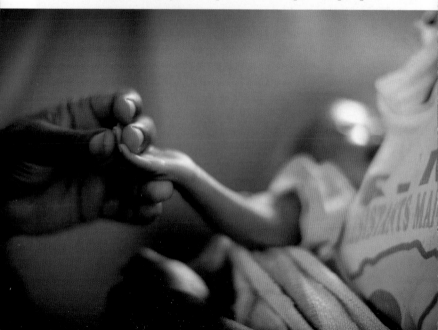

Augustin Katumba Mwanke, variously styled as Joseph Kabila's Rasputin, Karl Rove or Grand Vizier. 'He knew how to run the political networks and the business networks,' says an ex-minister. 'Katumba's work was to create a parallel state.'

Joseph Kabila, the second in an improbable dynasty of Congolese rulers, presides over a country the size of western Europe, groaning with natural wealth and in a state of near-total collapse.

Crude oil has poisoned the waterways where inhabitants
of the Niger Delta wash, drink, fish and worship.

The home of Nigeria's oil industry – Africa's biggest – groans with crude spilt from
the pipelines of Royal Dutch Shell and other multinationals. Run your way through
the water and chances are you'll see the tell-tale refractions of petroleum.

The cabal that held Nigeria to ransom as Umaru Yar'Adua, president from 2007 to 2010, lay dying illustrated the extent to which organised crime had infiltrated the highest levels of power.

Goodluck Jonathan has presided over a binge of corruption and embezzlement that was dizzying even by Nigerian standards.

The People's Democratic Party's presidential primary is a high point in the calendar of Nigeria's patronage politics. 'It's not a political party,' says a veteran human rights activist. 'It's a platform to seize power and then share the resultant booty.'

One of the few official photographs of Sam Pa (*third from left*). It shows him alongside Dubai's Sheikh Ahmed Bin Saeed Al Maktoum, signing a deal to build an oil refinery. The Dubai government's media office described Pa as the chairman of China Sonangol.

The key companies in Sam Pa's network are registered to Two Pacific Place at 88 Queensway in Hong Kong, the address from which is derived its informal name: The Queensway Group.

Asher Avidan (left) of Guernsey-registered BSG Resources, with Mamadie Touré, the fourth wife of the Guinean dictator Lansana Conté. The company denied her claims that she received millions of dollars to help it win valuable iron-ore prospects.

A billionaire and scion of an Israeli diamond family, Beny Steinmetz (*third from right*) is the main beneficiary of BSGR. The company lost mining rights worth billions of dollars after a Guinean inquiry, which BSGR denounced as a sham, concluded that they had been acquired corruptly.

Captain Moussa Dadis Camara seized power in Guinea's 2008 coup.
His security forces slaughtered opposition demonstrators at the national
stadium before an assassination attempt forced him into exile.

Raiders killed some 150 people in an attack on the village of Kuru Karama, outside the central Nigerian city of Jos. The violence is couched in ethnic terms but beneath it lies the struggle to control oil rent.

Christian killers in Jos daubed the name of the state governor, Jonah Jang, on the wall of a burned-out house in the Muslim quarter. 'He's an extremist,' says a moderate who has held high office in the state. 'He has very strong tribal views.'

Robert Mugabe lost control of the Zimbabwean finance ministry in a 2008 power-sharing deal that followed disputed elections. To raise some off-budget funding to help prolong his rule, he set about brutalising the diamond fields of Marange.

Cecil Rhodes, described as 'the first of the new Dynasty of Money Kings which has evolved in these later days as the real rulers of the modern world', was the archetype of those who fuse political conquest with control of Africa's resources.

African diamond miners, like these ones in the remote Central African Republic, earn only a fraction of the value of the stones they find. From Zimbabwe to Sierra Leone, African diamonds have begotten war, repression and dispossession.

in the form of a signature payment when Tandja granted China National Petroleum Corporation, China's second giant national oil company alongside Sinopec, rights to develop an oil block that Western companies had spurned. 'It was because Tandja had Chinese money that he felt he could mock the EU, Ecowas, the US,' Mohamed Bazoum, a leading member of the political opposition to Tandja, told me.[3] 'He wanted to be the king of Niger.' There were other sources of funds too. During Tandja's decade in power, an inquiry would later find, $180 million vanished from Niger's state coffers through embezzlement and corruption.[4]

Tandja steamrolled the institutions designed to check the president's powers, caring little for the discontent that was brewing on the streets and in the barracks. But if he thought having China in his corner meant Beijing would help in his hour of need, he was mistaken. His cabinet meeting was in session when the shooting started. Soon a plume of smoke was rising from the presidential palace. At least three people lay dead.[5] A band of rebel soldiers had secured the palace and taken Tandja and his ministers captive.

The military coup against Tandja deepened fears in Africa that China's competition with the old powers for the continent's resources was giving rise to a new and ruinous rivalry like that of the Cold War, which had allowed dictators to play Communist and capitalist suitors against one another.

This, however, was a coup – and a rivalry – with roots not in ideology but in the pursuit of economic interests, specifically control of natural resources. Perhaps it was always this way. In Angola the Cold War at times looked more like some ultraviolent version of *Alice in Wonderland*, with Cuban troops fighting to protect oil facilities run by an American company, the revenue from which sustained a Communist government whose rebel opponents enjoyed the support of Washington and its ally, apartheid South Africa.[6] Now, however, Beijing was offering Niger and other African states a genuinely new bargain: infrastructure without interference. China proposed to build roads and ports and refineries on a scale scarcely countenanced by the European colonizers or the cold warriors. In exchange it sought not allegiance to a creed so much as access to oil, minerals and markets.

For a country like Niger, such an offer was tempting. Uranium may be the only commodity to rival oil for strategic import, both for its use in nuclear energy and in nuclear weapons, but you cannot eat it. When I arrived in Niger in the wake of the coup, after passing through the smuggling domain of Dahiru Mangal in northern Nigeria with its godforsaken border post, I visited the feeding stations of the south. Poor rains and a rise in food prices had consigned millions to the latest of Niger's periodic bouts of starvation. One impossibly spindly three-year-old I encountered, his skin tight over his skeleton as he stared at the ceiling from his bed, weighed about half as much as he should have. Had he been made of uranium ore, he would have been worth $700. Instead, he looked certain to end up among the one in eight Nigerien children who die before the age of five. As in eastern Congo, the emaciated youngsters were a silent – or softly whimpering – rebuke to the presence of great natural wealth beside the most basic failures to sustain human life.

Faced with such deprivation, the prospect of massive Chinese investment to spur the development of a more robust economy was enticing – all the more so when there was next to nothing to show for decades of Western imperial domination and postcolonial commercial exploitation.

Audiences with Chinese emissaries to Africa are rare, but I had a hunch that Beijing's man in Niamey might be keen to speak out, given that the abrupt end to Tandja's rule threatened China's new-found access to Nigerien uranium and crude. I was shown into a well-appointed meeting room in the Chinese embassy, a refuge from the intense heat outside. Inside was a wall-length painting of the Three Gorges, the site of the hydroelectric dam that produces almost as much electricity as the whole of sub-Saharan Africa, excluding South Africa. It might have been an advertisement for the abundance of what the most populous nation could offer the most impoverished continent.

In strode Xia Huang, a graceful, assured man who had previously been posted in Paris and spoke impeccable French. The ambassador chose his words with care, but his message was clear. 'There has been exploitation of uranium in this country for nearly forty years,' Xia said.[7] 'But when one sees that the direct receipts from uranium are more or less equivalent to those from the export of onions each year, there's a problem. Uranium is a strategic energy resource, very important. When one sees this equation, there's a big problem. China's presence here, on this continent, the fact that China is engaged in exploration projects, in production projects, in projects of transformation – that gives another option to African countries.' Did he mean that China was proffering an alternative to what the West offered, I asked. The diplomat chuckled, wary of departing too far from the script that depicts China's rise as unthreatening to the old powers. 'No, I'm just saying "another option": perhaps a more lucrative option, a more profitable option for their economic development and their social progress.'

China, Xia said, was providing Niger and other African countries a route to true economic progress. Rather than continually being reduced to haggling over the terms at which foreigners carried off their natural resources, these countries could begin to industrialize, using Chinese-built infrastructure as the bedrock for their own manufacturing base – in other words, an antidote to Dutch Disease. 'Industrialization,' the ambassador declared, 'is an unavoidable step for this country to emerge from poverty.'

The Chinese message was not lost on the Nigeriens. Although there were the same complaints that followed Chinese companies around Africa – that they imported their own labour or, when they employed locals, did so for poor pay and in poor conditions – there were also tangible signs that China was turning its promises into bricks and mortar in Niger. Under Tandja the Chinese had built a second bridge over the River Niger and a hydroelectric dam to harness its power, and Chinese state companies had launched a $5 billion project to drill Niger's first crude from the Agadem oil block and construct Niger's first refinery, improbably turning a land-locked zone of penury into one of the few west African countries able to start to move away from the economic lunacy of exporting crude while shipping in refined petroleum products or relying on bootleg fuel.

There was a frisson of excitement that, at last, someone was interested in doing more than agreeing to fund a few token community projects to accompany massive mines. The president of Niger's chamber of commerce, Ibrahim Iddi Ango, was one of the converts, albeit a cautious one.

A thoughtful industrialist with investments in telecoms, cement and in-surance, he, like other Nigerien businessmen and politicians I spoke to, was delighted by China's readiness to do what Western companies had told Niger could not be done. Over the years Elf, the French forerunner to Total, Exxon of the United States, and other oil majors had been granted rights to assess the Agadem oil block. 'Each time the government said, "You want the oil? Build a refinery,"' Iddi Ango told me.[8] 'Each time they said it was impossible. The Chinese came and said, "You want a refinery? What size?"'

China was offering the states of Africa a helping hand in emulating its own transformation. Compared with the substantial share of the world's supplies of diamonds, gold, energy and metals Africa has yielded over more than a century, the continent has received a paltry return in terms of the basic architecture of economic progress. In 2008 sub-Saharan Africa, with a population of 900 million, produced as much electricity as Spain, with a population of 47 million.[9] When economists compared data for 2001 for all poor countries they found that those outside Africa had an average of 134 kilometres of paved roads for every 1,000 square kilometres of land; in Africa the figure was 31 kilometres (countries outside Africa classed as 'upper-middle income' had 781 kilometres).[10] Over the decades since the European empires dissolved, other parts of the world have hauled them-selves from poverty by industrializing, outstripping a continent that has largely been left without the means to become anything more in economic terms than a source of exported raw commodities. In 1970 sub-Saharan Africa had three times as much electricity capacity per million people as south Asia. By the turn of the century, after three decades during which African oil, gas and other fuels had fired the power stations of the world, south Asia had twice as much electricity capacity per million people as sub-Saharan Africa.[11] The World Bank estimated in 2010 that Africa needs $93 billion – equivalent to the cost of six London 2012 Olympic Games – every year to meet its infrastructure needs, more than double the current outlay.[12]

In the years following its first pact with Angola in 2004 Beijing struck similar multibillion-dollar resources-for-infrastructure deals in Congo and Sudan and spread its largesse into every corner of the continent. A third of all Chinese overseas contracts are in Africa. In recent years Chinese funding has accounted for two-thirds of Africa's spending on infrastructure.[13] By 2007 China had signed up to provide the bulk of the finance for ten major African hydroelectric dams, which, between them, represented a third of the continent's entire electricity capacity.[14]

Some vaunted transport undertakings, such as a Mauritanian railway, failed to materialize, and there have been reports of rain washing away shoddy Chinese-built roads. Nonetheless, the quality of Chinese construction work in Africa has improved over the decade since Beijing began its courtship. In Ethiopia mobile phone calls buzz along Chinese cables, and cargo pours through a Chinese-built airport. The tallest building in the capital, Addis Ababa, completed in 2012 at the cost of $200 million, is the new headquarters of the African Union, a magnificent curved edifice that stands as the emblem of China's African ambition.

Beijing picked up the bill for the AU headquarters. For other projects Chinese state-owned banks have provided much of the credit through which African governments finance infrastructure projects. These Chinese loans have interest rates higher than what traditional donors like the World Bank offer but lower than those available from commercial banks. Often, as in Angola, the repayments are not in cash but in natural resources.

The sums of money at China's disposal are stupendous. A senior manager at China's state-owned Exim Bank, the source of most Chinese finance to Africa, predicted in 2013 that the Chinese state would, by 2025, channel a trillion dollars to Africa in investments and loans, the equivalent of three-quarters of the entire gross domestic product of sub-Saharan Africa in 2013. 'We have plenty of money to spend,' said Zhao Changhui, one of the architects of China's trade relations with Africa.[15] The $3.5 trillion in foreign currency reserves that China has amassed as the world's largest exporter could not simply be parked in US government bonds, the investment equivalent of sticking your cash under the mattress. 'We need to use part of them in overseas investments,' Zhao said. 'Africa for the next twenty years will be the single most important business destination for many Chinese mega-corporations.'

Niger, with its oil, its uranium, and its president keen to shake off the former colonizers' shackles, was a prime target. Tandja's descent into despotism and the coup that followed marked the first major political upheaval in Africa for which the roots could be traced directly to China's challenge to Western control of the continent's resources. But it also demonstrated that the new powers in Africa and the old had more in common than either would care to admit.

It was Charles de Gaulle who devised the French system of influence over its former African colonies. De Gaulle had led the exiled French government during the Second World War and became the towering statesman of postwar French politics, assuming the presidency in 1958 as France was in tumult and facing revolt in Algeria. He granted Algeria its sovereignty. To France's possessions in west Africa he offered a deal to which their leaders almost universally acquiesced and under which they retained French protection after independence at the price of preserving French economic interests and letting Paris dictate foreign and defence policy. Such was de Gaulle's hold on French-speaking Africa's growing band of post-independence tyrants that, when he died in 1970, Jean-Bédel Bokassa, the self-styled emperor of the Central African Republic, sobbed at the funeral of a man he called 'Papa'.[16]

The French system in Africa, perpetuated primarily by Gaullists after their leader's death, developed into a network of resource deals, slush funds and corruption that its moniker neatly summarizes. To the eye, *Françafrique* reads like a harmless amalgam of *France* and *Afrique*, suggesting two peoples joined in common cause. Spoken aloud, however, it conjures something closer to the truth: *France à fric* – a play on the French for 'cash', which might be loosely translated as 'France's cash machine'.

In its heyday Françafrique was indeed a mutually beneficial arrangement, only not one for the benefit of the population at large but for the African autocrats and French mandarins who ran it. In the late 1990s an indefatigable investigative magistrate in Paris called Eva Joly followed the thread of some dubious transactions and discovered a huge, hidden pipeline of dirty money running through the African arm of Elf, the French state oil company. 'I felt like I was penetrating an unknown world, with its own laws,' said the Norwegian-born Joly, who received death threats as she delved deeper.[17]

Elf's division in Gabon was the centre of this unknown world. It used oil money to pay bribes to French politicians, buy luxury flats in Paris, and swell the fortune of Omar Bongo, under whom the Gabonese endured abysmal living standards while their rulers were reputed to have made the country the world's biggest per capita consumer of champagne. And Elf's tentacles spread beyond the francophone sphere as the oil company secured crude across Africa. A former Elf executive testified in 2000 that one beneficiary of the Elf slush fund was Angola's José Eduardo dos Santos.[18] (Dos Santos denied the allegation.)

Joly's investigation shook the French establishment, exposing a shadow state to match any African regime in its readiness to trade access to resources for illicit influence and personal benefit. Elf was privatized and its catacombs of corruption sealed off. Dozens of Elf employees went to jail. French politicians, among them Nicolas Sarkozy, declared that the era of Françafrique was over, and France's direct influence over many of its former colonies did indeed wane. But French corporate power in Africa remained strong. Total, the privatized successor to Elf, which ranks alongside Exxon Mobil, BP, Shell, and the other giants of the industry, holds some of the best oil rights in Angola and Nigeria, the continent's two top crude producers, and still pumps oil in Gabon.

In Niger, where Areva began operations two years before independence in 1960, France has maintained its strategic interest in uranium through systems that are, though strictly legal, hardly equitable.

Areva's contracts are not published, but reporters from Reuters got hold of its most recent decade-long agreements, which ran to the end of 2013. The documents showed that Areva was exempt from paying duties both on the mining equipment it imported and the uranium it exported. The royalty, a particular type of payment that mining companies make to governments based on the quantity of minerals they extract, was 5.5 per cent on the uranium it mined, well below that charged by other, wealthier countries and locked in by a clause exempting the company from any increase in the rate under new mining laws.[19] The mining industry defends such stipulations as necessary so as to allow long-term investment. Nonetheless, a French expatriate in Niamey, discussing the anti-French feeling on which Tandja had capitalized to whip up support for his burgeoning tyranny before the coup, encapsulated the antipathy that Areva's miserly terms engendered: 'There's a sense of neocolonialism, especially of Areva. There's a sense that France has no friends, only interests.'

The core of China's offer to Niger as well as to other African resource states was, as the ambassador explained to me, based on a contrast between Beijing's munificence and the niggardliness of the old powers. There are, however, elements of China's pursuit of African resources that replicate the old tricks of the traditional lords of African resources. Beneath the rhetoric of universal progress Beijing has proved just as willing as its European predecessors in Africa to use middlemen to cultivate personal ties to the most influential members of the ruling classes who control access to the continent's oil and minerals.

The search for one of those middlemen led me to Niamey's zoo. It lies in the centre of Niger's sand-blown capital, close to the junction of Rue de l'Uranium and Avenue Charles de Gaulle and not far from the presidential palace where the soldiers toppled Tandja. When I visited, not long after the coup, the hyenas were looking irritably mangy. A desiccated hippopotamus slouched in a shallow concrete bath. Schoolchildren squealed with delight as a long-suffering ostrich quick-marched laps of its cage in time with their clapping. The star attractions, the zoo's seven lions, were cramped. But better times lay ahead for them in the form of a planned new 1,000-square-metre lion enclosure soon to be erected at a cost of $60,000.

The lions' benefactor was a consultancy called Trendfield, a company registered in the secretive tax haven of the British Virgin Islands but based in Beijing. Trendfield had helped China's state-owned nuclear company, Sino-U, secure its uranium permits in Niger in 2006 and ended up with a 5 per cent stake in the project for itself.[20] Guy Duport, a Frenchman with an MBA from the University of Liverpool who was Trendfield's chief executive, wrote on his LinkedIn page, 'My negotiation skills were instrumental in the organisation and framework of the establishment of the strategic partnership between China National Nuclear Corporation [Sino-U] and the Republic of Niger for uranium exploration and exploitation.'[21]

In 2009, as the uranium project took shape, Trendfield pledged to rehabilitate the lion enclosure at Niamey's zoo, a microcosm of the infrastructure that Beijing along with companies linked to it were lavishing on Africa's resource states. 'Taking on this project was an essential part of our community development programme and it is something we take seriously,' Duport said in a press release.[22] 'This could also be the platform that creates more direct community activity by foreign companies to assist in the development of not only the Niamey National Museum and Zoo, but the community at large.' Trendfield also arranged for a veterinarian from a zoo in Missouri to fly in and give the lions their first checkup in a decade. (He did the full rounds, Trendfield reported, attending to '22 mammals, 28 birds, 4 reptiles', as well as the lions.)

An insider from the Tandja regime, who said he could not be named because of the sensitivity of the work he had done, told me that, as well as befriending the creatures of Niamey zoo, Trendfield had been close to Tandja and his family, in particular the president's son, Ousmane, who was Niger's commercial attaché in China.

I tracked down Trendfield's local office on a quiet Niamey side street. 'We don't usually talk to journalists,' remarked a British geologist who worked there. But El-Moctar Ichah agreed to speak to me. A Tuareg who had spent twenty years at Areva exploring for uranium in northern Niger as well as dabbling in politics, Ichah was the head of Trendfield's subsidiary in Niger.[23] He told me Trendfield had helped Sino-U with the standard things that consultancies do: arranging visas and site visits and requesting permits. 'We helped to introduce China here, because Niger was not well known.'[24] I asked him to clarify Trendfield's relationship with Tandja's son. 'That is just speculation. He was in China. That does not mean we had "relations".' Ichah went on, 'That question does not concern us, so we are not going to respond.' Later he added, 'We do our work to the highest ethical standards.' I sent Guy Duport questions about Trendfield's business in Niger. He did not reply.

In the weeks before the soldiers made their move, the crisis sparked by Tandja's attempts to prolong his rule had become feverish. Ethnic rivalries were bubbling. In the barracks of the Nigerien army some had seen enough. There are differing accounts of the manoeuvring within the military immediately before the coup. According to some versions two separate groups of officers – one composed of senior commanders, the other a younger cohort – simultaneously decided that this was the day to depose the president. The streets emptied as the sound of shooting rang out. By late afternoon national radio was broadcasting nothing but military music – a classic signal of a successful coup. The president who had thrown in his lot with Beijing was spirited away and incarcerated. Seated in front of army brass in camouflage fatigues, a spokesman for the newly installed junta said it had suspended the constitution and the institutions of state. Salou Djibo, a colonel hitherto unknown to the public, was declared Niger's new ruler.

For all the anxiety in Niamey, there was also relief, particularly among the Western diplomats who had criticized Tandja's authoritarianism and feared the constitutional crisis could plunge Niger into chaos in which the Islamist affiliates of al-Qaeda that roam the Sahara could flourish. Others had commercial reasons to welcome the coup.

Olivier Muller appeared thoroughly at ease with the turn of events – and well he might. He was Areva's boss in Niger. Geological maps of Niger's uranium deposits lined the walls of his office. When I went to see him he had just come from a meeting with Djibo, the leader of the junta. 'I met the president for one hour this morning,' the jocular Frenchman told me.[25] 'He's very happy we are here, and he wants us to do more. Nice guy. If you have one hour with the president, it's going well. If not, you get five minutes,' Muller went on. 'Obviously,' he made sure to add, 'we don't talk politics, just business.' With Tandja, by contrast, negotiations had been 'tough'. Now the thorn had been removed from Areva's side. 'Are France and Areva going to reinforce their presence here?' Muller said. 'Yes, I think so.'

Like the Chinese ambassador, however, Muller was wary of depicting an all-out battle for resources between the new powers and the old. Quite the opposite: Muller described a future in which the need to guarantee the smooth running of the resource trade outweighed national goals, even when state-owned companies from East and West vied for African governments' favour. 'Honestly, there is not competition,' Muller said. 'In the next ten years there are going to be smaller discoveries. People will be forced to cooperate. All these so-called competitors will share infrastructure.'

He was right – and not just about uranium in Niger. South of the border in Nigeria Total of France has formed a partnership with a Chinese oil company to extract crude from beneath the seabed. French and Chinese colleagues from the joint venture can be seen drinking together in the bars of uptown Lagos – hardly a scene of economic warfare over natural resources. In Guinea the Anglo-Australian mining house Rio Tinto is developing the vast iron-ore deposit at Simandou with the backing of Chinalco, the Chinese state-owned miner that is also Rio's biggest shareholder.

China spends two-thirds of its worldwide outlay on foreign corporate acquisitions in the resources sector.[26] Between 2009 and 2012 Chinese state-owned groups spent $23 billion buying Western companies with African resource assets that stretched from Sierra Leone to South Africa.[27] Alongside 'Angola Mode', the barter deals swapping infrastructure and cheap credit for natural resources under opaque terms, this is China's second path to African resources: buying its way into established Western companies of the sort that have long profited from the continent's oil and minerals. It is an approach that Sam Pa's Queensway Group has mimicked.

I met Nik Zuks in the bar of a Conakry hotel days before the first round of Guinea's presidential elections in June 2010. Greying and grizzled, the Australian mining entrepreneur had the bearing of a frontiersman. Zuks had spent years first in Angola, then in Guinea, and he knew the turf. His company, Bellzone, was listed on Aim, the junior London stock market used by a procession of small mining companies of varying quality to raise capital from investors prepared to take risks for the prospect of high returns. Bellzone had secured rights to an iron-ore prospect near Guinea's coast – not on the scale of Simandou but substantial nonetheless, and easier to export than the remote deposit over which Rio Tinto and Beny Steinmetz were grappling.

Zuks was in good spirits – I saw him and his colleagues drinking champagne on the eve of the polls – and it was easy to see why. The Queensway Group had struck a deal with Bellzone that would serve as an insurance policy should the winner of the imminent election tear up China International Fund's opaque $7 billion mining and infrastructure agreement with Dadis's junta.

CIF, the Queensway Group's infrastructure and mining arm, was, Zuks believed, breaking open the resources industry, creating a way to bypass the dominance of the traditional multinationals like Rio Tinto and offering new sources of funding outside the big Western banks and multilateral lenders like the World Bank. 'They are nimble-footed,' he told me, 'and they make decisions quickly.'[28]

That nimble-footedness allowed the Queensway Group to retain its interests in Guinea's resources even after the new government scrapped its $7 billion megadeal. 'Since I came to power Sam has not been to Guinea,' Alpha Condé told me when I interviewed him in Paris after his election victory. Air Guinée International, the new Guinean flag carrier backed by China International Fund whose launch I had attended in Conakry, was wound up before it ever flew. But Pa *was* still present in Guinea – not in person but via the London stock market. CIF reclaimed most of the $100 million it had wired to Guinea to prop up the junta – the same amount China Sonangol, the group's partnership with Angola's state oil company, would spend buying shares in Bellzone.[29]

A month before the election Bellzone announced an agreement with China International Fund under which the CIF would combine an iron-ore permit the junta had granted it with Bellzone's adjacent prospect. The two companies would develop them jointly, with CIF to provide $2.7 billion of funding.[30] Setbacks and delays dogged their work, but in December 2012 they shipped what Bellzone said was the first iron ore exported from Guinea since 1966.

The tie-up with Bellzone offered the Queensway Group a way to expand its interests deeper into the Western resource industry. Bellzone and CIF struck a deal under which both had rights to sell their share of the ore to Glencore, the vast commodities house that had also done business with Dan Gertler in Congo.

Sam Pa was graduating from Chinese spook-cum-fixer to a player in the global resources industry, adding some London guanxi to his connections in Beijing and African capitals. The Queensway Group also sought out allies in Toronto, another stock exchange favoured by mining companies, lending money to a company called West African Iron Ore, which had an iron-ore permit close to those that Bellzone and CIF were developing in Guinea. It was an alliance of middlemen: West African Iron Ore was led by Guy Duport, the man who had brought the Chinese into Niger's uranium industry through Trendfield, the benefactor of Niamey's lions.[31] In Angola the Queensway Group amassed minority stakes in oil ventures led by some of the industry's foremost Western companies: BP of the UK, Total of France, Eni of Italy, Statoil of Norway, Conoco Phillips of the United States.

As one of the foremost middlemen in China's advance into Africa, Sam Pa has adopted the tactics of Françafrique: fuse the power of those who hold offices of state with private business interests so as to enrich both from the exploitation of African natural resources. The Queensway Group was even said to have tapped the old networks of Françafrique. According to a US congressional report, China Sonangol enlisted Pierre Falcone, the French arms dealer who supplied weapons worth $790 million to the MPLA regime in Angola during the civil war in exchange for oil and who is known, according to a separate US Senate report, as a 'close associate' of José Eduardo dos Santos.[32] (Falcone, who has set up a consultancy based in Beijing, denies having had a commercial relationship with China Sonangol.)

Like Elf before them, Queensway Group companies appear to have funnelled money to African officials in countries whose resources they coveted. The ledger of payments published by a Hong Kong court in the dispute between the Queensway Group's founders and Wu Yang, the Chinese oilman who claimed he had not received his dues for making some valuable introductions, offers a glimpse of how the Queensway Group uses cash to 'curry favour' with African governments. One entry, in a section listing financial transactions made in 2009, reads simply: 'Antonio Inacio Junior: Loan for project (HK$2,340,000).'[33]

That indicates that a Queensway Group company made a loan in 2009, worth about US$300,000, to someone called Antonio Inacio Junior. There is nothing to suggest anything untoward – unless you know that Antonio Inacio Junior is the name of Mozambique's ambassador to China.[34] He appears, close-cropped and sharp-suited, in photographs of diplomatic engagements in China. I called the Mozambican embassy in Beijing to ask the ambassador about the loan and, as requested, sent a fax listing my questions. No reply came.

Mozambican government records show that a joint venture between China International Fund and a local company was created in November 2008.[35] The company, Cif-Moz, was formed to pursue opportunities in agriculture, industry, minerals, the production of construction materials, and other sectors. It established a foothold for Sam Pa and his allies in a country that was undergoing one of the great commodity rushes of recent years, as the giants of the resource business jostled for untapped stocks of coal and natural gas. In November 2009 – the same year as the loan to the ambassador – Cif-Moz was awarded a permit to prospect for a limestone mine south of the capital, Maputo.[36] Plans for a $35 million cement factory nearby followed.[37] When I asked a lawyer for a Queensway Group company why a loan had been granted to a serving official in a country where the group was seeking to do business, he declined to answer.[38]

Mozambique was just one target in the Queensway Group's quick-fire expansion across Africa from its Angolan base. Mahmoud Thiam, the Guinean mining minister who brokered the deal through which the Queensway Group bailed out the country's murderous junta, added to his position as minister a role as an ambassador for the group's interests. Following a coup in Madagascar, Thiam took part in negotiations between emissaries from the Queensway Group and the putschists' energy minister. 'It was all the same things they were doing in Guinea – trying to find projects that were interesting and doing good-faith advances,' Thiam told me.[39] China Sonangol tried to wrest an oil prospect from a rival but eventually lost out.[40]

At the same time Thiam served as an envoy for the Queensway Group to the leaders of Niger's coup. He told me that the group made a 'good faith' payment to Niger's junta of $40 million and expressed an interest in Agadem, the oil block that CNPC, the Chinese state-owned oil group, was drilling for the country's first crude – an indication of the Queensway Group's readiness to challenge China's national interests when doing so offered a chance for profit. 'But the president of the transitional government wisely decided not to touch that money until there was a full agreement,' Thiam told me.[41] 'It was never reached, so the payment was returned.' (Thiam insists that he ceased to work with China Sonangol and the Queensway Group once he stopped being a minister.)

The Queensway Group's forays into Madagascar and Niger came to nothing, but they illuminate a key element of its approach: Sam Pa offers pariah governments a ready-made technique for turning their countries' natural resources into cash when few others are prepared to do business with them. Governments installed by military coups are 'starving for funding,' Thiam told me. 'These guys come and they say, "We will fund you when no one else will." If you have the interest of your people and your own survival at stake, you will take that money.'

There is a distinct whiff of hypocrisy to Western criticism of China's advance into Africa. Beijing was vilified when it sought to protect its access to Sudanese oil by preventing George W. Bush from tightening sanctions against Omar al-Bashir, the dictator who has presided over campaigns of state-sponsored terrorism against his opponents. But China was merely adopting the same sort of resource realpolitik that Washington demonstrated when Condoleezza Rice, Bush's secretary of state, extended a warm welcome to Teodoro Obiang Nguema, the kleptocrat from Equatorial Guinea who consigns his enemies to the hideous recesses of Black Beach prison but has laid out the red carpet for American oil companies. The opacity of China's infrastructure-for-resources deals has been justifiably castigated, but when US lawmakers introduced pioneering new transparency rules to force oil and mining companies to disclose their payments to foreign governments, the American Petroleum Institute, the US oil industry body, went to court to try to block them. Although there was legitimate uproar when a Chinese ship that docked in South Africa was found to contain weapons bound for Robert Mugabe's regime in Zimbabwe, any notion that China is the sole or even the main source of the oceans of weapons that slosh through Africa is misplaced. One study by two Norway-based academics, based on years of arms import statistics and governance indicators, found that the United States had a greater propensity than China to sell weapons to repressive African governments.[42] The Chinese exported fewer weapons to Africa between 1992 and 2006 than Ukraine did, the study found.

It is too simplistic to see China's quest for African resources as a Manichean struggle for nature's treasure between East and West. There is competition, but there is also cooperation in the business of resource extraction. And for all its increased attractiveness to rival investors from overseas, much of Africa remains locked at the foot of the global economy.

Ibrahim Iddi Ango, the industrialist who headed Niger's chamber of commerce, told me that Niger's rulers had sold the country short in their negotiations with the Chinese. 'They need strategic resources. You must say, "You are interested in that? These are the conditions. First, you must use local labour. Second, all the needs you have – for example, the transit – you must use at a minimum 50 per cent local operators." But when they came the government said none of this. The state took a percentage of the businesses and let the Chinese do what they want.' A brief window of opportunity to use China's desire for African minerals to insist on securing for Niger the skills and infrastructure that might help to salve the resource curse by broadening the economy was closing. 'To diversify, it's central,' Iddi Ango said – and with good reason. Niger is among the African states most acutely dependent on a handful of raw commodity exports, their economic fortunes yoked to the whims of far-off consumers. On the African Development Bank's index, where a higher score indicates a more diversified economy, relatively wealthy countries not shackled to the resource trade such as Mauritius and Morocco score 22 and 41, respectively. The average for the whole of Africa, including more prosperous North Africa, is 4.8. The most oil-dependent states, Angola and Chad, record the lowest scores, 1.1. Niger does only marginally better, with a score of 2.4.[43]

'But if you let China do what it wants – as many African countries have – they pay for the oil or the resources and use Chinese labour, Chinese trucks. It's a big problem,' Iddi Ango said. 'They are coming because the resources are here. This moment will not be repeated. We can't miss it. When the uranium or the oil is finished, they will leave.'

The fall of Tandja demonstrated the limits of China's readiness to get involved in domestic politics to protect African allies. But Xia Huang, the Chinese ambassador in Niamey, encapsulated how China's readiness to spend and build allowed Beijing to gain a foothold sufficiently strong that its interests could withstand a coup against an ally. 'Today there is a bridge between the two sides of the River Niger,' he told me. 'But there is also a bridge that links China and Niger.'

Yet the true value of China's offer to guide Africa on a path to economic diversification and industrialization – the road that led the rich world to prosperity – rests on whether its construction spree is geared primarily toward cultivating the rulers who govern access to resources or toward broadening the opportunities of the population at large. Neither railways that simply connect Chinese-owned mines to Chinese-built ports for the export of commodities nor vanity projects of great cost but little economic usefulness will lift resource states' inhabitants from their poverty. Martyn Davies, the chief executive of a South African consultancy called Frontier Advisory, who has worked as an adviser on Chinese deals in Africa, told me, 'When you have a commodity-driven economy, where a lot of people are excluded, it's a silo economy. It's very difficult to build infrastructure that supports inclusive growth. Is Chinese-financed infrastructure going to provide diversification? Which comes first?' He added, 'African governments should never assume that responsibility for the development of our continent has been outsourced to Beijing.'

Beijing appears to be undercutting its side of the deal. Chinese goods like the counterfeit textiles flooding into northern Nigeria drown out hopes for industrialization, regardless of how many roads and railways Chinese companies lay. Lamido Sanusi, governor of Nigeria's central bank from 2009 to 2014, put it well: 'So China takes our primary goods and sells us manufactured ones. This was also the essence of colonialism. The British went to Africa and India to secure raw materials and markets. Africa is now willingly opening itself up to a new form of imperialism.'[44]

By the time Tandja was deposed, the bridge over the River Niger was built, China's oil project was in progress, its refinery was completed, its uranium mine was taking shape, and the lion enclosure in Niamey zoo was marked out. Xia Huang, the ambassador, told me that the junta's leader had assured him that China's position was not under threat. Both China and France pressed on with their plans for Niger's commodities. Areva pushed ahead with a new $2.6 billion mine that would double the company's output of Nigerien uranium. The Chinese found more oil than they had first thought, setting Niger on a course to join the middle ranks of African oil producers.

The soldiers who ousted Tandja were good to their word. They arranged elections, which international observers deemed legitimate, and went back to their barracks in April 2011, fourteen months after the coup. The elected president, Mahamadou Issoufou, was, like Alpha Condé in Guinea, a seasoned opposition leader who launched an anti-corruption campaign upon taking office. While jihadists ran riot across the border in

Mali, Issoufou won a reputation as a bulwark of stability in a tumultuous region.

When I met Issoufou during a trip to London a year into his presidency, he was eloquent and impressive, his chunky figure animated with the force of his grand plans to transform Niger.

Issoufou was determined to balance the competing interests of the great powers that sought Niger's resources rather than allow them to consume him as Tandja had done. He would not bow down before China, he told me. 'Their business has been aggressive in Africa – in natural resources, in uranium, in oil. We are an open country – open to investors from anywhere. But we want win-win partnerships, and that is our relationship with China. We will defend our interests, and they will defend theirs.'[45]

Issoufou took the fight to the French too. He embarked on eighteen months of negotiations with Areva over the share of uranium revenues it pays to the state. The talks were fractious. Areva closed its mines for a month, ostensibly for maintenance but also sending a signal of its power to choke off the government's income.[46] In May 2014 the two sides reached a deal. Areva agreed to pay higher royalties and to build a road linking the capital to the northern uranium region, but it retained some tax breaks under an unpublished contract.[47]

Even in what appeared to be triumph, however, Niger and its president were reminded of the extent to which the fortunes of a resource state are dictated by the twists of a global economy whose raw ingredients it supplies. Following the Fukushima disaster in Japan in 2011 governments around the world turned away from nuclear power, sending the price of uranium tumbling. On the day it announced its new deal in Niger Areva also revealed that it was shelving the development of a huge new uranium mine because the depressed price rendered the project uneconomic.

Nonetheless, Niger had joined a small but growing group of resource states in west Africa that were edging from decades of havoc toward more representative rule and a modicum of stability, among them Guinea, Sierra Leone and Liberia. But the lesson of their most stable near-neighbour, Ghana, is that the resource curse can still bite where there is peace – abetted by the global institutions charged with alleviating Africa's poverty and a financial system that drains away the proceeds of the continent's natural wealth.

» 7 «

Finance and Cyanide

L IFE FOR THE FAUNA around the hamlet of Kwamebourkrom in central Ghana got a little easier in late 2009. A pair of hunting dogs, Skimpy and Don't Forget, which had spent their lives catching the bushmeat that supplemented their owner's diet of fish and staple crops, barked their last after their master threw them a couple of fish from the day's catch. Now the antelope, crested porcupines and plump grass cutters that inhabit the tall grasses had two fewer predators to fear. Only later did Kofi Gyakah come to believe that Skimpy and Don't Forget had been poisoned.

Beyond the pond where Gyakah cast his nets each day and above the tousled shrubs, the red arm of a crane rose against the sky. Usually the hamlet's thirty residents heard the boom of explosive blasts each day at around noon. At night the sound of machines crushing rocks kept them awake.

Newmont, the biggest American gold-mining company, had completed the first phase of the $700 million Ahafo mine three years earlier, with the support of the International Finance Corporation, the arm of the World Bank that lends money to private-sector projects. Three years before the IFC made its loan to Newmont's new mine in Ghana, the World Bank had conducted an internal review of its programmes in Ghanaian mining. The Bank and the IFC had been trying to revive Ghana's ailing mining sector since the early 1980s. The Bank's programmes aimed to rehabilitate state-owned mines, attract private investment and assist small-scale miners. By and large, they failed. The internal review noted numerous shortcomings, including a 'patently untrue' claim that mining in Ghana caused little environmental damage.[1] The review, submitted to the Bank's board, concluded that because of low taxes on foreign mining companies, modest employment of locals, and scant recompense for people living near the mines, 'it is unclear what [the mining sector's] true net benefits are to Ghana.'

Nonetheless, the IFC had gone ahead and furnished Newmont with $125 million of finance for the new mine at Ahafo. The company uprooted ninety-five hundred people, but Kofi Gyakah and the other residents of Kwamebourkrom stayed put in their mud-and-thatch cottages, growing crops, fishing and hunting bushmeat as they always had. Soon the school where they sent their children closed down. The noise grew insufferable. Then came the cyanide.

Sodium cyanide is used in gold mining to separate the metal from the ores that come out of the ground. On 12 October 2009, Newmont issued a statement saying that a faulty sensor had caused a 'minor overflow' of fluid containing cyanide from the Ahafo mine. It said the spill had been 'contained and neutralized within the mine site' and that 'no pollution of the water sources downstream from the plant site has been found' but that its staff were still trying to establish the cause of 'a short-term environmental impact of fish mortality'.[2]

The adulterated liquid that flowed from the mine into the waterways around Kwamebourkrom and its neighbouring hamlets was too diluted to be a threat to human life, but aquatic life fared less well. Shortly after Newmont's spill Gyakah and his fellow fishermen found the fish in their ponds floating belly-up. A delegation from Newmont brought the hamlet some clean water – although the villagers recalled that the security man on the team had been sure to bring his own personal supply. Six months after the spill Newmont announced that it would comply with an order from Ghana's environment ministry to pay compensation, even though it stressed that a government panel that had investigated the spill 'found no evidence of adverse consequences to human life or property'.[3] The money would be split between the 'development needs of the affected communities' and two national regulatory bodies. Based on Ahafo's production figures and the gold price at the time of the settlement, it would have taken Newmont about three and a half days to earn back the $4.9 million it agreed to pay out.

When I visited the area a month after the spill the word 'cyanide' had entered the local dialect of Twi, Ghana's main indigenous language. Kofi

Gyakah told me he did not trust the emissary from Newmont who had come to the hamlet to reassure its residents that the water was safe. As far as he was concerned, the demise of Skimpy and Don't Forget appeared to indicate the contrary. Sporting a tattered shirt and a neat moustache, Gyakah showed me the hamlet's pond. I asked him how many fish had died. He looked stern as his young daughter peeked bashfully from behind his leg. 'Plenty,' he said. We sat down in the dry-earth yard between the hamlet's huts. A local teacher who had accompanied me translated. 'Living here is not comfortable at all,' Gyakah said. 'We are powerless.'

When the International Finance Corporation announced in 2005 that it was planning to invest in Newmont's development of the Ahafo mine, Newmont's market capitalization, the total value of all its shares on the New York Stock Exchange, stood at $17.5 billion, twice the size of Ghana's economy. Its quickly rising annual revenues were $4.5 billion, and it made $434 million in profits from operations on four continents that produced 9 per cent of the gold mined worldwide. The Ahafo concession alone was sitting on gold worth some $12 billion. The following year the IFC approved a loan for the Ahafo mine from its own account of $75 million and arranged a further $50 million from commercial banks, including Rothschild and Royal Bank of Scotland. The total package represented a modest 7 per cent of Newmont's $1.9 billion total debt.

Newmont had a good credit rating and could easily borrow from commercial banks without the IFC's assistance. According to its charter, the IFC is not meant to lend to companies that can borrow with reasonable terms elsewhere. But since it was set up in 1956 as an adjunct to the World Bank, its role has expanded. The driving force behind the creation of the IFC was Robert L. Garner, a Wall Street banker. The World Bank and the International Monetary Fund, mandated respectively to assist with post-war reconstruction and to ensure stable exchange rates, only worked with governments. Garner saw a need for a multilateral body that would support private investment in underdeveloped countries that traditional moneymen deemed excessively risky. 'It was my firm conviction that the most promising future for the less developed countries was the establishing of good private industry,' Garner said.[4]

With Garner as its first president, the IFC began work from headquarters in Washington, DC, with twelve staff, authorized capital of $100 million, and a limited mandate to make loans. Over time it effectively became an investment bank, except that its shareholders were, like those of the World Bank and IMF, member states – 184 of them, in the IFC's case. Its role expanded to investing in companies directly and raising its own funds by issuing bonds on international capital markets. It undertook advisory work and funded privatizations. By 2013 it had assets worth $78 billion, a balance sheet that would, were the IFC a normal bank, place it among the top thirty banks in the United States. It consistently makes more than a billion dollars a year in profit from projects in a hundred countries. A fifth of its commitments are in sub-Saharan Africa, where it backs everything from Ivorian poultry and Kenyan housing to oil prospecting along the Central African Rift. As an arm of the World Bank, its stated aim has widened from simply furnishing finance where it is scarce to helping to end extreme poverty by 2030 and a mission to 'boost shared prosperity in every developing country'.

The IFC accounts for most World Bank spending in the oil, gas and mining industries. Between 2000 and 2012 it provided as much as $800 million annually in financing for such projects. Investments in oil and mining account for only a small fraction of the IFC's overall outlay, but it is involved in some very large – and very contentious – projects in these industries, in partnership with some of the sector's most powerful companies, especially in Africa. Some have gone spectacularly wrong.

In 2000 the World Bank and the IFC agreed to back a $3.5 billion oil venture in Chad, an expanse of deprivation and warfare sandwiched between Niger and Sudan. It was meant to be a flagship project to demonstrate that oil revenues could be managed for the greater good, but it started badly when Chad's president, Idriss Déby, immediately began to divert the oil rent to the military that had helped keep him in power since 1990.[5] The $4.5 million Déby channelled to the army came from the signature bonus that Chevron and other oil companies paid for the rights to drill Chad's crude and build a pipeline to export it through Cameroon to the coast, not directly from the $200 million the IFC drummed up for the project. But it quickly became apparent that the commitments the IFC had extracted from Déby's government in exchange for its support were worthless. Déby's government had agreed to an innovative mechanism designed to ensure that revenues went to 'priority sectors' like health, education, and water supplies for the desert nation. Once the crude was flowing, however, he simply added 'security' to the list of priorities, allowing the oil money to slosh into his armed forces' coffers. Chad's economy grew by 30 per cent thanks to the start of oil production, the fastest rate of any country in 2004, but the overwhelming beneficiary was Déby's regime. Strengthened by oil money, Déby is, at the time of writing, approaching his quarter-century in office.

The shambles in Chad dealt a severe blow to the notion that the IFC's involvement could alter the ruinous effects of resource rents. Nonetheless, the IFC pressed on, its bosses determined to secure a place for themselves at the top tables of an industry that comprised the world's richest and most powerful corporations. In Guinea the IFC took a stake in Rio Tinto's much-delayed project to develop the iron-ore deposit at Simandou. Among some senior Guinean officials there was a sense that the IFC was on the wrong side of a struggle between a poor country and a giant mining house that appeared in no rush to embark on what would be the biggest industrial development in African history.[6] The IFC could argue, as Rio Tinto did, that complex undertakings on the scale of Simandou were always going to take many years to bring to fruition. Yet the IFC was at times prepared to act with undue haste. Such was its eagerness to keep pumping in funds and retain its influence that in 2012 it made a further $150 million equity investment toward the costs of development at Simandou before social and environmental assessments of the mine's impact had been completed. The IFC signed off on the investment even though its most powerful shareholder, the US government, refused to support the decision, noting that it might have been wise to assess the project's effect on what the IFC itself had called a 'bio-diversity hotspot' before proceeding.[7]

As they expanded their portfolio of African oil and mining interests, the IFC's leaders professed an abiding faith in the resource industry's potential to serve the greater good, despite a sorry history of evidence suggesting otherwise. In 2006 the IFC proposed investing in a British company called Lonmin that mined South Africa platinum 'to assist Lonmin [to] achieve world class safety and efficiency throughout it[s] mining operations, and to promote sustainable economic development in the area surrounding the mining operations'.[8] The stated aim of the IFC's partnership with Lonmin was lofty – to alter the miserable course of South African mining. Its bosses told the World Bank's board that, if successful, the partnership 'will set a new standard for the mining industry's relationship with the country and community in South Africa, and will forge a sustainable and mutually beneficial partnership with the community surrounding the operations.'

The IFC invested $50 million in Lonmin and provided another $100 million in credit. But its strategy was flawed from the outset. As the World Bank's ombudsman subsequently found, the IFC failed to monitor adequately the mounting tension between Lonmin's management and miners at its mines near Marikana, who were growing increasingly angry over their working conditions. In August 2012 the tensions erupted into bloodshed. Far from the new dawn in South African mining that the IFC had conjured when it invested in Lonmin, the scenes of police firing on demonstrators served as a reminder of the gulf that persists between those who profit from the country's natural riches and those who dig them out of the ground.

As well as exposing the IFC's failure to foresee the explosion of violence at its own project, the inquiry by the World Bank's ombudsman in the wake of the Marikana massacre called into question the IFC's whole approach to such investments. By taking a minority stake in publicly traded companies, the IFC could expect dividends like any other investor. But, despite its efforts to look and act like a private investment bank, the IFC's mandate is to influence those companies' behaviour. Minority investors, however, have little such influence. With its Lonmin investment and elsewhere the IFC was putting taxpayers' money at the service of large private oil and mining companies whose primary concern was to enrich their shareholders and over which the IFC held little sway. Its management's argument was that, by investing in the industry, the IFC could apply pressure for reform. But long before Skimpy and Don't Forget perished beside Newmont's Ghanaian gold mine, the IFC had received the clearest of warnings about the dangers of its support for oil and mining in Africa and elsewhere.

In June 2001 Emil Salim got a call from James Bond.[9] Salim was an illustrious economist with a PhD from Berkeley who had served for a decade as Indonesia's environment minister. Bond was a former head of mining at the World Bank. James Wolfensohn, an Australian banker then in his second term as head of the World Bank, had decided to launch an independent review to establish whether its projects to promote the extractive industries – oil, gas and mining – contributed to its mandate to reduce poverty. Salim, Bond informed him on the telephone, was the man to run it.

It was a moment when the stewards of the global economic order – the World Bank, the IMF and the World Trade Organization – were coming under unusually forceful scrutiny. The previous year tens of thousands of protesters had descended on the WTO summit in Seattle, denouncing it as the patsy of global capital and fighting pitched battles with riot police. Thousands picketed the annual World Bank and IMF meetings in Washington to voice a string of demands that included that the Bank end investment in oil and mining. Salim accepted the job, he wrote, 'with full confidence that the [World Bank] is genuinely willing to move away from a conventional "business as usual" approach into sustainable development'.[10]

Salim spent the next two years overseeing half a dozen research projects and marshalling teams that visited World Bank-backed oil and mining ventures and held forums in Africa, South America, Eastern Europe and Asia. Despite campaigners' concerns that the exercise would produce a whitewash – Salim had served under Suharto's dictatorship in Indonesia and seemed at times to be in thrall to the industry – when he published his findings in December 2003 they were damning.[11]

Salim's researchers ploughed through the World Bank's own data on countries with economies that were dependent on exporting natural resources. They found that between 1960 and 2000 poor countries that were rich in natural resources grew two to three times more slowly than those that were not. Over that period, of forty-five countries that failed to sustain economic growth, all but six were heavily dependent on oil or mining.[12] Without exception, through the 1990s every country that borrowed from the World Bank did worse the more it depended on extractive industries. The game, Salim and his team concluded, was rigged – and the World Bank appeared to be on the wrong side. 'The knowledge, power, financial, and technical resource gaps between major extractive industry companies, civil society, developing-country governments, and local communities throughout the world are profound,' Salim's research concluded. 'The inequalities between local communities and transnational companies are not just economic in nature; they include access to political power and information and the ability to know and use the legal system to their advantage.' In the dry language of the World Bank Salim was describing the looting machine: the alliance between shadow governments and the resource industry that tramples over the people who live where oil and minerals are found.

Salim's review examined the record of the World Bank and its two arms that work with private companies – the IFC and the Multilateral Investment Guarantee Agency, or Miga, which provides insurance against political upheaval for companies investing in volatile countries. Although, Salim concluded, the IFC and Miga had at times succeeded in making the oil and mining industries behave better, the Bank, the IFC and Miga were doing very little to assess whether oil and mining investments did anything to make people less poor. Salim noted the propensity of the resource industry instead to *create* poverty through pollution (including cyanide spillages), forced resettlement and the loss of grazing lands. His review quoted statistics that showed that mining was the world's most hazardous occupation, employing less than 1 per cent of all workers but accounting for 5 per cent of all deaths on the job, a tally of some fourteen thousand a year. The industry appeared to be a force that ran counter to everything the World Bank existed to promote.

Salim's recommendations were explosive. His review recommended that the IFC and Miga 'should only support investments where net benefits can be secured, counting all externalities, and where revenues are used transparently for sustainable development'. In policy-speak, he meant that the two organizations should seek to determine whether investments they supported actually did any good for the community at large and whether the investors met the full costs of their activities, including environmental and social costs as well as the usual outlays of doing business. And the IFC and Miga should only go ahead with investments in instances in which revenues would not simply be gobbled up by the corrupt or be siphoned out of the country. Staff, Salim went on, should no longer be rewarded simply for the amount of money they allocated but for whether their projects reduced poverty. Forced resettlements to make way for oil and mining projects should never be supported. Contracts should be published and revenues disclosed. The World Bank should phase out investments in oil within five years on environmental grounds. 'There is still a role for the World Bank Group in the oil, gas, and mining sectors,' Salim wrote, 'but only if its interventions allow extractive industries to contribute to poverty alleviation through sustainable development.'

Salim and his team had skewered some of the myths oil and mining companies propagate about their contribution to reducing poverty and challenged the World Bank to take specific steps to alter the most harmful aspects of its support for the industries. Nine months after Salim published his report the World Bank's management published its response. It proclaimed that it had 'considered these recommendations seriously' and then proceeded to ignore almost all of them.[13]

Where Salim's review had demanded that no one should be resettled from the path of an oil project or a mine without having given 'free, prior and informed consent', the Bank's management agreed only to insist that companies secure the Orwellian-sounding 'free, prior informed consultation'. Oil investment would continue. Salim did not conceal his displeasure. In a bitter echo of the commitment he believed he had won when he began his work, he described the World Bank management's approach as 'business as usual with marginal changes'.[14]

Barely a month after the World Bank brushed aside the bulk of Emil Salim's conclusions, a day of brutality in Congo threw renewed focus on the kind of projects it backs.

Miga's management had been warned that there were serious questions about Anvil Mining's copper mine at Dikulushi in southern Congo well before government troops brought death and destruction to the nearby town of Kilwa. In August 2004 a group of Congolese and foreign human rights organizations wrote to Miga's board about the Anvil project, which was then under consideration for a Miga risk guarantee.[15] The groups raised concerns about the development benefits the mine's backers claimed it would bring, about employment conditions, and about security. In very clear terms the groups warned Miga's board that Augustin Katumba Mwanke, the architect of Joseph Kabila's shadow state, had connections to the project.

Undeterred, Miga's board approved the issuance of guarantees worth $13 million a month after receiving the warning – the first such approval since Salim's review was published. Like other transactions by Miga and the IFC, the significance was greater than the relatively small sum involved: by backing a project, they confer the legitimacy that comes with the approval of the World Bank, supposedly the guardian of economic rectitude. The following month the army responded to a small and farcically ill-equipped rebellion in Kilwa by slaughtering a hundred people, an onslaught for which they made use of Anvil's equipment.

The following year Miga sought to explain itself to the human rights groups that had raised the alarm. By then an emissary from one of the groups, Patricia Feeney, an expert on African mining with Oxford-based Rights and Accountability in Development, had been leapt on by guard dogs when she visited Anvil's offices in the Congolese mining capital of Lubumbashi for a meeting during which, according to Feeney's notes, the company's local representative expressed no remorse for the military's actions at Kilwa.[16] Miga wrote in a letter to the campaigners that it had been unaware of the scale of what had happened at Kilwa when it signed off on the guarantees for Anvil in May 2005, seven months after the massacre.[17] Miga said it had contacted Anvil following the massacre and had been told that the military had commandeered Anvil's equipment. Miga assured the rights groups that it had looked into Anvil's relationship with Katumba but that 'no evidence of impropriety was provided'. It saw nothing untoward in Katumba's seat on the board of Anvil's local subsidiary or the fact that the company rented its headquarters from him.

Others had availed themselves of the facts of the matter far more quickly than Miga, a body that had put public money at the service of the mining company. In November 2004, a month after the massacre, a US embassy cable named Katumba as a shareholder in the mine and reported, 'The allegations of a massacre of civilians by government troops are entirely believable, and – given the high-level Kinshasa interest in Dikulushi mine – we can expect [Congolese government] authorities to obstruct any investigation.'[18]

When the World Bank's ombudsman, at the request of the rights groups, conducted its own audit of Miga's decisions regarding the Anvil mine, it found failures in the due diligence Miga performed before agreeing to provide a guarantee.[19] It repeated a finding of Emil Salim's review – that Miga lacked the expertise to monitor the social impact of the projects it supported but ploughed on regardless. The ombudsman said that questions about Anvil's relationship with Katumba were outside its mandate and referred them to the Bank's Department for Institutional Integrity, its in-house corruption watchdog. In 2014, a decade after the massacre, I asked the World Bank whether anything had come of the case. The Department for Institutional Integrity had followed up on the referral from the ombudsman, I was told, 'but in line with its disclosure policy, details of investigative processes cannot be disclosed'.[20]

Miga's guarantee remained in place until Anvil ran into financial trouble and stopped mining Dikulushi in 2009. In 2010 Anvil sold the mine to another Australian mining company, Mawson West, in exchange for shares. In 2012 Minmetals, a Chinese state-owned group, bought Anvil for $1.3 billion.

Miga's work with Anvil yielded an 'implementation toolkit' for companies that wanted their security operations to take human rights into account. But attempts in Congo to bring the perpetrators of the massacre to justice came to nothing.

When the IFC set about facilitating Newmont's investment in Ghana's gold, it was dealing with a very different environment from the chaos of Congo, the volatility of Guinea or the simmering grievances of post-apartheid South Africa. Ghana, the received wisdom goes, is different. Even as the rest of west Africa almost without exception endures some combination of war, insurgency and venal dictatorship, Ghana has since the 1990s emerged from its own troubles as one of a handful of African states where political parties fight close elections and the loser consistently leaves office. It surveys its hulking near-neighbour Nigeria with the attitude of the respectable professional who finds himself sitting next to an unruly drunk. After the Jubilee oil field was discovered in 2007 off Ghana's coast, high-minded businessmen in Accra, the capital, shuddered at the resultant influx of Nigerian bankers, convinced that the combined effect of crude and corruption would turn Ghana into a smaller version of Nigeria's petro-nightmare. Those fears were a little unfair – there are some upstanding Nigerian bankers – but understandable. Ghana had something to protect: a reputation for handling natural resources better than most.

Such was the mineral wealth of what would become Ghana that European traders and slavers knew it as the Gold Coast. Legend has it that the soul of the Ashanti people, once the most powerful of the territory's kingdoms (whose capital, Kumasi, lies 100 kilometres from the site of Newmont's IFC-backed mine at Ahafo), resides in a golden stool that descended from the heavens. When a colonial administrator demanded that, as the representative of the British Crown, he be afforded the honour of sitting on it, war ensued. Four decades after Ghana, in 1957, became the first African colony to win independence, Ashanti Goldfields became the first African company to list its shares on the New York Stock Exchange. Gold mined both by corporations and artisanal miners is Ghana's biggest export. It had known years of single-party rule, but by the time it discovered oil Ghana had achieved something almost unique on the continent: it had yielded up great quantities of commodities while building a functioning, democratic state.

Yet glitter as it may, Ghana's gold has not made it rich. It is one of only ten countries in sub-Saharan Africa to have achieved 'medium development', according to the UN's Human Development Index (all the rest are classed as 'low development', with a handful too chaotic or authoritarian for reliable data to be available).[21] But Ghana's relatively comfortable status among African countries should not mask the privation that persists; it sits between Iraq and India in the rankings. Ghana comes close to the top of the UN index that ranks countries by their success in turning GDP per head into improved living standards (scoring 22, compared with -97 for Equatorial Guinea), but Ghanaians' average income is a tenth of Lithuanians' and one in three Ghanaians cannot read or write, the same level of illiteracy as in Congo. Inherent in the praise that is heaped on Ghana is a troubling undertone that mitigated penury is the best that Africans can aim for.

Like the rest of Africa's resource states, Ghana bowed to the orthodoxy that the World Bank and the IMF imposed from the early 1980s in the form

of 'structural adjustment programmes'. Based on a set of neoliberal economic policies known as the Washington Consensus, these programmes
made loans to poor countries dependent on their adherence to strict conditions, including deep cuts to public spending, privatizing state-owned
assets, and lifting controls on trade. Foreign investment was deemed essential to economic growth. African and other poor countries were exhorted
to bend over backward with tax breaks and other incentives in order to
attract multinational corporations. When it came to oil and mining, a policy of beggar thy neighbour emerged, as resource states competed to offer
ever easier terms to foreign companies. In gold mining the standard rate of
mining royalties – a levy charged on mineral production, based on volume,
value, or profitability – settled at about 3 per cent across the continent,
among the lowest anywhere in the world.[22]

When a surge of demand from China and other rising economies sent
commodity prices rocketing in the mid-2000s, it became increasingly apparent to African governments that they were being fleeced. In Zambia,
one of the world's top copper producers, mining companies were paying
lower tax rates than the half a million Zambians employed in the industry.
In 2011 only 2.4 per cent of the $10 billion of revenues from exports of Zam-
bian copper accrued to the government.[23] Across the border in Congo the
figure is fractionally higher but still negligible: 2.5 per cent. Shortly after
I met Kofi Gyakah in the shadow of Newmont's mine in 2009 I went to
Ghana's Chamber of Mines in Accra and analysed the data it kept on the
mining industry. The previous year the industry generated $2.1 billion. Of
that, the sum of royalties, taxes and dividends from government stakes in
mining ventures paid to the state was $146 million, or 7 per cent – and that
is before factoring in the cost to the state of the subsidized electricity the
mines use. It is a pittance compared with the 45 to 65 per cent that the IMF
estimates to be the global average effective tax rate in mining.[24] Over the
eighteen previous years Ghana had produced 36 million ounces of gold,
enough to make ninety thousand standard gold bars. A senior banker I
interviewed in Accra put it simply: 'People are asking: how did the country
earn nothing from a hundred years of mining?'

I put a version of that question to Somit Varma. Varma, an Indian, was
the IFC's associate director for oil, gas, mining and chemicals when the
decision to invest in Newmont's Ahafo mine was taken and had since been

appointed head of the joint IFC–World Bank department in charge of all
financing and advisory work in those sectors. Later, like several other senior IFC officials, he would switch to a private company that had benefited
from IFC financing – in Varma's case, Warburg Pincus, the New York–
based private equity firm whose energy company, Kosmos, had received a
$100 million loan agreement from the IFC for its oil venture in Ghana on
Varma's watch.[25]

'In all extractive projects we ask: Is the deal fair to the government and
the private sector?' Varma told me.[26] 'Is the royalty regime fair, the tax regime?' He emphasized the ancillary benefits from Newmont's mine. Newmont had created fifteen thousand jobs, spent $272 million in 2008 within
Ghana, and allocated $1 for every ounce of gold sold from Ahafo and 1 per
cent of the mine's net profit to community development projects – an impressive array by industry standards.

But there were other aspects to Newmont's deal in Ghana that the company was less keen to publicize. It was paying a meagre 3 per cent royalty
on the gold it mined, and like other foreign mining companies across the
continent, it had secured a 'stabilization agreement' guaranteeing that its
payments to the state were kept low. The result is like an inverted auction, in which poor countries compete to sell the family silver at the lowest
price. What governments lose under generous deals with resource groups
is frequently made up by foreign aid, which constitutes a significant share
of many resource states' income – effectively subsidizing private oil and
mining companies with taxpayer funds from donor countries.

Emil Salim had recommended that the World Bank should strive to bro-
ker oil and mining deals to 'maximize the benefits retained in the country'.
But the IFC was content to back Newmont's stabilization agreement. 'It's
not that hundreds of companies are lining up to invest in the mining sector in Ghana,' the IFC's Varma told me when I asked whether Newmont's
deal was fair. 'They have lots of options worldwide. We have to encourage
companies to go into countries where they might not otherwise.'

Ghana's minister of finance, Kwabena Duffuor, was clearly less
convinced that the apportioning of revenues between his country and the
American mining house was equitable. In late 2009, not long after Newmont's cyanide spill, he declared that he wanted to raise the royalties due

from foreign miners from 3 per cent to 6 per cent. He said the government would address 'the whole mining sector fiscal regime'.[27]

Duffuor was echoing his counterparts in other African resource states, who were watching as the fruits of the boom in commodity prices were passing them by. Their demands for renegotiation of the terms prompted dire warnings from the industry about resurgent 'resource nationalism'. The perennial threat was repeated anew: even modest increases in royalties or taxes would scare off investors. It was an argument that three top economists from the African Development Bank who studied past efforts to increase African countries' share of the spoils deemed to be 'seldom backed by empirical evidence'.[28] But faced with the veiled menace of foreign advisers warning them to remain 'investor friendly', African governments tend to cave. The multinationals have grown accustomed to getting their way. When I asked Jeff Huspeni, Newmont's senior vice president for Africa, what he made of Ghana's plan to increase royalties, he said, 'Our investment agreement supersedes the mining law.'[29] Ghana, its fellow gold producer Tanzania and copper-rich Zambia all ended up diluting their plans to increase royalties.

Even when African governments ignore the threats and blandishments of the World Bank and the resources industry and manage to secure a greater share of the revenues from their oil and minerals, there is little they can do to stop the torrent of money that flows out of their countries through tax fiddles made possible by the globalization of finance. Such illicit outflows are not limited to the oil and mining industries, but those industries are particularly well suited to squirrelling money out of poor countries, where they often account for the bulk of exports. Two-thirds of trade happens within multinational corporations. To a large extent those companies decide where to pay taxes on which portions of their earnings. That leaves ample scope to avoid paying taxes anywhere or to pay taxes at a rate far below what purely domestic companies pay.

Imagine a multinational company making rubber chickens, called Fowl Play Incorporated. Fowl Play's headquarters and most of its customers are in the United States. A subsidiary, Fowl Play Cameroon, runs a rubber plantation in Cameroon. The rubber is shipped to a factory in China, owned by another subsidiary, Fowl Play China, where it is made into rubber chickens and packaged. The rubber chickens are shipped to Fowl Play's parent company in the United States, which sells them to mainly US customers.

Fowl Play could simply pay taxes in each location based on an honest assessment of the proportion of its income that accrues there. But it has a duty to its shareholders to maximize returns, and its executives want the bonuses that come from turning big profits, so its accountants are instructed to minimize the effective tax rate Fowl Play pays by booking more revenues in places with low tax rates and fewer revenues in places with high tax rates. If, for example, Fowl Play wanted to reduce its tax liability in Cameroon and the United States by shifting profits to China, where it has been granted a tax holiday to build its factory, it would undervalue the price at which the rubber is sold from the Cameroonian subsidiary to the Chinese one, then overvalue the price at which the Chinese subsidiary sells the finished rubber chickens to the parent company in the United States. All this happens within one company and bears scant relation to the actual costs involved. The result is that the group's overall effective tax rate is much lower than it would have been had it apportioned profits fairly. Many such tax manoeuvres are perfectly legal. When it is done ethically 'transfer pricing', as the technique in this example is known, uses the same prices when selling goods and services within one company as when selling between companies at market rates. But the ruses to fiddle transfer pricing are legion. A mining company might tweak the value of machinery it ships in from abroad, or an oil company might charge a subsidiary a fortune to use the parent's corporate logo.

Suppose Fowl Play gets even cannier. It creates another subsidiary, this time in the British Virgin Islands, one of the tax havens where the rate of corporation tax is zero. Fowl Play BVI extends a loan to the Cameroonian subsidiary at an astronomical interest rate. The Cameroonian subsidiary's profits are cancelled out by the interest payments on the loan, which accrue, untaxed, to Fowl Play BVI. And all the while Fowl Play and the rubber chicken industry's lobbyists can loudly warn Cameroon, China and the United States that, should they try to raise taxes or clamp down on fiddling, the company could move its business, and the attendant jobs, elsewhere. (The BVI company is only a piece of paper and doesn't employ anyone, but then there is no need to threaten the British Virgin Islands – its tax rate could not be lower.)

Numerous studies have concluded that, although such tax dodging is a problem, no one knows the scale of it, particularly in poor countries, where reliable data are scarce.[30] The Organisation for Economic Co-operation and Development, the club of the world's richest nations, acknowledged in 2013 that 'multinationals have been able to use and/or misapply' the rules that govern transfer pricing 'to separate income from the economic activities that produce that income and to shift it into low-tax environments'.[31] Noting that 'tax policy is at the core of countries' sovereignty', the OECD called for 'fundamental changes' to the ways in which multinationals are taxed.

If multinational companies were genuinely declaring profits where they were made, one might expect a broad correlation between the size of the profit and the size of the economy. In 2009 Jane G. Gravelle, an economics specialist working for the research unit of the US Congress, made just such an analysis.[32] In the seven richest countries after the United States, American-controlled companies' pretax profits were, on average, equivalent to 0.6 per cent of the gross domestic product of the countries where the profits were declared. That was Gravelle's benchmark for her experiment. A higher ratio would suggest that companies were booking disproportionate amounts of profit in countries relative to the business they actually did there.

Gravelle then took ten of the larger countries considered to be tax havens. The profit-to-GDP percentage jumped: to 2.8 per cent in Hong Kong, 3.5 per cent in Switzerland, 7.6 per cent in Ireland, and 18.2 per cent in Luxembourg. That suggested that multinationals were artificially switching revenues into low-tax countries, depriving the governments of the countries where the companies had their mines or banks or factories of the tax revenues to which they were entitled.

Finally, Gravelle looked at the tiny islands that form the heart of the offshore world. In the Channel Island of Jersey, the profit-to-GDP ratio reached 35.3 per cent. In three British Crown dependencies – the British Virgin Islands and the Cayman Islands in the Caribbean and Bermuda in the North Atlantic – as well as the Marshall Islands, an outpost in the Pacific partly controlled by the United States, the figure exceeded 100 per cent. Bermuda topped the chart with a profit-to-GDP ratio of 647.7 per cent. At this point the notion that multinationals that use tax havens apportion profits fairly becomes absurd: the total profits declared by American companies were several times the size of each tax haven's entire economy.

The United States alone is losing as much as $60 billion a year to tax dodges based on income shifting, according to estimates Gravelle cited – and the United States probably has the most advanced system to enforce payment and hunt down tax evaders. In a time of austerity multinationals that pay minute tax bills compared with their earnings have faced popular outrage, among them Starbucks and Amazon in the UK (not to mention Bono, a vocal antipoverty campaigner whose band, U2, switched part of its business affairs from Ireland to the Netherlands to reduce its tax exposure in 2006). When it comes to poor countries, estimated losses represent far greater shares of governments' overall tax take. Global Financial Integrity, a Washington-based pressure group that has helped propel multinational tax avoidance into the political debate, estimates that illicit outflows from the developing world amounted to $947 billion in 2011 and $5.9 trillion over the preceding decade. Four in every five dollars of those flows were due to trade mispricing, when companies manipulate the prices at which they sell goods and services, either between their own subsidiaries or in transactions with other companies; the rest was the proceeds of corruption, theft and money laundering. In Africa the outflows amounted to 5.7 per cent of GDP, the highest proportion of any region and growing at a rate of 20 per cent a year. African losses from trade mispricing alone are roughly equivalent to the continent's income from aid.[33]

The resources industries are ripe for trade mispricing – it serves as the camouflaged conduit of the looting machine. The Norwegian arm of the Publish What You Pay transparency campaign combed the published 2010 accounts of ten of the biggest oil and mining companies, including Exxon Mobil, Shell, Glencore and Rio Tinto, which together made $145 billion in profits on $1.8 trillion in revenues that year.[34] Between them the ten companies had 6,038 subsidiaries, a third of which were registered in so-called secrecy jurisdictions, tax havens where all but the most basic company information can be concealed and that are thought to be crucial conduits for profit shifting. With their weak, corrupted institutions, African resource states are sitting ducks for such fiddling. By another estimate, the poor country that suffered the heaviest illicit outflows through transfer mispricing in the three years starting from 2005 was Nigeria. Ghana came sixth, and Chad ninth.[35]

Next to all of that, the IFC's support for Newmont's unpublished deal to keep its royalty payments low might seem insignificant. But it is all part of the same machinery of legitimized plunder. The international financial system, from the institutions charged with helping poor countries escape destitution to the vast architecture of offshore secrecy, is stacked against African states getting a fair cut from their natural resources.

Many highly intelligent people of good faith and sound judgment work for the World Bank, its assorted arms, and the International Monetary Fund. Often they work in difficult conditions, driven by a desire to further the greater good. I have met dozens of them in African capitals and found many to be astute critics of the ruination the resource industries cause. But when it comes to the institutions' relationship with multinational oil and mining companies, something has gone awry. Perhaps institutions whose mandate is to alter the course of the global economy simply cannot avoid coming to an accommodation with what is, alongside banking, its most powerful industry. Perhaps some of their officials are seduced by the sheer wealth and glamour of oil and mining, where chief executives are paid tens of millions of dollars a year, dine with presidents, and inhabit a world of vintage wine, corporate jets and dick-swinging machismo. Whatever their motivations, the Bank and the Fund have felt compelled to embrace the oil and mining industries and have, through bodies like the IFC, foisted resource ventures of dubious merit on African countries again and again.

For decades the Bank and the Fund enjoyed unchallenged positions as the arbiters of orthodox economic policy in Africa. They could ram home their arguments by controlling the flow of loans. Sometimes they were right, sometimes they were catastrophically wrong, but their sway scarcely wavered. In recent years, however, that influence has been punctured by the rise of China, a power that can match the old institutions in financial firepower but is prepared to ask far fewer questions in exchange for influence over the management of African governments' oil and mineral resources.

Not long after Paul Wolfowitz took charge at the World Bank in June 2005, he made it clear that he wanted to fight back against China's thrust into Africa. It was becoming evident that China's easy credit was proving a seductive alternative for African governments to the conditions the Bank and the IMF demanded. In the decade leading up to 2010, lending to Africa by China Exim bank, the state-owned bank through which China funnels most of its loans to the continent, reached $67 billion, $12 billion more than the World Bank's tally over the same period.[36] Wolfowitz, formerly a hawkish member of the US defence establishment and a leading advocate of the 2003 invasion of Iraq, spotted the trend early. In an interview in 2006, although accepting that past Western lending to Africa, especially to the Congolese kleptocracy of Mobutu Sese Seko, had been ruinous, the World Bank's new boss warned that China risked repeating the madness of saddling African states with debt while their rulers wallowed in luxury. 'Let's be honest, what the US did with Mobutu . . . was really terrible,' Wolfowitz said. 'It was a scandal actually. Just because the US did it . . . isn't the reason that China has to do it all over again, and I hope they won't, but hope isn't good enough.'[37] Chinese banks, Wolfowitz argued, disregarded the Equator Principles, the voluntary code of conduct, drafted under the IFC's lead, governing social and environmental considerations for investments. He foresaw 'pretty frank and direct discussion with the Chinese'.

This was a little rich coming from the head of an institution whose role in oil and mining, in Africa and elsewhere, had been condemned by Emil Salim in its own review three years earlier. But Wolfowitz's point was valid. Access to easy Chinese loans might have looked like a chance for African governments to reassert sovereignty after decades of hectoring by the Bank, the IMF and Western donors, but like a credit card issued with no credit check, it also removed a source of pressure for sensible economic management.

James Wolfensohn, Wolfowitz's predecessor as World Bank president, in an interview reflecting on his tenure, captured the link between the surge in competition between China and the West for Africa's oil and minerals and the reduction in the World Bank's ability to press for reform. 'What we're seeing now is a rush for natural resources in Africa,' Wolfensohn said in 2011.[38] 'I think there's a lot less concern about the internal development of the countries than would be thought of by, say, the African Development Bank or the World Bank. But you do have ready money going into too many of these countries. And the issue of corruption and the issue of trying to get good governance is, I think, under less pressure now in a number of these countries than it was when I was around. It's going to be a long road.'

It was not just the World Bank that found its influence in Africa's resource states diminished. The IMF, its sister institution charged with maintaining the stability of the world financial system, already had a bad reputation in Africa, with reformers and kleptocrats alike, for imposing the strictures of the Washington Consensus, under which African states had become test tubes for the unfettered free-market philosophy that would also beget the subprime crisis and subsequent near-collapse of the Western banking system. Emil Salim's review of the World Bank's record in the oil and mining industries reported that, in the cases it had studied, 'the IMF's approach to the extractive sectors was mainly one that promoted aggressive privatization of significant mining and hydrocarbon assets for short-term financing of the [government's budget] deficit. This did nothing to ensure the creation of competition, efficiency gains, development of a domestic private sector, or environmentally and socially sound development strategies for the extractive sectors.'

The backlash to the stringent conditions it imposed under its structural adjustment programmes has chastened the IMF, but there were also reasons to be concerned about its increasing readiness to lend money to African governments with fewer stipulations. Using loans as leverage is easily caricatured as a neocolonial bludgeoning of sovereign African states, but it has its uses. In 2012 the IMF suspended a $500 million lending programme to Congo to put pressure on Joseph Kabila's government to disclose the details of one of its murky copper deals with Dan Gertler.[39] Elsewhere, however, the IMF has been far more pliant in its dealings with corrupt governments of African resource states that can play off traditional lenders against deep-pocketed Beijing.

In the aftermath of Angola's civil war the refusal of the IMF and Western donors to lend while the government declined to explain where its money was going helped push the country into the arms of the Chinese. By 2007, according to Angola's finance ministry, the country had secured at least $4 billion in credit lines from China's state-owned Exim Bank, plus another $2.9 billion arranged by Sam Pa's Queensway Group through China International Fund.[40] As the emerging economic powerhouses of Asia and Latin America guzzled commodities, the price of a barrel of oil, on which Angola's government depends for three-quarters of its income, had risen from $25 at the start of the decade to $140 by the middle of 2008, pouring money into Sonangol and burnishing the Futungo's sense of indestructibility. But when, in September of that year, Lehman Brothers came crashing down, sending tremors through the global economy, demand for oil fell dramatically. By December 2008 a barrel of crude was selling for $35. Petro-states that had grown accustomed to the high life suddenly found themselves unable to fund their own budgets. Angola was a case in point. For the IMF it was a chance to get a foot back in the door.

José Eduardo dos Santos's government needed money fast. In July 2009 it approached the IMF for emergency funding and said it was prepared to clean up its act to get it.[41] Emissaries from the IMF flew to Luanda for talks. Global Witness, which had spent years documenting misrule by Angola's oil- and diamond-funded elite, warned that the IMF would be 'condoning corruption' if it failed to impose sufficiently stringent conditions for the proper management of Angola's opaque state finances before extending a loan.[42]

In November 2009 the IMF announced that it would lend Angola $1.4 billion to tide it over for two years. It declared that the deal included a 'focused reform agenda'.[43] The government, the IMF said, had agreed to 'better oversight of major state-owned enterprises, especially Sonangol, the state-owned oil company', including ending its 'quasi-fiscal operations', a wonkish term for Sonangol behaving like a state in its own right, taking out loans and spending money with little oversight. 'The authorities' intention to enhance fiscal transparency, especially in the oil sector, is welcome,' Takatoshi Kato, the IMF's acting chairman, said when the loan deal was announced.[44]

What transpired was superficial reform at best. For every loan it makes to a government, the IMF conducts periodic reviews to see how the national finances are being managed and whether its conditions are being met. As they were poring over Angola's accounts, the IMF's economists noticed a discrepancy in the numbers. They totalled up all the revenue Angola should have received – mostly from oil sales – between 2007 and 2010 and compared the figure with how much had actually arrived at the treasury. The gap between the former and the latter was enough to make even seasoned IMF officials' jaws drop: $32 billion.[45] Even once much of the missing money had been traced to Sonangol's web of financial dealings, $4.2 billion was still completely unaccounted for. Angola's government had not been strapped for cash merely because of the turmoil in the global economy; the Futungo's shadow state had looted its treasury. But the IMF continued to hand over its loan, bit by bit, and to repeat assurances it received from the government that reforms were at hand. Sonangol did start disclosing more information about its dealings, even publishing audited accounts, and dos Santos agreed to shift much of Sonangol's spending on to the government's books, although he exempted oil-backed loans – precisely the vehicles used by Chinese state-owned banks and the Queensway Group, whose infrastructure projects the Angolan government had bailed out to the tune of $3.5 billion in 2007. Several other conditions of the IMF loan remained unfulfilled.

Ricardo Soares de Oliveira, the Angola expert at Oxford University who has spent years probing the Futungo, was scathing of the IMF's leniency: 'It is not just the IMF that has gone soft. Many western states supposedly worried about China's dealings were among the first to backtrack on reform. . . . [W]hile Angola's oil economy has never been more transparent, the impact of this on the governance of the country is trivial and even strengthens the regime.'[46] The cryptocracy evolved, but it kept its most secretive recesses – such as China Sonangol, the oil partnership with the Queensway Group – out of sight behind offshore companies and undisclosed contracts. The Futungo was able to enjoy the legitimacy conferred by the IMF's engagement, selectively implement the reforms that made commercial sense, and twist others to entrench its authority.

In 2012, as stipulated in the terms of its loan from the IMF, Angola set up a sovereign wealth fund, a commonly used vehicle for countries that make lots of cash from exports to invest some of it at home and abroad. It was a sensible idea in an economy so skewed by oil. Norway's sovereign wealth fund is arguably the main reason it has been able to dodge the resource curse – by keeping most of its oil revenues well away from the budget, to be invested for posterity, rather than inflicting Dutch Disease on the economy and allowing the political elite of the day to reward its cronies with fast cash. Angola's sovereign fund was given $5 billion of oil revenues to invest.[47] The choice of leadership for the fund, however, did little to allay fears that it would simply serve as another vehicle for the Futungo – the new fund was to be chaired by José Filomeno dos Santos, the president's son. By early 2011 the oil price was back above $100 a barrel. Even after the full loan had been issued, in 2013 the IMF's inspectors were still reporting that the government's endeavours to account for the missing billions were 'continuing'.[48] As Barnaby Pace, an oil specialist at Global Witness, put it, 'The Angolan government effectively treated the IMF as their overdraft.'[49]

Little of the detail of such elaborate financial manoeuvres reaches the slums of Luanda, the hamlets of central Ghana or the scarred mining towns of the Congolese copperbelt. But when their inhabitants detect, as Kofi Gyakah did beside a poisoned pond, a nagging sense of powerlessness, it is this manoeuvring they are sensing. Like the rumbles of a mine out of sight beyond the foliage, there is an alignment of political elites and transnational corporate networks subverting public institutions to dredge power and wealth upward into their own grasp, along with the oil and minerals they take from beneath African soil to fuel the richer parts of the world. The means are complex, sometimes even well intentioned, but the result is the accumulation of Africa's natural wealth by the few. For the rest, little remains but dead dogs and promises.

» 8 «

God Has Nothing
to Do with It

WHEN THE WARLORDS of Nigeria's oil province assembled for a conclave in late 2005 and resolved to shake the world with a campaign of kidnapping and sabotage, they entrusted the task of launching the onslaught to one of their most feared confreres. Farah Dagogo was short and slight, but he had established a reputation for daring and ruthlessness. Born in the east of the Niger Delta, where west Africa's mighty waterway divides into countless creeks and empties into the Gulf of Guinea, he grew up watching oil desolate his homeland. The lush mangroves of the world's third-largest wetland, an area the size of Ireland, groan with spilt crude. If you reach out from one of the canoes that ply the creeks and run your hand through the water, chances are you'll see the telltale rainbow refractions of petroleum. Pillars of flaming gas have raged day and night for fifty years, a technique of oil extraction known as 'flaring' that richer countries banned long ago.

The Niger Delta, as Dagogo and every last one of his 30 million fellow Deltans know, yields the oil that brings in 70 per cent of the Nigerian government's income and almost all the foreign currency that the country needs to pay for imports. Dictators did not hesitate to unleash the military if the Delta grew too restive. For men of Dagogo's generation the path of life led toward violence.

Dagogo was bright and received a basic education. 'He could be any mother's son,' Annkio Briggs, a veteran Niger Delta activist who has known him for years, told me.[1] 'He's a nice-looking young man. They were all young men growing up and who were not able to finish secondary school because there was nothing in the communities. Poverty drove them out, and they had no direction.'

Dagogo gravitated toward the man, formidable both in bulk and bombast, who was whipping up the Delta's resentment into a storm. Mujahid Asari-Dokubo was the figurehead of the armed struggle that broke out in the Niger Delta in the years after the end of military rule in 1999. He gave voice to the bruised pride of the Ijaw, the main ethnic group in the Delta and the fourth-biggest in the land, who had been excluded from the highest reaches of Nigerian power since independence as the Hausa of the North, the Igbo of the East and the Yoruba of the Southwest took turns at the trough. Baptized into Christianity like most Deltans, Asari converted to Islam, taking the name Mujahid, or holy warrior, and began to taunt the authorities. More militant than some of his fellow Ijaw agitators, he formed a private army, the Niger Delta People's Volunteer Force, and declared a guerrilla war against the Nigerian state and foreign oil companies, demanding that the people who lived there retain a greater share of the tens of billions of dollars that the Delta's oil fetches every year.

Asari drew in members of armed gangs, such as the KKK and the Greenlanders, which had evolved from university confraternities and bought weapons with the proceeds of the trade in heroin, cocaine and marijuana.[2] Commanders of the militias that blended crime with the cause of liberation joined him too, among them Farah Dagogo, who placed his own burgeoning paramilitary organization under Asari's banner. Dagogo made himself indispensable, acting as a personal aide to the boss, organizing logistics and keeping arms caches stocked. As Asari's forces battled rivals for territory in the eastern Delta, oil companies panicked and retreated. Crude output dropped. When the rattled government arrested Asari in 2004 and charged him with treason, Dagogo supplanted him as leader.

Along with military men and politicians, Farah Dagogo and his fellow warlords were captains of the trade in stolen crude oil known as 'bunkering'. Usually working by night, with the dank air and lapping waters of the creeks making their hands slippery as they smashed open the pipelines that snake through the Delta like black veins, bunkering gangs used two techniques: siphoning oil from a functioning pipeline ('hot-tapping') or blowing up the pipe and carting off the crude that spills out ('cold-tapping'). The trade was highly lucrative, even if its practitioners risked incineration. The UN estimated that, with a turnover of $2 billion a year, Nigeria's illicit oil rackets matched the west African cocaine trade in value.[3] Once the cargoes that were misappropriated at export terminals were added to the crude siphoned directly from pipelines, bunkering accounted for one hundred thousand barrels of crude a day, equivalent to one in every twenty barrels of Nigeria's oil production or the entire oil output of Chad. Army and navy officers were complicit in the bunkering networks, and an authoritative investigation into the illicit oil trade pointed to 'high-level civilian involvement'.[4]

There was also money to be made from ballot stuffing and intimidating voters during elections 'characterised by monumental fraud'.[5] In the gangs the Delta's politicians had a ready-made weapon to secure victory. Between polls 'the boys', as they are known, were left to their own devices.

Farah Dagogo emerged as one of the dons of the eastern Delta. Around the end of 2005 the overlord of the western Delta, Government Ekpumopolo, better known as Tompolo, called for a gathering. Tompolo had built a sophisticated enterprise funded by extortion and oil theft. To a greater extent than his fellow warlords, he was also more like a traditional Nigerian chief, a benefactor to the civilians in his territory, and a skipper to the three thousand armed men under his command. He combined guerrilla warfare with a social safety net. He had an ideology that drew on the Delta's rich heritage of intellectual agitation for self-determination. Tompolo could claim spiritual authority too, as a follower of Egbesu, war god of the Ijaw. Under his aegis the commanders of the Delta's militias agreed to coordinate their forces and merge their oil-theft operations. The Movement for the Emancipation of the Niger Delta – MEND – was born.

By the time MEND came together Dagogo was known as a reliable operator. He had demonstrated both his flair for spectacle and his ability to humiliate the authorities, such as when he staged a jailbreak in Port Harcourt, the Delta's oil city, to spring a crime lord called Soboma George from prison.[6] With another warlord, Boyloaf, he was nominated to undertake a mission that would announce MEND's formation. On 11 January 2006, Dagogo and Boyloaf kidnapped four foreign oil workers in a raid on a Shell platform in the shallow coastal waters of the Delta.[7] The abduction, coupled with a blast that knocked out one of the Delta's main pipelines, marked the start of Nigeria's oil war.

There had been kidnappings before. There had been pipeline attacks and raids by canoe-born gunmen. Nor were the grand threats to hold the federal government ransom by cutting oil production new. What changed was the scale of the onslaught. At the peak of its campaign MEND curtailed Nigeria's oil production by 40 per cent, equivalent to cutting off the entire oil production of the UK.

From the outset there were indications that MEND's leadership was, like Laurent Nkunda's coltan-funded militia in eastern Congo, at least as devoted to self-enrichment as to the political causes it espoused. There was little to indicate that Farah Dagogo was concerned with anything other than lucre. He set up his base close to civilian settlements in the creeks of the eastern Delta, so as to better ward off military attacks. When the kidnap squad arrived back at MEND headquarters it took six days to agree on the demands they should make. Alongside the release of the incarcerated Asari and a state governor with close ties to the gangs, MEND called for total local control of oil revenues and a payment of $1.5 billion from Shell as the price of the hostages' liberty. None of the demands was met, but the four were freed unharmed after nineteen days, following a ransom payment from the local authorities.[8]

But MEND succeeded in generating fear, a commodity as valuable as the crude itself. Claims of responsibility and threats of new attacks e-mailed out to journalists sent shivers through oil markets (though their author, Jomo Gbomo, was nothing more than a Yahoo! account used by a band of eloquent Deltans on whose literary flair MEND's fighters drew to magnify the impact of their raids). As well as Shell, the two biggest American oil companies, Exxon Mobil and Chevron, came under fire, as did other European groups operating in the Delta. Even the giant offshore fields that the oil majors had constructed in the Nigerian waters of the Gulf of Guinea were not safe. In June 2008 MEND gunmen in speedboats struck Bonga, Shell's flagship oil field 120 kilometres out to sea, temporarily crippling the $3.6 billion facility and knocking out a tenth of Nigeria's crude output.

MEND was always a fractious coalition of rebel groups and criminal syndicates. The divisions that emerged over how to apportion the first ransom payment only widened, and MEND became a franchise for plunder under the banner of resistance, with no unified leadership. But it nonetheless represented an informal army of as many as sixty thousand men, and its attacks received worldwide attention because of what they did to the price of oil. It so happened that the unrest in the Delta broke out just as oil prices were approaching record levels, as the fast-growing economies of China and India acquired a prodigious thirst for petroleum, and lost Nigerian production drove the price of a barrel higher still.

In October 2009 Farah Dagogo cashed in some of his chips. Following other senior commanders from MEND, he emerged from the creeks to accept an offer of amnesty that Umaru Yar'Adua, Nigeria's president, had extended in desperation after a surge of attacks on oil-industry installations. 'In line with conditions attached to this amnesty offer, we are surrendering all weapons under our direct control,' Farah said in a grandiose statement.[9] 'It is my sincere desire that the government immediately embarks on dialogue to forestall a resurgence of violence in the Niger Delta.'

The rhetoric was of a peace bargain to settle decades of resentment. In reality the whole affair was little more than a way to slug cash into the Delta to buy a lull in hostilities. All the principal warlords took the amnesty. Some decamped to begin luxurious semi-retirement in Abuja, the capital, or in the gaudy splendour of uptown Lagos, their pockets lined by the government and their oil-theft empires intact and even expanding. They simply ditched their political demands from the years of 'freedom fighting'.

The Delta is the scene of the most direct struggle for a share of Nigeria's oil. But the same struggle has consumed the entire Nigerian political system. As in Africa's other resource states, there is a finite pot of oil – or gold, or copper, or diamonds – so it is a zero-sum game: for me to win, you must lose.

Umaru Yar'Adua lured the warlords from the creeks with the classic bargain of the rentier state: pledge yourself to the status quo, and we shall cut you in on the resource money. It is the unspoken pact that governs Nigeria – and that catalyses the oil of the Delta into the violence that stalks the nation.

In Kano, northern Nigeria's ancient trading city that is the gateway to the expanses leading up to the Sahara, I met a man who was present at the country's birth. Yusuf Maitama Sule served as a young minister in Nigeria's first government. Over the following half-century he had seen how resource states produce predatory governments, both at home and as the chair of the UN's committee against apartheid. By January 2010, when I sought him out, he had long since retired to his residence in Kano, its stone walls cool against the searing heat of the arid North, but a humble dwelling by the standards of his fellow politicians. Now eighty, age had taken his sight but not the skill for oratory that had earned him his nickname, the Gramophone.

The problem, Sule declared, was that Nigeria's political leaders had departed from the golden rule that Ahmadu Bello, the Sardauna of Sokoto and elder statesman of the North at independence, had imparted to his protégés, Sule among them: 'Sardauna used to tell us that you can't be running and scratching your buttocks at the same time. You have to do one or the other. You can't be in government and do business at the same time. He said, "Any of my ministers that is interested in business should resign."'

Perhaps Sule's hankering for the mores of the first republic was tinted with the need of an old man to feel he had done some good. Historians would note that it was the northern elders who transplanted the feudal structures of the old caliphates onto the new country they created, helping to perpetuate the colonial pattern of control by a narrow elite and engendering a political system that was ripe for hijacking by home-grown plunderers. Yet it is hard to argue with the Gramophone's contention that the trajectory from those first years of nationhood has been downward.

'Today, our main problem is oil,' Sule went on. The seven-year rule of Ibrahim Babangida, the northern general who seized power in a 1985 coup that deposed the previous northern general, marked the inception of the class of oligarchs and officials who used public office to award themselves stakes in the oil business, Sule explained. 'It was during Babangida's regime that for the first time private individuals started getting oil blocks, and they made a lot of money. Today, unfortunately, all of us have interest in one thing – materialism. Everybody wants to make money. The housewife wants to make money. Her husband wants to make money. The ruler wants to make money. The traditional ruler who used to command a lot of respect because he had no interest in anything but his rulership, today he is interested in making money. The politician, he's not thinking of the national interest but his own personal interest, making money. All of us, unfortunately, have interest in one thing, and that is why we are having problems. That is why there is chaos in politics.'

Corruption is bad enough. But something else had happened, something darker still. 'Having tasted power, they wanted to go on with it,' Sule said of the class of petro-politicians that emerged. To do that, they 'started appealing to the tribal or religious sentiments of their people'.

In resource states ethnicity takes a terrible form. As resource rents beget a ruling class that is not accountable to the people, power is maintained through patronage. Public service is largely abandoned. With no record of service to point to, politics becomes a game of mobilizing one's ethnic brethren. *For us to win, they have to lose*. The social contract is replaced with a compact of violence.

Some eighteen thousand Nigerians died in ethnic, religious and political violence between the return of democracy in 1999 and 2012 (a tally that does not include the additional thousands killed by Boko Haram and the part-inept, part-vindictive army response to the insurgency).[10] At its heart this violence is the result of Nigeria's poisonous petro-politics, often dressed up as religious zealotry or ethnic chauvinism. In these direct acts of violence alone – not counting all of the children slipping away in dilapidated hospitals, the drivers who meet their end on roads where maintenance contracts have been embezzled, and the victims of a police force that is more predator than protector – the Nigerian looting machine claims a life every six hours. The common thread between the Niger Delta's warring militias, the gangs that sack northern villages, and the armed vote-riggers who rampage nationwide at election time on behalf of their masters at every level of Nigeria's federal government is the life-and-death pursuit of oil money.

I had been sitting with Maitama Sule for many hours when he grew tired and his aides shepherded him away. That evening in Kano my phone rang. Something terrible had happened in Jos.

From the commotion emanating from one of the burned-out dwellings I sensed that even the members of a burial detail accustomed to macabre sights had been rattled by their latest discovery. Dressed in white robes, they were systematically extracting the corpses from the rubble. One of them emerged from the blackened husk of a hut carrying the first receptacle that had come to hand, a small cardboard box that had once contained spaghetti branded with 'a promise of quality'. The tiny form within was on its side, its arms tucked under its chin, as though sleeping. It was so charred that it could have passed for a lump of charcoal. From the baby's size, I guessed its life had ended before its first birthday.

The burial detail moved through the village, which is known as Kuru Karama. Almost every house and hut had been burned, the squat mosque too. Debris shifted underfoot. The flames had peeled first the clothes, then the skin from the women whose bodies had been dumped into wells, there to distend with water for the three days that had passed since their death. An old man, known as the village simpleton, had had his neck broken before his killers shoved him into a hole. His head was twisted at a grotesque angle; his lifeless eyes looked up and out. The other bodies were like the baby's: scorched to the point that they might never have been flesh.

The killers had come on a Tuesday morning in January 2010, descending out of the hills that ring the village. They had guns, blades and machetes. Many of the villagers who had tried to flee into the scrubby farmland were hacked down as they ran. Clothes, long since dry, fluttered uncollected on a washing line.

Under Islamic custom the dead must be promptly interred. By now it was Friday. The first burial detail had arrived from the main mosque in the nearby city of Jos the previous day, but the scale of the slaughter had been so great that another had had to come to complete the task. The undertakers were working quickly, looking warily up at the hills. Corpses are heavy. These ones made a dull thud of lifelessness as they joined their neighbours in a mass grave. By the time the sun slipped toward the horizon on the second day of burials, a hundred and fifty bodies had been consigned to the ground.[11]

Abdullahi Wase had left the village on business the day before the attack. He came back in time to watch his wife's body being heaved into the burial pit. His children were nowhere to be found. Around him other residents who had dared to return salvaged what they could, scampering to catch their chickens and goats and manhandle them into the trunks of waiting cars. Perhaps they would head to the primary schools in Jos, which had been turned into refugee camps over the past few days, joining the eighteen thousand people who had been driven from their homes. From there they would try to start rebuilding their lives. Until the next time.

I had arrived in Jos the previous day. On the road down from Kano into the Middle Belt that marks Nigeria's religious division we passed twenty roadblocks manned by soldiers and police deployed to stop the turmoil in Jos from spilling outward. Behind the scrap yards on the outskirts of the city, a lone man was praying. The workshops were deserted, so too the streets. Toward the centre of the city a family was cramming belongings and relatives into a hopelessly overloaded red Volkswagen as the early evening curfew, which the military had shoot-on-sight orders to enforce, drew near. A charred body lay within the estate they were fleeing, they said, but no one dared enter to retrieve it.

I made it to a hotel just before the curfew descended and called Mohammed Lawal Ishaq. Ishaq was a lawyer and a leader of Jos's Hausas. A majority across the North, the Hausa are regarded as outsiders or 'settlers' in Jos by the Berom and the other ethnic groups deemed 'indigenes' of the state. 'The so-called indigenes dominate government patronage,' Ishaq told me, as rifle fire echoed around the city. 'So the so-called settlers, they venture into business. Some of them happen to be very successful. That is a trigger. The presence of the settlers in large numbers is threatening the political power of the indigenes. The people who consider themselves the indigenes, they happen to be Christians. The "settlers" happen to be Muslims. The government is supposed to be for all. But the so-called settlers believe the government is behind what is happening today. Now it's every man for himself.'

There were conflicting accounts of how the trouble had started. The most reliable seemed to be that a Hausa man had been trying to repair the damage done to his house in a previous bout of destruction. There had been an altercation with some young Christian men. In such crucibles of hatred that is all it takes – the city burned. Ishaq said fifty bodies had been brought to the central mosque so far. I had heard that at least two hundred people had died, both Christians and Muslims. Goodluck Jonathan, tentatively in charge while Yar'Adua was lying in a Saudi Arabian hospital, had sent in the troops. The presence of the army, traditionally dominated by northerners, had calmed the Hausa population, who regarded the local security forces as loyal to the Berom, just as the Berom believed the military had arrived to avenge slain Muslims. Burial teams from the central mosque had begun to venture, under military escort, to the outlying Hausa areas.

Jos was once a boom town. The Second World War stoked demand for the tin that lay in rich seams beneath its rocky outcrops. The colonial authorities brought in labour, adding to the flow of migrants who had been arriving since the previous century. Hausas from the Islamic North settled among the Berom and other local tribes, many of whom had been converted to Christianity by colonial missionaries. When the going was good, harmony prevailed. Nigerians of a certain age and class wistfully recall eating strawberries in Jos in the 1970s, caressed by cool breezes. Future prime minister John Major did a stint in one of the city's banks before returning to Britain and entering politics. But the tin mines fell into decline, their stocks exhausted and their administration beset by corruption. Hausas, better educated than the local inhabitants and connected to trade networks stretching across the North, weathered the changes well. They had secured titles to land; they prospered. Among the Christians the relative success of the newer arrivals bred resentment.

The Berom and their ilk amount to mere specks in Nigeria's ethnic tapestry. However, under the federal constitution, designed in the wake of the Biafran War to ensure that opportunities for patronage were widely distributed, they were designated the 'indigenes' of Plateau State. That gives them first claim to every public office and, in turn, to the share of Nigeria's oil revenue that represents almost the entire income of state governments – it gives their leaders a stake in the looting machine. For more than two decades Hausas' attempts, often backed by the federal government, to secure local government positions have triggered what amount to street battles over oil rent. In September 2001 a thousand people died in seven days.

In 2007, eight years into civilian rule, the governorship of Plateau State became vacant. Joshua Dariye, the governor since 1999, had succumbed to the consequences of his own greed. He had been detained on money-laundering charges during a visit to the UK in 2004 but absconded, beginning what would become a tradition for Nigerian governors who enjoyed impunity at home but fell foul of the authorities in Britain, where much of their looted wealth ended up. Back in Nigeria, Dariye was suspended from office by Olusegun Obasanjo, then president, for failing to prevent – and even, it was suggested, instigating – the near-constant ethnic violence in his state. A vociferous Christian and member of a small indigene tribe, Dariye described Jos's Hausas as 'unruly tenants'. He clung to the governorship for a while until charges of embezzling $9 million of public funds eventually brought him down.[12] (The case became bogged down in Nigeria's tortuous legal system, and in 2011 Dariye won a senate seat.)

Dariye was a prime example of what is known in Nigeria as an 'ethnic entrepreneur', the kind of politician that Maitama Sule feared was taking over the country. His successor was less clownish and more politically astute but belonged to the same category. As a senior officer in the Nigerian air force, Jonah Jang had twice served as a military governor of two states near Plateau during army rule. Born in Du, at the heart of Berom country, Jang was a Christian, a theologian, and a Pentecostal pastor. His official hagiography describes him as a 'jolly good fellow'.[13] He left the military once the soldiers relinquished power, helping to form the People's Democratic Party. He lost the 1999 gubernatorial race to Dariye but clinched the post in the shambolic elections of 2007.

The Christians of Nigeria's Middle Belt have long feared subjugation by Islamic invaders from the North, real and imagined, and men like Jang portray themselves as their defenders. On Jang's watch the Hausa in Jos were not only excluded from representation in public office but also felt that their housing and the markets where they traded were under threat.[14] 'The governor has become an evangelist of the assertiveness of Berom hegemony,' a high-ranking Christian cleric told me.[15] 'He has become very paranoid.' A moderate Berom in Jos who had held high office in the state government saw Jang as the embodiment of what was becoming a campaign of ethnic cleansing: 'He's an extremist. He has very strong tribal views. Politicians . . . manipulate feelings. That's what people have come to call the Berom Agenda: capture power, capture the resources, the state and the patronage, mostly to the Berom. Now this has become: "The Hausa imperialists, they must be curtailed and controlled.'"[16] Jos's indigenes were prepared to kill in the name of their governor. On the walls of a burned-out house in a Hausa quarter of the city, where a scorched torso and two human limbs lay scattered among the debris, the killers had daubed, 'God bless Jang.'

I wanted to meet this man who epitomized both Jos's tragic spirit of violence and the politics of ethnic patronage through which the Nigerian petro-state is controlled. Once the nightly curfew was over I set off for the governor's offices, edging through the roadblocks. At the state government headquarters I had arranged to see Jang's spokesman, James Mannock. The prospects of an interview with the governor were slim, he told me.[17] Instead, Mannock introduced me to Toma Jang Davou.

Davou was large, aging and enraged. As the head of the local Berom parliamentary forum, Davou shared with the governor a birthplace and a political creed. Jos's suffering could be blamed squarely on the northerners, he said. 'They have made concerted attempts to destroy democratic structures and impose upon Nigerians an Islamic sultanate,' Davou thundered. 'In order to achieve this aim, they have connived with al-Qaeda.' There were, it was true, the first signs of links between northern Nigerian jihadists and al-Qaeda affiliates in the Sahara. But what outraged Davou most was the way the northern dictator Ibrahim Babangida had tinkered with Berom dominance of Plateau State's patronage system in 1991 by creating a new constituency with a natural Hausa majority. 'He made Jos North exclusively for them. That was what triggered the problem, up to today.'

In 2008, a year into his tenure as governor, Jonah Jang decided to hold long-postponed elections that would include a contest for the chairmanship of the Jos North local government. The governor had been warned that staging an election would be fraught with danger.[18] He proceeded nonetheless. The Hausa would probably have had a majority in a free vote, but this would not be a free vote. Such was the PDP's dominance that, as with most other elections for every office from the presidency downward, the decisive contest would be the party primary to choose a candidate. Jang refused demands to nominate a Hausa; instead, he shipped in a Berom from his hometown to be the PDP candidate for Jos North. When the election came, the Hausa voted for an opposition party. Discovering that the vote count had been moved to a Berom-dominated part of Jos

North, Hausas began to muster outside it, suspecting foul play.[19] Chanting PDP partisans descended too, and PDP officials were seen entering the building. Late into the night the police told the crowds to disperse. Stones flew through the air. The next day, as Muslim and Christian, Hausa and Berom set upon one another's women and children, it was announced that the PDP had won Jos North and every other local government chairmanship in the state.

Davou begrudgingly acknowledged that there had been violence on both sides in Jos, in 2008 and now. But he insisted that hundreds of Christian bodies would shortly be discovered, claims for which I did not find any proof, although the Red Cross confirmed that there were Christians among the dead, and Berom neighbourhoods were as fraught with fear as Hausa ones.

The next day I negotiated the checkpoints again, heading for Ignatius Kaigama's church. Jos felt, if not calm, at least numbed, like a fist fighter who realizes, as the adrenalin subsides, that he has gone too far and beaten his opponent to a pulp.

Kaigama managed a hearty, gap-toothed smile of greeting despite the misery engulfing the city whose Catholics he had watched over for a decade. I had listened to Hausa and Berom alike vowing that there would be no peace until their enemies yielded. Kaigama's was one of the few pacific voices, though it was seldom heard above the clamour for vengeance. His position as the chair of the Christian Association of Nigeria had not shielded him from being accused of treachery by other Christian leaders when he had sought to set up an interreligious committee for peace with his Muslim counterparts.

Ushering me into his rectory, he dismissed the rumour that the likes of Davou had circulated that the latest trouble had begun when a church was attacked. The church in question was untouched, Kaigama said. Such fictions were part of Jos's theatre of violence: facts are mutilated, history is maimed. In any case, as far as the archbishop was concerned, God had nothing to do with it.

'No crisis in Jos is religious,' Kaigama told me. 'You get some religious leaders on both sides who use their preaching to say, "They are the enemy." The real issue is the competition for who owns Jos. It's ethnic and political.' Like the Niger Delta, where the rhetoric of resistance serves as a cover for a vast criminal enterprise, the cloak of religion provides a disguise for the Middle Belt's looters who will use any means to secure their share of the resource rents. Their henchmen enjoy impunity. 'How many cases have we had?' the archbishop went on. 'Who has ever been punished? People have been arrested. After a month or two we hear nothing more of it. They just get released.'

Like the Futungo in Angola, Nigeria's rulers had abdicated the stewardship of the common good, Kaigama believed. 'I suffer the consequences of their failure,' he told me. 'Every day there is a queue here' – he gestured toward the door of the rectory. 'They are not coming for spiritual guidance. I end up being a social worker or giving money to people whose wife needs a blood transfusion. Nobody is talking about the HIV pandemic, hunger, youth unemployment.' By contrast, the struggle for patronage was all-consuming. 'There's no room for merit: it's survival of who knows who. It's about numeric superiority and territorial controls, then it's put in religious garb.'

I was about to leave when Kaigama's genial expression became grave. 'A culture of violence is developing,' the archbishop said. 'Young people who are growing up know nothing but hatred and violence. They don't see the sanctity of life. They are ready to kill. God is not such a weakling that we must kill for him. Any politician who has failed resorts to religion. If he doesn't win a contract or a position, he will say it is because I am a Christian or a Muslim. It is religion politicized and used as a weapon.'

A governor of one of Nigeria's thirty-six states is effectively president of his own fiefdom. He has immunity from prosecution and controls the state security budget. The chairman of each of the 774 local governments is answerable to the state governor. To win a presidential primary a candidate needs two-thirds of the states to back him. That backing is in the gift of the governors. The Governors' Forum is perhaps the most potent gathering in the land. Only about half of Nigeria's oil revenues are allocated to the federal government. A fifth goes to the local governments. The governors control the quarter of oil revenues that goes to the states.

Oil-producing states receive an additional 13 per cent share of Nigeria's oil income before it is divided between the tiers of government. The state houses of the Niger Delta are powerful pistons of the looting machine. When he agreed to meet me in late 2010, Timipre Sylva had succeeded Goodluck Jonathan as governor of Bayelsa, one of the Delta's three main states. I had hoped to interview him at Gloryland, the gubernatorial palace set well apart from the shacks that house his constituents. Instead, I was summoned to the penthouse suite of a five-star hotel in Lagos, where Sylva was staying with his entourage during a visit to the commercial capital.

A tall and intelligent man, Sylva was under pressure. Politics in the Niger Delta is unremittingly volatile. Gunmen drift between the militias of MEND, crime gangs and squads of political thugs that freelance for competing aspirants to power. As Sylva's rivals sought to force him from office, loyalists were exchanging tit-for-tat attacks with his enemies. Relations with Jonathan, recently elevated to the presidential palace by Yar'Adua's death, had soured. Little wonder, I suggested, that others coveted his job: his immediate predecessor had found himself president and the one before had siphoned off so much cash that he, like Joshua Dariye and James Ibori, the former governors of Plateau and Delta States, had snapped up enough assets abroad to earn the attention of the British police.

Sylva accepted that there had been widespread corruption among the governors. But he was, he pleaded, just a cog in a patronage system not of his making. 'If a chief walks into my office, he expects me to take care of his problems because that is what the military used to do,' Sylva said. 'That's what he's used to. If I don't, I've got a very big political enemy.'

So you have to 'settle' them, I suggested, using the Nigerian term for the dispensing of cash.

'Yes. And you will read that as corruption. But me, I probably will read that as political survival, because I have to survive before I become incorruptible.'

'And you use public funds to do that?' I asked.

'What does he expect me to do? I don't have that kind of money; the kind of money he's expecting. Even if I have it privately, I won't do that with it. And he's coming to me because I'm governor. If, for example, the big chief comes, and he has to go for a medical check, it shouldn't be my problem. But it is. If a very big traditional ruler dies somewhere, and they want to do an elaborate burial ceremony, they come to me. I have to do it.'

Me, I probably will read that as political survival. To justify corruption, Sylva reached for the same word – 'survival' – that Mahmoud Thiam had chosen when he explained why pariah states are willing to deal with the likes of Sam Pa and the Queensway Group. Said Djinnit, the UN's man in west Africa, called the competition to control political power in the resource states 'a struggle for survival at the highest level'. Paul Collier talks about the law of 'the survival of the fattest' in rentier states. Plenty of political careers in Nigeria and Angola, Zimbabwe and Guinea have ended in untimely death. The gulf between the captains of the looting machine and the masses is vast in material terms, but it is just that – a gulf. Fall off the looting machine, and you are precipitously back in the world of Kuru Karama, wondering when your house will burn.

Keen to shift our conversation away from his own diversions of public money, the governor pointed out that Nigeria's looters have had willing overseas accomplices: 'Of course, most of the time corruption is supported by foreigners. They come here with the perception that everything goes here. They just do all kinds of things, and that's how they actually corrupted our people.'

Corruption does not start or end at the borders of Nigeria or Angola or Equatorial Guinea. Its proponents include some of the world's biggest companies, among them the blue-chip multinationals in which, if you live in the West and have a pension, your money is almost certainly invested.

In recent years, as US officials energetically enforced the Foreign Corrupt Practices Act, settlement agreements published by the Department of Justice have exposed details of foreign companies' participation in Nigeria's looting machine. Willbros, listed in New York, made 'commitments' to Nigerian officials and politicians running into millions of dollars through the mid-2000s to secure contracts to build natural gas pipelines through the Niger Delta.[20] Shell admitted paying bribes worth $2 million to Nigerian customs officials between 2004 and 2006. One instalment of a $5 million bribe paid by Kellogg, Brown & Root (KBR) was so bulky when converted into naira that it had to be loaded onto vehicles for delivery. As part of a slush fund worth some $180 million deployed over ten years to 2004, the kickbacks helped to win KBR contracts to build one of Nigeria's biggest oil facilities, the $6 billion liquefied natural gas plant at Bonny Island, on the lip of the Niger Delta. At the time KBR was a subsidiary of the American engineering giant Halliburton, whose chief executive, Dick Cheney, departed in 2000 to be George W. Bush's vice president.

Bribe by bribe, these companies and others help to make Nigeria's public servants instruments of illicit private gain. And these are merely the cases in which the foreign perpetrators of corruption have been caught. Nigeria has the distinction of being the African nation most frequently involved in international bribery schemes exposed by anti-corruption prosecutors, behind only Iraq and China worldwide.[21] Other transactions are structured in an effort to enrich officials without crossing the threshold of illegality. In 2011 Shell and the Italian oil company Eni paid $1.3 billion to the Nigerian government for the rights to a choice offshore oil prospect. The government promptly transferred $1.1 billion to an offshore company called Malabu. One substantial shareholder in Malabu was, as a UK High Court judge found in 2013, a man called Dan Etete.[22] Etete, a convicted money-launderer, awarded his own company the rights to the prospect while serving as oil minister under the military dictator Sani Abacha. The deal was described by a fixer involved in the deal as a 'safe sex transaction' in which the government served as a 'condom' protecting Etete and the oil companies.[23] In September 2014 Italian prosecutors opened an investigation into Eni's role in the OPL 245 deal. British police have also commenced an investigation into allegations of money laundering connected to the deal. Eni and Shell, which has not been placed under investigation, denied they had done anything wrong. Both said they had legitimately paid the government for the oil rights and had made no payment to Malabu.[24]

Another oil block adjacent to the one for which Shell and Eni paid handsomely is designated as Oil Prospecting Licence 256 (OPL 256), a potentially prodigious 2,500-square-kilometre concession. The licence was previously held by Devon Energy, an American company that decided to sell off its African interests in 2007. There are conflicting accounts of what happened next to OPL 256, but it ultimately ended up in the hands of Sam Pa's Queensway Group.

A spokesman for Devon Energy told me it sold its rights to OPL 256 in late 2009 to a Nigerian company called Fusion Grid Limited.[25] I had never heard of Fusion Grid and neither had knowledgeable contacts of mine in the oil industry. When I got hold of its registered owner, a Lagos lawyer called Koye Edu, he told me that Fusion Grid was nothing more than a shell company and that it had never held the rights to OPL 256.[26] They had been returned to the government when Devon pulled out, Edu said. A spokesman for Statoil, the Norwegian oil company that had held a minority interest in the block alongside Devon, told me the rights had been handed back to the state in 2008.[27]

By mid-2009 the oil industry press was reporting that China Sonangol, the Queensway Group's partnership with Angola's state oil company, had secretly acquired OPL 256.[28] Nigeria's rulers have long awarded oil rights at their discretion. Even when open auctions are held, blocks have been awarded to obscure companies whose hidden owners include powerful members of the political elite and the security forces, who subsequently flip them on to foreign oil companies at a profit that might otherwise have accrued to the Nigerian people.[29] There was no open tender for OPL 256. When I asked about the block some Nigerian officials and lawmakers told me the state still held the rights. But three well-connected contacts I spoke to in 2013 – a serving senior official, a former senior official and an industry insider – told me that China Sonangol was the proprietor.[30]

A former presidential aide who served under both Umaru Yar'Adua, president when China Sonangol appears to have secured the licence, and under Goodluck Jonathan agreed to speak to me in 2013. Although he was usually candid when explaining the oil industry, he became nervous when I asked him about OPL 256. 'I would not like to talk about the owner,' the former aide said, asking me not to print his name. 'They went through a lot of controversy in acquiring it.'[31] I asked whether the owner was China Sonangol. 'You might not be wrong, but I can't confirm if China Sonangol is the owner. As far back as Yar'Adua's time there was a lot of controversy on that block.' The former aide knew the oil industry well, and I asked him what he thought of China Sonangol. 'There are many people, almost cannibals of the industry, who just buy their way into these things, just by serious, serious political connections, but that does not make you a good player in the industry. China Sonangol is in that category.' Another contact, who was also well versed in Nigerian oil and had held senior official positions, told me in early 2014 that China Sonangol had begun drilling wells on its prospect.[32]

There were other indications that China Sonangol was moving large sums of money in connection with OPL256. The transactions ledger published in the Hong Kong court dispute between the Chinese oilman Wu Yang and his former allies in the Queensway Group recorded a payment in 2008 or 2009 by China Sonangol International Holding of nearly 20 million Hong Kong dollars (about US$2.5 million). It was marked as 'Nigeria 256'.

It is not clear who in Nigeria opened the door for the Queensway Group. This was not Guinea or Madagascar or Niger, whose coup leaders desperately needed any investor prepared to do business with them. Nor was it Angola, smarting from Western donors' refusal to fund postwar reconstruction and eager to embrace investors from China. All the biggest Western majors and, increasingly, the national oil companies from the emerging powers have interests in Nigerian oil. I was told that Andy Uba had facilitated China Sonangol's entry to the Nigerian oil industry. As an aide to Olusegun Obasanjo, president from 1999 to 2007, Uba's roles had included, according to *Africa Confidential,* 'representing his interests in business deals'.[33] Uba also has 'extensive oil and gas interests' of his own. Some of the industry figures whom I asked about Uba's role suggested his power had waned significantly since Obasanjo's departure from office, but another of my contacts, who has worked with oil companies in Nigeria for years and was relaying information from within the industry, told me, 'Anything that China Sonangol do in Nigeria is Andy Uba.'[34]

Alliances between powerful foreign companies and Nigeria's kleptocrats sustain a ruling class that has shown itself willing to whip up violence to protect its interests. But there are also more direct connections between the multinationals that profit from the country's crude and the gunmen who enforce Nigeria's compact of violence.

Mutiu Sunmonu is an inscrutable man. Solidly built, he has a way of breathing that gives his voice a lulling quality. As I prepared to take a seat beside him on a stage in central London one evening in early 2012, I recalled attending the party two years earlier to celebrate his promotion to Shell's managing director in Nigeria. At a ritzy venue in Lagos, used for gigs by Nigeria's superstar rappers, the big men of the business scene raised flutes of champagne to the man assuming what is arguably the second-most important office in the land, after the presidency but at least on a par with senior cabinet posts.

A Nigerian friend of mine had arranged for Sunmonu to come to London and deliver a lecture and had asked me to put some questions to him once he had spoken. It would be a rare opportunity to call the company's leadership to account in public. Shell's revenues of $484 billion in 2012 were almost twice the entire annual output of the Nigerian economy. It pumps about half of Nigeria's daily crude output of 2.5 million barrels. Shell's Nigeria boss answers to the Africa boss, who answers to the top team, then led by Peter Voser, a Swiss national who fought off rivals in 2009 to become chief executive, a position for which he was paid $16.5 million in 2011.

Sunmonu, like his predecessors, wore two hats. He was Shell's top man in Nigeria and the head of the Shell Development Petroleum Company of Nigeria (SPDC), the country's biggest company, of which the Nigerian state is the largest shareholder. Shell has 30 per cent of SPDC and is the operator. It drills the wells and pumps the crude but funds only 30 per cent of the expenditure and, thus, is entitled to only 30 per cent of the profits. The head of SPDC has two masters: the management of Shell and the Nigerian state.

For his London appearance, even though public relations handlers prepped him, Sunmonu looked uncomfortable. 'As a Nigerian,' he said, 'the situation in the Delta actually brings tears to my eyes. I see it, I feel it.'

He went on, 'The people in the Delta, they don't have access to clean water, and they don't have access to good medical care. They don't have access to education. There are no jobs, so everyone is trying to fend for himself, and they have seen this oil as an easy source to make money.'

It was a clear-eyed diagnosis of the maladies of the Delta, but it had one glaring omission: the role of the oil companies.

On a November morning in 1995 Shell's activities in the Niger Delta became headline news across the world. The dew was still fresh on the grass when Ken Saro-Wiwa and eight fellow activists were hanged in Port Harcourt prison on the orders of Nigeria's military government.[35] The men were leaders of a campaign by the Ogoni ethnic group, which had forced Shell to withdraw from their polluted corner of the Delta. Sani

Abacha, a world-class embezzler who had ruled Nigeria since he seized power in 1993, would brook no such dissent. The Ogoni resistance was a threat to Shell's operations and, thus, to the oil money that funded his regime. Some of Saro-Wiwa's critics have argued that he had more in common with the venal Nigerian politicians he lambasted than his crusading image suggested.[36] Nonetheless, from the jail cell where he was awaiting trial in late 1995, he rejected anything short of full compensation for the oil slicks that had poisoned Ogoniland. On 31 October a kangaroo court pronounced a death sentence on the Ogoni Nine. Horrified protests from world powers and African elders went unheeded.

Shell was accused of having offered to secure Saro-Wiwa's release if he called off a propaganda offensive that was damaging its reputation.[37] That allegation has never been proven, and Shell has always denied wrongdoing in the Saro-Wiwa case. In 2009, while maintaining those denials, it paid $15.5 million to settle a case brought by Ogoni plaintiffs in an American court related to allegations of complicity in Saro-Wiwa's death.[38]

When the gunmen of MEND launched their oil war a decade after Saro-Wiwa's uprising Shell faced a new threat. It responded with a mixture of co-option and confrontation. In 2006 Shell admitted that it had given contracts to companies connected to MEND.[39] Shell executives were also privy to the details of operations conducted by the Joint Taskforce, or JTF, the special contingent of the Nigerian military stationed in the Delta to keep the oil flowing and known for its heavy-handed tactics.[40]

Given its links to both the militants and the military – and what MEND fighters had told me during my trips to the Delta about Shell and other oil companies paying them protection money – when he finished speaking I asked Sunmonu whether he thought his company played a role in sustaining the conflict.

'It's a very difficult question,' he responded. 'I believe that some of the things we do in the Delta could indeed unintentionally provoke conflict. I will be the first to admit that the dynamics in the Delta are very complex. In one vein, the oil company might be thinking of promoting development within a community, but they may not realize that that community is not a homogenous one. So you are looking at it as a single community, well united. It's only when you go in there that you will find that there are factions within the community, and so your efforts of promoting development could in some cases actually lead to conflict. I think the point you are talking about, the oil companies using some of the militants as civilian guards, I can tell you that, as far as Shell is concerned, our business principle is very clear. We do not pay protection money. However, you also have to admit that except if a guy has a label on his forehead saying, "I'm a militant," you do not know who is a militant and who is a genuine contractor. There could be cases in the past where you have been told you are employing the genuine, bona fide contractor, and yet he's probably a militant or a warlord.'

Sunmonu conceded that such a situation could have arisen 'in the past' but insisted Shell acted 'always with the best of intentions'. Even if you credit his insistence that, contrary to the accounts I heard from militants during my trips to the Niger Delta, his company did not pay protection money, it is a startling admission: Shell's top executive in Nigeria was aware that company money might – even if unintentionally – be ending up in the warlords' coffers.

In a roundabout way, it seemed to me, Sunmonu was talking about the alignment of commercial interests that underpins Nigeria's compact of violence. I wanted to hear the warlords' take on their relationship with Shell. The next time I was in the Delta, in April 2013, a year after Sunmonu's talk, I sent word through an intermediary to Farah Dagogo. Dagogo had taken the amnesty, but like other senior figures from MEND, he was still very much in business, running his bunkering operations and his protection racket. I was told he was willing to meet me but could not. The government had taken to using poachers as gamekeepers and had given him and some fellow senior militants a surveillance contract to protect an oil facility. Some of his partners believed he had ripped them off, pocketing the payment for himself. The traditional Delta way of settling such disputes is with guns, so Dagogo had gone into hiding. But one of the militia commanders who had broken with him did agree to meet with me.

I was hanging around in Port Harcourt, a city as oversupplied with suspicion as it is with weapons, when the call came toward noon on a Saturday. With George, one of the unflappable drivers on whose courage and calm foreign correspondents in Nigeria rely, I drove away from the supermarkets and pizza joints of the city centre into the slums that spill out to the edge of the creeks. The roads became more pothole than tarmac, flanked by fetid open drains. We arrived at the designated spot, and I called my intermediary. He led me down a narrow alley, past cobwebs of electricity cables that had not carried a current in years. A teenager standing watch moved aside to let me into a discreet backroom in the warren of dwellings.

The General looked uneasy. He sported a navy blue vest, long white shorts and a goatee beard. His dark brown eyes scanned me. Swigging from a bottle of Guinness, he told me that some of the foot soldiers he had brought with him from their base in the creeks were loitering down the street. They would soon start to wonder what their commander was up to, so the General cut to the chase.

Now thirty-three, the General was born in Buguma, a settlement in the creeks beyond Port Harcourt. After elementary schooling in his village he came to the city to study business at university, an apt preparation for a career that required at least as much commercial as military acumen. Then he felt the lure of the gun. In 2003 he signed up with Mujahid Asari-Dokubo, the first of the Delta's superstar commanders. 'Along the line Asari betrayed us. He was making money alone.' So he switched his allegiance to Farah Dagogo, who stepped into the power vacuum left by Asari's arrest. The General carved out his own domain within Dagogo's territory in the eastern Delta, controlling a handful of settlements and the waterways between them. 'We accepted the amnesty, but it's not working out. We have nothing to show for it.' He maintained five camps, he said, with five thousand men at his command, a tally that seemed high but perhaps not grossly exaggerated. Now, on account of the allegations that he had swindled his partners in a pipeline surveillance contract, Dagogo too had been deemed a traitor, and the General had transferred his loyalty to yet another warlord of the eastern Delta, Ateke Tom.

The General paused. 'Do you smoke?' I offered a cigarette. 'No,' he corrected me, looking slightly put out, 'marijuana.' The General expertly rolled himself a chunky joint, lit it, exhaled a thick cloud, and continued.

'We have a cause to fight. The spillage has really affected our communities. Every place is downtrodden. No water; we cannot afford food. All our livestock are dying because of the pollution. Bunkering is our means of survival,' the General said. Kidnapping for ransoms brought in some money alongside the revenues from oil theft. He explained why he would not agree to let me publish his name, only his rank in the Delta's shadow military. Doing so might endanger another important income stream: his illicit contractual arrangements with the oil industry.

The General rattled off half a dozen areas in the eastern Delta where he claimed that, indirectly, the militants had succeeded in getting a cut of Shell's community development contracts. The militants would set up front companies. 'Through these companies we get pieces from Shell,' the General said, though I was not permitted to see the contracts. The General's militia was also indirectly given work cleaning up oil spills, he said, splitting the proceeds fifty-fifty with an official contractor.[41]

Under Shell's Global Memoranda of Understanding, introduced in 2006 following unrest in the Delta that crippled its installations to replace ad hoc corporate social responsibility projects with a more comprehensive approach to mollifying resentment, representatives of each settlement where the company operates inform Shell of their priorities. The projects Shell funds range from town halls to printing presses and scholarships, with each contract worth between 12 million and 60 million naira (US$80,000 to $400,000).[42] Shell says the programme 'represents an important shift in approach, placing emphasis on more transparent and accountable processes, regular communication with the grassroots, sustainability, and conflict prevention.'[43]

Before I met the General, a Port Harcourt go-between, well connected to the militants and whom we shall call Arthur, explained to me how Farah Dagogo and a fellow militia boss, who borrowed his *nom de guerre* from the American rapper Busta Rhymes, had diverted some of Shell's largesse to their own war chest.[44] Shell would send liaison officers for consultations with the Delta's inhabitants on the projects they wanted, Arthur told me. Dagogo and Busta Rhymes surreptitiously inserted themselves into the process, sending 'fictitious youth leaders, fictitious elders, fictitious women's groups, fictitious chiefs' to meet Shell's emissaries. SPDC, Shell's joint venture with the Nigerian state, keeps a list of the outside companies it has registered as contractors, and only these companies can be awarded contracts to undertake the community development projects that SPDC funds. 'So,' Arthur said, 'Dagogo and Busta Rhymes formed alliances with some of these contractors and told them, "This is the percentage that you will pay us.""

The General corroborated Arthur's account. If the hospitals and schools did not get built, it was because Shell's liaison officers were creaming off too much for themselves on top of the funds siphoned off by the likes of Dagogo and Busta Rhymes, the General insisted, making grabbing motions in the air. He reckoned that only half of the contracts that were paid out were actually fulfilled.

Before long the General decided he had to get back to the creeks. He mentioned an intermediary for Shell, a Nigerian known as Dr Frank, who had, possibly unwittingly, helped the militants secure their contracts. I was unable to track down Dr Frank or even to confirm his role. I tried to talk to two Shell managers who I had heard were involved in pipeline protection and community development in order to see what they knew of the militants' racket. In both cases Shell's press office in Lagos got wind of my approaches and told the managers not to talk to me.

When I e-mailed the press office and asked about Farah Dagogo and his cohorts benefiting from Shell contracts, a spokesman would only say that 'cluster development boards' composed of community representatives, not by SPDC itself, awarded contracts for development projects.[45] When I asked about protection money being paid to militants in the form of pipeline surveillance contracts, I was told, 'We do not award contracts to armed groups, and it is completely against our company policy to do so.' Surveillance contracts employed 'more than nine thousand unarmed people, primarily indigenes of the communities through which the pipelines traverse'. The spokesman declined to answer my questions about what safeguards Shell had put in place to prevent money from its community programmes flowing to militants.

I heard differing accounts about the extent to which the diversion of money from Shell's community programmes was the result of the actions of a few rogue contractors or whether knowledge of such diversions went higher up the company's chain of command. A former Shell employee, who spoke to me on the condition that I did not name him, told me, 'Shell has quite stringent mechanisms in place but Nigeria is a difficult place to adhere to any kind of rules.'[46] He suggested that complicity in such schemes was limited to low-level Shell employees and added, 'The whole community liaison system is incredibly corrupt . . . It was difficult to quantify how many Nigerian staff were in bed with the bad guys.'

One former Shell manager in the Delta did agree to talk to me on the record. A native of the Niger Delta, Harriman Oyofo spent twenty-nine years at Shell. He held various posts in Shell's Nigerian and African divisions before, in 1999, joining the external relations department in the Delta for SPDC, Shell's joint venture with the Nigerian state, and becoming, in his own words, Shell's de facto spokesman for the whole of its Nigerian operation. He left in 2010 to set up his own oil consultancy.

I asked him whether he knew of Shell money ending up with armed groups. 'Shell has never made policies because of armed groups. If you have a community of ten people, there may be one who is bent. You are not going to tailor your project just for that one person. When you build a health centre or a school or develop seedlings for a community, that's not because of any armed group; it's just that it makes sense to put back into the community.'[47] He conceded, however, that it was hard to discern between 'communities' and armed groups and that some community liaison officers had been 'reprimanded for one type of misdemeanour or another'. 'Some communities had hidden agendas,' he added.

When I asked Oyofo whether the pipeline-surveillance contracts that Shell doled out amounted to protection money, he waxed gnomic. 'If you ask someone to look after your bag, are you asking them not to steal it? No. You are asking them to look after it.' He steadfastly absolved Shell of responsibility. Wasn't it oil that had destroyed his homeland? 'Oil maybe – not Shell. Oil itself may be a problem, but the administration of the proceeds of oil is not in the hands of Shell. Shell is not the political administrator of Nigeria. Shell is just a company.'

Shell may be just a company, but it is one of the biggest in the world, richer than many governments. It has been part of Nigeria since before independence. Between 2007 and 2009 it spent at least $383 million on security in Nigeria.[48] The scale of its 'community development' spending in the Niger Delta is vast. By the end of 2011 these programmes covered 290 communities. Shell's Nigerian spokesman told me that in 2012 it spent $103 million 'addressing social and economic development challenges in the region'.[49] Shell has since sold off some of its oil fields in the Niger

Delta, preferring to concentrate on offshore operations that are harder to attack, but it remains a powerful force in the creeks.

Aaron Sayne, a languid American lawyer who worked on foreign corruption prosecutions before becoming one of the best-informed due-diligence investigators in Nigeria, has tried to put a figure on the overall amount of cash the oil companies slosh into the Delta. 'Each year the majors distribute over half a billion dollars in contracts, cash, compensation, jobs, donations, and development programs to Niger Delta communities—by one tally over $350 million in community development alone,' Sayne wrote in 2010.[50] He adds, 'That practices of Shell . . . and others stoke unrest in the Niger Delta is not news to analysts or the companies themselves. They are part of the Niger Delta conflict system, in spite of the money they spend on communities – or sometimes because of it.'

Local activists told me they had warned senior managers at Shell that the community development programmes were being abused, to no avail. 'They are pragmatic,' said one, who has spent years campaigning against the Delta's noxious cocktail of environmental degradation, violence and corruption.[51] 'They will do anything to make sure the oil will continue to flow.' He was equally scathing of the warlords who claimed to be warriors in the Delta's cause. 'The majority of the militants, especially the leadership, initially they were flagging up environmental things,' the activist told me, fuming with the anger of the betrayed as we spoke in a quiet corner of a Port Harcourt bar. 'Then the money came and the amnesty came. None of these fuckers ever talk about it anymore.'

In January 2011, a year after he sent troops to restore order in Jos, Goodluck Jonathan walked into Eagle Square, Abuja's parade ground, to be invested as captain of Nigeria's looting machine. He had already assumed the presidency after Yar'Adua's death, becoming the first son of the Niger Delta to hold the highest office in a political system fuelled by the region's oil. Now the People's Democratic Party presidential primary was about to nominate him to serve a full term. His name and that of his wife, Patience, could not have been more apt for the occasion.

Twelve years earlier Jonathan had been an obscure zoologist in a backwater of the Delta. As the founders of the PDP cast around for candidates as they prepared to inherit power from the military in the 1999 elections, they sought someone for whom a particular ethnic group in a corner of Jonathan's home state of Bayelsa might be persuaded – or, if necessary, coerced – to vote. Jonathan, a minor local environmental official, was reluctant but could not refuse when the local elders insisted. He was nominated as the PDP candidate for deputy governor of Bayelsa. The party won the presidency and the bulk of the governorships, as it has at every election since.

From there Jonathan's rise was as meteoric as it was fortuitous. In 2005 the governor of Bayelsa, Diepreye Alamieyeseigha, was arrested in London on money-laundering charges in connection with his $3.2 million of ill-gotten wealth that the Metropolitan Police said it found in cash and bank accounts.[52] He skipped bail and made it back to Nigeria but, having fallen foul of his political masters at home, was impeached and, eventually, jailed. He was two years into his second and final term as governor when his deputy, Goodluck Jonathan, was automatically promoted in his stead.

That might have marked the peak of Jonathan's ascent had it not been for the machinations that were then under way in Abuja, the city the political class crafted out of the bush in the centre of the country in the 1980s after the erstwhile capital of Lagos had become bloated with the masses of the poor. The 2007 elections were drawing near, and Obasanjo was trying to tinker with the constitution to permit himself a third term. Although he was thwarted, he remained Nigeria's political godfather, the kingmaker of the PDP, and he anointed Umaru Yar'Adua as the party's candidate to succeed him. For the second name on the ticket the PDP needed a state governor from the Niger Delta. The oil province was restive. The newly formed MEND was destabilizing the font of the patronage system. Other candidates had made too many enemies as they rose through Nigerian politics and were so mired in corruption that their rivals had enough dirt to stymie their aspirations.

Jonathan was a political minnow, but with his fedora hat and his Ijaw blood, he fitted the bill. After elections that observers deemed the most fraudulent in Nigeria's short democratic era, Jonathan became vice president.[53] When Yar'Adua's allies failed to cling to power as the president's health faded, Jonathan was sworn in to serve out the remaining year of the presidential term.

As vice president, Jonathan had been routinely snubbed by the members of Yar'Adua's inner circle. Even after he stepped into Yar'Adua's shoes, the heavyweights of the PDP regarded him as a pawn, someone who lacked the heft to challenge their interests, even if he had wanted to. For that very reason the party barons and their allies among the oligarchs who controlled the economy felt comfortable with the new man and threw their weight behind him for the forthcoming elections, opting to risk the wrath of the northern establishment by ditching an unwritten rule that rotates power between ethnic blocs, under which the North's turn had been cut short by Yar'Adua's death.

As acrobats cartwheeled around Eagle Square, thirty-four hundred delegates from across the nation converged to select the PDP presidential candidate for an election due three months later. Such was the party's grip on power that no one was in any doubt that the delegates were effectively selecting the next president. 'We have never had the presidency before,' Rotimi Amaechi, the governor of Rivers, the Niger Delta state that includes Port Harcourt, told me.[54] 'So we want to have a bite.'

The PDP, which likes to call itself the biggest political party in Africa, is simultaneously rife with competing ethnic claims on power and patronage and the vehicle through which Nigeria's revolving cast of rulers privately set aside their differences to ensure the continued hegemony of the looting class. It is also the political home of some brilliant lawmakers and scrupulous reformers. But they are in the minority. 'It's not a political party,' said Clement Nwankwo, who founded Nigeria's first human rights organization in the days of military rule, did two stints in jail, failed in his attempt to stand for the national assembly as a PDP candidate because he couldn't afford to pay the required bribes to party officials, and now ranks as one of Nigeria's most astute political analysts.[55] 'It's a platform to seize power and then share the resultant booty.'

Guarded by secret service agents, Nigeria's potentates had gathered in the VIP stands of Eagle Square as dusk descended. Louis Armstrong's voice lilted from giant speakers, singing 'What a Wonderful World'. Night fell, unleashing mosquitoes. The representatives of north, south, east and west – Muslims, Christians, and animists, speakers of half a dozen different languages – eyed one another with mistrust. Tempers frayed as supporters of Atiku Abubakar, a northern businessman and former vice president who had taken on the quixotic task of challenging an incumbent president for the PDP nomination, started to realize that they had been outmanoeuvred and outspent. Jonathan's victory had been ordained in advance. Each delegate received a cash bribe of $7,000 to vote for him, roughly five times the average Nigerian's annual income.[56] Bidding for the loyalty of all thirty-four hundred delegates would have cost the Jonathan campaign some $24 million. And that was just the basic payoff – higher-ranking officials could have expected much more. In the days leading up to the primary so much hard currency changed hands in Abuja that the dollar–naira exchange rate moved.

It was past 10 p.m. when the count started. Under the night sky PDP officials read the name written on each ballot. 'Jonathan, Jonathan, Goodluck Jonathan.' Just after 6 A.M. the victor emerged from the bowels of Eagle Square. The party's call-and-answer chant greeted him: 'PDP! Power!' Triumphant, Jonathan waved an arm and vowed to break with 'the corruption of the past that had held us down for too long'.

As he consolidated his position, Goodluck Jonathan's senior aides told me and other foreign journalists in hotel-room briefings that he was what he claimed to be: 'an agent of transformation'. He was using the dinosaurs of Nigerian politics to get him to the presidency, they said, but in time he would consign them to history and unleash Nigeria's potential. And there were encouraging signs. Jonathan appointed Attahiru Jega, an upstanding northern professor, to head the electoral commission. The April 2011 elections were deeply flawed but marked an improvement on previous polls, though the resentment in the North that a southern Christian was usurping its stint in the presidency triggered three days of rioting that left eight hundred people dead.[57]

The promised reforms began. Power stations were privatized, taking them out of the hands of a corrupt bureaucracy and raising the prospect that Nigeria's crippling electricity shortages might ease. Nigeria's image was improving – though, in many cases, it was no thanks to Jonathan. Babatunde Fashola, the governor of Lagos State and a leading light in one of the main opposition parties, started to restore a sense of civic pride to his city – laying roads, reining in the predatory police, and persuading

Lagosians to pay their taxes. With much fanfare, Nigeria officially overtook South Africa as the continent's biggest economy.

But Jonathan had little charisma. He lacked Yar'Adua's depth of thought and the natural authority that Obasanjo possessed as a war hero and master tactician. The only way to maintain his grip on power was to open the sluice gates of the looting machine. Jonathan presided over a binge of corruption and embezzlement that was dizzying even by Nigerian standards.

Nigeria's pot of oil rent is enormous. Unlike the mining industry, from which African states glean a minimal share of the profits, between 65 per cent and 85 per cent of the income from oil extraction typically accrues to the governments who license oil companies to pump it.[58] In recent years Nigeria's annual oil income has ranged between $20 billion and $60 billion, depending on the price of oil and the level of violence in the Delta.[59] The latter figure, for 2011, was one and a half times the profits Exxon Mobil, the world's most profitable company, recorded that year. Jaw-dropping quantities of these revenues go missing each year and, although the nature of corruption is that it is hard to quantify, the theft appeared to accelerate under Jonathan.

There were those who tried to stem the deluge. 'I'm emotionally drained because I'm swimming against the tide,' a reform-minded minister in Jonathan's cabinet told me in August 2010, adding, with some understatement, that 'the fight against corruption is not going well'.

Lamido Sanusi, a blue-blooded banker from Kano whom Umaru Yar'Adua had appointed as central bank governor with the task of cleaning up a financial system imploding under the weight of malpractice, came to the fore. He used the central bank's powers as best he could to arrest the perilous decline in Nigeria's foreign currency reserves as the politicians splurged.

As the plundering started to run out of control, Sanusi compiled a dossier showing that scams involving NNPC, the national oil company that serves, like Sonangol to the Angolan Futungo, as the engine of Nigeria's looting machine, were bleeding a billion dollars a month from the treasury.[60] When Sanusi went public with his allegations in early 2014 Jonathan forced him out of the central bank, dealing a blow to the independence of one of the few Nigerian institutions with the power to check the excesses of the country's rulers – though he could not prevent Sanusi's appointment as Emir of Kano, an influential position in the North's religious hierarchy.

A short, wiry man with a penchant for bow ties, Sanusi understood that Nigeria's petro-politics lay beneath the violence that was mounting across the nation, including the barbaric insurgency in the North launched by the jihadists of Boko Haram. 'There's a clear, direct link between the uneven distribution of resources and the rise in violence,' Sanusi said.[61] 'That's not to say that the political system is not corrupt all over, but the most critical element is the poor infrastructure that makes it difficult for industrialization and job creation to take place.' Addressing the economic ills that helped to feed Boko Haram's cause was next to impossible, however, while the looting machine was in such high gear. 'What we have seen with Boko Haram and all the violence in the country should give politicians pause,' Sanusi went on. 'Maybe it's time to start asking if the very opportunistic identity politics . . . is not endangering the entire system.'

As Jonathan's regime devoted itself to guzzling oil rents, Boko Haram, whose name means 'Western education is forbidden', sowed terror. From its heartland in the remote northeast its fighters bombed cities and burned villages across the North. Thousands died. The region's idle young men, their prospects as bleak as those of the mill hands whose textile factories had been felled by Dutch Disease, were ready recruits. Abubakar Shekau, the sect's megalomaniac leader, posted rambling videos online and established himself among the world's most notorious jihadis. The corruption of the ruling class, as much as its bellicose interpretations of Quranic law, was Boko Haram's rallying cry.

Like the Delta militias before them, Boko Haram's guerrillas struck Abuja, the bubble of the elite, with car bombs, though that was nothing compared with the havoc it unleashed in the North. The military, incapacitated by corruption and its budgets embezzled, was no match for the gun-toting jihadists. When a raiding party abducted two hundred schoolgirls from the village of Chibok in April 2014, the extent to which the oil-sickened Nigerian state had become incapable of its most basic duty, to safeguard its citizens, was plain for all to see.

What has happened to Nigeria is not the result of some innate facet of the African spirit, as some observers suggest with a shrug of casual racism. British members of Parliament have shown themselves willing to sell their right to ask parliamentary questions, and the pork-barrel politics of Capitol Hill in Washington, DC, looks very much like a patronage system. Lobbyists in every major capital inject money into politics on behalf of vested interests. The difference between a corrupted resource state and a state that can still call itself a place of representative rule is the extent to which such subversion of public office for personal benefit is the scandal or the norm. It is the degree to which the institutions of state – legislative bodies, the police, the courts – serve as instruments of the mighty or as checks on arbitrary power.

'If you had a government in the UK or the US that could get away with these levels of corruption, they would do it,' Clement Nwankwo, the astute Nigerian political analyst, told me, sitting in his simple office on an Abuja side street. 'But there are always institutions. In Nigeria people have not overcome their diversity enough to realize that they could make a difference, they could challenge this fear of authority. They resign themselves to what is. People exploit the divisions: ethnic, religious, regional. They represent themselves as protecting these interests, and they call on their people to protect them. The reality is that the generality of people don't benefit.'

Chinua Achebe, the late Nigerian writer, wrote in 1983, 'The trouble with Nigeria is simply and squarely a failure of leadership. There is nothing basically wrong with the Nigerian character. There is nothing wrong with the Nigerian land or climate or water or air or anything else. The Nigerian problem is the unwillingness or inability of its leaders to rise to the responsibility, to the challenge of personal example which are the hallmarks of true leadership.'[62]

That remains an unsurpassed diagnosis of his nation's malady. There is, though, something else Achebe wrote that captures the strange dissonance I witnessed time and again when I spoke with the lords of the looting machine.

The General in the Niger Delta told me he kidnapped to pay school fees. Shell's Mutiu Sunmonu had a lump in his throat as he recalled the terrible state of his homeland, despoiled by the oil industry he helps to run. Manuel Vicente lamented the hunger that surrounded him in Luanda, even when confronted with evidence of how the Futungo hoards the benefits of Angola's oil. Joseph Kabila, the Congolese president whose shadow state is partly responsible for the violence that stalks his country, once said, 'The worst thing I have ever seen is the sight of a village after a massacre; you can never erase that from your memory.'[63] These men and thousands less prominent have enough empathy to feel the suffering caused by the system they perpetuate. But they are somehow able to subordinate that empathy to the need to keep the machine going and to ensure that they remain at the controls rather than joining the countless others who are crushed beneath it.

Achebe's poem 'Vultures' might have been written of the perpetrators of the horrors in Jos or eastern Congo or the national stadium in Conakry, who have mothers and brothers and lovers just as their victims did. He pictures the vulture that picks the eyes of a swollen corpse in a trench before nestling its head against its mate. He imagines the commandant at Belsen who stops off on his way home after a day's work at the concentration camp to:

> pick up a chocolate
> for his tender offspring
> waiting at home for Daddy's
> return . . .

It would be ludicrous to compare the resource industry in Africa to the Holocaust, but I think Achebe was seeking to make a wider point about the human spirit: it is capable of loving and of participating in horrors in the same afternoon. Perhaps it is a source of hope for Africa's resource states that those who wield power are coming to see the terrible cost of the trade in oil and minerals. Or perhaps the looting machine has just enough humanity to allow it to keep on turning.

» 9 «

Black Gold

W HEN NCHAKHA MOLOI was looking for a name for his mining company he settled on *motjoli*. In Sesotho motjoli is the word for the leading bird in a V-shape formation, guiding the others toward their destination. Moloi had grown up in QwaQwa, a homeland beside the Drakensberg mountains of central South Africa to which the apartheid regime consigned Sesotho-speaking blacks. There were no mines in QwaQwa, but the menfolk would disappear for months on end to the mines of the Witwatersrand, under which lie the seams that have yielded a third of the gold mined worldwide over the past 150 years, returning only at Easter and Christmas to spend their wages.

Moloi took up one of the few places the authorities allotted for black students, at the prestigious University of the Witwatersrand in Johannesburg, to study medicine. But he found cutting up cadavers too gruesome and decided to switch subjects. He had never heard of geology, but once university staff told him that it addressed 'all the big questions' he was hooked. He studied the nature of the Earth out of fascination rather than any grand design for a career, but after graduation Moloi went to work as a prospector for Anglo American, the mining house that Ernest Oppenheimer had founded in 1917, which had grown to become the world's biggest mining conglomerate. After a while Moloi moved to the Oppenheimer family's diamond company, De Beers.

As they bumped around the diamond fields in their pickup truck, the members of Moloi's team paid little heed to the different colours of their skin. But when he went to De Beers's head office to make his reports, Moloi was subjected to the indignities apartheid imposed on black South

Africans. He still recalls the strictures: 'They can't come here, they can't go there. You get offended.'[1] Ignoring his bosses' objections, Moloi joined the National Union of Mineworkers, a bulwark of resistance to apartheid. His relationship with De Beers soon soured, and he took a job at Rio Tinto, working on a copper mine close to the Kruger National Park, where the racial division was even more apparent. 'I was working on the mine, in production, and I was really exposed to how things are,' Moloi remembers.

By 1990 mass protests and international sanctions had brought the apartheid regime to the verge of collapse. F. W. de Klerk released Nelson Mandela and lifted the ban on the African National Congress. The party set up working groups to prepare itself for government, and Moloi joined the one on science and technology. By 1993 the leading lights of the ANC's economics team had identified the usefulness of a man who knew the mining business from the inside. Moloi was brought onto the party's economic planning team as it made ready to face the sky-high expectations of black South Africans, many of whom believed that their imminent liberation would bring swift deliverance from poverty. After the triumph of Mandela and the ANC in the 1994 elections, Moloi was deployed to various senior positions in the mining ministry. A decade later he founded Motjoli Resources and took his place among the generation of black entrepreneurs seeking to do to a mining industry still predominantly in white hands what the ANC had done to politics – wrest control from the minority and enfranchise the black majority. But as Moloi discovered, looting machines are not so easily supplanted.

From the country's birth, South Africa's white rulers relied on income from exports of minerals, primarily gold. In 1912, the year when the forerunner to the ANC was formed to press for black rights, gold and diamonds accounted for 78 per cent of exports. Manufacturing developed, but throughout the apartheid decades South Africa remained a resource economy. The relationship between the English-speaking tycoons who controlled the biggest mining companies and the Afrikaner politicians who ran the apartheid system was at times uneasy, but they reached an accommodation that kept racist rule in place and secured the flow of cheap black labour to the mines.

In 1970, the year the Olympic movement expelled South Africa, the government passed legislation formally stripping blacks of their citizenship and restricting them to destitute 'homelands', and the authorities appointed a barbaric new commanding officer at Robben Island prison to watch over Mandela and his fellow inmates, South Africa produced some 62 per cent of the gold mined worldwide. From the early 1970s to 1993 gold, diamonds and other minerals accounted for between half and two-thirds of South Africa's exports annually.[2]

South Africa's gold and diamonds provided the financial means for apartheid to exist. In that sense white rule was an extreme manifestation of the resource state: the harnessing of a national endowment of mineral wealth to ensure the power and prosperity of the few while the rest are cast into penury and impotence. None of Africa's resource states today come close to the level of orchestrated subjugation of the majority that the apartheid regime achieved. Neither do they employ apartheid's racial creed, even if ethnicity has combined poisonously with the struggle to capture resource rent in Nigeria, Angola, Guinea and elsewhere. But as their rulers, in concert with the multinational corporations of the resource industry, hoard the fruits of their nations' oil and minerals, Africa's resource states have come to bear a troubling resemblance to the divisions of apartheid.

While the children of eastern Congo, northern Nigeria, Guinea and Niger waste away, the beneficiaries of the looting machine grow fat. Amartya Sen, the Nobel Prize-winning Indian economist who has examined with great insight why mass starvation occurs, writes, 'The sense of distance between the ruler and the ruled – between "us" and "them" – is a crucial feature of famines.'[3] That same reasoning could be applied to the provision of other basic needs, including clean water and schooling. And rarely is the distance Sen describes as wide as in Africa's resource states.

Many of Africa's resource states experienced very high rates of economic growth during the commodity boom of the past decade. The usual measure of average incomes – GDP per head – has risen. But on closer examination such is the concentration of wealth in the hands of the ruling class that that growth has predominantly benefited those who were already rich and powerful, rendering the increase in GDP per head misleading. A more revealing picture comes from a different calculation. Each year the United Nations ranks all the countries for which it can gather sufficient data (186 in 2012) by their level of human development, things like rates of infant mortality and years of schooling. It also ranks them by GDP per head. If you subtract a country's rank on the human development index from its rank on the GDP per head index, you get an indication of the extent to which economic growth is actually bettering the lot of the average person in that country. In countries that score zero – as Congo, Rwanda, Russia and Portugal did in 2012 – living standards are roughly where you might expect them to be, given that country's GDP per head. People in countries with positive scores enjoy disproportionately pleasant living conditions relative to income – Cuba, Georgia and Samoa top the table with scores of 44, 37 and 28 respectively. A negative score indicates a failure to turn national income into longer lives, better health, and more years of education for the population at large. Of the ten countries that come out worst, five are African resource states: Angola (–35), Gabon (–40), South Africa (–42), Botswana (–55), and Equatorial Guinea.[4]

Equatorial Guinea's score (–97), comfortably the worst in the world, is all the more remarkable because its GDP per head is close to $30,000 a year, not far below the level of Spain or New Zealand and seventy times that of Congo.[5] For a tiny nation of seven hundred thousand people, you might expect that to mean widespread prosperity. But the economy is acutely concentrated on oil, which accounts for 75 per cent of GDP and 90 per cent of government revenue. Oil sales generate 98 per cent of exports, a figure only slightly higher than the share of the vote that Teodoro Obiang Nguema, president since 1979, usually secures in sham elections. His son, Teodorin Obiang, officially received only a modest salary for the ministerial positions he has held but has nonetheless been the proud owner of a $30 million mansion in Malibu, properties in Cape Town and the Avenue Foch in Paris, a fleet of Ferraris and Rolls-Royces, a Gulfstream jet, paintings by Renoir and Matisse, and one of Michael Jackson's crystal-encrusted gloves.[6] The rest of Equatorial Guinea endures living standards ranked 136 out of 186 countries, behind Guatemala (GDP per head: $5,000), and has the same life expectancy, fifty-one years, as Somalia. The average length of schooling is eight years, about the same as in Afghanistan.

Mining was always going to be central to the ANC's plans to redress the economic injustices of apartheid – an experiment in whether South Africa could break the link between resource wealth and extreme inequality. The industry had served both as the test tube for apartheid policies and the breeding ground of resistance to white rule.

The ANC inherited a country in which the mining industry, like the rest of the economy, was controlled by a white minority that had surrendered political but not commercial hegemony. The new government's solution was a policy called Black Economic Empowerment, or BEE, under which the owners of South Africa's biggest companies would transfer a chunk of their shares to blacks and other previously disadvantaged ethnicities. The owners would lend the buyers money to finance the purchase of the shares, to be repaid from future dividends. The idea was to transform South Africa's economy to reflect the rainbow nation it aspired to be. The reality, however, has been different. 'Most people are fully supportive of the need for an ambitious transformation agenda,' Martin Kingston, the head of the South African office of the investment bank Rothschild's and one of Johannesburg's most influential and well-connected bankers, told me.[7] 'But it's been flawed in design and implementation, and it's been abused. There was an expectation that BEE would be a panacea for impoverished black South Africans. It has not been. Some have benefited, but they are at the top, not the bottom.'

The volatility of the Johannesburg Stock Exchange played havoc with BEE deals. Many black investors got burned as falling share prices left them struggling to pay for the stock they had acquired in empowerment transactions. But there were some who profited spectacularly – in particular, a handful of black men who combined a sense for business with impeccable connections to the ruling party.

Patrice Motsepe, an astute former lawyer with family ties to the ANC, who founded African Rainbow Minerals, became South Africa's first black billionaire. Tokyo Sexwale, whose charisma helped him make a seamless transition from freedom fighter to mining mogul, gained a foothold in the platinum industry and expanded into other sectors and beyond South Africa's borders before returning to government as housing minister in 2009. Cyril Ramaphosa's journey was the most remarkable of all. As the tenacious young leader of the National Union of Mineworkers, he led the strikes in the 1980s that struck at the heart of the apartheid economy, and as secretary general of the ANC he played a central role in the negotiations with the National Party that averted civil war and led to the free elections of 1994. Ramaphosa won a reputation for fearlessness and integrity. Then, after he lost out to Thabo Mbeki in the race to succeed Mandela as president, he switched from politics to business. He struck the first big BEE deal, becoming chairman of an Anglo American subsidiary. The transaction fared badly, but other deals followed, and Ramaphosa went into business with Glencore, the Swiss commodity trading house. His fortune made, Ramaphosa, like Sexwale, returned to politics, becoming the deputy leader of the ANC in 2012 and, following the 2014 elections, deputy president of South Africa.

Nchakha Moloi was never ANC royalty like Ramaphosa or Sexwale. Nonetheless, Motjoli Resources made headway through BEE deals, especially in coal. When we met at a sushi restaurant among the smart malls of uptown Johannesburg in 2013, Moloi, though past fifty, was dressed more like a Silicon Valley entrepreneur than the double-breasted executives of mining boardrooms. He wore a red baseball cap, a G-Star Raw T-shirt, and a funky watch.

Moloi was eyeing up new opportunities in iron ore, another metal abundant in South Africa's cornucopia of minerals, but he acknowledged that BEE had proved badly flawed. Black ownership of the mining industry was still 'minuscule'.[8] Many of BEE's beneficiaries had been content to receive a share of revenue from pre-existing mines rather than investing in digging their own ones.

'It's very hard because the stage was set before black people came into the mining industry,' Moloi told me. The white barons of South African mining had clung to the choicest cuts, he maintained. 'The resources, the best of the best have been carved up. Whatever was left that was good, they kept it for themselves. The world-class deposits are kept by the historical owners, and they have created conditions of entry for black people. They said, "You can come in at 26 per cent; we will determine the cost of finance, when the interests vest, the value." In terms of world-class deposits in South Africa, there's no chance of black people getting in – just the remnants.'

Perhaps he overstated his case – Patrice Motsepe, for one, has acquired some plum assets – but the argument carries weight. First the colonialists and then the apartheid regime carried off the cream of South Africa's natural wealth. South Africa's mineral resources are still by far the world's most valuable, estimated at $2,494 billion, way ahead of second-place Russia and enough money to buy Apple, Exxon Mobil and the rest of the nine biggest listed companies in the world.[9] But by the time black South Africa came into its inheritance, mining output was slowing, many of the richest remaining seams lay dangerously deep underground, and the industry's money men were wary of investing in a country run by a party with a socialist tradition.

Handing a slice of the mining industry to Ramaphosa, Sexwale and the rest helped to create a class of black South African tycoons. Only the churlish would deny that many of them had made great sacrifices for their compatriots' freedom. Perhaps, as their admirers suggested, they gave other black South Africans something to aspire to. But Black Economic Empowerment does nothing to change the fundamental structure of the mining industry, one that channels rents narrowly to those who control it, whatever the level of melanin in their skin. Conditions for the average mine worker remained grim while the new black moguls dreamed, as Tokyo Sexwale told his aides, of becoming 'the first black Oppenheimer'.[10]

Apartheid in South Africa was racial in philosophy and spatial in execution.

Whites had their cities and their ranches; black, Indian and mixed-race people were consigned to urban ghettoes and rural 'homelands'. Men from the homelands, or 'Bantustans', were carted off to the mines, where their movement was tightly controlled. The townships beside the cities were meant to be close enough to supply whites with black labour by day but also sufficiently distant to allow them to sleep soundly in their beds at night.

Nowadays the inequity that has outlived apartheid is most apparent in South Africa's urban geography. The extraordinary women who work in the Leratong Joy for One AIDS orphanage in Alexandra, a particularly tough township that lies on what must be one of the most stark economic fault lines anywhere, can see the glittering towers of the corporate head-quarters and exclusive hotels of Sandton, the business district a few hundred metres to the east. The sight of the orphans – some of whom did not yet know they had the virus that had killed their parents and none of whom could yet grasp how poor were the cards South Africa's inequitable economy had dealt them – belting out 'If you're happy and you know it, clap your hands!' is one of the most heartbreakingly ironic things I have ever seen.

Under apartheid, when whites made up at most 20 per cent of the population, they garnered between 65 and 70 per cent of the national income. In 2009, fifteen years after Mandela became president, the richest 20 per cent of South Africans garnered 68 percent of the national income; the figure reached 70 per cent in 2011.[11] By some measures the gap between rich and poor has widened since the end of apartheid.[12] That is the legacy of apartheid-era urban planning, two-tier education and countless other lingering distortions of white rule. But it also fits the pattern of inequality that stems from the resource curse.

When the simmering rage of black South Africans who were still barely scraping by after two decades of majority rule finally exploded, the detonation came, inevitably, at a mine. Marikana lies on the Bushveld Complex, a vast subterranean saucer of minerals that contains by far the planet's largest stocks of platinum. In August 2012 miners launched wildcat strikes. They demanded that Lonmin, the mine's London-listed owner, which enjoyed the backing of the IFC, grant them a hefty pay raise.

Many of the miners lived in informal camps beside a mine that private guards with shotguns patrolled, their shared toilets a humiliating contrast to the high-tech facilities used to extract ore. In the buildup to the strike new currents of radicalism had emerged. The National Union of Mineworkers had been a decisive force in the struggle against apartheid, but large numbers of miners believed it had grown too close to the ANC government and the Lonmin management. They had decamped to its militant rival, the Association of Mineworkers and Construction Union. There were violent clashes between members of the two unions and between strikers and security forces. Cyril Ramaphosa, the former NUM leader who had grown rich through BEE mining deals and sat on Lonmin's board, described the

unrest as 'plainly dastardly criminal' and urged the police to act.[13] The
tension mounted. On 16 August armed police opened fire on the strikers.
They killed perhaps a dozen miners instantly. Others, as the South African
photojournalist Greg Marinovich painstakingly established, were executed
nearby.[14] In all, thirty-four miners died. It was South Africa's bloodiest day
since the end of apartheid.

The strike and its consequences triggered national soul-searching. 'The
Marikana phenomenon,' declared Mamphela Ramphele, a doctor, aca-
demic and former anti-apartheid activist, 'is a logical outcome of an extractive industry model, where people could walk past shacks of the very
people who are producing the platinum that makes them so fabulously
rich, without thinking something is remiss.'[15]

Marikana laid bare that which has not changed – or at least, not changed
quickly enough – since the end of apartheid. It gave grist to the arguments
of those seeking to overturn Mandela's vision of a 'nonracial' society, such
as Julius Malema, the firebrand former head of the ANC's youth league
who combined choruses of 'Shoot the Boer' with calls for the nationaliza-
tion of the mining industry. For those who pondered it soberly, though,
Marikana revealed something that was not necessarily about race at all, but
about the curse of natural resources.

South Africa is in many ways different from the continent's other resource states. Its economy is more sophisticated, and its institutions have
generally proved more resistant to political manipulation. But there are
troubling parallels between South Africa and Angola, Nigeria and the
other African nations that oil and minerals have ruined. 'Where there is an
asymmetrical concentration of political and economic power, the resource
economy on the African continent often falls prey to a narrow, extraction-
ist elite whose outlook, despite its democratic pretensions, is feudal, and
its behaviour more similar to old tribal chiefs than modern government,'
Songezo Zibi, who worked in public relations for the mining house Xstrata
before becoming one of South Africa's most incisive commentators and
the editor of the authoritative *Business Day* newspaper, told me.[16]

The embodiment of that chiefly style of rule in South Africa today is
Jacob Zuma. His folksy charm and populist touch have kept him afloat
through a succession of corruption scandals. In March 2014 he won a

second term as president – although the ANC's majority decreased. Two months before the election South Africa's corruption ombudsman found Zuma guilty of misconduct over $20 million of improvements to his private residence at Nkandla, the president's birthplace in the Zulu heartlands.[17] The improvements, ostensibly to upgrade security at the residence, included a swimming pool, a chicken run, and an amphitheatre. Some of the money spent on the Nkandla residence was diverted from the Department of Public Works' budget for inner-city regeneration, the body charged with remoulding the physical legacy of apartheid.

South Africa aspires to be part of the vanguard of a new world order. Alongside Brazil, Russia, India and China, it belongs to the so-called BRICS nations, a grouping of fast-growing industrial economies that began as an acronym of the five countries, coined by the Goldman Sachs economist Jim O'Neill, and has evolved into a club that has its own summits and, as of 2014, its own bank, a counterweight to the World Bank and the IMF. At the BRICS summit in Brazil in July 2014, Zuma told his fellow heads of state that he recognized that the South African economy 'needs to be more inclusive, more dynamic, with the fruits of growth shared equitably'. If Zuma is sincere in that endeavour, he will need to break the spell of southern Africa's stupendous natural riches, which have brought violence and dispossession ever since an English vicar's son called Cecil John Rhodes first set foot in the diamond fields of the Highveld.

The New Money Kings

ROBERT MUGABE had a serious problem. Hunger was rife in what had been, in the early years of his rule, a relatively prosperous nation, and cholera was spreading rapidly. Zimbabwe's currency was worthless. But the most pressing difficulty, as far as the eighty-four-year-old president was concerned, was political. In March 2008 the usual tactics of Mugabe and his Zanu-PF party – trumpeting his record as a hero of African liberation while intimidating the opposition and rigging the vote – had failed to deliver the usual resounding victory in presidential elections. In the first round of voting Morgan Tsvangirai, a former mineworker who had risen through the union movement to become the head of the opposition, had beaten him into second place. Tsvangirai pulled out of the runoff after a campaign of violence against his supporters, and Mugabe's coronation as the victor had been such a naked fraud that regional leaders forced their elder statesman to submit to a coalition government with his rival. 'Robert Mugabe's world,' wrote his biographer, Heidi Holland, 'was constructed from his delusions of omnipotence.'[1] Now, after steadily gathering power unto himself since the end of white rule in 1980, he had been forced to share it.

Once unthinkable, calls from within Mugabe's own party for the old man to step aside were growing louder. Most urgently Mugabe needed cash to ensure that the security forces, the foundation of his regime, remained loyal. Under the power-sharing deal Mugabe's Zanu-PF had kept control of the security apparatus but had surrendered the finance ministry to Tsvangirai's Movement for Democratic Change. To compensate for losing direct access to the treasury, the aging autocrat required some off-budget funding. He lost little time.

Shortly after dawn on 27 October the residents of Chiadzwa, a town close to the high peaks that mark Zimbabwe's border with Mozambique, heard the sound of rotor blades. Five military helicopters buzzed into view and began spraying bullets and tear gas.[2] Army trucks disgorged eight hundred soldiers, who chased those who fled into the hills, firing their assault rifles indiscriminately. Operation No Return had begun.

Chiadzwa's misfortune was to lie on one of the world's greatest untapped repositories of diamonds. For many years the Marange area's inhabitants had thought little of the sparkling flecks in the earthen walls of their houses. De Beers had prospected the site in the 1990s but turned its attention elsewhere. From around 2006 local villagers started to realize that Marange was awash with alluvial diamonds, stones that have been dislodged from the subterranean volcanic pipes in which they formed and deposited on the surface. Fortune seekers from across the land descended on the Marange fields, panning for stones by day and bedding down in the bush at night. A superstition took hold among miners that a death would bring diamonds – collapsing ground could prove fatal for the unfortunate miner standing on it but would often expose a fresh trove of precious stones.

In a country where Mugabe's programme of farm seizures had contributed to the collapse of a flourishing economy, where even the central bank's massaged version of the inflation rate was above 2 million per cent, diamonds offered a ready way to make some dollars or South African rand from the South African and Lebanese traders and smugglers who sprang up as the diamond rush gathered steam. The police brutally ensured they got their cut. For a while it suited Mugabe to let the free-for-all continue. At the peak of the rush thirty-five thousand miners were working the fields.[3] But then circumstances changed. With Tsvangirai as prime minister and the finance ministry in the MDC's hands, Mugabe's shadow state could no longer rely on looting the treasury directly. His eyes turned to the diamond fields.

For three weeks the armed forces pummelled Marange. The bodies of many of the two hundred and fourteen miners who died were consigned to mass graves. Survivors were ordered to pitch tents for the soldiers, even to sing for them. 'Marange has become a zone of lawlessness and impunity,' concluded researchers from Human Rights Watch who conducted more than a hundred interviews in Marange in the aftermath of Operation No Return, 'a microcosm of the chaos and desperation that currently pervade Zimbabwe.'

Before long, obscure companies with links to Mugabe's security forces were being awarded concessions to mine diamonds at Marange.[4] Annexing the diamond fields had the added bonus of starving the MDC-controlled finance ministry of funds, helping to make its already improbable task of reviving the Zimbabwean economy next to impossible and undercutting its credibility as a party that could govern effectively. Measured by carats, Zimbabwean diamonds accounted for 9 per cent of the world's supply in 2012. Its reserves, estimated at 200 million carats, were the largest anywhere outside Russia.[5] But only about 10 per cent of the $800 million in revenues from official exports of Zimbabwean diamonds between 2010 and 2012 found their way to the treasury, despite the Zimbabwean state owning large stakes in some of the mining ventures.[6] Tendai Biti, the MDC's brightest strategist who became finance minister in the power-sharing government, said what everyone suspected: 'There might be a parallel government somewhere in respect of where these revenues are going.'[7]

That parallel government, like the shadow states of Joseph Kabila in Congo or the Futungo in Angola, had secured off-the-books funding from Zimbabwe's natural resources. As the 2013 elections approached, Mugabe was determined not to repeat the mistakes of 2008. With the diamond fields firmly in his grip, he set about planning to use them to recapture absolute power.

In July 2013, days before the election I drove over the heights of Christmas Pass and headed down toward the dusty plains of the Marange diamond fields. I stopped off at the newly built settlements to which former residents of the mining areas had been forcibly relocated, exchanging under duress their communities and grazing lands for scrubby plots and isolation that cut their income and forced them to pull their children out of school. At the checkpoint guarding the entrance to the mining zone I attempted to assume the bearing of a foreign diamond trader not to be messed with and passed through, enduring only some probing glances.

Msasa trees, with their beanpole trunks, stood sparsely between the boulders, offering a modicum of shade for the longhorn cattle. At a half-built hangout on the fringes of the mining zones miners told me tales of the frenzied diamond rush. One remembered ruefully how he found a clear, high-quality, five-carat diamond but parted with it for only a thousand dollars because he had not then known that that was a mere fraction of its value. There was boozing and violence on the fields: miners could make princely wages compared with the average Zimbabwean's fast-dwindling income, even after they had paid off the soldiers. But there was little to show for the sacks of precious stones that had departed. A stretch of tarmac road next to where we were speaking abruptly gave way to a dirt track.

Trymore, who asked me not to use his family name, came down from Harare to his home village in the diamond fields a few months before Operation No Return. Some days he found nothing; on others he might make $700. The police used to hassle the miners, but it was nothing compared with what followed once the military took control and brought in the mining companies.

One day, Trymore told me, his brother had been cleaning out the village well when private security guards from one of the mining companies confronted him. They accused him of mining illegally and took him to a place whose name brought a shudder from everyone in Marange who uttered it: the Diamond Base. At the time the base was located close to Trymore's village. (It was subsequently moved to a hilltop, a piercing eye surveying all those below.) The base housed soldiers and military police. Terrible stories spread about what happened within, of people being rolled in ashes and ordered to beat one another. 'They will do anything there,' a human rights activist in Marange told me. 'There are no records. A lot of people have never come out.'

With his eyes fixed straight ahead, Trymore recounted what he had been able to discover about his brother's final hours at the Diamond Base. He was beaten so savagely that he had been vomiting and shitting blood before he died.

Trymore stopped speaking. The only sound was the scrape of a bricklayer's trowel nearby. Trymore was an MDC supporter, and the half-formed building where we were sitting was taking shape as a bar for opponents of the regime. The proprietor swept in, a hefty ball of energy called Shuah Mudiwa. Mudiwa was jovial despite being in the thick of a perilous task: trying to win reelection as the MDC MP for the area. He had been arrested the previous day for staging an unsanctioned rally.

Mudiwa told me he believed diamond money was paying for Zanu-PF's campaign regalia, adding that the MDC wanted to cancel all the mining companies' contracts if, as many of its supporters earnestly believed in those final days before the poll, the party was finally on the verge of shunting Mugabe aside.

But they had underestimated their opponents. Perhaps the MDC's lacklustre performance in the coalition government would have dented its support in a free vote, but Zanu-PF had no intention of leaving the allocation of power to the whims of voters. According to local election monitors, more than 750,000 voters in towns and cities, the bedrock of MDC support, had been left off the electoral roll.[8] The MDC had been prevented from examining the roll, and more than a million excess ballots had been printed. Some 300,000 voters were turned away from polling stations on election day, and another 200,000 were 'assisted' in casting their ballots.[9] The margin of Mugabe's victory looked resounding – a 61 per cent share of the vote – but the 940,000 votes by which he beat Tsvangirai were well within the tally of dubious ballots. Tsvangirai called the results a 'massive fraud', but there was no hiding the fact that his old foe had comprehensively outflanked him.

Shuah Mudiwa would lose his seat as Zanu-PF claimed a two-thirds majority in Parliament. Before he bustled off for a final few laps of the campaign trail I asked him about one of the lesser-known companies doing business in the Marange fields, which I had heard was linked to the Central Intelligence Organisation, Mugabe's secret police. 'It's the military of China and the CIO,' Mudiwa said. 'They are trading diamonds.'

The company was called Sino Zim Development. It was part of the Queensway Group.

The terrorizing of Marange is only the latest chapter in the sorry history of African diamonds. The discovery of diamonds in the centre of what would become South Africa in the 1860s marked the start of industrial diamond mining, the excavation of underground pipes formed by cooling magma that contain the nuggets of crystallized carbon that have bewitched mankind since antiquity. Until the 1930s South Africa accounted for virtually the world's entire supply of rough stones. New discoveries elsewhere in southern Africa followed – in Namibia, Angola, and Congo – then in west Africa.

In recent decades the trade has broadened, as Russia, Canada and Australia also became important sources of stones. But Africa still accounts for well over half of the global rough diamond supply.[10] Its most famous stones grace the temples of power. The Star of Africa, cut from the Cullinan diamond, the largest ever found at more than three thousand carats, is mounted on the Sovereign's Sceptre in the British Crown Jewels, kept at the Tower of London. (Like many African diamonds since, the Cullinan left the continent through subterfuge. After its discovery in South Africa in 1905 it was sent to Britain as a gift for King Edward VII. The heavily guarded steamer ostensibly carrying the stone was a decoy designed to hoodwink potential thieves; the diamond itself went by registered post.) Other celebrated African stones have fetched tens of millions of dollars at auction and reside in private collections. A few sit in the Smithsonian, the museum between the US Capitol and the White House in Washington.

Against the beauty of Africa's diamonds glares the ugliness of what they have been used to do. In recent decades diamonds have provided the funds that sustained two of the continent's most horrendous wars.

When the collapse of the Soviet Union brought an end to the Cold War, factions in proxy conflicts that had relied on the financial support of one of the two superpowers suddenly found themselves in need of new sources of cash to buy weapons. In Angola José Eduardo dos Santos's Communist government controlled the coast: it could rely on oil from the Cabinda enclave that then produced most of the country's crude, as well as the flourishing new reserves offshore. Inland, Jonas Savimbi's Unita rebels turned to the diamonds strewn under their territory in the Angolan interior. Diamond sales brought in $700 million a year for the rebels through the 1990s, when both sides increased the ferocity of their campaigns following Savimbi's rejection of a 1992 election that was meant to bring peace. Hundreds of thousands died; entire cities were destroyed.[11]

In 1998 the United Nations imposed sanctions on Unita's diamond sales. But diamonds lend themselves to smuggling – a single half-decent gem can fetch as much as several tons of iron ore. Unita's exports were not curtailed, merely inconvenienced. Traders simply carried the stones across the border and declared them to be Congolese or Zambian. From there they would flow to Antwerp or other centres of the rough diamond trade and were again sold on, chiefly to De Beers, then still a cartel that controlled 80 per cent of the world trade in rough diamonds.[12] Cut, polished and mounted, the diamonds would end their journey on the earlobes and ring fingers of the wealthy and the amorous.

The notion of a 'blood diamond' strengthened as consumers came to realize that beautifying their hands came at the cost of African limbs. In Sierra Leone rebels under the tutelage of Charles Taylor, a warlord in neighbouring Liberia, severed hands and feet as they waged a campaign devoid of any cause beyond amassing power and wealth. From the time of its formation in 1991 the principal goal of the Revolutionary United Front and its army of child soldiers was to maintain control of Sierra Leone's diamond fields, channelling the stones into Liberia for export to the world market. For a decade government troops, rebels and a regional Nigerian-led force vied to outdo one another with the scale of their violence and looting. All the while the diamond trade dripped fuel into the conflict. As in Angola, when the United Nations imposed an embargo on diamonds from Sierra Leone in 2000, the stones flowed out through Taylor's Liberia instead, where declared exports far exceeded domestic production.[13] One lawyer in Freetown, Sierra Leone's bullet-ridden capital, said, 'It is strange to say but I believe that without diamonds this country couldn't have been in this state of exploitation and degradation.'[14]

A British military intervention in 2000 helped to end Sierra Leone's war. Two years later, in Angola, when government troops hunted down Jonas Savimbi and killed him, there was the prospect of lasting peace for the first time since independence in 1975. The same year, the public tarnishing of the resource industry's most illustrious commodity gave rise to the first international mechanism designed to break the link between natural wealth and bloodshed.

Campaigners from Global Witness generated such outrage with their investigations of the links between diamonds and war that De Beers's claims that it had ceased to buy blood diamonds were insufficient to prevent more concerted action. The Kimberley Process, named after the South African mining town that was the scene of the first mining rush in the 1870s, was designed to stop rebel movements like Unita and the RUF from selling diamonds into the world market, either directly or via neighbouring states, by ensuring that every rough stone carried a certificate of origin. Drawing together governments, campaign groups and companies that mined and marketed diamonds, the Kimberley Process was voluntary and often fractious. But its membership grew until it accounted for 99.8 per cent of the diamond trade.[15]

The Kimberley Process helped to stem the flow of blood diamonds, but it had a glaring flaw. Its chief targets were rebel movements. Governments that broke the rules were occasionally sanctioned – and risked losing the premium that came with Kimberley certification – but even atrocities such as those that Mugabe's security forces perpetrated at Marange were not enough to consign a country to the blacklist. In 2011, after the Kimberley Process agreed to certify Zimbabwe's diamonds, Global Witness withdrew in disgust from the organization it had helped found. 'It has become an accomplice to diamond laundering – whereby dirty diamonds are mixed in with clean gems,' said Charmian Gooch, one of the group's founding directors.[16]

Even where a local diamond industry has been managed in exemplary fashion, the vagaries of operating at the lowest rung of the resources industry can be as severe as in countries supplying less glamorous fare like iron, copper or crude oil. Botswana, where diamonds account for three-quarters of exports, is a rare example of an African state that is rich in resources but has not succumbed to war and grand corruption. In part that is because it is so small – the population is 2 million people, fewer than all but five countries of the African mainland – and relatively ethnically homogenous. It was one of the earliest southern African nations to gain independence, in 1967, and had its own functioning institutions in place by the time two gargantuan diamond mines were discovered, helping the government drive a hard bargain with De Beers. Botswana enjoys peace and living conditions that are much better than those of most other Africans. The government has taken a stake in De Beers and forced the company to move some of its cutting and polishing operations to Botswana, part of a concerted effort to begin the long journey from resource economy to industrialization. Yet when the global financial crisis caused demand for diamonds to seize up in 2008, Botswana was reminded of its economic fragility. The United States, which accounts for half of the world's diamond sales each year, slipped into recession, causing diamond prices to tumble.

'There is no doubt we are facing a huge challenge,' Ian Khama, Botswana's president, told me in March 2009.[17] 'The main reason is because we have been very dependent on revenues from minerals, especially diamonds, ever since they were found in the seventies.'

When I turned up at Jwaneng, the De Beers mine in southern Botswana rated as the most valuable on the planet, the scene was a far cry from the Hollywood bash hosted by Khama's predecessor as president a few weeks earlier – in the resplendent company of the supermodel Helena Christensen, the actress Sharon Stone and the burlesque starlet Dita Von Teese – to try to speed the resuscitation of the diamond industry on which his country depends.[18] The rickety dwellings of the informal settlement that had grown up around the mine were emptying out. De Beers had decided to mothball the mine until the world economy picked up and demand for diamonds returned. The mood in the *shebeens*, the unlicensed drinking dens selling potent brews and sorghum beer, was grim. 'I came here as a boy,' Edwin Phaladi, a fifty-two-year-old cobbler, told me. 'Now I'm going back to my village.'[19]

No matter whether they are trading in copper or gold or natural gas, repressive regimes need middlemen to turn their control of resources into money. The diamond industry is peculiarly closed and complex, however, with stones sold either under long-term contracts or at private auctions, their value determined by gauging the aesthetics of refracted light or the relative merits of a hint of pink to a tinge of yellow. The barons of the diamond trade rank among the most powerful figures in the African resource game. Dan Gertler, whose grandfather founded Israel's diamond exchange, got his start in Congo by winning a diamond monopoly in exchange for funds to help arm Laurent Kabila's forces. Long before the scandal over payments to the wife of a Guinean dictator cost his mining company its multibillion-dollar iron-ore rights in Guinea, Beny Steinmetz had expanded the family diamond business into the biggest supplier to De Beers and had struck a deal to provide gems from postwar Sierra Leone to Tiffany's. (Steinmetz's marketing strategy includes furnishing Formula One cars with steering wheels encrusted with diamonds, a touch that adds 'a real bit of bling to the cars', according to one of the lucky drivers, Lewis Hamilton.) [20]

Lev Leviev, the third kingpin of African diamonds, is, like Steinmetz and Gertler, a billionaire and a citizen of Israel, one of the three centres of the diamond trade alongside Belgium and India. Unlike his two compatriots, however, Leviev was not brought up in one of the great diamond families. He was born in Uzbekistan, then still a Soviet satellite, before moving with his Jewish parents to Israel as a teenager. Penniless but ambitious – 'I knew from the time I was six that I was destined to be a millionaire,' he has said – he left school and began an apprenticeship in the diamond trade, learning the art of cutting and polishing stones.[21] But the best rough diamonds were reserved for the privileged 'sightholders' anointed by De Beers. Leviev muscled his way into that club – then took on the cartel. First in Russia, then in Angola, he went directly to the authorities, bypassing De Beers. No one had attempted so bold a challenge before, and Leviev's audacity started to loosen De Beers's stranglehold on the industry.

When Leviev arrived in Angola in the mid-1990s the war was entering its final stages. He co-founded a company to buy Angolan stones and secured an 18 per cent stake in Catoca, a choice diamond prospect in territory that the government had, by the time mining began in 1998, reclaimed from the rebels. It would become one of the world's great mines.[22]

Having elbowed out De Beers, Leviev was made. His cutting and polishing operation became the world's largest.[23] He built a business that ran the length of the diamond trade, from mines in Angola, Namibia and elsewhere to jewelry stores on Bond Street and Madison Avenue. Africa Israel, a sprawling multinational conglomerate listed in Tel Aviv of which Leviev took control in 1996, has dabbled in everything from bikinis to US petrol stations to the construction of Israeli settlements in occupied Palestinian territory.[24] A devout adherent of the Chabad, a fundamentalist branch of

Judaism, Leviev ploughed part of his fortune into advancing the cause, building schools and synagogues and orphanages in Russia and beyond. For himself, he built a $70 million mansion in the exclusive north London enclave of Hampstead, complete with movie theatre, swimming pool and an armour-plated front door behind which he, his wife, and two of his nine children took up residence in 2008.[25]

Following the September 11 attacks in New York in 2001, Leviev snapped up bargain stakes in the New York Times Building, Madison Avenue's Clock Tower, and other downtown Manhattan real estate he planned to convert into luxury condominiums. When the financial crisis struck in 2007, the properties' values collapsed along with the rest of the US real estate market. Leviev had borrowed heavily to fund the acquisitions and now found himself, in the words of one associate, 'on the balls of his ass'. He sought to offload some of the portfolio, and in November 2008 struck a deal to sell his most illustrious property, 23 Wall Street, the former home of J.P. Morgan bank, across the road from the New York Stock Exchange. The buyer agreed to pay $150 million for it, a generous sum in a plunging market. 'No one could understand why anyone would pay $150 million for that,' a businessman familiar with the deal told me. 'The most optimistic scenario you could create in November 2008 was $75 million.'

The buyer was China Sonangol, the joint venture between the Queensway Group and the Angolan state-owned oil company, and the deal was part of a string of transactions that secured for Sam Pa's network a piece of Wall Street and an entry to the African diamond trade.

While Lev Leviev's property acquisitions were submerged in debt, the Queensway Group had money to burn after coming through its 2007 crisis. Its first Angolan oil field had started producing crude; other ventures were taking shape. A Western businessman who worked with China Sonangol was told that the company was generating $100 million after expenses each month. Property was the group's new frontier, from luxury apartments in Singapore to a planned office development in North Korea. Through deals hatched in the recesses of the financial system, the Queensway Group and its allies in the Futungo began to turn commodities deep beneath Africa's oceans and soils into cash, and to turn that cash into prestigious bricks-and-mortar assets within the exalted citadels of global commerce.

Before the sale of 23 Wall Street Leviev's company announced that China Sonangol would also be buying its stakes in the Clock Tower and the New York Times Building. But property records show no sign of those transactions taking place. Nonetheless, court documents show that Leviev's US property company agreed to waive half a million dollars from the J.P. Morgan building sale 'to preserve the important business relationship between the parties'.[26]

The acquisition of the J.P. Morgan building was only the most visible link between the Queensway Group and Leviev.[27] In late 2009 Leviev sold China Sonangol his 18 per cent stake in Catoca, the Angolan diamond mine that yields stones worth hundreds of millions of dollars every year, for $250 million. China Sonangol had bailed out Leviev's adventures in Manhattan real estate; now Leviev had made China Sonangol the first Chinese company to own a stake in an African diamond mine.

At a dinner in Hong Kong in 2009 Pa and Leviev could be seen chatting away. But the relationship would sour. In 2014 a Leviev spokesperson told me that, despite corporate records that showed an enduring connection, 'the Leviev Group has no joint business with Mr Sam Pa or with any companies associated with him.' Yet Sam Pa was already broadening his interests in African diamonds – into Zimbabwe's Marange fields.

The campaign ad's soundtrack belonged in some wholesome 1950s caper; the woman's voice narrating it was silky and chipper. A cartoon showed pots of glittering mineral treasures strewn across Africa, particularly Zimbabwe. But this wealth was not serving those it should. Little single-prop airplanes zoomed away with all that treasure, generating billions of dollars for foreign companies. Meanwhile, the narrator explained, 'Africa, the richest continent, remains poor.' The solution was the 'indigenization' of the mining industry. Transferring stakes in foreign mining companies' local subsidiaries to indigenous owners or to the state would cause a greater share of the revenues to stay in the country. Cartoon hospitals and cartoon schools bloomed like flowers across Zimbabwe.

The ad chimed neatly with the footage that ZBC, Zimbabwe's state broadcaster, had aired immediately before it, showing one of Robert Mugabe's final rallies before the July 2013 election. Despite being only a few months short of ninety, the president's speeches had lost little of their polish or rage and none of their length. Zanu-PF supporters decked out in the party's yellow and green – some genuine, some probably dragooned – held up banners declaring, 'Zimbabwe is not for sale.' 'Down with those who would sell Zimbabwe,' boomed the emcee, denouncing the opposition MDC's support in the West.

The rally and the campaign cartoon captured the essence of Mugabe's message: the work of the liberator who threw off the yoke of white rule was unfinished. Imperial forces still kept Zimbabwe down.

They had a point. The export of oil, gas and minerals in raw form contributes to keeping Africa's resource states trapped at the foot of the global economy, unable to industrialize. Zimbabwe has a bounteous share of southern Africa's minerals: nickel, platinum and gold as well as the diamonds of Marange. The idea of indigenization seems reasonable. Across the region the post-liberation redistribution of land, mineral wealth and other economic interests has lagged far behind political emancipation. Mugabe's government has repeatedly ordered foreign mining companies operating in the country to hand over a 51 per cent stake of their local subsidiaries to indigenous black owners. Ministers described the policy with more wrath than detail, but it was broadly supposed to follow the model of South Africa's Black Economic Empowerment programme, under which mining groups lend money to locals to buy the stakes, with the loans to be repaid out of the dividends that the new owners would earn from future profits.

Critics of the South African programme point out that it has contributed to maintaining the sort of inequitable economic structures that prevailed under apartheid by creating a new rentier class of black moguls. But Zimbabwe's indigenization has not even got that far, in part because the authorities have been more interested in personal rather than national enrichment. Solomon Mujuru, the former army chief whose wife became Mugabe's vice president in 2004, provided a telling example when he neatly combined venality and geopolitics. According to a leaked account by the head of the local subsidiary of Impala Platinum, the biggest platinum miner in Zimbabwe, Mujuru privately offered to shield the company from Chinese designs on its assets if it agreed to select him as its 'indigenous partner and protector'.[28] Such machinations have helped to stymie any large-scale transfer of ownership even to the crony class, let alone ordinary Zimbabweans.

Mugabe has long sought to blame Zimbabwe's economic collapse on Western sanctions. In reality those sanctions are aimed at his personal interests and those of his coterie. Even after the European Union bowed to lobbying by Belgium, the heart of the diamond trade, in September 2013 and permitted the sale of Zimbabwean stones in Europe by lifting sanctions on the state-owned mining company, which has stakes in several Marange ventures, Mugabe stuck to his narrative.[29] 'Our small and peaceful country is threatened daily by covetous and bigoted big powers whose hunger for domination and control of other nations and their resources knows no bounds,' he said in a speech later that month to the UN General Assembly in New York.[30]

But just as Angola's José Eduardo dos Santos fought against apartheid South Africa only to preside over an elite that has used oil money to cut itself off from the rest, Robert Mugabe sits atop a feudal ruling class that resembles in structure – if not skin colour – the minority rule he waged a guerrilla war to overthrow.

In many African resource states the oil and mining industries took hold before independence, before the newborn nations had had a chance to develop institutions to steward the common good and circumscribe arbitrary power. When giant oil fields were discovered in the North Sea in 1969, Norway and the UK had the institutions in place to mitigate the destructive force of oil money. Not so with countries such as Nigeria, where Shell was pumping oil before British colonial rulers departed.

'The British and the rest, they were like the Spanish conquistadores,' Folarin Gbadebo-Smith, a Nigerian polymath who qualified as a dentist before studying at the Kennedy School of Government at Harvard, serving in the Lagos local government, running the Nigerian-Asian chamber of commerce, and founding a think tank called the Centre for Policy Alternatives, told me when we met one afternoon at a mutual friend's house in Abuja.[31] 'The colonial powers set up a machine, a machine to extract resources. When they left, it passed to the next leaders, like DNA. In so many places the military took over to capture the rent. It is incredibly difficult to change that structure. The foreign partners remain with their collaborators. It's like a virus, transmitted from the colonial regime to the post-independence rulers. And these extractors, they are the opposite of a society that is governed for the commonwealth, for the public good.'

The archetype of these extractors, those who use the conquest of natural resources to advance political power and vice versa, was Cecil John Rhodes.[32] Arriving in the central plains of what would become South Africa during the diamond frenzy of the 1870s, Rhodes rose from small-time digger to lord of the diamond trade. He founded De Beers and, when gold was discovered to the north of the diamond fields, launched Gold Fields of South Africa, which still ranks among the biggest gold miners, with mines from Australia to Peru.

Rhodes, who served as prime minister of the Cape Colony for five years beginning in 1890 and had private armies at his command, was an avowed imperialist. He sought relentlessly to expand northward the interwoven projects of British colonial rule and his own corporate interests by way of treaties, force of arms and duplicity. His most hegemonic venture, the British South Africa Company, had a royal charter affording it powers akin to those of a government. The region's black inhabitants, from the Xhosa of the eastern Cape – Nelson Mandela's people – to Robert Mugabe's Shona ancestors in Rhodesia, were gradually subjugated and marginalized.

Rhodes died in 1902, humbled by his support of the disastrous Jameson Raid into Boer territory. W. T. Stead, the great crusading newspaperman of Victorian Britain, called Cecil Rhodes 'the first of the new Dynasty of Money Kings which has evolved in these later days as the real rulers of the modern world'.[33] That description echoes down the century that followed and past the turn of the millennium. Areva in Niger, Shell in Nigeria, Glencore in Congo – they and others like them replicate in their sheer power over African nations the empires that came before them. Twice when I asked seasoned mining executives in Africa what they made of the Queensway Group, they drew an analogy with Rhodes. 'It's Rhodes all over again . . . a huge mafia,' said one I spoke to in Zimbabwe. In Angola another executive, who had watched the group penetrate the inner circles of power and then launch its expansion across the continent, told me, 'It has megalomaniac tendencies. It's like Rhodes, trying to conquer Africa all over again.' The Western businessman who had dealings with the Queensway Group updated the language: 'They are an old imperialistic company. They have mineral rights, and they have connections into the highest levels of corrupt governments, which gives them the right to take whatever the fuck they want.'

The power structures of the new resource empires differ from those that the likes of Rhodes built in one striking way: they comprise a lot more black faces at higher levels. There are plenty of examples of African complicity in the exploitation of the continent by foreign powers, from the slave trade onward. The classic imperial ploy, perfected by the British, was to foster a client elite whose authority would be buttressed by London, provided that that elite maintained London's interests. Today in Africa's resource states the local potentates are equal partners with the oil executives, the mining magnates and the globetrotting middlemen. There have even been some direct reversals of the old order: Sonangol, the Futungo's vehicle for broadcasting its power and wealth, has bought stakes in Portuguese banks and utilities and holds Portuguese sovereign debt. When Portugal's prime minister went to Luanda after the EU agreed to bail out his country's stricken economy, he said his government would look 'very favourably' on Angolan investment.[34]

As Rhodes knew, to profit from natural resources, one has need of armed forces to protect both the terrain under which they lie and the political status quo. Oil and mining groups routinely use armed private security companies to guard their facilities; bands of mercenaries are still prepared to go to war on the promise of resource dollars. But these days raising a fully fledged private army is generally deemed beyond the pale. For a would-be latter-day Rhodes, the trick is to forge an alliance with the local purveyors of violence. Sam Pa and the Queensway Group sought out Robert Mugabe's secret police.

The Zimbabwean security forces are the heart of Mugabe's regime, and the Central Intelligence Organisation is the heart of those security forces.

Mugabe inherited the organization when he displaced Ian Smith, Zimbabwe's last white ruler, in 1980 and retained its boss, Ken Flower. As the first hopeful years of Mugabe's reign gave way to terror, the CIO became the lead violin in his orchestra of fear.

'Apart from its core mandate of intelligence-gathering, the CIO has also engaged in paramilitary operations and is heavily implicated in Zimbabwe's culture of violence,' writes Knox Chitiyo, a Zimbabwean authority on the security services who has taught at the army staff college.[35] 'The CIO is notorious for abductions and the use of torture to extract information.' With as many as ten thousand personnel inside Zimbabwe plus its informal operatives and agents abroad, the organization reaches into every corner of society. At election time its mandate is to intimidate Zanu-PF's opponents and induce voters to cast their ballots for the ruling party or not at all.[36] When artisanal miners in Marange notice someone they suspect of being a CIO agent drawing near, they warn one another by saying that there are cattle eating in the fields, a harbinger of starvation reapplied to signal a different kind of danger.

The CIO reports directly to Mugabe and is funded through the office of the president, where the budget is off-limits to parliamentary scrutiny. The secret police does business on the side too, after the fashion of the Russian intelligence services or General Kopelipa, the head of Angola's military bureau.[37] The Zimbabwean army, police force and CIO have all been linked to the obscure mining companies that were assigned rights to mine Marange's diamonds.[38] 'In a country filled with corrupt schemes,' a US diplomat wrote in a 2008 cable, 'the diamond business in Zimbabwe is one of the dirtiest.'[39]

Sam Pa's dealings with the CIO stretch back at least to early 2008, before the elections that year that brought about Zimbabwe's power-sharing government. In February 2008 Pa's private plane began arriving at Harare airport, according to documents purporting to be internal CIO reports, obtained by Global Witness.[40] On his monthly visits Pa bought diamonds from the military and the CIO, which were already plugging themselves into Marange before taking full control with Operation No Return. In exchange Pa pumped money into Mugabe's shadow state. According to the leaked documents, his payments to the CIO reached $100 million by early 2010, a sum almost equivalent to the entire annual budget of the government department that includes the secret police. He also threw in a fleet of Nissan off-road vehicles.[41]

Two well-connected Zimbabwean businessmen told me that Sam Pa's ultimate business partner in Zimbabwe was Happyton Bonyongwe, the head of the CIO and Mugabe's spymaster. I have not seen anything on paper recording such a partnership. There is, however, a paper trail that connects the Queensway Group to the CIO.

While Sam Pa was trading stones that others were mining at Marange, a company called Sino Zim Development won the chance to dig for itself. The Zimbabwean government granted it a concession to mine diamonds in the Marange fields. This was the company that Shuah Mudiwa, the opposition MP in Marange, told me was 'the military of China and the CIO'. The Chinese military does not appear to have had any direct interest; perhaps Mudiwa had got wind of Sam Pa's arms dealing and his ties to the Chinese intelligence services. While a handful of other companies began to churn out stones from Marange, Sino Zim's prospect came up dry. According to Queensway Group lawyers, by 2012 Sino Zim had given up its concession without exporting 'a single carat'.[42] But Sino Zim appears to have served another purpose: it formalized the Queensway Group's business connection to the CIO.

By 2009 the Queensway Group was increasingly using Singapore as a base for its worldwide operations. The companies at the apex of its corporate structure remained registered in Hong Kong, but the city-state across the South China Sea offered many of the same opportunities for corporate secrecy while also allowing the Queensway Group to advance its transition to a fully fledged multinational not tethered to its Chinese and African roots. On 12 June 2009, a few months after Operation No Return had torn through Marange, Sino Zim Development Pte, Ltd. was registered in Singapore. Its sister company, also called Sino Zim Development but registered in Zimbabwe, received a diamond concession in the Marange fields, and the Singaporean company shifted $50 million into the country on behalf of the Zimbabwean company.[43] Both companies were tied to the Queensway Group's leading figures.

As usual, Sino Zim's ownership looped through the opaque recesses of the financial system. The Singaporean company had two shareholders;

both were companies registered in the British Virgin Islands, where ownership is secret but signatories, if they are not one of the agents who each tend to act on behalf of thousands of companies, usually have at least an influence over the company and are likely to own it in part or in whole.

The signatory for the company that held 70 per cent of Sino Zim's shares was Lo Fong-hung, Sam Pa's principal partner, who holds stakes in a score of other Queensway companies. The signatory for the company that held the remaining 30 per cent of Sino Zim was a new addition to the Queensway constellation: Masimba Ignatius Kamba, who gave as his address the seventh floor of Chester House in central Harare.[44] In the days leading up to Zimbabwe's elections in July 2013 I went looking for Kamba at his Harare address. I wanted to try to verify what I had heard: the Queensway Group's business partner in Zimbabwe was a member of Mugabe's secret police. The Zimbabwean press had named Kamba as a member of the CIO, and the opposition had named him as the organization's director of administration.[45]

Harare's business district is livelier than the sleepy, verdant avenues of the suburbs, but it is positively genteel compared with the furore of Lagos or Luanda. Not far from Harare's main bus terminal, a block over from Robert Mugabe Road, Chester House is a bland concrete high-rise of offices. In the dingy reception I signed my name in the visitors' book and was informed that the lift was broken. I set off up the winding flights of stairs. The signs on the entrances to the offices on the lower floors said they belonged to the Ministry of Education and Culture. I reached the seventh floor, which Kamba lists as his address in Sino Zim's company filings, but, for the moment, I clambered on upward, suspecting that if there were a CIO presence in the building, it might have something to do with the organization whose headquarters occupy the ninth and tenth floors, the Zimbabwean Congress of Trade Unions.

Before he became the opposition leader, Morgan Tsvangirai used to run the ZCTU. The photographs of bruised and battered unionists on the walls of its head office testified to the organization's active resistance to the regime. I asked one unionist what went on on the lower floors. 'The sixth and seventh floors, that's where we have the CIO guys,' the unionist told me. 'We don't relocate because they just follow us.' So Ignatius Kamba was using a CIO office with a mandate to spy on trade unionists as his official address for business dealings with the Queensway Group.

Struggling to keep thoughts of the CIO's penchant for brutality out of my head, I walked back down the stairs. 'Zelgold Investments: Registered Money Lender' read the blue and yellow sign beside the entrance that led from the stairwell to the offices on the seventh floor, Kamba's registered address. I walked in and popped my head in the first door. Inside was a sparsely furnished room with freshly whitewashed walls. A burly, smartly dressed man sat at a desk bellowing into a telephone. His colleague, also in suit and tie, looked startled when I said I was looking for Masimba Ignatius Kamba.

He missed a beat. 'What company?'

'Sino Zim,' I said.

The man informed me that Sino Zim's offices were on another street a few blocks away, and it was clear from the atmosphere in the room that it was time to leave.

Two days later I followed the directions to Sino Zim that the man at Kamba's registered office had given me. At the reception I asked again for Kamba. 'This is a Chinese company, and our bosses are in a meeting,' came the reply. This, it turned out, was not the office of Sino Zim Development, the company that had secured the diamond concession at Marange, but of a company with a similar name that ran the Queensway's Group's cotton venture in Zimbabwe. To find Sino Zim I was told to head back out and carry on past the headquarters of Megawatt House, the dilapidated state electricity company. I reached Livingstone House, an angular and imposing twenty-two-story building that was the city's tallest when it was constructed under white rule and named after the Scottish missionary pioneer immortalized in Western imaginings of Africa through his encounter in 1871 with the British explorer Stanley ('Dr. Livingstone, I presume?'). Today the skyscraper houses, among other things, Zimbabwe's ineffectual anticorruption commission. Its proprietors were the same outfit that has snapped up another office complex across town and a hotel that is popular for weddings in the suburbs – the Queensway Group.[46]

The lobby at Livingstone House was only slightly less grand than that of Luanda One, the Queensway Group's Angolan skyscraper. At the entrance to the third floor I finally saw the official logo of Sino Zim, opposite the office for the local branch of Coca-Cola. Sino Zim's reception area opened onto a large balcony covered with AstroTurf and overlooking a thicket of trees. The executives worked out of the seventh floor, I was told. I took the lift up and entered a well-appointed office with abstract art on the walls. An elegant secretary informed me that Sino Zim's management had gone home for the day. As I wrote out a note (which was never answered) I asked the secretary whether Sam Pa ever visited the office. She smiled. 'He comes and goes.'

The air was laden with humidity as I walked through the manmade canyons of Hong Kong. Glittering skyscrapers were interspersed with besmirched high-rise tenements and the occasional dilapidated edifice swathed in bamboo scaffolding. It was a Monday morning in May 2014, and the front pages of newspapers on sale in the bustling streets reported on the protests that had broken out in Vietnam after China sent an oil rig into disputed waters, the latest regional provocation by an increasingly assertive power. I walked past the spot where, nine years earlier, a close-range volley of tear gas floored me as I reported on a march on the World Trade Organization summit taking place within the Hong Kong Exhibition Centre by Korean farmers demonstrating against the privations of globalization.

I reached the address I was looking for: Pacific Place, the crown of towers at 88 Queensway. I went through the mall at street level, with its luxury boutiques and moody lighting, and up to the courtyard between the towers, decorated with greenery. An expensive café catered to the cosmopolitan financiers who work here. China Sonangol, China International Fund and assorted more discreet companies of the Queensway Group are registered at Hong Kong's corporate registry at the tenth floor of Two Pacific Place, the second tower with the curved veneer of mirrored glass.

The spacious lobby was decorated with little paintings on the walls in a jaunty 1940s style, depicting businessmen carrying briefcases and playing golf and women walking tiny dogs and having their skirts blown upward like Marilyn Monroe. I emerged from the lift – all marble and mirrors – on the tenth floor and saw, behind glass doors, the logo of China Sonangol.

Inside there was a waiting room off to the left and a knee-high statue of an African woman, carved in dark stone. I buzzed the intercom, and a woman in glasses and blue blouse let me in. Before I could introduce myself another woman emerged. She was short, with a rounded face and black hair in a bob and wearing a black blouse and black trousers. She asked who I was. I explained that I worked as a reporter for the *Financial Times* and was writing a book in which China Sonangol would appear. Both women smiled politely, but a distinct awkwardness remained in the air.

I rattled off the names of other companies in the Queensway Group registered to the address where we were standing: China International Fund, New Bright, Dayuan. I named Lo Fong-hung, who has listed this office as her address. The woman in black told me she didn't know of these companies. I asked about China Sonangol, whose logo was on the wall beside us. She told me to look at the website. I explained I had sent countless e-mails, none of which had received a reply. She insisted I send another one. I asked whether there was anyone at the office who could answer my questions. She told me she was not 'senior', that there were no managers here, that I must have the wrong place. I asked whether I could leave a written message for a manager. She declined. I asked for the name of someone I could contact. She declined. I asked her name. She declined. I pointed to a stack of brochures including copies of *CIF Space*, the in-house newsletter of China International Fund, a company the woman had said she knew nothing about. I asked to have one. 'We cannot distribute them,' she said, then added, 'I think you should leave.' I stepped out, the door clicked behind me, and the woman vanished. I buzzed the intercom again and tried to ask after Sam Pa. 'No,' said the receptionist.

It was the same story at the office on the forty-fourth floor of the next tower along the main road, the Lippo Centre at 89 Queensway, a building that resembles a giant Jenga stack and to which the group had recently switched some of its registered addresses. There, I didn't even make it through the door of another China Sonangol office before being asked to leave.

I did, however, get hold of Sam Pa's mobile number. I called it repeatedly. Mostly it rang out or went to a message suggesting he was out of Hong Kong. Twice he answered, and I explained that I was going to write about him. He spoke English with a thick accent. The first time he said he was at lunch; the second time he said he was in a meeting. Both times he told me he would call back. He never did. As far as I know he has never given an interview.

The one person from the Queensway Group who would speak to me was China Sonangol's lawyer, Jee Kin Wee. We exchanged e-mails in 2014. I wrote a detailed letter to him, posing fifty-two questions about the Queensway Group and its activities. A letter came back, signed China Sonangol, which answered four of them. 'Due to confidentiality agreements and our legitimate desire for privacy, which private companies are entitled to, we will not be providing you with any additional information than is necessary [sic],' the letter read. 'We do however reserve our rights to pursue legal remedies if you repeat or publish defamatory statements.' It went on, 'We are not a listed company and the Law does not require us to disclose all our business dealings in the same manner as listed companies.'[47]

Sam Pa travels constantly. His jet rarely stays put for more than a few days. In the first months of 2014 alone it shuttled between Hong Kong, Singapore, Mauritius, Madagascar, the Maldives, Angola, Zimbabwe, Indonesia (where China Sonangol has a slice of a natural gas field) and Beijing.[48]

Like Rhodes before him, Pa's African horizons are forever widening. In December 2013 Ernest Bai Koroma, the president of Sierra Leone, a nation scarred by its diamond-funded war but where peace has started to take hold, stopped off in Angola on his way home from Nelson Mandela's memorial service in South Africa. Over dinner and red wine at Luanda One, the Queensway Group's golden skyscraper, Koroma held what a statement from his office described as 'fruitful discussions with Chinese Business Tycoon and Vice Chairman of China International Fund Limited, Mr Sam, on key infrastructural developments to be implemented in Sierra Leone'.[49] A photograph shows Koroma engrossed in conversation with Pa, who is dressed in his usual dark suit and spectacles, a mobile phone on the table in front of him, gesturing as through ticking off items on a checklist. (Another photograph, taken a year earlier, shows Pa looking on as Koroma signs a memorandum of understanding between Sierra Leone, China International Fund and China Railway Construction Corporation, a giant

Chinese state-owned company that employs 240,000 people, for a slew of projects ranging from diamonds to fisheries.) [50]

The Queensway empire is expanding to new frontiers far from its heartlands in Africa's oil fields, mineral seams and diamond pipes. China Sonangol recruited Alain Fanaie, a former senior resource-industry banker at Crédit Agricole, a French bank that had helped it arrange multibillion-dollar loans. Fanaie was installed as chief executive of China Sonangol, operating out of its Singapore headquarters. (In July 2014 China Sonangol issued a brief statement saying that Fanaie had resigned.) [51] But even as it acquired the outward trappings of a regular company, Sam Pa remained its chief emissary.

In September 2013 Sam Pa posed for photographs at a signing ceremony in Dubai beside Sheikh Ahmed bin Saeed al-Maktoum, a senior member of the oil-rich emirate's royal family. They had just put ink to a deal for China Sonangol to build what Dubai's official press release called a 'state-of-the-art refinery' to process crude oil.[52] In May 2014 Pa attended another ceremony, this time in Beijing. He sat next to Marat Khusnullin, the deputy mayor of Moscow, and Hu Zhenyi, the vice president of China Railway Construction Corporation. Pa was representing China International Fund in an agreement to build a new metro line in Moscow. Khusnullin, the deputy mayor, was in town as part of the delegation accompanying Vladimir Putin to China. Two months earlier Putin had annexed Crimea following the fall of the pro-Russian president of Ukraine, prompting the United States and Europe to impose sanctions on Putin's inner circle and Russia's oil industry. It was a deal straight out of the Queensway Group's African playbook: cultivating a regime recently placed under international sanctions, denounced as a pariah in the West, mired in corruption and rich in natural resources.

J. R. Mailey, an American researcher who was part of the congressional research team that first identified the Queensway Group and coined its name, has developed an encyclopedic knowledge of Sam Pa's corporate empire. I asked him what he thought would become of the Queensway Group. 'Even if Queensway's business empire crumbles, everything that allowed Sam Pa to rise in the first place is still there. He still has the Rolodex; he still knows how to get close to elites in fragile states. Most importantly he knows how to operate under the radar and just beyond the reach of law enforcement. If it weren't him, it would be someone else. The system is still there: these investors can still form a company without saying who they are, they can still anchor their business in a country that is not concerned about investors' behaviour overseas, and, sadly, there's no shortage of resource-rich fragile states on which these investors can prey.[53]

Sino Zim gave up its concession in Zimbabwe's diamond fields, saying it was 'commercially unviable'. It was said in Harare's mining circles in 2013 that the company was looking at another corner of Marange as well as mineral prospects. China International Fund, the Queensway Group's outward face, denied giving money to Mugabe's secret police.[54] But Sam Pa carried on coming and going from Harare.

In April 2014, eight months after Robert Mugabe rigged his way back to total control of a country he had already ruled for thirty-three years, the US Treasury added Sam Pa's seven names to its list of 'specially designated nationals'. The Zimbabwean Sino Zim Development was also added to the list, though not the Singaporean company with the near-identical name. The people and companies on the list are those 'owned or controlled by, or acting for or on behalf of' the rulers of countries subject to US sanctions. American companies are prohibited from doing business with them, and their US assets are frozen. Beijing had already tried to put some distance between itself and the Queensway Group. The Chinese embassy in Harare said in 2009 that the Chinese government had 'nothing to do with the business operations of a company named China International Fund'.[55] (Even the Queensway Group itself maintains a fig leaf of separation between its corporate structure and the man who jets round the world striking deals on its behalf: China Sonangol's lawyer told me that Sam Pa was merely an 'adviser' to the company.) [56]

But Chinese companies carried on winning contracts in Africa's resource states on the coat-tails of the Queensway Group. The US authorities stopped short of adding to the sanctions list China Sonangol, whose partners in Angolan oil ventures include the biggest American oil companies and on whose behalf Sam Pa jets around the world signing deals.[57]

Nothing that we have done is reversible. Those were Mahmoud Thiam's words as he prepared to leave Guinea and go back to New York, his mining deals complete. The sentiment might seem ludicrous in hindsight: the elected government that followed the junta Thiam served ejected Sam Pa and Beny Steinmetz, both of whom he had supported. In another way, though, he was right. Sam Pa's reign as a baron of the African resource trade might endure, or he might return to obscurity as rapidly as he rose from it, felled by the fickle politics of resource states. But the looting machine has known many captains in many guises: King Leopold, Cecil Rhodes, Mobutu, Mugabe, and hosts of executives from Western oil and mining companies and their new Chinese counterparts. They are rivals ostensibly, yet all of them profit from the natural wealth whose curse sickens the lives of hundreds of millions of Africans.

The empires of colonial Europe and the Cold War superpowers have given way to a new form of dominion over the continent that serves as the mine of the world – new empires controlled not by nations but by alliances of unaccountable African rulers governing through shadow states, middlemen who connect them to the global resource economy, and multinational companies from the West and the East that cloak their corruption in corporate secrecy. We prefer not to think of the mothers of eastern Congo, the slum dwellers of Luanda and the miners of Marange as we talk on our phones, fill up our cars and propose to our lovers. As long as we go on choosing to avert our gaze, the looting machine will endure.

EPILOGUE

Complicity

Around the corner from where I now live, in east London, there is a café with a chalkboard sign that reads, 'Ethically sourced organic coffee here!' The coffee comes from a company founded by Bob Marley's son Rohan, which gets its beans in from Jamaica, Central America and Ethiopia. In the supermarket further down the road the label on a packet of dates says they were grown in Israel; the grapes are from Chile. There is less attention to provenance in the other shops, selling jewelry and mobile phones and fizzy drinks in aluminium cans, or in the real estate agents offering houses with copper wiring and stainless steel kitchens, or in the gas station, with its assorted grades of gas and diesel. Commodities from every continent blend together in the snaking supply chains of the global economy, and it is safe to say that there are incognito nuggets of Africa for sale on my east London high street just as there are in the malls of Los Angeles and the boutiques of Rome. Likewise, through our pension funds invested in their shares, we all enjoy the profits of the giant corporations of the oil and mining industries.

When something undesirable, rather than shipments of treasure, arrives from Africa there is uproar. African migrants – some refugees, some driven by poverty to take desperate risks – die in their hundreds every year as they attempt to cross the Mediterranean in pitifully unseaworthy vessels trying to reach Europe. In late 2014 Italy's government announced that it would end a search-and-rescue operation that had saved 150,000 lives in the year since it began (but that had, it could be argued, prompted the people smugglers who organize the boats to pack ever more passengers onto ever more hopeless craft). The fact that tankers carrying African crude that has despoiled and corrupted the countries in which it was pumped are free to ply the same routes did not enter the debate. After two American aid workers in Liberia became infected with the Ebola virus in July 2014 and were flown back to the United States for treatment, Donald Trump wrote on Twitter, 'Stop the EBOLA patients from entering the U.S. Treat them, at the highest level, over there. THE UNITED STATES HAS ENOUGH PROBLEMS!' *Newsweek* ran a picture of a monkey on its cover, alongside an improbable story about the danger that imports of African bushmeat would unleash the virus on America.[1] Few made the connection between the debilitating effects of a looting machine that funnels African wealth to the rich world and the inability of the countries where Ebola was rife to fight the virus. By October Ebola and the haemorrhagic fever it induces had visited the most terrifying deaths imaginable on five thousand people in Guinea, Liberia and Sierra Leone, countries that were tentatively emerging from war and dictatorship. In all three the virus fed off the resource curse, which had helped to enfeeble health services and corrode the state's ability to safeguard its citizens. There was no talk of closing Western borders to these countries' diamonds, bauxite and iron ore.

Indeed, industrialized countries' hunger for African resources only grows. The commodity boom that fattened the pot of rent in Nigeria, Angola, Congo and the rest of Africa's resource states has prompted oil and mining companies to spend lavishly on exploring virgin territory. New gas finds in east Africa are estimated to exceed the entire reserves of the United Arab Emirates, not far behind those of the United States.[2] Mining companies are digging deeper underground and prospecting the expanses of the African interior. All but five African countries are either producing crude oil or looking for it.[3] There are already signs that the corrosive effects of the resource trade are spreading in tandem with the industry's new discoveries.

One December night a few years ago I went to a club in London to see Nneka, one of Nigeria's most exciting young musicians. I had seen her play in Lagos and met her a couple of times. A daughter of the Niger Delta, she sings and raps about the hardships oil has visited on her people. One track – 'VIP,' or Vagabond in Power – goes:

> You dey break my heart
> You dey take my soul away
> They make my pikin [child] dey suffer
> They make Africa dey suffer
> Vagabond in Power
> You dey break my heart

As she prepared to launch into a rendition of 'VIP', Nneka reminded the crowd of the role that Shell and other multinational resource companies headquartered in the West play in Nigeria's daily corrosion. She gave an instruction, one that applies to all of Africa's looted nations: 'Don't think you're not involved.'

AFTERWORD

The Sofitel in Beijing is a sumptuous place, its foyer all marble and chiaroscuro. The hotel stands only minutes from the great halls of the Communist Party, and guests have included visiting rulers such as the sultan of Brunei. At least one celebrated Asian pop star has reportedly arranged an extramarital liaison at the hotel. The proprietor, one of China's richest men, celebrated a deal by throwing an early-morning champagne bash in the ballroom. Similar to the Chinese approach in Africa, the architects drew on classic French style with 'Chinese inspiration'. It is like some climate-controlled equivalent of a medieval castle, a way station for VIPs of the twenty-first-century's transnational elite.

It was at the Sofitel, on a Thursday evening in October 2015, that Sam Pa discovered that his *guanxi* had run dangerously low.

It is not clear precisely who led Pa away from the hotel that night. By one account, he was drinking with some contacts from Chinese naval intelligence when the operatives arrived. They do not appear to have been from the police, nor indeed from any of the state security agencies. Most likely, they were emissaries from the Party itself, probably its Central Commission for Discipline Inspection, an agency whose name makes those familiar with its methods shudder.

As I write, no one I have spoken to can say categorically what has become of Pa. Perhaps he will smooth his way out of trouble, just as he did in 2007, when changes in the Chinese leadership threatened his young empire. Perhaps he will remain in detention until the Party's interrogation techniques extract the required confession.

I have tried to imagine how Pa felt when he saw the Party operatives approaching. Did he froth with anger, as he does when one of his Queensway functionaries displeases him? Did his stomach vault from a shot of adrenalin as he realized that, at last, the game was up? Do the lords of the looting machine know fear, or does such power flow from the troves of natural riches they control that they feel invincible, even as the mine shaft is collapsing around them?

Pa would have had an inkling of what was coming. The previous day, the Party had announced the defenestration of Su Shulin, the governor of Fujian province. Su was the first sitting governor to be ensnared by the anti-corruption campaign Xi Jinping launched after he assumed the presidency in 2013, promising to purge both 'tigers and flies'. Su was placed under investigation for 'suspected serious disciplinary offences'.[1] The details of such cases rarely become public until the Party has established the narrative to its satisfaction, but Su's arrest seemed to be linked to his tenure as the boss of Sinopec. The vast state-owned oil company had led China's worldwide search for crude supplies. Now an audit had raised some alarming questions about its heavy spending on overseas acquisitions.

Su had not been in charge when Sinopec negotiated its first Angolan deals with the Queensway Group in 2004. But a photograph from 2008 shows Su, flanked by aides, on one side of a stately conference table. Facing him over the floral centrepieces is the Queensway triumvirate. Manuel Vicente, Angola's Mr Oil, looks affable in a dark suit. Lo Fong-hung, in a striped cardigan, is smiling too. And there beside his partners, sporting a loud pink jersey and a chunky wristwatch, is Sam Pa, looking as he must have felt: untouchable.

After Pa's detention, Jee Kin Wee, the lawyer for China Sonangol's arm in Singapore and still the only person within the Queensway Group who has publicly answered my questions, insisted that the company could survive the fall of its frontman. 'In each country in which the company has business interests,' Wee told me, 'the relationship is one between the corporate entity and others, and the contractual obligations of the company and the company's commitment to honouring them do not depend on what happens to any individual.'[2] But an associate of Pa's, who got back in touch with me as news of Pa's detention spread, thought differently.

He foresaw the demise of the Queensway Group. 'A relationship cannot be bought nor transferred,' he said. '[It] takes years of voyage together to build trust.'

When one of its most adept operators falls, the looting machine can appear fragile. If it is no more than a loose affiliation of chancers, schmoozers, wildcatters and bent politicians, held together by bribes, handshakes, complicity in corruption and the fickle loyalty of kleptocrats, then it will gradually fall apart.

Sam Pa is not the only boss of the African resources business who has discovered that the arm of the law is longer and less feeble than an observer of the industry might have surmised. A couple of weeks before Pa's detention, the Metropolitan Police in London arrested and bailed Diezani Alison-Madueke on suspicion of corruption offences (as I write, she has not been charged). Her ruinous stint as Nigeria's oil minister had ended when Nigerians despaired of the venality of Goodluck Jonathan's government and ditched him in March 2015's elections. It was the first time a sitting Nigerian president had been removed from office by the ballot.

Jonathan's replacement was a tall, austere, seventy-two-year-old retired general from the North, Muhammadu Buhari. Buhari had ruled Nigeria once before, at the head of a military government from 1983 to 1985 that is remembered for severe discipline. As I write in Lagos, Nigerians are allowing themselves to hope that the general will stem the pillage of their nation (even if some wag, perhaps jaded by past disappointments, has scrawled 'looting is permitted in all premises' on a wall at the airport).

Xi Jinping's anticorruption campaign in China appears to be a purge of his enemies as much as it is an attempt to clean up politics and remove obstacles to economic reform. But elsewhere, assaults on corrupt elites have been startling in the way they have shaken entrenched power. Brazilian prosecutors exposed a web of corruption that extracted billions of dollars from Petrobras, the state oil company. A scandal over whether the Malaysian prime minister, Najib Razak, was involved in the misappropriation of vast sums from state coffers has consumed that country's politics. On his first visit to Washington after unseating Jonathan, Nigeria's Buhari won a promise that American investigators would help him track down his country's looted oil money. That is, if they have time: a team of them has been busy exposing FIFA as the epitome of a transnational kleptocracy.

Other notable corruption cases still seem a long way from a reckoning. Cobalt International Energy finally sold up in Angola. In August 2015, the company announced it was selling its stakes in offshore Angolan oil prospects to Sonangol, the state oil company. Sonangol agreed to pay Cobalt $1.8 billion of Angolans' money for the stakes. The US Securities and Exchange Commission dropped its civil investigation into Cobalt's Angolan dealings but the Department of Justice's criminal one is still going. And the company continues to deny wrongdoing. Despite three of the most powerful men in Angola having admitted in writing to me that they owned concealed stakes in Cobalt's offshore oil venture, no one has been charged with corruption.

BSG Resources and Beny Steinmetz remain embroiled in half a dozen legal battles related to their claim to the Simandou iron-ore deposit in Guinea. A New York judge threw out Rio Tinto's claim that BSGR had conspired with Vale to steal Rio's rights to half the mountain. Frederic Cilins finished his sentence for obstructing justice and was deported to France. But the criminal investigations continued. A team from the Swiss prosecutor's office investigating the corruption allegations travelled to Conakry, Guinea, in June 2015 to interview witnesses. There have been no charges against the company or Steinmetz in either the Swiss case or the American one, and they maintain that they have done nothing wrong. Indeed, they continue to insist that they are the victims of the machinations of Alpha Condé, a man they strive to style as an evil despot. He won a second term as president in October's elections. There were violent clashes between the security forces and supporters of the opposition, which alleged rigging. But foreign observers considered the elections valid.

Elsewhere, fragile democratic institutions are crumbling. In Congo, Joseph Kabila's apparent attempts to extend his rule beyond its constitutional limit have already caused the electoral timetable to slip. He is part of a growing trend among African nations where the looting machine operates: like Kabila, the rulers of Burundi, Rwanda and Congo-Brazzaville have either ignored term limits designed to prevent dictatorship or look to be trying to do so.

As ever, few have drawn the connection between these countries' political upheavals and the global industries that feed on their natural resources. But some in the West seem to be awakening to the fact that corruption, like football and finance, has gone global.

In a speech in Singapore in July, David Cameron noted what everyone who understands the global financial laundry already knew: that properties in London 'are being bought by people overseas through anonymous shell companies, some with plundered or laundered cash'. He plans a corruption summit in 2016. That will mark a test of whether he can deliver on a promise to push Britain's crown dependencies and overseas territories – which include islands in the Caribbean and English Channel that rank among the world's most secretive tax havens – to create registries of 'beneficial ownership'. That would reveal for the first time the identity of the many thousands who have hitherto been able to incorporate companies there in anonymity – provided, that is, that the registries themselves are made public.

If the leaders who gather at Cameron's summit actually want to choke off an artery of the looting machine, there would be a simple way to do it. To secure new prospects, oil and mining companies either buy a smaller company that has already struck gold or oil or iron ore, or they embark on exploration themselves, often taking a local partner. Vale tried to do the former with its deal to buy BSGR's Guinean assets; Cobalt did the latter when it went into business with Nazaki Oil & Gáz in Angola. With varying degrees of enthusiasm and competence, these oil and mining companies conduct due diligence. Often, the ultimate owners of the target company or the prospective partner will be obscured behind an anonymous shell company. The three officials who secretly held stakes in Nazaki used just such a mechanism. In many cases, the oil or mining company is unable or unwilling to ascertain who is the ultimate owner and proceeds with the deal nonetheless. If it later emerges that the company it bought or took as a partner was in fact used to benefit corrupt officials, the executives can profess horror and innocence.

But what if companies were subject to a duty of care to prevent corruption?

Imagine a criminal offence that made a company liable if it proceeded with a transaction without having identified the ultimate beneficiaries of its target or prospective partner – and that transaction were subsequently shown to have enriched officials. The company would be treated before the law as though it had knowingly concocted a corrupt scheme. At a stroke, one of the chief conduits for corruption would be stoppered.

It would be pretty straightforward to stopper a major outflow of the looting machine, too: simply require the buyers of property to declare their true identity, rather than that of the offshore vehicle they are using either to conceal the source of their wealth, dodge tax, or both. That might also offer some explanation as to why the average Londoner or New Yorker struggles to buy a home: kleptocrats in need of bricks and mortar with which to launder the cash they have stashed in a tax haven are prime customers for Western real estate.

Corruption and money-laundering have a way of evolving, and doubtless would do so again, but that is no reason not to try to stamp out each mutation. Perhaps, though, the propensity of the oil and mining industry to generate more corruption than any other part of the global economy will decline not because the industry gets cleaner but because it withers.

The agreement at the December 2015 Paris climate summit to seek an end to energy produced by fossil fuels capped a miserable year for the resources industry. In June 2014, a barrel of crude sold for $115. Then word got around that the expansion of China's economy, the engine of the world economy, was slowing. By early 2016, oil was down to $30 a barrel. Normally, Saudi Arabia would cut production to push the price back up. This time, the kingdom kept on pumping in an attempt to squeeze rivals, like Brazil and Russia, whose reserves lie so far under the seabed that lower prices make them uneconomic to extract. Executives at oil companies cut their spending plans dramatically. Prices for metals and diamonds tumbled too. Even mighty Glencore was humbled. As its revenues fell, the giant commodity house's debt burden grew, forcing it to sell some assets in haste. From April to September 2015, its shares lost two-thirds of their value. Even Ivan Glasenberg, Glencore's chief executive, felt the chill of austerity: his personal fortune sank below a billion dollars. At a conference in London in October, Glasenberg exhorted African governments to sweeten the terms they offered mining companies: 'You are competing for our money,' he told them.

He was right. And that is why, though from time to time it crushes one of its captains, the looting machine grinds on. Those who control the oil and mineral industries control African kleptocrats' access to the global economy. The fall in commodity prices caused the rulers of African resource states to slash spending on public services. But when it came to sustaining their own control, the straitened times only increased the kleptocrats' determination.

As José Eduardo dos Santos entered his thirty-seventh year as Angola's president, his prospects were looking shaky. Sam Pa, the Futungo's crucial Chinese middleman, was detained. Oil revenues had plunged. Mutterings of discontent grew louder. The response of a regime whose power flows from the looting machine was to lash out.

Dos Santos's security forces threw a group of young Angolans in jail. For months, they were held without charge, before being released to house arrest. One of them, a rapper called Henrique Luaty da Silva Beirão, spent thirty-six days on hunger strike. Eventually, the state brought charges of conspiring to overthrow the president. Their crime had been to attend a political reading group and to study a particular text. It was a manual on non-violent resistance, written in 1993 by Gene Sharp, an American science professor, called *From Dictatorship to Democracy*.

Tom Burgis
London and Lagos, November 2015–January 2016

Notes

INTRODUCTION: A CURSE OF RICHES

1. The name was coined by researchers working for a US congressional commission set up to study China and its expanding role in the world. It was first used in Lee Levkowitz, Marta McLellan Ross and J. R. Warner, 'The 88 Queensway Group: A Case Study in Chinese Investors' Operations in Angola and Beyond', US-China Economic and Security Review Commission, 10 July 2009, http://china.usc.edu/App_Images/The_88_Queensway_Group.pdf. The people and companies that form the Queensway Group do not use the term themselves, and the term does not connote a formal business but rather is an informal shorthand for a corporate network.

2. These commodity prices are calculated with World Bank data that convert the nominal price for each year into their value in 2010 dollars. (Global Economic Monitor (GEM) Commodities, World Bank, http://databank.worldbank.org/data/views/variableselection/selectvariables.aspx?source=global-economic-monitor-(gem)-commodities.) The oil price is for Brent crude, one of the main benchmarks in the industry.

3. Unless otherwise stated, 'Africa' in this book refers to sub-Saharan Africa, excluding the North African states whose histories and economies broadly diverge from those of the countries south of the Sahara. (Sudan lies between the two; the UN classifies it as part of north Africa, and the World Bank and others classify it as part of sub-Saharan Africa, of which it would be the forty-ninth country). When I refer to resources I mean oil, gas and other fossil fuels, minerals, ores and precious stones, not agricultural commodities.

4. Macartan Humphreys, Jeffrey D. Sachs and Joseph E. Stiglitz, *Escaping the Resource Curse* (New York: Columbia University Press, 2007), 1.

5. Richard Dobbs, McKinsey Global Institute, *Reverse the Curse: Maximizing the Potential of Resource-Driven Economies* (New York: McKinsey and Company, December 2013), 5, www.mckinsey.com/insights/energy_resources_materials/reverse_the_curse_maximizing_the_potential_of_resource_driven_economies.

6. The share of national income spent on education tends to decline once resource revenues start to flow, as do enrolment in secondary school and girls' education. Oil exporters spend between two and ten times as much on their militaries as other countries do. Humphries, Sachs and Stiglitz, *Escaping the Resource Curse*, 10–13.

7. Said Djinnit, telephone interview with author, May 2010.

8. World Bank, 'Concept Note for a Trust Fund Proposal for the Legal and Local Sustainable Local Development Aspects and Transparency of Extractive Industry Development', 5 October 2012, http://siteresources.world bank.org/WBEUROPEEXTN/Resources/268436-1322648428296/8288771 -1326107592690/8357099-1349433248176/Concept_Note_Trust_Fund_Proposal .pdf.

9. Ecobank, 'Six Top Trends in Sub-Saharan Africa's (SSA) Extractives Industries', 23 July 2013, www.ecobank.com/upload/20130813121743289489uJud Jb9GkE.pdf.

10. These figures are for the whole African continent, not just sub-Saharan Africa. Merchandise Trade, World Trade Organization, www.wto.org/english /res_e/statis_e/its2011_e/its11_merch_trade_product_e.htm; OECD, Stats, http: //stats.oecd.org/qwids/#?x=2&y=6&f=3:51,4:1,1:1,5:3,7:1&q=3:51+4:1+1 :1+5:3+7:1+2:262,240,241,242,243,244,245,246,249,248,247,250,251,231+6:2003 ,2004,2005,2006,2007,2008,2009,2010,2011,2012.

11. According to the US Energy Information Administration, sub-Saharan Africa supplied 7 per cent of the liquid fuels produced worldwide in 2012. Author's calculation based on International Energy Statistics, http://www.eia.gov/cfapps/ ipdbproject/IEDIndex3.cfm?tid=5&pid=53&aid=1.

12. Charlotte J. Lundgren, Alun H. Thomas and Robert C. York, 'Boom, Bust, or Prosperity? Managing Sub-Saharan Africa's Natural Resource Wealth' (Washington, DC: International Monetary Fund, 2013), www.imf.org/ external/pubs/ft/dp/2013/dp1302.pdf; Oxford Policy Management, 'Blessing or Curse? The Rise of Mineral Dependence Among Low- and Middle-Income Countries', December 2011, www.opml.co.uk/sites/opml/files/Bless-ing%20or%20curse%20The%20rise%20of%20mineral%20dependence%20 among%20low-%20and%20middle-income%20countries%20-%20web%20 version.pdf.

13. World Trade Organization data for 2010, cited above. Africa here means the entire continent.

14. Source for Nigeria: author's calculations based on Nigeria, International Monetary Fund, www.imf.org/external/pubs/ft/scr/2014/cr14103.pdf, p. 25;

source for Angola: author's calculations based on Angola, International Monetary Fund, www.imf.org/external/pubs/ft/scr/2014/cr14274.pdf, p. 31.

15. Andrew Mackenzie, Speech to the Melbourne Mining Club dinner, London, 6 June 2013, www.bhpbilliton.com/home/investors/reports/Documents/2013/130606%20-%20Andrew%20Mackenzie%20%20Melbourne%20Mining%20Club%20Speech%20final.pdf.

CHAPTER 1. FUTUNGO, INC.

1. See the 2013 cost-of-living rankings by Mercer, www.mercer.co.in/newsroom/2013-cost-of-living-rankings.html.

2. Ricardo Soares de Oliveira, 'Business Success, Angola-Style: Postcolonial Politics and the Rise and Rise of Sonangol', *Journal of Modern African Studies* 45, no. 4 (December 2007): 595–619, 603, 610.

3. Paula Cristina Roque, 'Angola: Parallel Governments, Oil and Neopatrimonial System Reproduction', Institute for Security Studies, Pretoria, June 2011, www.issafrica.org/uploads/SitRep2011_6JuneAngola.pdf.

4. Jacques Marraud des Grottes, telephone interview with author, June 2012.

5. The IMF's first analysis of the hole in Angola's accounts and the reasons for it can be found in 'Angola – Fifth Review Under the Stand-By Arrangement with Angola', International Monetary Fund, IMF Country Report No. 11/346, 8 December 2011. This and all other IMF reports on Angola are at www.imf.org/external/country/ago.

6. See, for example, 'Angola: Officials Implicated in Killing Protest Organizers', Human Rights Watch, 22 November 2013, www.hrw.org/news/2013/11/22/angola-officials-implicated-killing-protest-organizers.

7. 'Cobalt International Energy', *Exceptional* (Americas edition), July 2013, www.ey.com/US/en/Services/Strategic-Growth-Markets/Exceptional-magazine-Americas-edition-July-2013---Cobalt-International-Energy.

8. Benjamin Wallace-Wells, 'The Will to Drill', *New York Times*, 14 January 2011, http://query.nytimes.com/gst/fullpage.html?res=9D06E6D61E3DF935A25752C0A9679D8B63.

9. Jennifer Dawson, 'Cobalt Expands Houston HQ After Angola Discovery', *Houston Business Journal*, 27 April 2012, www.bizjournals.com/houston/print-edition/2012/04/27/cobalt-expands-houston-hq-after-angola.html?page=all.

10. *Africa Confidential* profile of General Manuel Hélder Vieira Dias Júnior (Kopelipa), www.africa-confidential.com/whos-who-profile/id/836.

11. 'A Crude Awakening', Global Witness, December 1999, www.global witness.org/library/crude-awakening.

12. 'Global Enforcement Report 2013', TRACE International, March 2014, www.traceinternational.org/Knowledge/ger2013.html.

13. The other oil venture in which José Domingos Manuel was a shareholder alongside Vicente, Dino and Kopelipa was called Sociedade de Hidrocarbonetos de Angola, which was said to have interests in Guinea Bissau. *Diário da República* (Angola's official journal), 14 April 2008.

14. Rafael Marques de Morais, 'The Angolan Presidency: The Epicentre of Corruption', Maka Angola, July 2010, http://makaangola.org/wp-content/uploads/2012/04/PresidencyCorruption.pdf.

15. Rafael Marques de Morais, 'President's Three Henchmen Lead the Plunder of State Assets in Angola', Maka Angola, 30 July 2010, http://makaangola.org/maka-antigo/2010/07/30/trio-presidencial-lidera-o-saque-aos-bens-do-estado-angolanopresident%E2%80%99s-three-henchmen-lead-the-plunder-of-state-assets-in-angola/?lang=en; see also 'Marques Takes Them On', *Africa Confidential*, 20 January 2012, www.africa-confidential.com/article-preview/id/4305/Marques_takes_them_on.

16. A US lawyer who asked not to be identified and who investigated Nazaki in 2008 on behalf of a different foreign oil company told me in February 2012 that he had been told by that company that Nazaki was controlled by Manuel Vicente and other officials.

17. Tom Burgis and Cynthia O'Murchu, 'Angola Officials Held Hidden Oil Stakes', *Financial Times*, 15 April 2012, www.ft.com/cms/s/0/effd6a98-854c-11e1-a394-00144feab49a.html#axzz3ERem2oDu.

18. Manuel Vicente, interview with author, Luanda, June 2012.

19. Defence accounted for an average of 16.4 per cent of South African government expenditure in the 1980s, with a high of 22.7 per cent in 1982 and a low of 13.7 per cent in 1987. See 'South African Defence Review 2012', South African Department of Defence, 89, www.sadefencereview2012.org/publications/publications.htm.

20. Manuel Alves da Rocha, economist at the Universidade Católica de Angola, interview with the author, Luanda, May 2012.

21. Comments by Elias Isaac, witnessed by author, Angola country director for the Open Society Initiative for Southern Africa, at Chatham House in London on 17 September 2013.

22. Manuel Vicente, interview with author.

23. António Tomás Ana, interview with author, Luanda, June 2012.

24. See, for example, Alexandre Neto, 'Government Uses Military in Mass Forced Evictions', Maka Angola, 5 February 2013, http://makaangola.org/maka-antigo/2013/02/05/aparato-de-guerra-usado-nas-demolicoes-em-cacuaco/?lang=en.

25. Rosa Palavera, interview with author, Luanda, June 2012.

26. Paulo Moreira (Portuguese PhD student living in Chicala to study the Angolan government's slum policies), interview with author, Luanda, June 2012.

27. The World Bank data for 2009 put 43 per cent of Angolans below the international poverty line of $1.25 a day, adjusted for purchasing power parity. World Development Indicators, World Bank, http://data.worldbank.org/indicator/SI.POV.DDAY.

28. Delta Imobiliária's role as the estate agent for Kilamba and other Chinese-built housing developments is confirmed in a 28 August 2013 press release by Sonip, the real estate arm of Sonangol, titled 'Lista de beneficiários de habitações na centralidade do Kilamba atendimento de 02 a 06 de setembro de 2013'. Delta was announced in the *Diário da República*, Angola's official journal, of 13 October 2008, alongside sister companies of Nazaki, the company through which Vicente, Kopelipa and General Leopoldino Fragoso do Nascimento held their concealed stakes in the Cobalt International Energy venture, although the documentation I have seen does not disclose Delta's owners. For an account of Delta's ownership and its role in Kilamba, see Rafael Marques de Morais, 'Kopelipa e Manuel Vicente – Os Vendedores de Casas Sociais', Maka Angola, 26 September 2011, http://makaangola.org/maka-antigo/2011/09/26/the-ill-gotten-gains-behind-the-kilamba-housing-development. Marques expanded on this in an e-mail exchange with the author, November 2013, saying that Grupo Aquattro Internacional, the same anonymously owned holding company through which Vicente, Kopelipa and Dino held their stakes in Nazaki, owned Delta.

29. Rafael Marques de Morais, 'Pro-Dos Santos Militias Attack Activists at Home', Maka Angola, 23 May 2012, http://makaangola.org/maka-antigo/2012/05/23/milicias-pro-dos-santos-atacam/?lang=en.

30. Paula Cristina Roque, 'Angola's Second Post-War Elections: The Alchemy of Change', Institute for Security Studies, Pretoria, May 2013, www.issafrica.org/uploads/SitRep2013_23May.pdf.

31. Ibid.

32. Magali Rheault and Bob Tortora, 'Most African Leaders Enjoy Strong Support', Gallup, 25 April 2012, www.gallup.com/poll/154088/african-leaders-enjoy-strong-support.aspx.

33. Tom Burgis, 'Cobalt to Fight SEC Corruption Allegations', *Financial Times*, 5 August 2014, www.ft.com/intl/cms/s/0/ad3700c6-1cac-11e4-88c3-00144feabdc0.html#axzz3ERem2oDu..

34. The share sales are net. See Tom Burgis, 'Cobalt's Returns from Angolan Venture Raise Wider Concerns', *Financial Times*, 20 November 2013, www.ft.com/intl/cms/s/0/36e28cf6-4bb5-11e3-a02f-00144feabdc0.html#axzz3ERem2oDu.

35. Ibid.

36. Tom Burgis, 'Cobalt Cuts Ties with Two Angola Oil Partners', *Financial Times*, 28 August 2014, www.ft.com/intl/cms/s/0/c6c7028a-2e94-11e4-bffa-00144feabdc0.html#axzz3ERem2oDu.

37. Isaías Samakuva, interview with author, London, January 2014.

38. See, for example, 'Chinese Company to Build 5,000 Social Houses in Angola', Macauhub, 31 August 2011, www.macauhub.com.mo/en/2011/08/31/chinese-company-to-build-5000-social-houses-in-angola, which quotes Fernando Fonseca, minister for urbanism and construction, as saying that a further phase of the Kilamba project was to be developed as a partnership between the Angolan government and China International Fund. A ceremony at which President dos Santos laid the founding stone for this new phase of Kilamba was reported in the February 2012 edition of *CIF Space*, China International Fund's internal newsletter (in Chinese), www.chinainternationalfund.com/UserFiles/Upload/20131868175041.pdf, p. 5.

CHAPTER 2: 'IT IS FORBIDDEN TO PISS IN THE PARK'

1. Pindar, 'Olympian 1', translated by Diane Arnson Svarlien, Perseus Digital Library, 1990, www.perseus.tufts.edu/hopper/text?doc=Perseus:text:1999.01.0162.

2. UN Development Programme, Human Development Indicators, at 2011 prices (http://hdr.undp.org/en/content/gni-capita-ppp-terms-constant-2011-ppp). Data from some countries, including Somalia and North Korea, are so hard to collect that they are not included in the rankings.

3. Michael Nest, *Coltan* (Cambridge: Polity, 2011).

4. Blaine Harden, 'The Dirt in the New Machine', *New York Times*, 12 August 2001, www.nytimes.com/2001/08/12/magazine/the-dirt-in-the-new-machine.html.

5. Ibid.

6. UN Security Council, 'Final Report of the Panel of Experts on the Illegal Exploitation of Natural Resources and Other Forms of Wealth of the Democratic

Republic of the Congo', 12 April 2001, contained in Kofi Annan's letter to the United Nations Security Council, www.pcr.uu.se/digitalAssets/96/96819_congo_20021031.pdf.

7. Nest, *Coltan*, 12–13.

8. Ibid., 13.

9. Harden, 'The Dirt in the New Machine'.

10. Ibid.

11. Nest, *Coltan*, 23; corroborated by author's interviews.

12. US Geological Survey, 'Mineral Commodity Summaries: Cobalt', January 2013, http://minerals.usgs.gov/minerals/pubs/commodity/cobalt/mcs-2013-cobal.pdf.

13. Katumba's story is drawn from interviews with former colleagues and rivals in Kinshasa and Goma, July 2013, and from his posthumously published memoir, *Ma Vérité* (Nice: EPI, 2013) (all quotations from this text translated by author).

14. Mawapanga Mwana Nanga, interview with author, Harare, July 2013.

15. Katumba, *Ma Vérité*, 75.

16. Oscar Mudiay, interview with author, Kinshasa, July 2013.

17. Lutundula Commission, 'Lutundula Report' (author's translation), December 2005, part 1, www.conflictminerals.org/pdf/lutundula_commission_report_contractreview.pdf.

18. Katumba, *Ma Vérité*, 152. In French, Kabila addresses the much younger Katumba as 'petit', an English approximation of which would be 'kiddo'.

19. Mawapanga, a Congolese army officer present at the fall of Pweto, and a Congolese businessman who knows the Kabila family, each recounted versions of events similar to this in interviews with the author, Kinshasa and Goma, July 2013. The account of Katumba scrambling for fuel comes from *Ma Vérité* alone (152–153).

20. UN Security Council, 'Final Report of the Panel of Experts on the Illegal Exploitation of Natural Resources and Other Forms of Wealth of the Democratic Republic of the Congo', October 2002.

21. 'Gertler's Assets Multiply', *Africa Confidential*, 24 May 2013 www.africa-confidential.com/article-preview/id/4907/Gertler%e2%80%99s_assets_multiply.

22. Olivier Kamitatu, interview with author, Kinshasa, July 2013.

23. The account of the massacre at Kilwa is drawn from Monuc, 'Report on the Conclusions of the Special Investigation into Allegations of Summary Executions and Other Violations of Human Rights Committed by the FARDC in Kilwa (Province of Katanga) on 15 October 2004', ABC News, www.abc.net.au/4corners/content/2005/MONUC_report_oct05.pdf.

24. Lutundula Commission, 'Lutundula Report'.

25. Sally Neighbour, 'The Kilwa Incident Transcript', Four Corners (ABC), 6 June 2005, www.abc.net.au/4corners/content/2005/s1386467.htm.

26. Rights and Accountability in Development, Global Witness, Action Contre l'Impunité pour les Droits Humains and Association Africaine de Défense des Droits de l'Homme, 'Kilwa Trial: A Denial of Justice', 17 July 2007, www.globalwitness.org/sites/default/files/pdfs/kilwa_chron_en_170707.pdf. In 2007 a Congolese military court found not guilty Anvil Mining and soldiers accused of being responsible for the massacre at Kilwa, a verdict that drew protests from, among others, Louise Arbour, the UN high commissioner for human rights.

27. Monuc, 'Report on the Conclusions of the Special Investigation . . .'

28. The Monuc team recorded that Anvil accepted that the army used its vehicles but denied that they were used to transport loot or corpses, and that it admitted paying some of the soldiers.

29. Bill Turner, e-mail exchange with author, October 2014.

30. US Embassy Kinshasa, 'Augustin Katumba, President's Alleged Treasurer and Enforcer, Steps Down as Head of National Assembly's Ruling Coalition; His Influence Could Remain', 14 December 2009, WikiLeaks, 1 September 2011, www.wikileaks.org/cable/2009/12/09KINSHASA1080.html.

31. UN Security Council, 'Fourth Special Report of the Secretary-General on the United Nations Organization Mission in the Democratic Republic of the Congo', 21 November 2008, www.securitycouncilreport.org/atf/cf/%7B65BFCF9B-6D27-4E9C-8CD3-CF6E4FF96FF9%7D/DRC%20S%202008%20728.pdf.

32. For the size of Nkunda's force, see 'Eastern Congo: Why Stabilisation Failed', International Crisis Group, 4 October 2012, www.crisisgroup.org/en/regions/africa/central-africa/dr-congo/b091-eastern-congo-why-stabilisation-failed.aspx. For the CNDP's recruitment of child soldiers, see 'DR Congo: UN Mission Says Recruitment of Child Soldiers Is Surging', UN News Centre, 14 December 2007, www.un.org/apps/news/story.asp?NewsID=25076.

33. Matthew Green, 'Congo's Rebel Leader Has Political Goal in His Sights', Financial Times, 15 November 2008.

34. East Congolese who has worked in both mining and intelligence and who asked not to be identified, interview with author, Kinshasa, July 2013.

35. Olivier Hamuli, interview with author, Goma, July 2013.

36. UN Security Council, 'Fourth Special Report of the Secretary-General on the United Nations Organization Mission in the Democratic Republic of the Congo'.

37. A map of military involvement in mining in the Kivus, published in August 2009 by the Belgium-based independent research institute, the International Peace Information Service, offers further evidence of the commercial relationship between Mwangachuchu and the CNDP. Drawing on interviews in the mining areas and official data, the researchers established that armed groups had positions at more than half of the mines in the Kivus, tapping into the trade in tin, gold, and tungsten as well as coltan. They found that in Bibatama and the surrounding mining areas the former CNDP cadres – by then theoretically absorbed into the national army – taxed miners $2 a month. See 'Militarised Mining Areas in the Kivus', International Peace Information Service, August 2009, www.ipis research.be/mining-sites-kivus.php.

38. 'A Comprehensive Approach to Congo's Conflict Minerals', Enough Project, April 2009, www.enoughproject.org/files/minerals_activist_brief.pdf. Other experts I spoke with deemed the Enough Project's figure of $185 million in minerals revenues to the armed groups a reasonable estimate.

39. UN Security Council, 'Final Report of the Group of Experts on the Democratic Republic of the Congo', 2 December 2011, www.un.org/ga/search/view_ doc.asp?symbol=S/2011/738. The experts reported, 'At Rubaya, Ntaganda gains large revenues from taxation levied by "parallel" mine police.' Rubaya is the main mining town in Mwangachuchu's concession; Bosco Ntaganda was chief of the military wing of the CNDP when it was incorporated into the Congolese army.

40. Foreign election observer, telephone interview with author, November 2013.

41. 'DR Congo: Rein in Security Forces', Human Rights Watch, 2 December 2011, www.hrw.org/news/2011/12/02/dr-congo-rein-security-forces.

42. 'Letter Dated 18 May 2012 from the Group of Experts on the Democratic Republic of the Congo addressed to the Chair of the Security Council Committee Established Pursuant to Resolution 1533 (2004) Concerning the Democratic Republic of the Congo', www.securitycouncilreport.org/atf/cf/%7B65BFCF9B -6D27-4E9C-8CD3-CF6E4FF96FF9%7D/DRC%20S%202012%20348.pdf.

43. 'Letter Dated 12 November 2012 from the Chair of the Security Council Committee Established Pursuant to Resolution 1533 (2004) Concerning the Democratic Republic of the Congo Addressed to the President of the Security Council', www.securitycouncilreport.org/atf/cf/%7B65BFCF9B-6D27-4E9C-8 CD3-CF6E4FF96FF9%7D/s_2012_843.pdf. The UN investigators found that 'the Government of Rwanda continues to violate the arms embargo by providing direct military support to the M23 rebels, facilitating recruitment, encouraging and facilitating desertions from the armed forces of the Democratic Republic of the Congo, and providing arms, ammunition, intelligence and political advice.

The de facto chain of command of M23 includes Gen Bosco Ntaganda and culminates with the Minister of Defence of Rwanda, Gen James Kabarebe.'

44. The record of the conversation between Kabarebe and Mwangachuchu is in 'DR Congo: M23 Rebels Committing War Crimes', Human Rights Watch, 11 September 2012, www.hrw.org/news/2012/09/11/dr-congo-m23-rebels-committing-war-crimes. The HRW report also notes Rwandan denials of UN findings that it backed M23: 'The Rwandan government, in its official response to the UN Group of Experts, said that the phone calls between Rwandan officials and Congolese individuals had "deliberately been taken out of context" and that those made by Kabarebe were "aimed at avoiding a return to violence and [to] promote political dialogue".'

45. US, Switzerland Back IOM Emergency Operations in Eastern Democratic Republic of Congo, International Organisation for Migration, 5 July 2013.

46. This trip to eastern Congo produced material for a series of articles as part of the *Financial Times*'s seasonal appeal on behalf of Action Contre la Faim (Action Against Hunger), published in November and December 2012, www.actionagainsthunger.org/taxonomy/partnerships/corporate/financial-times.

47. 'Kabila au deuil de Katumba Mwanke', YouTube, 13 February 2012, www.youtube.com/watch?v=kmNUYi3WVsE.

48. Franz Wild, Michael J. Kavanagh and Jonathan Ferziger, 'Gertler Earns Billions as Mine Deals Fail to Enrich Congo', Bloomberg, 5 December 2012, www.bloomberg.com/news/2012-12-05/gertler-earns-billions-as-mine-deals-leave-congo-poorest.html. A person with knowledge of Gertler's arrival in Congo confirmed this with the author.

49. UN Security Council, 'Final Report of the Panel of Experts on the Illegal Exploitation of Natural Resources and Other Forms of Wealth of the Democratic Republic of the Congo', 12 April 2001.

50. Mawapanga Mwana Nanga, interview with author.

51. UN Security Council, 'Final Report of the Panel of Experts on the Illegal Exploitation of Natural Resources and Other Forms of Wealth of the Democratic Republic of the Congo', 12 April 2001.

52. Former senior Congolese official, interview with author, Kinshasa, July 2013. The International Monetary Fund welcomed the abolition of the monopoly in its Article IV consultation of July 2001, www.imf.org/external/pubs/ft/scr/2001/cr01114.pdf, p. 25.

53. Katumba, *Ma Vérité*, 204. I asked a representative of Dan Gertler whether he would confirm that the party had taken place and that Geller had attended. The representative (by e-mail, November 2013) declined to confirm or deny the

visit but said that 'any reference to Uri Geller is gossip and tittle-tattle and simply not so'. In December 2013 Geller told me in a telephone interview that he had indeed attended the event on a yacht, though he declined to comment on who else was present. When I again asked Gertler's representative to confirm Geller's comments, the representative did not respond. The leaked US embassy cable from 14 December 2009 (US Embassy Kinshasa, 'Augustin Katumba', Wiki-Leaks) says, 'Gertler has invited Katumba to Israel often.'

54. Katumba, *Ma Vérité*, 208.

55. Former minister, interview with author, Kinshasa, July 2013.

56. Kamitatu, interview with author.

57. Katumba, *Ma Vérité*, 200.

58. Jason K. Stearns, *Dancing in the Glory of Monsters: The Collapse of the Congo and the Great War of Africa* (New York: PublicAffairs, 2011), xxiv.

59. Wild, Kavanagh and Ferziger, 'Gertler Earns Billions as Mine Deals Fail to Enrich Congo'.

60. The account of the SMKK deals is pieced together from public records. Much of the work in deciphering and publicizing this and other similar deals in Congo was done by Franz Wild, Michael Kavanagh and others at Bloomberg as well as by Daniel Balint-Kurti and others at Global Witness. The deals are summarized in 'Equity in Extractives', Africa Progress Panel, 2013, http://africaprogresspanel.org/wp-content/uploads/2013/08/2013_APR_Equity_in_Extractives_25062013_ENG_HR.pdf.

61. The Canadian junior was Melkior Resources. For the contract creating SMKK, see mines-rdc.cd/fr/documents/avant/gcm_melkior%20resources%20inc.pdf.

62. The reference to Gécamines having mined the SMKK site in the 1980s comes from a statement to the market by Camec titled 'Central African Mining & Exploration Company Plc Acquires Extensive Copper & Cobalt Assets in the DRC', 23 October 2008, www.infomine.com/index/pr/Pa687196.PDF.

63. Following a few prior related transactions beginning in November 2007, in October 2008 Camec, a London-listed company founded by Andrew Groves, a veteran of mining deals in misruled African countries, along with Phil Edmonds, a former England cricketer, bought 50 per cent of SMKK for $85 million from a company called Cofiparinter (see 'Central African Mining & Exploration Company Plc Acquires Extensive Copper & Cobalt assets in the DRC'). The ultimate owners of Cofiparinter, which, according to a company search, is registered in Luxembourg, were not revealed. But the deal was contingent on Camec, which had already done business with Gertler elsewhere in Katanga, buying out

a Gertler company, registered in Gibraltar and called Prairie International, from the joint venture they shared. (A Camec statement of 4 March 2008 titled 'DRC Update' announced the creation of a joint venture to run the Mukondo copper and cobalt mine between a Camec subsidiary and Prairie International, which is described as 'a company in which a Trust for the benefit of the family of Dan Gertler is a major shareholder'. Investegate, www.investegate.co.uk/article.aspx ?id=200803101030017150P). The agreement added to Camec's valuable portfolio in Congo, which included assets it took over from Billy Rautenbach, a Zimbabwean businessman close to Robert Mugabe who had once run Gécamines for Laurent Kabila before falling out with the Congolese authorities and ending up on the EU's Zimbabwe sanctions list. (The June 2006 report of the UN Panel of Experts on Congo describes Rautenbach as 'a major shareholder' in Boss Mining, which was subsequently acquired by Camec. 'Letter Dated 18 July 2006 from the Chairman of the Security Council Committee Established Pursuant to Resolution 1533 (2004) Concerning the Democratic Republic of the Congo Addressed to the President of the Security Council', www.un.org/ga/search/view_doc.asp?symbol =S/2006/525. Decision 2011/101/CFSP of the European Council, 15 February 2011, has Rautenbach's name on the list of people and entities subject to sanctions and describes him as a 'businessman with strong ties to the Government of Zimbabwe, including through support to senior regime officials during Zimbabwe's intervention in DRC'. Official Journal of the European Union, http:// eur-lex.europa.eu/LexUriServ/LexUriServ.do?uri=OJ:L:2011:042:0006:0023: EN:PDF.) In September 2009 ENRC announced it was buying Camec, which also had assets elsewhere, for £584 million, a 67 per cent premium on the predeal price of Camec's shares. First on the list of ENRC's rationales for the deal was that it would yield access to significant assets in Congo, which included Camec's 50 per cent share in SMKK in the Katangan copperbelt.

64. Eurasian Natural Resources Corporation, 'May 2010 Interim Management Statement and Production Report for the First Quarter Ended 31 March 2010', 13 May 2010, www.enrc.com/ru/regulatory_news_article/1993.

65. The memorandum of association that gives Emerald Star Enterprises Ltd.'s incorporation date as 29 October 2009 was published by Eric Joyce, a British MP who has unearthed details about Gertler companies operating in Congo (http://ericjoyce.co.uk/wp-content/uploads/2011/11/10-bvi-records-emerald-star -enterprises-ltd0001.pdf). See also Joyce's database of shell companies operating in Congo, http://ericjoyce.co.uk/wpcontent/uploads/2011/11/drc_shell_ companies.pdf.

66. ENRC's 'Announcement of 2010 Preliminary Results', 23 March 2011,

describes Emerald Star Enterprises Limited as 'an entity controlled by the Gertler family trust' (67), www.enrc.com/regulatory_news_article/2015.

67. 'Contrat de Cession des Parts entre la Générale des Carrières et des Mines et Emerald Star Enterprises Limited', Congo's Ministry of Mines, 1 February 2010, http://mines-rdc.cd/fr/documents/contrat_cession_parts_gcm_smkk_fev_2010.pdf.

68. 'The acquisition of [Emerald Star] was effectively completed and control obtained by the Group in June 2010.' ENRC, 'Announcement of 2010 Preliminary Results'.

69. The sale of 50 per cent of SMKK by Gécamines to Emerald Star would only come into force once a right of first refusal was waived by Cofiparinter, the vehicle through which the stake had been acquired by Camec, which ENRC had subsequently purchased. 'Contrat de Cession des Parts entre la Générale des Carrières et des Mines et Emerald Star Enterprises Limited', 15.

70. James Wilson, Jonathan Guthrie and David Oakley, 'ENRC "Should Have Set Off Alarm Bells",' *Financial Times*, 22 November 2013, www.ft.com/intl/cms/s/0/1995e548-5368-11e3-b425-00144feabdc0.html#axzz3EoUGcJ7h.

71. Caroline Binham, Jonathan Guthrie, Cynthia O'Murchu and Guy Chazan, 'UK Fraud Unit Seeks ENRC Answers', *Financial Times*, 11 July 2013, www.ft.com/intl/cms/s/0/2fceb4e0-ea48-11e2-b2f4-00144feabdc0.html#axzz3EoUGcJ7h.

72. The terms of the offer, including the £2.28 valuation, were set out in an ENRC statement to the market on 8 August 2013, headed 'Response to Offer', www.enrc.com/regulatory_news_article/3791.

73. The calculations in Africa Progress Panel's 'Equity in Extractives' report were based on the difference between the prices at which the state sold mining assets to companies linked to Gertler and either the price at which he sold them or valuations conducted by other companies that held stakes in them as well as by independent analysts. Representatives of Gertler told the author privately that the Africa Progress Panel report's description of these transactions and calculations based on them contained errors. The ten-page list of questions sent to Gertler's representatives in September 2013 seeking comments for this book included a breakdown of each of the transactions mentioned in the report as well as the author's own understanding of them. The author specifically asked whether there were inaccuracies in each of the descriptions of the transactions. Despite repeated assurances that a reply was forthcoming, none arrived.

74. According to the OECD/DAC International Development Statistics Database, the total humanitarian aid from all donors to Congo between 2010 and 2012

was $1.29 billion. Congo consistently ranks among the largest recipients of humanitarian aid. www.oecd.org/dac/stats/idsonline.htm.

75. 'Etude analytique sur la contribution du secteur minier au budget de l'Etat', Congolese Senate, January 2013, report in author's possession.

76. Michela Wrong, *In the Footsteps of Mr. Kurtz: Living on the Brink of Disaster in Mobutu's Congo* (New York: HarperCollins, 2001), 78–79, 108.

77. Africa Progress Panel, *Equity in Extractives*. See p. 58 and Annex 2 for details of the Mutanda and Kansuki transactions involving Glencore.

78. ENRC did not respond to questions I sent to the company in 2014 about the SMKK transaction; Glencore had no specific comment on the Africa Progress Panel report, though it challenged some of the report's assumptions. E-mails from the author to spokespeople for Glencore and ENRC, November 2014.

79. UN Security Council, 'Final Report of the Panel of Experts on the Illegal Exploitation of Natural Resources and Other Forms of Wealth of the Democratic Republic of the Congo', 12 April 2001.

80. Senior FARDC officer, interview with author, Goma, July 2013. Viktor Bout's connections to the coltan trade are detailed in 'Supporting the War Economy in the DRC: European Companies and the Coltan Trade', International Peace Information Service, January 2002, www.ipisresearch.be/download.php?id=197.

81. Senior FARDC officer, interview with author.

82. Katrina Manson, 'Central Africa: The Quest for Clean Hands', *Financial Times*, 18 December 2012, www.ft.com/cms/s/0/b69124a4-394f-11e2-8881-00144feabdc0.html#axzz3E0XwAFEn.

83. Michael Priester, 'Baseline Audits of Mining Companies in Democratic Republic of the Congo to the CTC Standard Set: Mwangachuchu Hizi International Baseline Audit Report', DRC Ministry of Mines and BGR, April 2012, www.bgr.bund.de/EN/Themen/Min_rohstoffe/CTC/Downloads/mhi_mine.pdf?__blob=publicationFile&v=3.

84. World Bank, 'Democratic Republic of Congo: Growth with Governance in the Mining Sector', May 2008, http://siteresources.worldbank.org/INTOGMC/Resources/336099-1156955107170/drcgrowthgovernanceenglish.pdf.

85. Pole Institute, 'Blood Minerals: The Criminalisation of the Mining Industry in Eastern DRC', Friends of the Congo, August 2010, www.friendsofthecongo.org/pdf/blood_minerals_pole_aug2010.pdf.

86. Fidel Bafilemba, Timo Mueller and Sasha Lezhnev, 'The Impact of Dodd–Frank and Conflict Minerals Reforms on Eastern Congo's War', Enough Project, June 2014, www.enoughproject.org/reports/impact-dodd-frank-and-conflict-minerals-reforms-eastern-congo%E2%80%99s-war.

87. 'As June 2nd Conflict Minerals Deadline Approaches, Global Witness Warns That First Reports Lack Substance', Global Witness, 29 May 2014, www. globalwitness.org/library/june-2nd-conflict-minerals-deadline-approaches -global-witness-warns-first-reports-lack.

88. Pole Institute, 'Blood Minerals'.

89. Wild, Kavanagh and Ferziger, 'Gertler Earns Billions as Mine Deals Fail to Enrich Congo'.

90. For example, the rights to the Kolwezi, Frontier and Lonshi mines passed to companies linked to Gertler after they were confiscated from Canadian mining company First Quantum Minerals.

91. Fleurette Group website, http://fleurettegroup.com, accessed January 2014.

92. Wild, Kavanagh and Ferziger, 'Gertler Earns Billions as Mine Deals Fail to Enrich Congo'.

CHAPTER 3: INCUBATORS OF POVERTY

1. The details of the smuggling operation are drawn from interviews with northern Nigeria politicians, officials, businessmen and textiles consultants in Abuja, Katsina, Kano and Kaduna between 2009 and 2013.

2. The professional estimates I have seen for smuggling textiles into Nigeria range from $1.5 billion to $2.2 billion annually. The comparison with total sector imports is based on UN Conference on Trade and Development data for 2009. UnctadSTAT database, unctadstat.unctad.org.

3. The poverty figure is from the World Bank for 2010, the most recent year available, http://data.worldbank.org/indicator/SI.POV.DDAY.

4. Industry consultant, interviews with author, various locations, 2009–2013; Volker Treichel, ed., *Putting Nigeria to Work: A Strategy for Employment and Growth* (Washington, DC: World Bank, 2010), 52.

5. Treichel, *Putting Nigeria to Work*, 52.

6. UN Industrial Development Organisation, 'Textile and Garment Industry Sector Study in Nigeria: Technical Report for the Federal Government of Nigeria', UNIDO, July 2009.

7. Hassan A. Karofi and Lawal Ibrahim, 'Dahiru Barau Mangal—Enter Yar'Adua's "Mr-Fix-It"', *Daily Trust*, 10 August 2008, http://allafrica.com/ stories/200808110682.html.

8. Northern Nigerian sources speaking to US embassy officials, as reported in US Embassy Cable, 'Nigeria: Kano Businessman Alleges Yar'Adua Corruption',

21 February 2008, WikiLeaks, 8 December 2010, www.wikileaks.org/plusd/cables/08ABUJA320_a.html. A textile industry consultant corroborates the estimated fee.

9. Ibid.

10. Nasir El-Rufai, interview with author, Abuja, April 2013.

11. Former EFCC official, interview with author, Abuja, April 2013. A November 2008 cable from the US embassy in Abuja, published in September 2011 by WikiLeaks, reported, 'Ribadu also expressed concern for his former EFCC colleague and friend, Ibrahim Magu; he claims Magu is in danger because of his specific knowledge of the President's relationship with Dahiru Mangal (an influential wealthy northern businessman who is currently under investigation and has ties to the Yar'Adua family and administration) and a money laundering operation which fronts as a legitimate company.' 'Nigeria: Further Harassment of Former Efcc Chair Ribadu', 25 November 2008, WikiLeaks, www.wikileaks.org/plusd/cables/08ABUJA2307_a.html.

12. Jan L. van Zanden, *The Economic History of The Netherlands 1914–1995: A Small Open Economy in the 'Long' Twentieth Century* (New York: Routledge, 1997), 165.

13. A Southern African Development Community study from 2000, cited in Economic Commission for Africa, 'Minerals and Africa's Development: The International Study Group Report on Africa's Mineral Regimes', November 2011, www.uneca.org/sites/default/files/publications/mineral_africa_development_report_eng.pdf.

14. UN Industrial Development Organisation (UNIDO) and UN Conference on Trade and Development (UNCTAD), 'Fostering Industrial Development in Africa in the New Global Environment, Economic Development in Africa Report', UNCTAD, July 2011, http://unctad.org/en/docs/aldcafrica2011_en.pdf.

15. Ecobank, 'Six Top Trends in Sub-Saharan Africa's Extractives Industries', 23 July 2013, www.ecobank.com/upload/20130813121743289489uJudJb9GkE.pdf; UNIDO and UNCTAD, 'Fostering Industrial Development in Africa in the New Global Environment'.

16. 'Equity in Extractives', Africa Progress Panel, 2013, http://africaprogresspanel.org/wp-content/uploads/2013/08/2013_APR_Equity_in_Extractives_25062013_ENG_HR.pdf.

17. 'Step Change', *The Economist*, 12 April 2014, www.economist.com/news/finance-and-economics/21600734-revised-figures-show-nigeria-africas-largest-economy-step-change.

18. Noo Saro-Wiwa, *Looking for Transwonderland: Travels in Nigeria* (Berkeley, CA: Soft Skull Press, 2012), 241.

19. Calculations based on data in African Development Bank, 'African Economic Outlook 2013', www.undp.org/content/dam/rba/docs/Reports/African %20Economic%20Outlook%202013%20En.pdf.

20. See, for example, Razia Khan (head of Africa research at Standard Chartered), *An Extra Strong MINT*, Chatham House, February/March 2014, www.chathamhouse.org/sites/files/chathamhouse/public/The%20World%20 Today/2014/FebMarch/WT0114Khan.pdf.

21. Paul Collier, *The Bottom Billion: Why the Poorest Countries Are Failing and What Can Be Done About It* (Oxford, New York: Oxford University Press, 2008), 42ff.

22. US Senate Permanent Subcommittee on Investigations, 'Keeping Foreign Corruption Out of the United States: Four Case Histories', February 2010. The committee's findings detail the channelling of ill-gotten funds into the United States by relatives of Omar Bongo of Gabon, Teodoro Obiang Nguema of Equatorial Guinea and Atiku Abubakar of Nigeria, among others.

23. In November 2010 Panalpina and its US subsidiary as well as five oil and gas companies, including Shell, admitted violations of the US Foreign Corrupt Practices Act and agreed to pay $237 million in criminal and civil penalties; Panalpina admitted bribery in Angola, Azerbaijan, Brazil, Kazakhstan, Nigeria, Russia and Turkmenistan. In the words of the US Department of Justice, Panalpina customers, including Shell, 'admitted that the companies approved of or condoned the payment of bribes on their behalf in Nigeria and falsely recorded the bribe payments made on their behalf as legitimate business expenses in their corporate books, records and accounts'. US Department of Justice, 'Oil Services Companies and a Freight Forwarding Company Agree to Resolve Foreign Bribery Investigations and to Pay More Than $156 Million in Criminal Penalties', 4 November 2010, www.justice.gov/opa/pr/oil-services-companies-and-freight-forwarding -company-agree-resolve-foreign-bribery.

24. Martin Meredith, *The State of Africa* (London: Simon and Schuster, 2006), 276; John J. Struthers, 'Nigerian Oil and Exchange Rates: Indicators of "Dutch Disease"', *Development and Change* 21, no. 2 (April 1990): 318–327.

25. Yakubu Dogara, telephone interview with author, May 2010.

26. US Embassy Cable, 'Nigeria'.

27. Tom Burgis and Matthew Green, 'Reformist Restrained by "Cabal" Capitalising on His Frailty', *Financial Times*, 6 May 2010, www.ft.com/intl/cms/ s/0/646dd1ae-58fb-11df-90da-00144feab49a.html#axzz3EoXwAFEn.

28. Caroline Binham and Tom Burgis, 'Ibori Pleads Guilty to Laundering Public Funds', *Financial Times*, 27 February 2012, www.ft.com/intl/cms/s/0/88b-b8bbe-6169-11e1-8a8e-00144feabdc0.html#axzz3EoXwAFEn.

29. Tom Burgis, 'Yar'Adua's Return Provokes US Warning', *Financial Times*, 24 February 2010, www.ft.com/cms/s/0/c628c23c-20d9-11df-b920-00144feab49a .html#axzz3HpltffT1.

CHAPTER 4: GUANXI

1. World Bank, 'Commodity Markets Outlook', January 2014, www.world bank.org/content/dam/Worldbank/GEP/GEPcommodities/Commodity_ Markets_Outlook_2014_January.pdf; US Energy Information Administration, International Energy Statistics, www.eia.gov/cfapps/ipdbproject/iedindex3.cfm ?tid=5&pid=5&aid=2&cid=regions&syid=1990&eyid=2013&unit=TBPD.

2. On 17 April 2014, the Office of Foreign Assets Control, the division of the US Treasury that handles sanctions, updated its Specially Designated Nationals List – the roster of those subject to financial restrictions and with whom US companies are prohibited from doing business. One new entry in the Zimbabwe sections read, 'PA, Sam (aka HUI, Samo; aka JINGHUA, Xu; aka KING, Sam; aka KYUNG-WHA, Tsui; aka LEUNG, Ghiu Ka; aka MENEZES, Antonio Famtosonghiu Sampo); DOB 28 Feb 1958; nationality China; citizen Angola; alt. citizen United Kingdom; Passport C234897(0). (United Kingdom)' (Resource Center, U.S. Department of the Treasury, www.treasury.gov/resource-center/sanctions/OFAC-Enforcement/ pages/20140417.aspx). When the Treasury lists passports and citizenships of over-seas nationals on its sanctions list, it does not necessarily mean that they hold those passports and citizenships, merely that the Treasury suspects they might.

3. Ibid.

4. Mahmoud Thiam, telephone interview with author, December 2013.

5. Beth Morrissey, Himanshu Ojha, Laura Rena Murray and Patrick Martin-Menard, 'China-Based Corporate Web Behind Troubled Africa Resource Deals', Centre for Public Integrity, 9 November 2011, www.publicintegrity.org/ 2011/11/09/7108/china-based-corporate-web-behind-troubled-africa-resource-deals.

6. See, for example, Peter Mattis, 'The Analytic Challenge of Understanding Chinese Intelligence Services', *Studies in Intelligence* 56, no. 3 (September 2012): 47–57.

7. Richard McGregor, *The Party: The Secret World of China's Communist Rulers* (London: Penguin, 2012), 114.

8. Nigel Inkster, interview with author, March 2014.

9. See Chapter 2. Senior FARDC officer, interview with author, Goma, July

2013; 'Supporting the War Economy in the DRC', International Peace Information Service, January 2002, www.ipisresearch.be/download.php?id=197.

10. See, for example, Simon Mann, *Cry Havoc* (London: John Blake, 2011).

11. Forum for Africa-China Cooperation website, www.focac.org, accessed 7 May 2014.

12. IMF Direction of Trade Statistics tabulated in 'Trade Levels Rise and Rise', Africa-Asia Confidential, 5 August 2013, www.africa-asia-confidential .com/article-preview/id/959/Trade_levels_rise_and_rise; see also Sarah Baynton-Glen, 'China-Africa—CNY Internationalisation', Standard Chartered, 9 April 2013, https://research.standardchartered.com/configuration/ ROW%20Documents/China-Africa_%E2%80%93_CNY_internationalisation_09_04_13_08_01.pdf.

13. Ecobank, 'Six Top Trends in Sub-Saharan Africa's (SSA) Extractives Industries', 23 July 2013, www.ecobank.com/upload/20130813121743289489u JudJb9GkE.pdf.

14. Angolan Embassy in London, 'Ministry of Finance Denies Misuse of Chinese Loans', 17 October 2007; Ana Cristina Alves, 'Chinese Economic Statecraft: A Comparative Study of China's Oil-backed Loans in Angola and Brazil', *Journal of Current Chinese Affairs* 42, no. 1 (January 2013): 99–130, 108.

15. 'Angola, China Vow to Forge Long-Term Stable Cooperative Relations', Xinhua, 25 February 2005, www.china.org.cn/english/international/121289.htm.

16. Pieter D. Wezeman, Siemon T. Wezeman and Lucie Béraud-Sudreau, 'Arms Flows to Sub-Saharan Africa', Stockholm International Peace Research Institute, December 2011, http://books.sipri.org/files/PP/SIPRIPP30.pdf.

17. 'Angola Unravels', Human Rights Watch, September 1999, section 141, www.hrw.org/reports/1999/angola; Indira Campos and Alex Vines, 'Angola and China: A Pragmatic Partnership', Centre for Strategic and International Studies, March 2008, http://csis.org/files/media/csis/pubs/080306_angolachina .pdf, 3.

18. Helder Bataglia, telephone interview with author, February 2014.

19. Lee Levkowitz, Marta McLellan Ross and J. R. Warner, 'The 88 Queensway Group: A Case Study in Chinese Investors' Operations in Angola and Beyond', US-China Economic and Security Review Commission, 10 July 2009, http:// china.usc.edu/App_Images/The_88_Queensway_Group.pdf. Quoting Venezuelan Presidential Press, President Chavez: 'The FTAA Has Died for the Good of Our People,' 3 April 2004, the '88 Queensway' report says, 'In April 2004, a Venezuelan television station reported that President Hugo Chávez had signed a letter of intent with Portugal and China to proceed with investment projects amounting

to $300 million in the energy, construction, communications, services, and aluminium sectors. Signing on behalf of Portugal was Helder Bataglia; on behalf of China was Lo Fong-hung, listed as a director of Beiya International Development. Following the signing of the letters, President Chávez announced that "The [Free Trade Area of the Americas between Venezuela and the United States] is dead. May the Washington government's plan to simply impose a model on us, rest in peace for the good. The signing of this agreement also gives a renewed boost to relations between China and Venezuela.'"

20. Thiam, telephone interview with author. See also Morrissey et al., 'China-Based Corporate Web Behind Troubled Africa Resource Deals'.

21. Decision of the High Court of the Hong Kong Special Administrative Region, Court of First Instance, HCMP 2143/2011, in *Wu Yang v. Dayuan International Development Limited et al.*, 4 June 2013, http://legalref.judiciary.gov .hk/lrs/common/search/search_result_detail_frame.jsp?DIS=87490&QS=%24 %28Dayuan%2CInternational%2CDevelopment%29&TP=JU.

22. *Aló Presidente*, transcript of episode 187, 4 April 2004.

23. Bataglia, telephone interview with author.

24. Lo Fong-hung is named as Wang Xiangfei's wife in company filings in Hong Kong for Nan Nan Resources, the Queensway Group's listed company. The details of Wang's career are drawn from Nan Nan filings and those of other companies where he serves as a director.

25. Morrissey et al., 'China-Based Corporate Web Behind Troubled Africa Resource Deals'.

26. Letter from China Sonangol in response to my questions ahead of the publication of a report on the Queensway Group in *Financial Times*, 18 July 2014, www.ft.com/chinasonangolresponse.

27. Extracts from the ledgers of Queensway Group companies contained in a court judgment refer to a cash advance by China International Fund of $1.5 million to 'Mr. Sam'. See Decision of the Hong Kong High Court. A press release by the Government of Dubai Media Office on 25 September 2013, announcing an agreement for China Sonangol to build an oil refinery, said 'Sam Pai, Chairman, China Sonangol Group' signed the memorandum of understanding. An 11 December 2013 press release by Sierra Leone's State House Communication Unit described a meeting between President Ernest Koroma and 'Vice Chairman of China International Fund Limited, Mr. Sam' (http://cocorioko. info/?p=2618).

28. Levkowitz, Ross and Warner, 'The 88 Queensway Group'.

29. Decision of the Hong Kong High Court.

30. Iain Esau, 'Shell Goodbye to Greater Plutonio', Upstream, 19 December 2003.

31. Carola Hoyos, 'Shell All But Withdraws from Angola', *Financial Times*, 9 April 2004.

32. See, for example, 'Sonangol Sinopec Acquires 50% Interest in Angola Block 18 from Shell', Global Markets Direct Financial Deals Tracker, 30 December 2004.

33. 'Zeng Peiyan—Politburo Member of CPC Central Committee', Xinhua, 15 November 2002, http://news.xinhuanet.com/english/2002-11/15/content_631108.htm.

34. Bataglia, telephone interview with author.

35. Manuel Vicente, interview with author, Luanda, June 2012.

36. According to the judge's account of Wu Yang's evidence in his dispute with other Queensway Group founders, the holding company through which China Sonangol's Queensway-based shareholders held their interests 'did not initially have any material assets'. See Decision of the Hong Kong High Court.

37. Beiya International Development Ltd was named as the 70 per cent shareholder of China Sonangol in its articles of association. This company's own company filings show that it had been incorporated a year before China Sonangol, also in Hong Kong. Its shares were also split 70/30, with the majority holding assigned to New Bright, the company owned by Lo Fong-hung and Veronica Fung, and the minority assigned to Beiya Industrial Group, a Chinese state-owned conglomerate. Wu Yang, the Chinese businessman who claims he helped engineer the deal between Sonangol and Sinopec in which China Sonangol served as the middleman, has said in court filings (see Decision of the Hong Kong High Court) that Beiya was merely a nominee for him and his business partner, both of whom were granted a stake in the venture in return for making introductions that led to the deal. Company filings show that the shares were formally transferred into Wu Yang's name in October 2004, giving him an indirect stake of 21 per cent in China Sonangol, through which he also received an indirect stake in Sonangol Sinopec International of 9.5 per cent. (Various filings from the Hong Kong Companies Registry, copies in author's possession.)

38. Letter from the board of China Petroleum and Chemical Corporation (also known as Sinopec) to shareholders setting out the terms of the transfer of Sinopec's holdings in SSI from a subsidiary to the parent company, 1 April 2010.

39. Ibid.

40. In 2010 Sinopec switched ownership of its stake in Block 18 from its subsidiary in Hong Kong to the parent company in mainland China. Sinopec valued

its 55 per cent of SSI's equity at $1.678 billion. By that valuation, China Sonangol's 45 per cent stake in SSI was worth $1.373 billion. Through its 70 per cent interest in China Sonangol, the Queensway Group's indirect stake in Block 18 was worth $960 million. See 'Sinopec's First Acquisition of Overseas Upstream Assets', Sinopec press release, 28 March 2010, http://english.sinopec.com/media_center/news/20100329/download/en-news100329d.pdf.

41. The average price of a barrel of Brent crude, the benchmark, in 2011 was $111, meaning Block 18's output of some 200,000 a day was worth $22 million. The Queensway Group's effective share of Block 18 was 15.75 per cent.

42. Manuel Vicente, interview with author.

43. Isaías Samakuva, interview with author, London, January 2014.

44. Vicente, interview with author; China Sonangol company filings from Hong Kong.

45. On 11 May 2006, the Chinese authorities issued an arrest warrant for Liu Guiting on charges of embezzlement and bribery, for which he was later jailed for life (see 'Former China Railway Group Chief Jailed for Life in Corruption Case', trans. BBC Monitoring, Xinhua, 1 April 2009, http://english.cri.cn/6909/2009/04/01/1241s470616.htm; 'Former Chairman of Beiya Group Receives Life Sentence for Embezzlement', Caijing, 1 April 2009). Liu had been the chairman of Beiya Industrial Group, the Chinese state-owned railway company that had been a minority partner in one of the Queensway Group's earliest holding companies, Beiya International Development. Through Beiya International Development, the Beiya Industrial Group initially held its stakes in China Beiya Escom, its joint venture with Helder Bataglia's company, and China Sonangol. Six days after the warrant for Liu went out, Beiya International Development submitted an application to the commercial authorities in Hong Kong to change its name to Dayuan International Development, wiping away any trace of its scandal-struck origins.

46. Company records show that China Beiya Escom, the Queensway Group's joint venture with Helder Bataglia's company, formed another joint venture with Cotrade, Congo-Brazzaville's state-owned oil trader, called Cotrade Asia. Cotrade Asia was never shown to have done anything illicit, but Cotrade was one of the companies that a British judge found to have participated in a scheme, orchestrated by the country's elite, to hide money that the country owed to its creditors. 'Those involved in creating and masterminding the use of the structure were dishonest in the relevant sense of the word because of this objective when creating and using the sham companies and transactions in question, to avoid enforcement of existing liabilities,' the judge ruled. See the judgment of Mr

Justice Cooke in *Kensington International Limited v. Republic of the Congo*, 28 November 2005, in the London High Court of Justice. Cotrade Asia is mentioned in subsequent court actions related to the scheme. See the judgment of Judge Carlson in *Kensington International Limited v. ICS Secretaries Limited*, 31 May 2007, in the Hong Kong High Court of First Instance.

47. China International Fund is owned through the same structure through which the Queensway Group holds its 70 per cent interest in China Sonangol. The holding company, which owns 99 per cent of CIF, was originally called Beiya International Development, then subsequently Dayuan International Development. Dayuan is owned 70 per cent by New Bright, the Queensway Group company that belongs to Veronica Fung and Lo Fong-hung; Wu Yang holds the remaining 30 per cent of Dayuan. Lo also holds 1 per cent of CIF shares directly. In 2012, after Wu Yang sued Dayuan, Lo and Fung, Dayuan's 99 per cent stake in CIF was transferred to another company, Magic Wonder Holdings Limited. The only information available about Magic Wonder is that it was incorporated on 26 April 2012, and that its address is a post office box in the British Virgin Islands. Dayuan International Development and China International Fund company filings in Hong Kong; British Virgin Islands Financial Services Commission, Registry of Corporate Affairs.

48. Angolan Embassy in London, 'Ministry of Finance Denies Misuse of Chinese Loans'.

49. 'Chinese Investors Claim 2.7 mln Yuan from Misleading Company', Xinhua, 27 December 2007, http://english.people.com.cn/90001/90776/90882/6328055.html; '3 Chinese Jailed for Insider Trading, Fined $11.2 mln', Xinhua, 4 February 2008, http://english.peopledaily.com.cn/90001/90776/90884/6351533.html. Following the scandal the contract was awarded instead to Citic.

50. Sinopec, 'Announcement on Resignation of Mr. Chen Tonghai as Director and Chairman of the Board', press release, 22 June 2007, http://english.sinopec.com/media_center/announcements/archive/2007/20070622/download/AM20070622157.pdf; 'Former Sinopec General Manager Expelled from Party on Corruption Charges', Xinhua, 25 January 2008, http://english.sinopec.com/media_center/announcements/archive/2007/20070622/download/AM20070622157.pdf.

51. 'Sinopec Ex-Chairman Chen Gets Death Sentence with Reprieve After Reporting Others' Crimes', Xinhua, 15 July 2009, http://news.xinhuanet.com/english/2009-07/15/content_11713262.htm.

52. Alex Vines, interview with author, London, September 2013. See also Alex Vines, Lillian Wong, Markus Weimer and Indira Campos, 'Thirst for

African Oil', Chatham House, August 2009, www.chathamhouse.org/sites/files/chathamhouse/r0809_africanoil.pdf.

53. US Embassy in Luanda, 'New China Credit Line Under Consideration', diplomatic cable, 27 January 2009, WikiLeaks, 8 December 2010, http://www.wikileaks.org/plusd/cables/09LUANDA51_a.html.

54. Angolan Embassy in London, 'Ministry of Finance Denies Misuse of Chinese Loans'.

55. Bataglia, telephone interview with author.

56. Decision of the Hong Kong High Court.

CHAPTER 5: WHEN ELEPHANTS FIGHT, THE GRASS GETS TRAMPLED

1. The details of Frederic Cilins's conversation with Mamadie Touré come from the transcript of the FBI's recording of their meeting, as incorporated in the 'Report and Recommendation of the CTRTCM [Guinea's Comité Technique de Revue des Titres et Conventions Miniers] on the Licenses and Mining Convention Obtained by VBG', April 2014, www.contratsminiersguinee.org/blog/publication-report-recommendation-VBG.html (in French, author's translation).

2. For copies of the 'contracts' in question, see the documents published by the Guinean government inquiry together with its report into BSGR's activities. 'Report and Recommendation of the CTRTCM . . .' (in French, author's translation), www.documentcloud.org/documents/1105518-declaration-de-mamadie-toure-et-pieces-jointes.html.

3. See 'About Beny Steinmetz', Beny Steinmetzwebsite, http://beny-steinmetz.com/about.html, and William MacNamara, 'Dealmaker with Eye for Wilder Frontiers', *Financial Times*, 19 February 2012, www.ft.com/intl/cms/s/0/c2dfocca-562a-11e1-a328-00144feabdc0.html.

4. Rebecca Bream, 'Nikanor and Katanga to Merge', *Financial Times*, 7 November 2007, www.ft.com/intl/cms/s/0/5e9f1a68-8ca1-11dc-b887-0000779fd2ac.html; Eric Onstad, Laura Macinnis and Quentin Webb, 'The Biggest Company You Never Heard Of', Reuters, 25 February 2011, www.reuters.com/article/2011/02/25/us-glencore-idUSTRE71O1DC20110225.

5. Martin Meredith, *The State of Africa* (London: Simon and Schuster, 2006), 67.

6. World Bank data for 2012, World Development Indicators, http://data.worldbank.org/indicator/SH.DYN.MORT.

7. Rio Tinto gives a history of the Simandou project at 'Simandou', Rio Tinto, www.riotintosimandou.com/ENG/project_overview/33_history.asp.

8. Powerscourt,'Response to Press Speculation', statement on behalf of BSGR, 9 May 2013, www.prnewswire.com/news-releases/bsgr-response-to-press-speculation-206749511.html.

9. Cilins gave an account of his activities to Steven Fox, an investigator with a firm called Veracity, which was hired as part of the investigation into BSGR that the Guinean government of Alpha Condé launched.

10. Mamadie Touré, Sworn Statement, Florida, 12 December 2013. This statement was published together with the report of the Guinean inquiry. 'Report and Recommendation of the CTRTCM . . .'

11. Ibid.

12. Ibid.

13. Tom Burgis, Helen Thomas and Misha Glenny, 'Guinea Reignites $2.5bn Mining Tussle', *Financial Times*, 2 November 2012, www.ft.com/cms/s/0/06d-895f4-24f7-11e2-8924-00144feabdc0.html#axzz3HUSpQnyc.

14. 'Corruption Perceptions Index 2006', Transparency International, www.transparency.org/research/cpi/cpi_2006.

15. Touré, Sworn Statement.

16. Asher Avidan profile, www.bsgresources.com/about/senior-management, accessed 2 May 2014, subsequently removed from BSGR's website.

17. Touré, Sworn Statement.

18. Burgis, Thomas and Glenny, 'Guinea Reignites $2.5bn Mining Tussle'.

19. Angolan Embassy in London, 'Ministry of Finance Denies Misuse of Chinese Loans', 17 October 2007.

20. Jon Lee Anderson, 'Downfall', *New Yorker*, 12 April 2010, www.newyorker.com/magazine/2010/04/12/downfall-3.

21. Mahmoud Thiam, e-mail exchange with author, April 2013.

22. Campaign contributions compiled by the Center for Responsive Politics, http://www.opensecrets.org/pres08/search.php?cid=ALL&name=&employ=UBS&cycle=2008&state=&zip=&amt=a&sort=n&page=14.

23. Tom Burgis, 'Rusal Seeks Help over Mining Dispute', *Financial Times*, 22 September 2009, www.ft.com/cms/s/0/b0ddbe9a-a6d2-11de-bd14-00144feabdc0.html#axzz3HUSpQnyc.

24. Tom Burgis, Tom Mitchell and Catherine Belton, 'Guinea Demands Share of UC Rusal Offering', *Financial Times*, 25 January 2010, www.ft.com/intl/cms/s/0/d2bb3c8a-0a1a-11df-8b23-00144feabdc0.html.

25. 'UC RUSAL Starts the Realization of Dian-Dian Project of State Importance in Guinea', Rusal press release, 10 July 2014.

26. Henry Bellingham, letter to Bakary Fofana, Guinean minister of state for foreign affairs, copied to Mahmoud Thiam and others, 28 September 2010 (copy in author's possession).

27. Mahmoud Thiam, telephone interview with author, September 2009.

28. See Rio Tinto's lawsuit of 30 April 2014, against Vale, Beny Steinmetz, BSGR, Mahmoud Thiam and others, www.riotinto.com/media/media-releases -237_10305.aspx.

29. Mahmoud Thiam, e-mail exchange with author, 30 April 2014. See also James Wilson, Tom Burgis and Joe Leahy, 'Rio Tinto Sues Vale and BSGR over Guinea Mine Controversy', *Financial Times*, 30 April 2014, www.ft.com/intl/ cms/s/0/8ef9c710-d06c-11e3-af2b-00144feabdc0.html#axzz3Ezf9d5kT.

30. Mahmoud Thiam, telephone interview with author, December 2013. The account of Thiam's initial dealings with the Queensway Group is drawn from this interview.

31. Manuel Vicente, interview with author, Luanda, June 2012; confirmed by Mahmoud Thiam, interview, December 2013.

32. Details of the events of 28 September 2009 are most comprehensively re-counted in 'Bloody Monday: The September 28 Massacre and Rapes by Security Forces in Guinea', Human Rights Watch, December 2009, www.hrw.org/sites/ default/files/reports/guinea1209webwcover_0.pdf, and in UN Security Coun-cil, 'Report of the International Commission of Inquiry Mandated to Establish the Facts and Circumstances of the Events of 28 September 2009 in Guinea', 18 December 2009, www.securitycouncilreport.org/atf/cf/%7B65BFCF9B-6D27-4 E9C-8CD3-CF6E4FF96FF9%7D/Guinea%20S%202009%20693.pdf.

33. Rukmini Callimachi, 'Civil War Feared in Guinea as Militia Grows', *Asso-ciated Press*, 6 December 2009, www.sify.com/news/civil-war-feared-in-guinea-as -militia-grows-news-international-jmgbujcggadsi.html. The presence of Israeli and South African instructors at the training camps in Forecariah is also reported elsewhere, such as US Embassy in Rabat, 'Guinea: Update on Dadis Camara's Health', diplomatic cable, 17 December 2009, WikiLeaks, 4 December 2010, https://wikileaks.org/cable/2009/12/09RABAT988.html.

34. Israel Ziv, LinkedIn profile, http://il.linkedin.com/in/zivisrael, accessed 2 May 2014.

35. Global CST website, accessed 2 May 2014; US Embassy in Bogota, 'Col-ombian Defense Ministry Sours on Israeli Defense Firm,' diplomatic cable, 1 December 2009, WikiLeaks, 6 April 2011, http://wikileaks.org/cable/2009/12/09 BOGOTA3483.html.

36. Multiple interviews with people who have investigated Global CST and Dadis's ethnic militia as well as associates of Kenan yielded an incomplete picture

of the work the company did in Guinea. The Comité Technique de Revue des Titres et Conventions Miniers, in a letter to BSGR of 30 October 2012, referred to 'the illegal sale of military material by the company Global CST to the army of the Republic of Guinea for a value of USD 10 million' (in French, author's translation). 'Promising Contracts', *Africa Confidential*, 28 May 2010, www.africa-confidential.com/article-preview/id/3544/Promising_contracts, describes Israel Ziv's arrival in Guinea to train an ethnic militia. The Israeli authorities announced in 2010 that they had fined Global CST over its Guinean contract. See 'Israel Fines Security Firm for Negotiating Deal to Supply Arms to Military Junta in Guinea', *Fox News*, 18 May 2010, www.foxnews.com/world/2010/05/18/israel-fines-security-firm-negotiating-deal-supply-arms-military-junta-guinea.

37. Mahmoud Thiam, e-mail exchange with author, April 2013.

38. Callimachi, 'Civil War Feared in Guinea as Militia Grows'.

39. Human Rights Watch, 'Bloody Monday'.

40. Mahmoud Thiam, e-mail exchange with author, April 2013.

41. US Embassy in Paris, 'Guinea: Das Fitzgerald's Consultations in Paris', diplomatic cable, 19 November 2009, Wikileaks, 1 September 2011, www.wikileaks.org/plusd/cables/09PARIS1532_a.html.

42. Mahmoud Thiam, telephone interview with author, December 2013.

43. 'Accord Cadre entre Fonds International De Chine Sa et le Gouvernement de la République de Guinée', 12 June 2009, in author's possession; 'République de Guinée et CIF Singapore Pte Ltd et China Sonangol International (S) Pte. Ltd, Pacte d'actionnaires', 10 October 2009, in author's possession; accompanying loan agreement between CIF Singapore and the Republic of Guinea, in author's possession.

44. Rusal, 'RUSAL Won a Three-Member ICC Arbitral Tribunal Case Against the Republic of Guinea', 21 July 2014, www.rusal.ru/en/press-center/news_details.aspx?id=10762&ibt=13&at=0.

45. UN Security Council, 'Report of the International Commission of Inquiry . . .'

46. The UN inquiry would name both Dadis and Toumba, as well as the anti-trafficking chief Moussa Tiégboro Camara, as the commanders for whom there were 'reasonable grounds to suspect individual criminal responsibility' for the atrocities of 28 September. UN Security Council, 'Report of the International Commission of Inquiry Mandated to Establish the Facts and Circumstances of the Events of 28 September 2009 in Guinea'. In an interview with RFI Toumba claimed that Dadis was trying to place all the blame for the massacre on him. 'Camara Betrayed Me, Says Diakité', RFI English, 16 December 2009, www1.rfi.fr/actuen/articles/120/article_6202.asp.

47. Promotional material handed out at the launch of the Air Guinée International named Hadja Halimatou Diallo as deputy chief executive (in author's possession). She was the wife of Cellou Dalein Diallo, the candidate of the Union des Forces Démocratiques de Guinée, widely regarded as the frontrunner ahead of the elections. He ultimately lost in a run-off to Alpha Condé.

48. China South Locomotive and Rolling Stock Corporation, '5 CSR locomotives & 22 Carriages Exported to Guinea', press release, 6 May 2010, www.csrgc .com.cn/g981/s2889/t59603.aspx, describes a ceremony marking the embarkation of rolling stock for Guinea in the presence of officials from the company and from China International Fund and Guinea's ambassador to China.

49. Mahmoud Thiam, interview with author, Conakry, June 2010.

50. 'Guinea Soldiers Arrested for Attack on President's Home', BBC News, 20 July 2011, www.bbc.com/news/world-africa-14197052; 'Presidential Guard Fall Out', Africa Confidential, 22 July 2011, www.africa-confidential.com/ article-preview/id/4109/Presidential_guard_fall_out.

51. The Palladino affair, involving a questionable loan deal with the state mining company, was a case in point. See 'A New Battle to Control the Mines', Africa Confidential, 22 July 2011, www.africa-confidential.com/article-preview/ id/4508/A_new_battle_to_control_the_mines.

52. Patrick Radden Keefe, 'Buried Secrets', New Yorker, 8 July 2013, www. newyorker.com/magazine/2013/07/08/buried-secrets.

53. See, for example, Powerscourt, 'Response to Press Speculation'.

54. When Mark Malloch-Brown and FTI settled the claim for €90,000, a statement issued by BSGR's new PR firm, Powerscourt, said Malloch-Brown and FTI had 'conceded defeat and agreed to pay substantial compensation and legal costs'. FTI countered, 'Neither FTI Consulting nor Lord Malloch-Brown has "conceded defeat" in any way.' See, for example, James Wilson and Cynthia O'Murchu, 'Steinmetz and Malloch-Brown Settle Guinea Damages Claim', Financial Times, 10 June 2013, www.ft.com/intl/cms/s/0/6f62f158-d1ce-11e2-b17e -00144feab7de.html#axzz3Ezf9d5kT. FTI said the €90,000 settlement was less than what it and Malloch-Brown would have spent on legal fees trying to have the claim struck out. Beny Steinmetz and three BSGR directors also sued Global Witness, seeking to force the group to disclose information it held on the company under the Data Protection Act. See, for example, Henry Mance, 'Beny Steinmetz Tests UK Data Laws in Global Witness Dispute', Financial Times, 10 March 2014, www.ft.com/cms/s/0/fc1d57a2-a606-11e3-b9ed-00144feab7de .html#axzz3EzpqJvFU.

55. BSG Resources, 'Opportunities Available for People of Guinea Being

Destroyed by Discredited Regime', 22 March 2013, www.bsgresources.com/media/opportunities-available-for-people-of-guinea-being-destroyed-by-discredited-regime.

56. Mahmoud Thiam, telephone interview with author, October 2012.

57. Powerscourt, 'Response to Press Speculation', and BSG Resources, 'Opportunities Available for People of Guinea Being Destroyed by Discredited Regime'.

58. Alpha Condé, interview with author, Paris, November 2013.

59. Keefe, 'Buried Secrets'.

60. Tom Burgis, 'US Court Allows Forensic Tests in Guinea Case', *Financial Times*, 16 January 2014, www.ft.com/cms/s/0/9b29f9f0-7ece-11e3-8642-00144 feabdc0.html?siteedition=uk#axzz3HUSpQnyc; Tom Burgis, 'French Businessman Pleads Guilty in Guinea Mining Case', *Financial Times*, 10 March 2014, www.ft.com/intl/cms/s/0/a138edec-a87c-11e3-b50f-00144feab7de.html.

61. Tom Burgis, 'French Businessman Jailed for 2 Years in Guinea Mining Case', *Financial Times*, 25 July 2014, www.ft.com/intl/cms/s/0/64fb3f4e-1427 -11e4-9acb-00144feabdc0.html#axzz3EzpqJvFU.

62. Responses to questions from the *Financial Times* by Powerscourt on behalf of Beny Steinmetz and BSGR, 10 March 2014, in author's possession.

63. The claim against Global Witness filed by Beny Steinmetz and three directors of BSGR filed at the High Court in London on 12 December 2013 described Steinmetz as the 'principal financial beneficiary of BSGR', in author's possession.

64. Touré, Sworn Statement.

65. Press statement issued by Powerscourt on behalf of BSGR, 7 March 2014, in author's possession. When I was reporting these developments for the *Financial Times* I sent representatives of BSGR and Steinmetz a list of questions about the version of events offered by Mamadie Touré (see Touré, Sworn Statement) and the final report of the Guinean inquiry. The representatives declined to answer them.

66. 'Report and Recommendation of the CTRTCM . . .'

67. Ibid.

68. Vale, 'Vale Informs on Simandou Developments', press release, 25 April 2014, http://saladeimprensa.vale.com/en/releases/interna.asp?id=22674.

69. See James Wilson, Tom Burgis and Joe Leahy, 'Rio Tinto Sues Vale and BSGR Over Guinea Mine Controversy', *Financial Times*, 30 April 2014, www.ft.com/intl/cms/s/0/8ef9c710-d06c-11e3-af2b-00144feabdc0.html#axzz3EzpqJ vFU, and Tom Burgis, 'Rio Tinto and Vale Step Up Battle over Guinean

Deposit', *Financial Times*, 1 May 2014, www.ft.com/intl/cms/s/0/e1ec7172-d141
-11e3-81e0-00144feabdc0.html.

70. Rio Tinto, 'Rio Tinto and Government of Guinea Sign New Agreement for Simandou Iron Ore Project', statement, 22 April 2011, www.riotinto.com/media/media-releases-237_6340.aspx.

71. Rio Tinto, 'Rio Tinto and Chinalco Sign Memorandum of Understanding to Form Iron Ore Joint Venture for the Simandou Project in Guinea', statement, 19 March 2010, www.riotinto.com/media/media-releases-237_1455.aspx.

72. 'Recommandation Concernant les Titres Miniers et la Convention Minière Détenus par la Société', Comité Technique de Revue des Titres et Conventions Miniers on the Vale-BSGR rights (held in a joint venture called VBG), 9 April 2014.

73. 'Guinea: Letter of Intent, Memorandum of Economic and Financial Policies and Technical Memorandum of Understanding', International Monetary Fund, 11 February 2012, www.imf.org/External/NP/LOI/2014/GIN/091814.pdf.

74. Harry Snoek, telephone interview with author, October 2012.

CHAPTER 6: A BRIDGE TO BEIJING

1. 'France Condemns Niger President's Emergency Powers', RFI, 2 July 2009, www1.rfi.fr/actuen/articles/115/article_4174.asp.

2. Ali Idrissa (head of Rotab, a Nigerien transparency campaign), interview with author, Niamey, April 2010. See also Tom Burgis, 'Strategic Resources: A Richer Seam', *Financial Times*, 20 May 2010, www.ft.com/cms/s/0/d9853fda
-6441-11df-8618-00144feab49a.html.

3. Mohamed Bazoum, interview with author, Niamey, April 2010.

4. 'Vast Embezzlement Under Previous Niger Regime: Report', Agence France-Press, 27 March 2011, http://en.starafrica.com/news/vast-embezzlement-under-previous-niger-regime-report-157192.html; 'L'ex-président nigérien Mamadou Tandja est sorti de prison', Jeune Afrique, 11 May 2011; 'Fire Consumes Niger's Anti-Corruption Files', Reuters, 3 January 2012, http://ca.reuters.com/article/topNews/idCATRE8021A720120103.

5. Abdoulaye Massalatchi, 'Niger Capital Calm, Business as Usual Day After Coup', Reuters, 19 February 2010, www.reuters.com/article/2010/02/19/idUSLDE61I0CG._CH_.2400.

6. Edward George, *The Cuban Intervention in Angola, 1965–1991: From Che Guevara to Cuito Cuanavale* (New York: Frank Cass, 2005), 190.

7. Xia Huang, interview with author, Niamey, April 2010.

8. Ibrahim Iddi Ango, interview with author, Niamey, April 2010.

9. Vivien Foster, 'Africa Infrastructure Country Diagnostic', World Bank, September 2008, http://siteresources.worldbank.org/INTAFRICA/Resources/AICD_exec_summ_9-30-08a.pdf.

10. Tito Yepes, Justin Pierce and Vivien Foster, 'Making Sense of Africa's Infrastructure Endowment: A Benchmarking Approach', World Bank, January 2008, http://elibrary.worldbank.org/doi/book/10.1596/1813-9450-4912.

11. Foster, 'Africa Infrastructure Country Diagnostic'.

12. Vivien Foster and Cecilia Briceño-Garmendia, 'Africa's Infrastructure: A Time for Transformation', World Bank, 2010, http://siteresources.worldbank.org/INTAFRICA/Resources/aicd_overview_english_no-embargo.pdf.

13. Simon Freemantle and Jeremy Stevens, 'BRIC and Africa: New Partnerships Poised to Grow Africa's Commercial Infrastructure', Standard Bank, 15 October 2010; 'China-Africa Economic and Trade Cooperation', Information Office of the State Council, Beijing, August 2013, www.safpi.org/sites/default/files/publications/China-AfricaEconomicandTradeCooperation.pdf.

14. Vivien Foster, William Butterfield, Chuan Chen and Nataliya Pushak, 'Building Bridges: China's Growing Role as Infrastructure Financier for Sub-Saharan Africa', World Bank, 2009, http://siteresources.worldbank.org/INTAFRICA/Resources/BB_Final_Exec_summary_English_July08_Wo-Embg.pdf.

15. Toh Han Shih, 'China to Provide Africa with US$1tr Financing', *South China Morning Post*, 18 November 2013, www.scmp.com/business/banking-finance/article/1358902/china-provide-africa-us1tr-financing.

16. Martin Meredith, *The State of Africa* (London: Simon and Schuster, 2005), 227–228.

17. Eva Joly, 'Est-ce dans ce monde-là que nous voulons vivre?', Arènes, 2003, quoted in Nicholas Shaxson, *Poisoned Wells: The Dirty Politics of African Oil* (New York: Palgrave Macmillan, 2007). I have also drawn on Shaxson's account for other details of the Elf affair.

18. Meredith, *State of Africa*, 615.

19. Daniel Flynn and Geert de Clercq, 'Special Report: Areva and Niger's Uranium Fight', Reuters, 5 February 2014, www.reuters.com/article/2014/02/05/us-niger-areva-specialreport-idUSBREA140AA20140205.

20. Trendfield website, 'Société des Mines d'Azelik SA (SOMINA): Teguidda', accessed 16 May 2014, http://trendfieldonline.com/niger.html.

21. Guy Duport, LinkedIn page, accessed 7 March 2014, https://cn.linkedin

.com/in/guyduport; management profiles, Trendfield website, accessed 7 March 2014.

22. Marketwired, 'Trendfield Lion Habitat', press release on behalf of Trendfield, Hong Kong, 15 April 2010, www.marketwired.com/press-release/trendfield-lion-habitat-1168639.htm.

23. Trendfield website, management profiles.

24. El-Moctar Ichah, interview with author, Niamey, April 2010.

25. Olivier Muller, interview with author, Niamey, April 2010.

26. Between 2007 and 2011 68 per cent of Chinese mergers and acquisitions abroad, measured by the value of the transactions, involved energy and resources. The second-biggest sector, accounting for 11 per cent of activity, was financial services, followed by industrial and chemical companies, with 10 per cent. See 'China Outbound M&A', Squire Sanders, May 2013, www.squiresanders.com/files/Publication/d54c8c99-e6a0-425e-80d4-4d8b122b7553/Presentation/PublicationAttachment/a18546e6-281d-43d2-adbc-4e01424eed20/Squire_Sanders_Briefing_May2013.pdf.

27. Ecobank, 'Six Top Trends in Sub-Saharan Africa's (SSA) Extractives Industries', 23 July 2013, www.ecobank.com/upload/20130813121743289489uJudJb9GkE.pdf.

28. Nik Zuks, interview with author, Conakry, June 2010.

29. Mahmoud Thiam interview, December 2013; Bellzone, 'CIF Strategic Investment and Proposed Fundraising', statement to the stock exchange, 1 March 2011.

30. Bellzone, 'Binding MOU Reached with Chinese Partner to Develop Rail and Port Infrastructure for the Kalia Iron Project and to Form a 50/50 Joint Venture to Develop Additional Iron Permits in Guinea, West Africa', statement to the stock exchange, 24 May 2010.

31. West African Iron Ore, 'West African Iron Ore Signs Binding Letter of Intent for a $30 Million Finance Facility and Offtake Agreement with Strategic Partner China International Fund', statement to the stock exchange, Newswire, 4 September 2012, www.newswire.ca/en/story/1029729/west-african-iron-ore-signs-binding-letter-of-intent-for-a-30-million-finance-facility-and-offtake-agreement-with-strategic-partner-china-internationa.

32. Levkowitz et al., 'The 88 Queensway Group'; 'Keeping Foreign Corruption Out of the United States: Four Case Histories'; US Senate Permanent Subcommittee on Investigations, Committee on Homeland Security and Governmental Affairs, February 2010, www.hsgac.senate.gov/subcommittees/investigations/hearings/-keeping-foreign-corruption-out-of-the-united-states

-four-case-histories. In Lee Levkowitz, Marta McLellan Ross and J. R. Warner, 'The 88 Queensway Group: A Case Study in Chinese Investors' Operations in Angola and Beyond', US-China Economic and Security Review Commission, 10 July 2009, http://china.usc.edu/App_Images/The_88_Queensway_Group .pdf, US congressional researchers write that 'China Sonangol is the client of a prominent international consulting firm called Pierson Asia.' Pierson was founded and is run by Falcone, who has based himself in Beijing since being released from prison following the Angolagate scandal in France. A person with close ties to the Futungo told me in April 2014 that Falcone was 'one of the architects' of the Queensway Group's arrival in Angola. Falcone, whom I have repeatedly asked for an interview, told me in an e-mail exchange in April 2014, 'For the sake of clarity, I do not have nor [have] had any working or commercial relationship of any sort with China Sonangol.'

33. Decision of the High Court of the Hong Kong Special Administrative Region, Court of First Instance, HCMP 2143/2011, in *Wu Yang v. Dayuan International Development Limited et al.*, 4 June 2013.

34. 'Missões Diplomáticas e Consulares da República de Moçambique', Mozambique government, www.embassymozambique.se/down/missoes_diplo maticas.pdf; 'Vice Minister Fu Meets Ambassador of Mozambique to China', Chinese Ministry of Commerce, http://english.mofcom.gov.cn/aarticle/photo news/200808/20080805705121.html.

35. Mozambique's government journal, the *Boletim da República*, series III, no. 36, 20 November 2009 announced that Cif-Moz had been registered on 16 September 2008. The company's joint owners were named as China International Fund, with 80 per cent of the equity, and SPI-Gestão e Investimento SARL, with 20 per cent.

36. The website of Mozambique's *cadastro mineiro*, the government body that oversees the mining industry, records that Cif-Moz applied for a licence to prospect for limestone in the Matutuine district, number 2564L, on 17 March 2008. The five-year licence was granted on 30 November 2009. It was cancelled at some point before 26 May 2014, when I checked the *cadastro*'s website, portals.flexi cadastre.com/Mozambique/EN.

37. 'Chinese Companies Plan to Prospect for Raw Materials in Mozambique', Macauhub, 6 December 2010, www.macauhub.com.mo/en/2010/12/06/chinese-companies-plan-to-prospect-for-raw-materials-in-mozambique; 'It's Mine', Africa-Asia Confidential, February 2011, www.africa-asia-confidential .com/article-preview/id/530/It%e2%80%99s_mine.

38. Letter from China Sonangol in response to my questions ahead of the

publication of a report on the Queensway Group in *Financial Times*, 18 July 2014, www.ft.com/chinasonangolresponse.

39. Mahmoud Thiam, telephone interview with author, December 2013. See also Laura Rena Murray, Beth Morrissey, Himanshu Ojha and Patrick Martin-Menard, 'African Safari: CIF's Grab for Oil and Minerals', Caixin, 17 October 2011, http://english.caixin.com/2011-10-17/100314766.html, and 'Top Salesman for China Sonangol', Africa Energy Intelligence, 12 January 2011, www.africaintelligence.com/AEM/oil/2011/01/12/top-salesman-for-china-sonangol,87388022-ART.

40. The Tsimoro oil field potentially held a billion barrels of crude. It already had a proprietor, a London-listed junior oil-exploration company called Madagascar Oil, but there were rumours that the government was planning to confiscate the oil field. Despite China Sonangol's efforts, Madagascar Oil clung to the Tsimoro field.

41. Thiam interview.

42. Paul Midford and Indra de Soysa, 'Enter the Dragon! Are the Chinese Less Likely to Extend Politico-military Support to Democratic African Regimes?', paper prepared for the International Studies Association's annual meeting, New Orleans, February 2010.

43. 'African Economic Outlook 2013', African Development Bank, www.undp.org/content/dam/rba/docs/Reports/African%20Economic%20Outlook%202013%20En.pdf.

44. Lamido Sanusi, 'Africa Must Get Real About Chinese Ties', *Financial Times*, 11 March 2013, www.ft.com/intl/cms/s/0/562692b0-898c-11e2-ad3f-00144feabdc0.html.

45. Mahamadou Issoufou, interview with author, London, June 2012. See also Tom Burgis, 'Niger Leader Urges Action on Mali', *Financial Times*, 12 June 2012, www.ft.com/intl/cms/s/0/37f4b60e-b49a-11e1-bb68-00144feabdc0.html.

46. Abdoulaye Massalatchi and Geert De Clercq, 'Areva's Niger Uranium Mines Shut for Maintenance as Licence Talks Continue', Reuters, 3 January 2014, www.reuters.com/article/2014/01/03/areva-niger-closure-idUSL6N0KD23620140103.

47. Abdoulaye Massalaki, 'Areva Signs Uranium Deal with Niger, Delays New Mine', Reuters, 26 May 2014, http://uk.reuters.com/article/2014/05/26/areva-niger-idUKL6N0OC2TB20140526; Alice Powell, 'Niger Finally Sign Uranium Contract, But Is It a Fair Deal?', Publish What You Pay, 27 May 2014, www.publishwhatyoupay.org/newsroom/blog/areva-%E2%80%93-niger-finally-sign-uranium-contract-it-fair-deal.

CHAPTER 7: FINANCE AND CYANIDE

1. 'Project Performance Assessment Report: Ghana, Mining Sector Rehabilitation Project (Credit 1921-Gh), Mining Sector Development and Environment Project (Credit 2743-Gh), Operations Evaluation Department', World Bank, July 2003, http://lnweb90.worldbank.org/oed/oeddoclib.nsf/docunidviewforjava search/a89aedb05623fd6085256e37005cd815/$file/ppar_26197.pdf.

2. Newmont Ghana Gold Ltd, Press statement, 12 October 2009.

3. Omar Jabara of Newmont Corporate Communications wrote a letter to the editor of the *Financial Times*, published 31 March 2010 (www.ft.com/cms/s/0/6a148c3e-3c5d-11df-b316-00144feabdc0.html?siteedition=uk#axzz3Hpltff T1) in response to my article on Newmont, the cyanide spill and Ghana's gold, 'Mining Fails to Produce Golden Era for Ghana', *Financial Times*, 22 March 2010, www.ft.com/intl/cms/s/0/0d3e06c4-35dd-11df-aa43-00144feabdc0.html#ax zz3F02grPqh.

4. 'IFC History', IFC, www.ifc.org/wps/wcm/connect/corp_ext_content/ifc_external_corporate_site/about+ifc/ifc+history.

5. 'The Inspection Panel Investigation Report', World Bank, 17 September 2001, http://siteresources.worldbank.org/EXTINSPECTIONPANEL/Resources/ChadInvestigationReporFinal.pdf.

6. Guinean government official, telephone interview with author, September 2013.

7. 'IFC Investment in Simandou Mine (Guinea)—US Position', US Treasury, 24 May 2012, www.treasury.gov/resource-center/international/development-banks/Documents/(2012-05-22)%20Guinea%20Statement_As%20Posted.pdf.

8. Compliance Advisor/Ombudsman, 'Appraisal Report on IFC Investment in Lonmin Platinum Group Metals Project, South Africa', World Bank, 30 August 2013, www.cao-ombudsman.org/cases/document-links/documents/CAO_Appraisal_LONMIN_C-I-R4-Y12-F171.pdf.

9. 'Striking a Better Balance – The World Bank Group and Extractive Industries: The Final Report of the Extractive Industries Review', Preface, December 2003, https://openknowledge.worldbank.org/handle/10986/17705.

10. Ibid.

11. Alan Beattie, 'The World Bank Digs a Hole for Itself', *Financial Times*, 25 February 2004.

12. 'Striking a Better Balance'.

13. 'Striking a Better Balance—The World Bank Group And Extractive

Industries: The Final Report of the Extractive Industries Review', World Bank Group Management Response, September 2004, http://siteresources.worldbank.org/INTOGMC/Resources/finaleirmanagementresponseexecsum.pdf.

14. Mark Drajem, 'World Bank Accepts New Oil, Gas Lending Controls; Call to Discontinue Programs Rejected', *Washington Post*, 4 August 2004, www.washingtonpost.com/wp-dyn/articles/A38174-2004Aug3.html.

15. Action Contre l'Impunité pour les Droits Humains, Nouvelle Dynamique Syndicale, Rights and Accountability in Development, Friends of the Earth and Environmental Defense, letter to Miga's executive director, 25 August 2004 (copy in author's possession).

16. Right and Accountability in Development et al., 'Anvil Mining Limited and the Kilwa Incident: Unanswered Questions', 20 October 2005, www.raid-uk.org/sites/default/files/qq-anvil.pdf.

17. Philippe Valahu, acting director of Miga's operations group, letter to Patricia Feeney of Rights and Accountability in Development and Colleen Freeman of Friends of the Earth US, 18 August 2005 (copy in author's possession).

18. US Embassy in Kinshasa, 'Possible Massacre at Kilwa', diplomatic cable, 18 November 2004, WikiLeaks, 1 September 2011, www.wikileaks.org/plusd/cables/04KINSHASA2118_a.html.

19. Office of the Compliance Advisor/Ombudsman, 'CAO Audit of Miga's Due Diligence of the Dikulushi Copper-Silver Mining Project in The Democratic Republic of the Congo', November 2005, www.cao-ombudsman.org/cases/document-links/documents/DikulushiDRCfinalversion02-01-06.pdf.

20. World Bank spokesperson, e-mail exchange with author, January 2014.

21. Human Development Index 2014, UN Development Programme, http://hdr.undp.org/en/content/table-1-human-development-index-and-its-components.

22. Ousman Gajigo, Emelly Mutambatsere and Guirane Ndiaye, 'Royalty Rates in African Mining Revisited: Evidence from Gold Mining', African Development Bank, June 2012, www.afdb.org/fileadmin/uploads/afdb/Documents/Publications/AEB%20VOL%203%20Issue%206%20avril%202012%20Bis_AEB%20VOL%203%20Issue%206%20avril%202012%20bis_01.pdf.

23. The figures on Zambia are drawn from 'Equity in Extractives', Africa Progress Panel, 2013, http://africaprogresspanel.org/wp-content/uploads/2013/08/2013_APR_Equity_in_Extractives_25062013_ENG_HR.pdf.

24. 'Fiscal Regimes for Extractive Industries: Design and Implementation, International Monetary Fund', April 2012, www.imf.org/external/np/pp/eng/2012/081512.pdf, cited in 'Equity in Extractives'.

25. Varma is not the only senior IFC official to switch between the institution

and companies it assists. Thierry Tanoh, a former IFC vice-president for Latin America, sub-Saharan Africa and western Europe, was designated as the next chief executive designate of a pan-African bank called Ecobank Transnational (ETI) a day before the IFC revealed it would increase its investment in the bank by $100 million. Lars Thunell, a former IFC chief executive, was in 2012 appointed to the board of Kosmos, the Texan oil explorer with interests in Ghana, which was backed by the IFC and private equity houses, including Warburg Pincus, the one Varma had joined in 2011. Following such moves, the IFC tightened rules designed to prevent conflicts of interest. See William Wallis, 'World Bank Unit Toughens Staff Rules', *Financial Times*, 23 December 2013, www.ft.com/cms/s/0/5a6a4054-6250-11e3-bba5-00144feabdc0.html#axzz3F0NBUX6g.

26. Somit Varma, telephone interview with author, November 2009.

27. Burgis, 'Mining Fails to Produce Golden Era for Ghana'.

28. Gajigo, Mutambatsere and Ndiaye, 'Royalty Rates in African Mining Revisited: Evidence from Gold Mining'.

29. Jeff Huspeni, telephone interview with author, November 2009.

30. Much of the literature is reviewed in 'Addressing Base Erosion and Profit Shifting', Organisation for Economic Co-operation and Development, 2013, www.loyensloeff.com/nl-NL/Documents/OECD.pdf.

31. 'Action Plan on Base Erosion and Profit Shifting', Organisation for Economic Co-operation and Development, 2013, www.oecd.org/ctp/BEPSAction Plan.pdf.

32. Jane G. Gravelle, 'Tax Havens: International Tax Avoidance and Evasion', *National Tax Journal* 62, no. 4 (December 2009): 727.

33. 'Equity in Extractives'.

34. Nick Mathiason, 'Piping Profits', Publish What You Pay (Norway), 19 September 2011, www.publishwhatyoupay.org/resources/piping-profits-secret -world-oil-gas-and-mining-giants.

35. Christian Aid, 'False Profits: Robbing the Poor to Keep the Rich Tax-Free', March 2009, www.christianaid.org.uk/images/false-profits.pdf.

36. 'The Africa-China Connection', Fitch Ratings, 28 December 2011, private note to clients.

37. Paul Wolfowitz, interview with *Les Echos*, 19 October 2006, http://web .worldbank.org/WBSITE/EXTERNAL/EXTABOUTUS/ORGANIZATION /EXTPRESIDENT/EXTPASTPRESIDENTS/EXTOFFICEPRESIDENT/ 0,,contentMDK:21102200~menuPK:64343277~pagePK:51174171~piPK:6425 8873~theSitePK:1014541,00.html.

38. James Wolfensohn, interview with *Forbes*, 17 January 2011, www.forbes

.com/2011/01/14/james-wolfensohn-world-bank-transcript-intelligent-investing.html.

39. Michael J. Kavanagh, 'IMF Halts Congo Loans over Failure to Publish Mine Contract', Bloomberg, 3 December 2012, www.bloomberg.com/news/2012-12-03/imf-halts-congo-loans-over-failure-to-publish-mine-contract-2-.html; International official, telephone interview with author, July 2013. The deal in question involved the undisclosed transfer of the state's 25 per cent stake in the Comide copper project to a British Virgin Islands company called Straker International, as part of a broader transaction involving Gertler companies.

40. Angolan Embassy in London, 'Ministry of Finance Denies Misuse of Chinese Loans', 17 October 2007.

41. 'Transcript of a Conference Call on Angola with Sean Nolan, Senior Advisor in the African Department, and Lamin Leigh, Angola Mission Chief', IMF, 25 November 2009, www.imf.org/external/np/tr/2009/tr112509.htm.

42. 'IMF Risks Condoning Corruption with New Loan to Angola', Global Witness, 5 October 2009, www.globalwitness.org/fr/node/3855.

43. Lamin Leigh, Yuan Xiao and Nir Klein (of the IMF's Africa department), 'IMF Lends Angola $1.4 Billion to Support Reserves, Reforms', International Monetary Fund, 23 November 2009, www.imf.org/external/pubs/ft/survey/so/2009/car112309b.htm.

44. 'IMF Executive Board Approves US$1.4 Billion Stand-By Arrangement with Angola', IMF, 23 November 2009, www.imf.org/external/np/sec/pr/2009/pr09425.htm.

45. The IMF's first analysis of the hole in Angola's accounts and the reasons for it is in the 'Fifth Review Under the Stand-By Arrangement with Angola', IMF, 8 December 2011. This and all other IMF reports on Angola are at www.imf.org/external/country/ago.

46. Ricardo Soares de Oliveira, 'Transparency Reforms Yield Little Change', *Financial Times*, 18 July 2012, www.ft.com/intl/cms/s/0/e8c819ce-c5f9-11e1-b57e-00144feabdc0.html#axzz3F0NBUX6g.

47. Andrew England and William Wallis, 'Angola Sets Up Fund to Preserve Oil Riches', *Financial Times*, 17 October 2012, www.ft.com/intl/cms/s/0/fb1db978-186d-11e2-8705-00144feabdc0.html#axzz3F0NBUX6g.

48. International Monetary Fund, 'IMF Concludes Second Post-Program Monitoring Mission to Angola', press release, 30 January 2013, www.imf.org/external/np/sec/pr/2013/pr1329.htm.

49. Barnaby Pace, interview with author, London, February 2014.

CHAPTER 8:
GOD HAS NOTHING TO DO WITH IT

1. Annkio Briggs, interview with author, Port Harcourt, May 2013.

2. Judith Burdin Asuni, 'Understanding the Armed Groups of the Niger Delta', Council on Foreign Relations, September 2009, www.cfr.org/nigeria/understanding-armed-groups-niger-delta/p20146.

3. UN Office on Drugs and Crime, 'Transnational Trafficking and the Rule of Law in West Africa: A Threat Assessment', July 2009, www.unodc.org/documents/data-and-analysis/Studies/West_Africa_Report_2009.pdf.

4. Christina Katsouris and Aaron Sayne, 'Nigeria's Criminal Crude: International Options to Combat the Export of Stolen Oil', Chatham House, September 2013, www.chathamhouse.org/sites/files/chathamhouse/public/Research/Africa/0913pr_nigeriaoil.pdf.

5. Transition Monitoring Group final report on the 2003 Nigerian elections, quoted in 'Nigeria's 2003 Elections: The Unacknowledged Violence', Human Rights Watch, June 2004, www.hrw.org/reports/2004/nigeria0604/nigeria0604.pdf.

6. Patrick Naagbanton, 'On the Denouement of Soboma George (Part 1)', Sahara Reporters, 31 August 2010, http://saharareporters.com/2010/08/31/denouement-soboma-george-part-1.

7. IRIN, 'Nigeria: Shell Evacuates Oil Platforms After Fresh Attacks', 16 January 2006,www.irinnews.org/report/57816/nigeria-shell-evacuates-oil-platforms-after-fresh-attacks.

8. Asuni, 'Understanding the Armed Groups of the Niger Delta'.

9. 'Statement by Farah Dagogo, Out-Going Commander of MEND', issued by Jomo Gbomo, 3 October 2009, in author's possession.

10. 'World Report 2013', Human Rights Watch, Nigeria chapter, www.hrw.org/world-report/2013/country-chapters/nigeria.

11. Published accounts of the massacre include 'Nigeria: Protect Survivors, Fully Investigate Massacre Reports', Human Rights Watch, 24 January 2010, www.hrw.org/news/2010/01/22/nigeria-protect-survivors-fully-investigate-massacre-reports.

12. Senan Murray, 'Profile: Joshua Dariye', BBC, 24 July 2007, http://news.bbc.co.uk/2/hi/africa/6908960.stm.

13. 'Biography', Plateau State, www.plateaustate.gov.ng/?ContentPage&secid=55&sub_cnt=sectionpage&sub_cntid=155.

14. Philip Ostien, 'Jonah Jang and the Jasawa: Ethno-Religious Conflict in Jos, Nigeria', Muslim-Christian Relations in Africa series, August 2009, www.

sharia-in-africa.net/media/publications/ethno-religious-conflict-in-Jos-Nigeria/ Ostien_Jos.pdf.

15. Northern Christian leader, interview with author, Kaduna, January 2010.

16. Former Plateau State official, interview with author, Jos, January 2010.

17. I requested an interview with Jonah Jang again when I was back in Nigeria in 2013 but was told he was not available.

18. US Embassy in Abuja, 'Nigeria: Jos Riots Not/not Caused by Outsiders from Niger and Chad', cable, 19 December 2008, WikiLeaks, www.wikileaks .org/plusd/cables/08ABUJA2494_a.html.

19. Ostien, *Jonah Jang*.

20. The details of the Willbros, Panalpina and KBR bribery schemes are detailed in settlements with the US Department of Justice at www.justice .gov and the Securities and Exchange Commission at www.sec.gov (Willbros: www.justice.gov/criminal/fraud/fcpa/cases/willbros-group.html; Panalpina/ Shell: www.justice.gov/opa/pr/oil-services-companies-and-freight-forwarding -company-agree-resolve-foreign-bribery; KBR/Halliburton: www.justice.gov/ opa/pr/kellogg-brown-root-llc-pleads-guilty-foreign-bribery-charges-and-agrees -pay-402-million).

21. 'Global Enforcement Report 2012', TRACE International, www.trace international.org/data/public/GER_2012_Final-147966-1.pdf

22. Judgment of Lady Justice Gloster, High Court, London, in *Energy Venture Partners Limited v. Malabu Oil and Gas Limited*, 17 July 2013, in author's possession.

23. 'Safe Sex in Nigeria', *The Economist*, 15 June 2013, www.economist .com/news/business/21579469-court-documents-shed-light-manoeuvrings -shell-and-eni-win-huge-nigerian-oil-block; 'The Scandal of Nigerian Oil Block OPL 245', Global Witness, November 2013, www.globalwitness.org/library/ scandal-nigerian-oil-block-opl-245-0.

24. Emilio Parodi and Oleg Vukmanovic, 'Large Part of Eni's Nigerian Oil Deal Cash Went on Bribes—Italian Prosecutors', Reuters, 1 October 2014, www.reuters .com/article/2014/10/01/eni-nigeria-investigation-idUSL6N0RW40720141001.

25. Chip Minty (spokesman for Devon Energy), e-mail exchange with author, October 2013.

26. Koye Edu, telephone interview with author, December 2013.

27. Bård Glad Pedersen (spokesman for Statoil), e-mail exchange with author, October 2013.

28. 'China Sonangol's Secret License', Africa Energy Intelligence, 8 July 2009, www.africaintelligence.com/AEM/oil/2009/07/08/china-sonangol-s-secret -license,65100549-GRA.

29. See, for example, Dino Mahtani, 'Nigeria Vows to Investigate $90m Oil Deal', *Financial Times*, 31 October 2006; Kate Linebaugh and Shai Oster, 'Cnooc Pays $2.27 Billion for Nigerian Oil, Gas Stake', *Wall Street Journal*, 10 January 2006, http://online.wsj.com/articles/SB113680307278841473.

30. There were also reports in the Nigerian press that corroborated what my contacts told me: China Sonangol had secured a 95 per cent stake in OPL 256, with the remaining 5 per cent held by the Nigerian Petroleum Development Company, an arm of the state-owned Nigerian National Petroleum Corporation. See Hamisu Muhammad, 'Most Indigenous Oil Blocks Not Producing—Report', Daily Trust, 19 March 2013, http://allafrica.com/stories/201303190385.html.

31. Former presidential aide, telephone interview with author, October 2013.

32. Former senior Nigerian official, telephone interview with author, January 2014.

33. 'Who's Who: Dr Andy Uba', *Africa Confidential*, 5 June 2014, www.africa-confidential.com/whos-who-profile/id/2603/Andy_Uba. This profile also says that Uba 'has a significant stake in China Sonangol', although I was unable to find company documents demonstrating as much.

34. Oil industry professional, telephone interview with author, September 2013.

35. Ike Okonta and Oronto Douglas, *Where Vultures Feast: Shell, Human Rights, and Oil* (Brooklyn: Verso, 2003), 134.

36. See, for example, Adewale Maja-Pearce, 'Remembering Ken Saro-Wiwa', in *Remembering Ken Saro-Wiwa and Other Essays* (Lagos, Nigeria: New Gong, 2005).

37. See, for example, Okonta and Douglas, *Where Vultures Feast*, 58.

38. Royal Dutch Shell, 'Shell Settles Wiwa Case with Humanitarian Gesture', press release, 8 June 2009, www.shell.com/global/aboutshell/media/news-and-media-releases/2009/shell-settlement-wiwa-case-08062009.html.

39. Dino Mahtani and Daniel Balint-Kurti, 'Shell Gives Nigerian Work to Militants' Companies', *Financial Times*, 27 April 2006.

40. A US diplomatic cable, 'Militants Ask Mittee for Help for Villagers Wounded in Rivers Conflict; Some Villagers Killed in JTF Attacks', 24 September 2008, WikiLeaks, https://wikileaks.org/plusd/cables/08LAGOS374_a.html, shows that Ann Pickard, then Shell's Africa chief, was aware of precise details of a JTF assault in the Niger Delta reported to have caused civilian casualties. I asked Shell for its comments on the cable, and a spokesman responded, 'Shell's Country Chairs regularly meet with government officials in the countries where we operate and discuss topics of mutual concern. There is nothing untoward

about this. It is not unusual for issues relating to the security of our facilities to be discussed in those meetings, in particular in Nigeria, but we cannot comment on the contents of documents which we did not produce.' Precious Okolobo, spokesman for Shell companies in Nigeria, e-mail exchange with author, July 2013.

41. I asked Shell's spokesmen in Nigeria and London to comment on the accounts I was told about the ties between the company and the Delta's militants. Part of their reply was: 'It is also SPDC policy that certain types of contracts are awarded to community contractors; yet even these contracts are based on transparent and auditable processes. SPDC does not award contracts to armed groups, this being against the Shell General Business Principles. All SPDC contractors (including community contractors) are subjected to a rigorous Integrity Due Diligence (IDD) check before registration as contractors and also before contract award or renewal.'

42. Shell's e-mail responses to questions from author, July 2013.

43. Shell briefing notes, 'Global Memorandum of Understanding', April 2013, http://nidprodev.org/index.php/programmes/current-projects/global-memorandum-of-understanding-gmou-deployment.

44. Niger Delta go-between, interviews with author, Port Harcourt, August 2010 and April 2013.

45. Shell's e-mail responses to questions from author, July 2013.

46. Former Shell employee, interview with author, April 2013.

47. Harriman Oyofo, interview with author, Warri, April 2013.

48. Ben Amunwa, 'Dirty Work: Shell's Security Spending in Nigeria and Beyond', Platform, August 2012, http://platformlondon.org/wp-content/uploads/2012/08/Dirty-work-Shell%E2%80%99s-security-spending-in-Nigeria-and-beyond-Platform-August-2012.pdf.

49. When I asked the company about the scale of its community development spending, it said, 'We calculate figures annually. In 2012, SPDC and SNEPCo [the Shell subsidiary that runs its offshore oil projects in Nigeria] directly invested $103.2 million toward addressing social and economic development challenges in the region. This has nothing to do with the security budget. The annual GMoU budget is based on the agreed mandate with the clusters. It may interest you to know that, in addition to the GMoU initiative, Shell operations in 2012, contributed over $178 million to the Niger Delta Development Commission (NDDC), as required by law.' Shell's e-mail responses to questions from author, July 2013.

50. Aaron Sayne, 'Antidote to Violence? Lessons for the Nigerian Federal

Government's Ten Percent Community Royalty from the Oil Company Experience', Transnational Crisis Project, February 2010, http://crisisproject.org/wp-content/uploads/2011/09/Antidote-to-Violence-Niger-Delta-Report-no.1.pdf.

51. Niger Delta activist, interview with author, Port Harcourt, May 2013.

52. 'Nigeria Governor to Be Impeached', BBC News, 23 November 2005, http://news.bbc.co.uk/2/hi/africa/4462444.stm.

53. See, for example, 'Nigeria: Presidential Election Marred by Fraud, Violence', Human Rights Watch, 26 April 2007, www.hrw.org/news/2007/04/25/nigeria-presidential-election-marred-fraud-violence.

54. Tom Burgis, 'Jonathan Wins Nigerian Ruling Party Primary', *Financial Times*, 14 January 2011.

55. Clement Nwankwo, interview with author, Abuja, April 2013.

56. Financier close to the PDP and a senior PDP politician, interviews with author, Lagos, May 2013.

57. 'Nigeria: Post-Election Violence Killed 800', Human Rights Watch, 17 May 2011, www.hrw.org/news/2011/05/16/nigeria-post-election-violence-killed-800.

58. 'Fiscal Regimes for Extractive Industries: Design and Implementation', International Monetary Fund, 15 August 2012, www.imf.org/external/np/pp/eng/2012/081512.pdf.

59. Oil revenue data from the International Monetary Fund, IMF Article IV Consultation reports on Nigeria, various years, www.imf.org/external/country/nga.

60. William Wallis, 'Nigeria Bank Governor Alleges Oil Subsidy Racket', *Financial Times*, 12 February 2014, www.ft.com/cms/s/0/6c4aea72-93cd-11e3-a0e1-00144feab7de.html#axzz3F0fTN4qv.

61. Lamido Sanusi, interview with author and William Wallis of the *Financial Times*, London, January 2012.

62. Chinua Achebe, *The Trouble with Nigeria* (London: Heinemann, 1983), 1.

63. François Soudan, 'Portrait: Joseph Kabila', *La Revue*, July/August 2006, quoted in Jason K. Stearns, *Dancing in the Glory of Monsters: The Collapse of the Congo and the Great War of Africa* (New York: PublicAffairs, 2011), 311.

CHAPTER 9: BLACK GOLD

1. Nchakha Moloi, interview with author, Johannesburg, July 2013.

2. T. Bell, G. Farrell and R. Cassim, 'Competitiveness, International Trade and Finance in a Minerals-Rich Economy: The Case of South Africa', in *Finance*

and Competitiveness in Developing Countries, ed. José María Fanelli and Rohinton Medhora, Routledge Studies in Development Economics (Ottawa, Canada: IDRC, 2002).

3. Amartya Sen, *Development as Freedom* (New York: Knopf, 1999), 175.

4. UN Development Programme, Human Development Indicators 2013, https://data.undp.org/dataset/Table-1-Human-Development-Index-and-its-components/wxub-qc5k. The non-African countries in the bottom ten were Qatar, Kuwait and Oman, all significant oil and gas producers, Bhutan, where fuel and minerals account for half of exports, and Turkey.

5. The GDP per head numbers are for 2012 and calculated by the World Bank using purchasing power parity at current international dollar prices. The living standards ranking is the United Nations Development Programme's Human Development Index for 2012.

6. The US Department of Justice enumerated the assets as part of an attempt to confiscate what it said were Teodorin Obiang's profits of corruption ('Second Vice President of Equatorial Guinea Agrees to Relinquish More Than $30 Million of Assets Purchased with Corruption Proceeds', 10 October 2014, www.justice.gov/opa/pr/second-vice-president-equatorial-guinea-agrees-relinquish-more-30-million-assets-purchased). French prosecutors have mounted a similar case.

7. Martin Kingston, interview with author, Johannesburg, July 2013.

8. The figures for black ownership of mining assets are disputed. A 2009 audit by the government's Department of Mineral resources concluded that 9 per cent of the mining industry was owned by 'historically disadvantaged South Africans', far below the 26 per cent target. The audit noted, 'Regrettably, the reported level of BEE ownership is concentrated in the hands of . . . a handful of black beneficiaries.' See 'Mining Charter Impact Assessment Report', Department of Mineral Resources, October 2009, www.dmr.gov.za/publications/finish/108-minerals-act-charter-and-scorecard/126-miningcharterimpact-oct-2009/0.html.

9. Craig Sainsbury, Clarke Wilkins and Daniel Seeney, 'Metals and Mining Strategy: Royalties, Riches and Taxes', Citi, 27 April 2010, www.crikey.com.au/wp-content/uploads/2010/05/100524_SAU08616-21.pdf.

10. Alec Russell, *Bring Me My Machine Gun: The Battle for the Soul of South Africa from Mandela to Zuma* (New York: PublicAffairs, 2009), 163.

11. The data on income distribution under apartheid are drawn from Murray Leibbrandt, Ingrid Woolard, Arden Finn and Jonathan Argent, 'Trends in South African Income Distribution and Poverty Since the Fall of Apartheid', OECD, May 2010, www.npconline.co.za/MediaLib/Downloads/Home/Tabs/

Diagnostic/Economy2/Trends%20in%20South%20African%20Income%20
Distribution%20and%20Poverty%20since%20the%20Fall%20of%20Apartheid
.pdf. The 2009 income distribution data are from the World Bank: World Bank,
World Development Indicators 2014, http://databank.worldbank.org/data/views/
reports/tableview.aspx#.

12. The Gini coefficient shows income distribution on a scale in which zero
shows perfect equality and 100 shows perfect inequality. In 1993, the year before
the end of white rule, South Africa's Gini coefficient was 59.3. In 2009 it was 63.1,
the highest level in the world after the Seychelles, Namibia and the Comoros.
World Bank, World Development Indicators 2014, http://databank.worldbank
.org/data/views/reports/tableview.aspx?isshared=true#.

13. Pascal Fletcher and Jon Herskovitz, 'South Africa Labor Hero Urged
Crackdown on "Criminal" Strike', Reuters, 24 October 2012, www.reuters.com/
article/2012/10/24/us-safrica-mines-ramaphosa-idUSBRE89N13B20121024.

14. Greg Marinovich, 'The Murder Fields of Marikana', *Daily Maverick*, 7
September 2012, www.dailymaverick.co.za/article/2012-08-30-the-murder-fields
-of-marikana-the-cold-murder-fields-of-marikana.

15. Andrew England, 'Ramphele Discreet on Her ANC Challenge', *Financial Times*, 11 February 2013, www.ft.com/intl/cms/s/0/3bf80aa4-7370-11e2-9e92
-00144feabdc0.html#axzz3F0fTN4qv.

16. Songezo Zibi, interview with author, Johannesburg, July 2013.

17. See, for example, Amogelang Mbatha and Franz Wild, 'South Africa's
Zuma Found Guilty of Misconduct by Ombudsman', Bloomberg, 19 March 2014,
www.bloomberg.com/news/2014-03-18/south-african-ombudsman-reports-on
-state-spending-on-zuma-s-home.html. See also the full report on the Nkandla
affair by Thuli Madonsela, the public protector, 'Secure in Comfort', March 2014,
www.publicprotector.org/library%5Cinvestigation_report%5C2013-14%5C
Final%20Report%2019%20March%202014%20.pdf.

CHAPTER 10: THE NEW MONEY KINGS

1. Heidi Holland, *Dinner with Mugabe: The Untold Story of a Freedom Fighter
Who Became a Tyrant* (London: Penguin, 2008), 159.

2. Several of the details of Operation No Return are drawn from 'Diamonds
in the Rough: Human Rights Abuses in the Marange Diamond Fields of Zimbabwe', Human Rights Watch, June 2009, www.hrw.org/sites/default/files/re-
ports/zimbabwe0609web.pdf.

3. Ibid.

4. See 'Diamonds: A Good Deal for Zimbabwe?', Global Witness, February 2012, www.globalwitness.org/library/diamonds-good-deal-zimbabwe.

5. Kimberley Process data, www.kimberleyprocess.com/en/zimbabwe; Bain and Company, 'The Global Diamond Report 2013', www.bain.com/publications /articles/global-diamond-report-2013.aspx

6. The 2013 budget statement by Tendai Biti's Ministry of Finance, published on 15 November 2012, said the ten companies mining Marange had collectively exported $800 million over the previous two years. The government had 50 per cent stakes in the biggest companies, so it was due dividends as well as taxes and royalties. But only $81 million, or 10 per cent of the value of the exports, had made its way to the state coffers. '2013 National Budget Statement', Ministry of Finance and Economic Development, www.zimtreasury.gov .zw/122-2013-national-budget-statement.

7. 'Chinese Firm Not Paying Diamond Proceeds to Zimbabwe: FM', AFP, 17 May 2012, https://ph.news.yahoo.com/chinese-firm-not-paying-diamond -proceeds-zimbabwe-fm-180120647--finance.html.

8. See, for example, Andrew England, 'Zimbabwe Opposition Challenges Mugabe Landslide', *Financial Times*, 9 August 2013, www.ft.com/intl/cms/ s/0/0a3e2d74-0108-11e3-8918-00144feab7de.html.

9. 'Zimbabwe Electoral Commission: 305,000 Voters Turned Away', BBC News, 8 August 2013, www.bbc.com/news/world-africa-23618743.

10. According to official production statistics recorded by the Kimberley Process, in 2012 Africa's sixteen diamond-producing countries together produced $7.5 billion of the $12.6 billion of diamonds produced worldwide. Data compiled by author from Kimberley Process country reports, www.kimberley process.com/en/documents.

11. 'A Rough Trade', Global Witness, 1 December 1998, www.globalwitness .org/library/rough-trade.

12. Ibid.

13. See, for example, UN Security Council, 'Report of the Panel of Experts Appointed Pursuant to Security Council Resolution 1306 (2000), Paragraph 19, in Relation to Sierra Leone', December 2000, www.un.org/sc/committees/1132/ pdf/sclet11951e.pdf.

14. Freetown lawyer Desmond Luke, quoted in Martin Meredith, *The State of Africa* (London: Simon and Schuster, 2006), 566.

15. Kimberley Process data.

16. 'Global Witness Leaves Kimberley Process, Calls for Diamond Trade to Be

Held Accountable', Global Witness press release, 5 December 2011, www.global witness.org/library/global-witness-leaves-kimberley-process-calls-diamond -trade-be-held-accountable.

17. Ian Khama, interview with author, Gaborone, March 2009.

18. 'Julianne Moore and A Diamond Is Forever Hosted a Private Pre-Oscar Dinner to Celebrate Diamonds in Africa', De Beers press release, Los Angeles, 21 February 2009, www.diamondintelligence.com/magazine/magazine.aspx ?id=7733.

19. Tom Burgis, 'Hard Times Ahead as Diamonds Lose Their Sparkle for Botswana', *Financial Times*, 12 March 2009, www.ft.com/intl/cms/s/0/be8c-680c-0ea7-11de-b099-0000779fd2ac.html.

20. Formula One, 'Diamond-Encrusted Steering Wheels for McLaren', press release, 12 May 2010, www.formula1.com/news/headlines/2010/5/10764.html.

21. Zev Chafets, 'The Missionary Mogul', *New York Times*, 16 September 2007, www.nytimes.com/2007/09/16/magazine/16Leviev-t.html?scp=1&sq=%22 Lev%20Leviev%22&st=cse&_r=0.

22. Christian Dietrich, 'Inventory of Formal Diamond Mining in Angola', in *Angola's War Economy*, ed. Jakkie Cilliers and Christian Dietrich (Pretoria: Institute for Security Studies, 2000).

23. Phyllis Berman and Lea Goldman, 'Cracked De Beers', *Forbes*, 15 September 2003, www.forbes.com/forbes/2003/0915/108.html.

24. In January 2014 Norway reinstated a ban on its $810 billion oil fund investing in Leviev's Africa Israel Investment and its construction subsidiary, Danya Cebus, 'due to contribution to serious violations of individual rights in war or conflict through the construction of settlements in East Jerusalem'. The ban, first imposed in 2010, had been lifted the previous August. Africa Israel expressed regret at Norway's decision. See 'Norway's $810 Bln Fund Excludes Two Israeli, One Indian Firm', Reuters, 30 January 2014, www.reuters.com/article/2014/01/30/ norway-sovereignwealthfund-idUSL5N0L417M20140130.

25. Anna Davis, 'Inside the £35m Hampstead Home of Diamond Billionaire', *London Evening Standard*, 8 January 2008.

26. See the motion to dismiss filed by the defendants in *Richard A. Marin v. AI Holdings (USA) Corp et al.* in the Supreme Court of the State of New York, County of New York, 1 June 2011. Marin was a veteran financier brought in by Africa Israel USA, the American arm of the Israeli conglomerate controlled by Lev Leviev, after the value of its property investments tumbled. He sued the company in 2011 after he was dismissed. The case was settled out of court.

27. As well as the Manhattan property and Catoca diamond deals, Leviev

companies bought minority stakes in the Queensway Group's sole listed company, the name of which has been repeatedly changed and is, at the time of writing, Nan Nan Resources. It appears to hold only some coal licences in China.

28. US Embassy in Harare, 'Zimplats Ceo on Chinese Interest In Platinum Sector, Internal Goz Politics', cable, 2 August 2005, WikiLeaks, 1 September 2011, http://www.wikileaks.org/plusd/cables/05HARARE1088_a.html, recounts a conversation between embassy staff and Greg Sebborn, then chief executive of Zimbabwe Platinum, the local subsidiary of Impala Platinum, in which Sebborn described Mujuru's approach.

29. Adrian Croft, 'EU to Lift Sanctions on Zimbabwe Diamond Mining Firm', Reuters, 17 September 2013, www.reuters.com/article/2013/09/17/zimbabwe-elections-eu-idUSL5N0HD2FE20130917.

30. Lesley Wroughton, '"Shame, Shame, Shame" Mugabe Tells US and Britain', Reuters, 26 September 2013, www.reuters.com/article/2013/09/26/us-un-assembly-mugabe-idUSBRE98P12A20130926.

31. Folarin Gbadebo-Smith, interview with author, Abuja, April 2013.

32. Martin Meredith's *Diamonds, Gold, and War: The British, the Boers, and the Making of South Africa* (New York: PublicAffairs, 2007) contains a magisterial account of Rhodes's life and the struggle for minerals and territory in southern Africa. I have drawn on it here.

33. Ibid., 475.

34. Peter Wise, 'Portugal Appeals to Angola for Funds', *Financial Times*, 17 November 2011, www.ft.com/intl/cms/s/0/9c1f123e-1132-11e1-ad22-00144feabdc0.html.

35. Knox Chitiyo, 'The Case for Security Sector Reform in Zimbabwe', Royal United Services Institute, September 2009, www.rusi.org/downloads/assets/Zimbabwe_SSR_Report.pdf.

36. See, for example, 'The Elephant in the Room: Reforming Zimbabwe's Security Sector Ahead of Elections', Human Rights Watch, June 2013, www.hrw.org/reports/2013/06/04/elephant-room. Local human rights groups such as Sokwanele have also documented the CIO's electoral abuses.

37. On General Kopelipa's alleged interests in diamonds, see, for example, 'Angola Investigates Top Generals in "Blood Diamonds" Case', Maka Angola, 3 March 2012.

38. See, for example, 'Diamonds: A Good Deal for Zimbabwe?'

39. US Embassy in Harare, 'Regime Elites Looting Deadly Diamond Field', cable, 12 November 2008, WikiLeaks, 8 December 2010, www.wikileaks.ch/cable/2008/11/08HARARE1016.html.

40. 'Zimbabwe: Financing a Parallel Government?', Global Witness, June 2012, www.globalwitness.org/sites/default/files/library/Financing_a_parallel_government_Zimbabwe.pdf.

41. Sam Pa was also named as having played a role in a clandestine arms deal through which Mugabe supplied weapons to Laurent Gbagbo, the president of Ivory Coast whose refusal to accept electoral defeat in late 2010 triggered a crisis that came close to civil war. See Jon Swain, 'Mugabe Secretly Arms Ivory Coast's Usurper President', *Sunday Times* (London), 23 January 2011, www.thesunday times.co.uk/sto/news/world_news/Africa/article519387.ece.

42. 'Update Following Financing a Parallel Government Report', Global Witness, 30 October 2012, www.globalwitness.org/library/update-following-financing-parallel-government-report.

43. Jee Kin Wee, Group Head of Legal at China Sonangol International (S) Pte. Ltd., the Singapore-registered arm of China Sonangol, told me by e-mail in April 2014 that the Singaporean Sino Zim Development 'was in fact a dormant company'. However, accounts dated 18 February 2011, and filed in Singapore by the Singaporean Sino Zim Development state that it transferred $50 million to its Zimbabwean account on 16 November 2009, to be held in trust for the Zimbabwean Sino Zimbabwean Development, which was incorporated later (in author's possession). On the concession, see, for example, Takunda Maodza, 'Chiadzwa: President on Fact-Finding Mission', *The Herald*, 16 June 2011, www.herald.co.zw/chiadzwa-president-on-fact-finding-mission/.

44. Company filings show that Kamba was a named director of the Singaporean Sino Zim Development and also named as the authorized signatory of a British Virgin Islands-registered company called Strong Achieve Holdings, which owned 30 per cent of it. Kamba's directorship, see, for example, Sino Zim Development Pte. Ltd., 2009 annual accounts, filed with the Singapore corporate registry (copy in author's possession). For Kamba as signatory for Strong Achieve Holdings of the British Virgin Islands, see, for example, Sino Zimbabwe Development Pte. Ltd, memorandum of association, 12 June 2009, filed with the Singapore corporate registry (copy in author's possession).

45. 'Zimbabwe: Financing a Parallel Government?'

46. In 2013 China Sonangol's website stated that the company owned the Highlands Park Hotel, Bard House and Livingstone House in Harare. By June 2014, after Sam Pa and Sino Zim Development were added to the US list of people and companies subject to sanctions in relation to Zimbabwe, the references to China Sonangol's Zimbabwean property assets had been removed from its website.

47. Tom Burgis, 'China in Africa: How Sam Pa Became the Middleman',

Financial Times, 8 August 2014, www.ft.com/intl/cms/s/2/308a133a-1db8-11e4 -b927-00144feabdc0.html. China Sonangol insisted in its letter that I not quote from it 'out of context'. The full letter is available at *Financial Times*, www. ft.com/chinasonangolresponse.

48. The Airbus jet that Sam Pa uses has the registration VP-BEX, according to multiple sources including 'Zimbabwe: Financing a Parallel Government?' I have tracked VP-BEX's flights using public flight-plan data.

49. Sierra Leone's State House Communications Unit, 'President Ernest Koroma Receives Red Carpet Welcome in Angola', statement, 11 December 2013, http://cocorioko.info/?p=2618.

50. Sierra Leone Presidency, 'Big Boost for President Koroma—as Chinese Consortium Signs MoU', statement, statehouse.gov.sl, 8 September 2012, www. statehouse.gov.sl/index.php/useful-links/550-big-boost-for-president-koromaas -chinese-consortium-signs-mou; the number of CCRC's employees comes from *Forbes*, www.forbes.com/companies/china-railway-construction.

51. 'Resignation of Group CEO', China Sonangol, undated and added to website in July 2014, www.chinasonangol.com/news_and_events.html.

52. Government of Dubai, 'Dubai to Set Up Crude Oil Refinery Project: MoU with China Sonangol International to Address Dubai's Increasing Energy Requirements', press release, 25 September 2013.

53. J. R. Mailey, interview with author, February 2014. Mailey (formerly J. R. Warner), was one of the authors of the first study of the Queensway Group, which coined its name after the researchers happened upon the web of companies emanating from the same Hong Kong address. See Lee Levkowitz, Marta McLellan Ross and J. R. Warner, 'The 88 Queensway Group: A Case Study in Chinese Investors' Operations in Angola and Beyond', US-China Economic and Security Review Commission, 10 July 2009, http://china.usc.edu/App_Images/The_88_ Queensway_Group.pdf.

54. After Global Witness published 'Zimbabwe: Financing a Parallel Government?', China International Fund, the Queensway Group's mining and infrastructure arm, sent Global Witness a statement through a lawyer, stating, 'China International Fund has not been involved in sending money to the secret police. While China International Fund has provided money to the government of Zimbabwe it has done so for legitimate business reasons.' The statement added that Sino Zim Development exported 'not a single carat' of diamonds from Zimbabwe. 'The mines with which that company was involved proved to be commercially unviable and hence were never active.' It said that 'a cutting factory designed to retain profits in Zimbabwe was also

never operational'. 'Update Following Financing a Parallel Government Report', Global Witness, 30 October 2012.

55. 'Embassy Says China Int'l Fund Ltd a HK Firm', Xinhua, *China Daily*, 30 December 2009, http://www.chinadaily.com.cn/china/2009-12/30/content_9249034.htm.

56. Jee Kin Wee (group head of legal, China Sonangol International Ltd.), e-mail exchange with author, March/April 2014.

57. Ibid.

EPILOGUE

1. Gerard Flynn and Susan Scutti, 'Smuggled Bushmeat Is Ebola's Back Door to America', *Newsweek*, 21 August 2014, www.newsweek.com/2014/08/29/smuggled-bushmeat-ebolas-back-door-america-265668.html.

2. US Geological Survey quoted in 'Equity in Extractives', Africa Progress Panel, 2013, http://africaprogresspanel.org/wp-content/uploads/2013/08/2013_APR_Equity_in_Extractives_25062013_ENG_HR.pdf.

3. 'Show Us the Money', *Economist*, 1 September 2012, www.economist.com/node/21561886.

AFTERWORD

1. 'Fujian governor under probe for suspected disciplinary offenses', Xinhua, 7 October 2015, news.xinhuanet.com/english/2015-10/07/c_134690018.htm

2. Jee Kin Wee, e-mail exchange with author, October 2015

List of Illustrations

Acknowledgments

I am more grateful than I can say to all those who have accompanied me during my African postings and through the three years it took to write *The Looting Machine*.

Michael Holman, Aaron Sayne, Greg Marinovich, Antony Goldman, Jolyon Ford and Tedd George read drafts, challenged my assumptions and spotted my missteps. For all their generosity and that of the dozens of others who have shared their wisdom, errors of fact or judgment are entirely my own. Many fine folk gave me shelter, cheer and chat along the way, especially Greg, Leonie, Luc and Madeline Marinovich, Ed Brown and Joy Brady in Johannesburg; Yinka Ibukun, Tolu Ogunlesi, Richard Akerele, the Bogobiri crew and my fellow members of the press pack in Lagos; Joe and Gillian Brock in Abuja; and Isabella Matambanadzo in Harare. Alagoa Morris guided me in the Niger Delta; Toyin Akinosho and Bismarck Rewane respectively helped me fathom Nigeria's oil industry and economy; Paula Cristina Roque, Ricardo Soares de Oliveira and Rafael Marques de Morais explained the mysteries of Angola; David and Sophie Kalinga and Patrycja Stys showed me the way in eastern Congo. Countless others – too many, alas, to name here – pitched in with contacts, leads and counsel. Gabriel Bawa, Gabriel Akinyemi, Jimoh Ahdine and George Ani in Nigeria did much more than just keep the car on the road. Nneka kindly granted me permission to quote her lyrics.

I have been privileged to work with other members, past and present, of the *Financial Times*'s Africa corps. I owe each of them more beers than I could ever carry. Dino Mahtani is always two steps ahead. Matthew Green is a chronicler of conflict with few peers and a friend in need. Katrina Manson in Nairobi, Tony Hawkins in Harare, Andrew England in Johannesburg and Xan Rice in Lagos never tired of my requests for help with the book. David White was an irrepressible companion in Angola. Richard and Fatima Lapper were convivial comrades in Johannesburg. First in South Africa, then in London, Alec Russell (alongside the wonderful Sophie, Mungo and Ned) poured encouragement into my tank. William Wallis, a man attached to Africa at the soul, gave me my shot as an *FT* correspondent and has provided boundless insight and merriment ever since.

I am grateful to the *FT* for allowing me to reuse material from my African postings and from my later work on the investigations team. With every 'Here's the thing…' Christine Spolar, the paper's investigations editor, imparted more of the canny judgment without which many of these stories would not have come off. Demetri Sevastopulo, Cynthia O'Murchu and Helen Thomas (my fellow Guinea Pig) were brilliant collaborators. Try as we might, we could never overturn the good humour of Nigel Hanson, the *FT*'s unflappable lawyer. Lionel Barber and John Thornhill backed our stories to the hilt. Alan Beattie set me straight on trade, James Kynge on China. Quentin Peel kept a sage eye on me. It is a testament to the paper that the other reporters, news editors, managing editors, subeditors, researchers and editorial assistants who deserve thanks for their skill, patience, courage and camaraderie are too numerous to list. This book is, however, my own endeavour, separate from my work for the *FT*.

J. R. Mailey has charted the Queensway Group like no one else and graciously answered my incessant questions. Numerous journalists, researchers and activists have added pieces to the Queensway jigsaw. I am indebted to Patrick Smith and others at *Africa Confidential*, that great chronicle of the continent. Within the oil and mining industries there are plenty of men and women of integrity. Some who spoke and sparred with me are named here, many are not. I am grateful to all of them.

Funds from the Royal Society of Literature Jerwood Awards and the Authors' Foundation kept a roof over my head and a plane ticket in my pocket. Martin Redfern at HarperCollins and Clive Priddle at PublicAffairs took a manuscript that was mumbling and made it sing. A great many of their excellent colleagues helped to bring the book to fruition. Kevin Conroy Scott of Tibor Jones and Sophie Lambert, now of Conville & Walsh, backed the idea when it was just a germ. Sophie's invaluable enthusiasm and nous have nurtured it all the way.

My mother and father never let on how worried they were each time I set off. They have been my rocks, as have the three most extraordinary siblings a man could wish for: Catherine, Joe and Felicity. When I met Camilla Carson this book was barely begun. By the time it was finished, she was my wife. She kept me smiling as I wandered and wrote. She has my love, now and always.

My greatest thanks and admiration go to those I cannot name. Most of them are Africans. They dared to tell me things others would prefer to keep secret, often taking serious risks to do so. I hope I have done you justice.

Index